Lecture Notes in Computer Science 8742

Commenced Publication in 1973
Founding and Former Series Editors:
Gerhard Goos, Juris Hartmanis, and Jan van Leeuwen

Editorial Board

T0184696

Stefan Sauer   Cristian Bogdan
Peter Forbrig   Regina Bernhaupt
Marco Winckler (Eds.)

Human-Centered Software Engineering

5th IFIP WG 13.2 International Conference, HCSE 2014
Paderborn, Germany, September 16-18, 2014
Proceedings

Springer

Volume Editors

Stefan Sauer
University of Paderborn, Germany
E-mail: sauer@s-lab.upb.de

Cristian Bogdan
KTH - Royal Institute of Technology, Stockholm, Sweden
E-mail: cristi@csc.kth.se

Peter Forbrig
University of Rostock, Germany
E-mail: peter.forbrig@uni-rostock.de

Regina Bernhaupt
University Paul Sabatier Toulouse, ICS-IRIT, France
E-mail: regina.bernhaupt@irit.fr

Marco Winckler
University Paul Sabatier Toulouse, ICS-IRIT, France
E-mail: winckler@irit.fr

ISSN 0302-9743   e-ISSN 1611-3349
ISBN 978-3-662-44810-6   e-ISBN 978-3-662-44811-3
DOI 10.1007/978-3-662-44811-3
Springer Heidelberg New York Dordrecht London

Library of Congress Control Number: 2014948051

LNCS Sublibrary: SL 2 – Programming and Software Engineering

Typesetting: Camera-ready by author, data conversion by Scientific Publishing Services, Chennai, India

Printed on acid-free paper

Springer is part of Springer Science+Business Media (www.springer.com)

Preface

The International Conference on Human-Centered Software Engineering (HCSE) is a single track working conference which aims at bringing together researchers and practitioners interested in strengthening the scientific foundations of user interface design, examining the relationship between software engineering and human-computer interaction and on how to strengthen user-centered design as an essential part of software engineering processes.

HCSE 2014 is the fifth edition of a series of conferences promoted by the International Federation for Information Processing (IFIP) Working Group WG 13.2 on Methodologies for User-Centered Systems Design. Previous events were held in Salamanca, Spain (2007), Pisa, Italy (2008), Reykjavik, Iceland (2010) and Toulouse, France (2012). While HCSE had initially been organized in conjunction with other conferences, it has grown over the years and is now held as a bi-annual standalone conference since HCSE 2012 in Toulouse. HCSE 2014 took place in Paderborn, Germany, during September 16–18, 2014. It was hosted and locally organized by the s-lab – Software Quality Lab of the University of Paderborn, in the context of the newly founded Software Innovation Campus Paderborn (SICP). Conference venue was the Heinz Nixdorf MuseumsForum, a modern conference center also hosting the world's largest computer museum.

HCSE 2014 welcomed 13 full research papers, describing substantial novel contributions and advanced results, and 10 short papers, presenting practice and experience reports, practical evaluations as well as late breaking results, which are all featured in this collection. The acceptance rate for qualified full research papers was 38%, the acceptance rate for short papers was 27%. All qualified submissions were independently reviewed by at least three reviewers, who were selected members of the Program Committee, occasionally supported by external reviewers. In addition, the papers and reviews were extensively discussed by the Program Committee to make the decisions. Seven full research papers were directly accepted, six were accepted in a second review round, after the authors had improved their contributions according to the first-round review results. Furthermore, seven papers that were originally submitted as full papers were included in the program as short papers. All submissions that were conditionally accepted in the first round were accessorily reviewed by a meta-reviewer in the second round. The reviewing process for short papers followed a standard procedure, leading to final decisions after one round. Our sincere gratitude goes to the members of our Program Committee and external reviewers, who devoted countless hours to provide valuable feedback to authors and ensure the high quality of the HCSE technical program.

We thank Prof. Dr. Margaret Burnett and Prof. Dr. Wil M.P. van der Aalst, our keynote speakers, who accepted to give inspiring speeches at HCSE and provided us with extended abstracts that are also presented in this proceedings volume. In addition, we express special appreciation to our Publicity Chair Holger Fischer and the local organizer team in Paderborn. We are indebted to our sponsors for their generous support in helping to make our conference special and successful. Finally our thanks go to all the authors who actually did the research work and especially to the presenters who sparked inspiring discussions with all the participants at HCSE 2014 in Paderborn.

Stefan Sauer
Cristian Bogdan
Peter Forbrig
Regina Bernhaupt
Marco Winckler

HCSE 2014 Technical Committee

General Conference Chair

Stefan Sauer — University of Paderborn, Germany

Technical Program Chairs

Peter Forbrig — University of Rostock, Germany
Cristian Bogdan — KTH - Royal Institute of Technology, Stockholm, Sweden

User Experience Chair

Regina Bernhaupt — University Paul Sabatier Toulouse, ICS-IRIT, France

Program Committee

Ahmed Seffah	Concordia University, Canada
Alistair Sutcliffe	Manchester Business School, UK
Anirudha Joshi	University of Mumbay, India
Anke Dittmar	University of Rostock, Germany
Ann Blandford	University College London, UK
Bertrand David	École Centrale de Lyon, France
Birgit Bomsdorf	University of Applied Science Fulda, Germany
Carmen Santoro	Istituto di Scienza e Tecnologie dell'Informazione, Italy
Christian Stary	Johannes Kelper University Linz, Austria
Corina Sas	University of Lancester, UK
Costin Pribeanu	University of Bucarest, Romania
Cristian Bogdan	KTH - Royal Institute of Technology, Sweden
Daniel Sinnig	Concordia University Montreal, Canada
David Benyon	University of Edinburgh, UK
Dominique Scapin	INRIA Rocquencourt, France
Ebba Hvannberg	University of Iceland, Iceland
Emilia Mendes	Blekinge Institute of Technology, Sweden
Fabio Paterno	Istituto di Scienza e Tecnologie dell'Informazione (ISTI), Italy

Francisco Montero	Universidad de Castilla La Mancha, Spain
Gaëlle Calvary	University of Grenoble, France
Gerd Szwillus	University of Paderborn, Germany
Gerrit van der Veer	Vrije University, The Netherlands
Hallvard Traetteberg	Norwegian University of Science and Technology (NTNU), Norway
Hermann Kaindl	Vienna University of Technology, Austria
Jose Campos	University of Minho, Portugal
Jose Gallud	Universidad de Castilla La Mancha (UCLM), Spain
Jürgen Ziegler	University of Duisburg, Germany
Karin Coninx	Hasselt University, Belgium
Marcelo Pimenta	Universidade Federal do Rio Grande do Sul, Brasil
Marcin Sikorski	University of Gdansk, Poland
Marco Winckler	University Paul Sabatier Toulouse, ICS-IRIT, France
Margaret Burnett	Oregon State University, USA
Maria Lozano	Universidad de Castilla~La Mancha (UCLM), Spain
Marta Lárusdóttir	Reykjavik University, Iceland
Matthias Rauterberg	University of Technology Eindhoven, The Netherlands
Michael Harrison	University of Newcastle, UK
Oscar Pastor	Universitat Politècnica de València (UPV), Spain
Paolo Bottoni	University of Rome "La Sapienza", Italy
Pedro Campos	University of Madeira, Portugal
Peter Forbrig	University of Rostock, Germany
Regina Bernhaupt	University Paul Sabatier Toulouse, ICS-IRIT, France
Scott D. Fleming	University of Memphis, USA
Simone Barbosa	Pontifical Catholic University (PUC) of Rio de Janeiro, Brasil
Stefan Sauer	University of Paderborn, Germany
Steve Goschnick	University of Melbourne, Australia
Victor López-Jaquero	Universidad de Castilla-La Mancha (UCLM), Spain
Xavier Ferré	Universidad Politécnica de Madrid, Spain

Additional Reviewers

Carlos Eduardo Silva	University of Minho, Portugal
João Carlos Silva	IPCA, Barcelos, Portugal

Proceedings Chair

Marco Winckler   University Paul Sabatier Toulouse, ICS-IRIT,
                                   France

Publicity Chair

Holger Fischer   University of Paderborn, Germany

Corporate and Institutional Sponsors

Platinum

Initiative "Paderborn überzeugt"
www.paderborn-ueberzeugt.de

s-lab – Software Quality Lab
s-lab.upb.de

SICP Software Innovation Campus Paderborn
www.sicp.de

Gold

www.c-lab.de

SFB901

ON - THE - FLY COMPUTING
DFG Colaborative Research Center
sfb901.upb.de

Silver

Leading-Edge Cluster in Germany
www.its-owl.de

PADERBORN IST INFORMATIK

Initiative "Paderborn ist Informatik"
www.paderborn-ist-informatik.de

Scientific Sponsors

International Federation for Information Processing (IFIP)
Technical Committee TC 13 Human-Computer Interaction
Working Group WG 13.2 on Methodologies for User-Centered
Systems Design

Supporters

www.interaction-design.org

Table of Contents

Research Papers

Late Breaking Results

Keynotes

Active Collaborative Learning: Supporting Software Developers in Creating Redesign Proposals

Anders Bruun[1], Janne Juul Jensen[1,2], Mikael B. Skov[1], and Jan Stage[1]

[1] Aalborg Universitity, Department of Computer Science, DK-9220 Aalborg, Denmark
[2] Trifork A/S, DK-8000 Århus C, Denmark
{bruun,dubois,jans}@cs.aau.dk,
jjj@trifork.com

Abstract. Redesign proposals have been suggested as means to improve the feedback from usability evaluation to software development. Yet redesign proposals are usually created by usability specialists without any involvement of the software developers who will implement the proposals. This paper reports from an exploratory study where redesign proposals were created in an active and collaborative learning process that involved both software developers and usability specialists. The focus was on the support that the developers needed in order to contribute constructively to improve the usability of the system. The findings show that this process had a considerable impact on the developers' understanding of the usability problems, especially the weaknesses of the system. They were able to contribute constructively to create redesign proposals, and they found the workshop very useful for their future efforts to eliminate the usability problems that have been identified.

Keywords: Usability evaluation, usability problem, redesign proposal, developer involvement, active collaborative learning, exploratory study.

1   Introduction

A usability evaluation is conducted to assess the usability of an interactive software system. Usability is the system's ability to help specified users achieve specified goals in a particular environment in an effective, efficient and satisfying way [10]. A formative usability evaluation is conducted to improve the interaction design. Formative evaluations are carried out during development, often iteratively, with the goal of detecting and eliminating usability problems [1]. A formative usability evaluation establishes a strong and useful basis for understanding and improving the design of a software system. Exploiting this requires feedback that significantly impacts how developers understand the usability of the system [7].

The classical feedback from a usability evaluation is a report that describes the usability problems that have been identified [18]. The aim is to present the results of the evaluation in a format that is useful for the developers that are going to eliminate the identified usability problems. Unfortunately, a substantial body of research documents that usability reports are of limited utility and effect, e.g. [5, 7, 15]. To overcome

S. Sauer et al. (Eds.): HCSE 2014, LNCS 8742, pp. 1–18, 2014.

this, it has been argued that evaluators who conduct a usability evaluation should not only describe what the usability problems are, but also suggest how they could be resolved, e.g. [11]. Such suggestions have been denoted as redesign proposals, and their advantages have been studied empirically, e.g. [6].

Redesign proposals are a great step forward in providing useful feedback about usability to developers of interactive systems. However, redesign proposals are usually created solely by evaluators who are usability specialist and subsequently handed over to the developers in an old-fashioned presentation style involving only one-way communication. This division in roles for evaluators and developers is similar to a traditional teaching approach.

In education, many authors have questioned the qualities of a traditional teaching style. Dewey's theory on education was based on the idea that education consists primarily in transmission through communication; a process of sharing experience until it becomes a common possession [4]. He emphasized that the traditional teaching's concern with delivering knowledge, needed to be balanced with a much greater focus on the students' actual experiences and active learning. The teacher should be acknowledged as the intellectual leader of a social group, not by virtue of official position, but because of wider and deeper knowledge and matured experience [17]. Dewey was a key proponent of experiential education with learning through action that embody teaching methods such as cooperative learning and active learning.

This paper explores how software developers can become actively involved in creating redesign proposals to resolve identified usability problems. We explore different patterns of collaboration between usability specialists and software developers based on Dewey's theory on education combined with the idea that redesign proposals should be a key vehicle for providing feedback from a usability evaluation. In section 2, we present related work on feedback from usability evaluations. In section 3, we describe our exploratory study where active collaborative learning was employed to understand the results of a usability evaluation and create redesign proposals. Section 4 describes our findings from the study. In section 5, we discuss the implications of the findings for software development practice. Finally, section 6 provides the conclusion.

2   Related Work

There is a rich body of research on feedback from usability evaluations. The classical approach from the first half of the 1990s suggested that the results of a usability evaluation should be provided in a written usability report where the key element is a list of the identified usability problems and a detailed description of each [18].

Research from the same period demonstrated significant difficulties with usability reports. An early paper on this topic was based on analysis of real usability reports. Many of these reports did not describe usability problems but redesign solutions; it was emphasized that it is extremely rare for an evaluator to simply describe a problem, unless it is deemed as not having an apparent solution. These observations led to a proposal for a general format for usability problem lists [11]. Other publications from the same time also deal with the format of the usability problem list [13, 16].

There is also a considerable number of empirical studies that deal with feedback from usability evaluations. The early works are primarily concerned with evaluation methods and only secondarily with report formats, e.g. [1]. More recent research has focussed on a more rigorous problem reporting format [14] and practical guidelines for making problem descriptions [3]. There has also been work on different types of support for structured usability problem reporting [9].

A different stream of work has documented the problems with the classical usability problem report. A comparative study showed that the usability report had a strong impact on the developers' understanding of specific usability problems and supported a systematic approach to deal effectively with problems, whereas observation of user tests facilitated a rich understanding of usability problems and created empathy with the users and their work [8]. Two other studies analysed in more detail the utility of problem descriptions for the developers who should eliminate the problems [15, 22].

A number of studies have dealt with redesign proposals as opposed to mere problem descriptions. A study on the impact of inspections on software development concluded that specific recommendations to fix specific problems had a considerable positive effect [19]. Another study tracked how attempts to resolve usability problems influenced the usability of the system. Their feedback included redesign proposals to individual usability problems [12]. A more recent study has developers assess the relevance of usability problem descriptions compared to redesign proposals, and it was concluded that developers assessed redesign proposals as having higher utility in their work than usability problem descriptions but no developers, however, wanted to receive only problems or redesigns [6]. This also led to a set of recommendations for describing usability problems in practical usability work. For an overview of suggestions for other kinds of feedback, see [8].

The research on usability problem descriptions and alternatives has been questioned by authors with a background in usability practice. For example, it has been argued that in much research on usability evaluation methods, the effectiveness of the different methods has been compared in terms of the usability problems identified with an assumption of a direct link to design improvements [20]. It has also been claimed that the literature on usability evaluation is fundamentally flawed by its lack of relevance to applied usability work, and a key flaw is the focus on finding, rather than fixing, usability problems [22]. There are also practitioners who have been more constructive by emphasizing that redesign proposals are too often quick fixes, and they are only as brief as many of the problem descriptions. Therefore, they suggest that a more developed form of redesign proposals is defined [5].

The usability reports and the variety of alternatives that have been suggested share a common feature. They are almost exclusively based on usability specialists acting as evaluators who are being active in describing problems and creating redesign proposals. The developers, on the other hand, are passively receiving the descriptions and proposals. This is not a very effective way of establishing a common ground for improving the system, as emphasized in the introduction with reference to key education theories.

3   Exploratory Study

Our exploratory study aimed to investigate the effects of integrating usability evaluation feedback into a tailored design activity in a workshop setting where the developers were actively involved. Thereby, we aimed to alleviate some of the inherent problems of merely presenting usability problem lists.

3.1   System

The evaluated system is a web-based building permit system that citizens and companies use to apply for building permits, e.g. for construction of new houses or factories and refurbishing of existing houses. The existing system was an interactive form that was directly inspired by a previous paper-based form, which was usually used by Danish municipalities. The form is an integrated part of a collection of web-based services that is provided for municipalities in Denmark.

3.2   Usability Evaluation

We conducted a classic think-aloud usability evaluation, cf. [18], of the building permission system to generate a usability problem list. This was done in a traditional manner using lab evaluations with pre-assigned tasks.

3.3   Participants

10 subjects (3 females and 7 males) participated in the evaluation of the system. The participants were from 29 to 64 years old. They all had experience with the Internet and web-based services in general, but had varied levels of formal training and education (from a self-taught to a PhD) and had varied experiences with filling in online municipality forms and also varied experience with building and refurbishing houses. None of the participants had any prior experience with the system that was evaluated.

3.4   Procedure

From understandings of the prospective users and system functionality, the evaluation team constructed usage scenarios and task assignments for the usability evaluation. In total, three tasks were defined.

The four authors of this paper conducted the evaluation. The ten participants were scheduled for participation in the evaluation over two days, with five participants each day. Before the sessions, the participants were given a written test instruction outlining the purpose and the procedure for the evaluation. Furthermore, the participants were asked to fill in a demographic questionnaire. The sessions were conducted in a classical usability lab with one-way mirrors, where the participants were placed in a test room with the test monitor. A data logger in an adjacent observation room observed the evaluation while making notes. The participants were asked to follow the think-aloud protocol during the test. After the test sessions, the participants were asked to fill in a NASA TLX test [24, 25] to assess how they perceived the mental workload.

Each day, after all evaluation sessions, we conducted a problem identification session using the Instant Data Analysis method [26]. This method was used to facilitate quick and efficient identification of the usability problems, which were needed in the subsequent design workshop. The usability problem identification procedure for both days were as follows 1) Problems observed from memory by the test monitor, 2) problems observed from memory by the test monitor or the logger, 3) problems identified from systematic walk-through of assigned tasks, 4) problems identified from systematic walk-through of logger's notes, and 5) severity categorization of each identified usability problem.

3.5   Result

We identified a total of 75 usability problems of which 7 were categorized as critical, 38 as serious, and 38 as cosmetic. Furthermore, we classified 4 of the problems as incomplete because we did not have adequate knowledge of the application domain to classify these problems according to the scale.

Considering the identified problems, we found that several of them were related to the basic concepts where the participants found it difficult to distinguish between the different kinds of permissions and applications. Furthermore, none of the participants could figure out which fields were mandatory, causing them to be uncertain about the completeness of the submitted form. Also, the division between building applicant and owner caused several problems for most of the participants. Finally, nearly none of the participants were able to attach appendices and drawings to their application. Accordingly, the NASA TLX test showed that the participants assessed mental workload and frustration as the most important contributors to the experienced workload.

3.6   Redesign Workshop

Previous research has demonstrated that usability evaluation feedback inherently involves several challenges and obstacles, as emphasized above in the overview of related work. To address some of these issues, we designed a redesign workshop with the aim of facilitating feedback through active developer participation and collaborative activities between developers and the usability specialists who had acted as evaluators.

The fundamental idea of the redesign workshop was to "look forward" through integrated design activities rather than having a retrospective approach only focusing on identified problems and, thereby, not focusing on overcoming the limitations of the current system. In the workshop, the software developers should become active in the evaluation of their own system. To achieve this, we integrated three components: 1) active involvement of the developers, 2) focus on the future system, and 3) support from usability specialists.

3.7   Participants

The participants in the redesign workshop were developers from the software company Dafolo A/S and usability specialists from Aalborg University. The participating developers represented different skills and job positions at the software company ranging from programmers over project leaders to a development manager. We will refer to them collectively as developers. In total, five developers participated in the workshop.

The usability specialists were the authors of this paper and are all researchers within interaction design and human-computer interaction and have extensive experience with usability evaluation. They held either a PhD or Master degree within human-computer interaction.

We divided the participants into three groups:

- Group 1: 3 Developers
- Group 2: 2 Developers + 1 usability specialist
- Group 3: 3 usability specialists

The overall aim was to explore to what extent the developers could contribute actively to the creation of redesign proposals and how much support they would need to do so. We also observed the group dynamics and assessed the redesigns they.

3.8   Preparation

We prepared the redesign workshop in the following way. We reduced the original list of usability problems from 75 to a short-list of 25 problems. For the reduced list we selected problems that were associated with one particular use scenario on applying for construction permit. Thus problems that were irrelevant to this particular scenario were omitted. Also, the reduction was done in order to create a basis for the redesign activity where the participants would be able to address all or nearly all problems. The reduced problem list contained 2 critical problems, 2 serious problems, 7 cosmetic problems, and 14 incomplete problems.

We also formed the three groups in advance. We divided the five developers and the four usability specialists into the three groups, where we strived for diversity in each groups with both junior and senior participants. Group 1 was formed with three developers only, and without any usability support. Group 2 was formed by combining two developers and a usability specialist who should provide support in the process. Group 3 was formed to provide product support for the other two groups; they conducted a redesign activity in advance of the workshop.

The participating developers received no information or results from the usability evaluation prior to the workshop as our experience was that this was counterproductive, because the developers would go into a defensive mode.

3.9   Activities

The design workshop consisted of three major activities (or elements):

1. Problem presentation and illustration
2. Redesign session
3. Plenary presentation and discussion

The first activity encompassed introduction to the workshop and presentation of the usability evaluation results. We scheduled this activity for an hour and it served the purpose of introducing the evaluation to the developers and more importantly presentation of the short-list of usability problems. The selected 25 problems were presented and illustrated in the interface and their severity was motivated. The usability specialists were leading this activity. All participants received a copy of the problem list.

The second activity was the redesign sessions. We gave the groups the task that they should produce a redesign of the system that addressed the shortlist of usability problems. Group 1 and 2 were placed in two separate rooms in our usability lab, allowing us to monitor them while working on the redesign. Two of the usability specialists from Group 3 acted as data loggers for each of the groups. The groups were instructed to 1) produce a written description of the redesign proposal, 2) illustrate the new interface layout and flow on a flip-over, and 3) note which problems they had addressed. Furthermore, they were instructed to prepare an oral presentation in the plenum session.

The third activity was a plenary session where group 1 and 2 presented their redesigns. After that, Group 3 presented the redesign they had prepared in advance. Each group presented their solutions for app. 15 minutes followed by questions and discussion for another 15 minutes. After the individual presentations, the solutions and design strategies were compared and discussed.

We measured the developers' attitudes to or perceptions of the strengths and weaknesses of the current system. This was done three times during the workshop: before they were introduced to the problem list, after the design session, and after the entire workshop. Each time, the participants were instructed to list 5 weaknesses and 5 strengths of the existing system.

4   Findings

In this section we present the finding from the explorative study with focus on the redesign proposals that were produced and the usefulness of the workshop.

4.1   Redesign Strategies and Design Proposals

This subsection describes the three redesign strategies and the design proposals that were developed during the design workshop.

Redesign Strategies. The two developer groups (1 and 2) adopted a bottom-up strategy where they mainly addressed usability problems at the low-level description. We identified no visible effect of introducing a usability specialist into a developer group (#2) compared to the group consisting solely of developers (#1).

The adopted strategies also implied that Group 1 and 2 addressed the usability problems rather explicitly and had no problems in assessing which usability problems their solution addressed or solved.

The lack of an overall design strategy caused problems for both groups, as they several times had to change or alter their solutions, e.g. order of data input.

The developer group (#1) addressed nine usability problems in total. They primarily focused on the critical and serious problems and intentionally left out cosmetic problems in the beginning of the activity. Of the nine problems addressed, three problems were critical, two were serious, and four were cosmetic. As stated above, their overall strategy was a bottom-up approach focusing on the problems one by one.

The developers and usability specialist group (#2) addressed a total of 12 usability problems. Of these, three were critical, two were serious and three were cosmetic. Group 2 also adopted the bottom-up approach where they addressed problems as they were listed in the problem list instead of focusing on solving critical issues first.

When the usability specialist group (#3) created their redesign proposal in advance of the workshop, they adopted a more top-down strategy where they started to discuss the overall future solution, e.g. the presentation order of the different elements of form filling. After creating the redesign, they retrospectively traversed the whole problem list to mark which problems they had resolved. while doing this, it seemed that they utilized their knowledge and experience from the actual usability evaluation. Sometimes they were uncertain if they had solved a usability problem because they had less knowledge about the application domain. They addressed a total of 16 problems, where four were critical, five were serious and seven were cosmetic.

Design Proposals. Group 1 presented the most technically advanced redesign proposal in which the main theme regarded process automation in a wizard based solution, see Figure 1. The wizard consisted of the following steps:

1. Type of construction work
2. Owner/Applicant and property information
3. Type of construction work (further questions)
4. Submission overview/receipt.

To illustrate this, we first need to review one of the experienced usability problems regarding users not knowing whether to submit a permit application for the construction work or a more simple notification. A permit application is needed in case the construction work conflicts with district plans, in which case the municipality must grant permission before construction may begin. A notification is used when the construction work obeys district plans. The users (citizens) in our evaluation were unable to decide, whether they were required to submit a "permist application" or a "notification", which was selected in the pdf form via radio buttons. Group 1 proposed an advanced solution for this, in which users would answer a set of questions regarding the type and size of the construction work. They also proposed to incorporate a Geographic Information System (GIS) component in which users could draw sketches of the buildings. By using this type of information, the system could potentially decide if the construction work would need permission or just a notification, hereby automating the process.

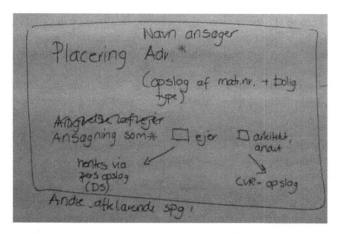

Fig. 1. A window from the redesign proposal from Group 1

Another automation was suggested in the case of finding information about land register, which was another problem encountered by users in the evaluation. Users did not know where to find this information and the format of a land register was also unclear. Group 1 suggested that this problem could be overcome by automatically looking up the land register based on the given address of the construction work.

Group 1 also addressed a problem with irrelevant input fields. As an example, some users were confused about the information required in input fields for "Applicant address", because there also were input fields for "Owner address". The users were confused about whether to fill in the same information in both cases, as they were applicants and owners at the same time. Group 1 suggested a solution where the system leaves out irrelevant fields based on previous selections in the wizard.

Group 2 also suggested a wizard based design solution, in their case with the following steps:

1. Owner/Applicant information
2. Information about property
3. Type of construction work.

The main theme for this design proposal evolved around contextual help providing more clear and simple examples of when, for instance, users should select "permit application" or "notification". This addressed problems concerning complex terminology. Another problem addressed was also identified during the usability evaluation and regarded some users who did not notice the "Save" button, which allowed them to save the pdf form on their computer. Group 2 addressed this by placing all buttons consistently in a toolbar at the same location of each page (at the bottom). This group also focused on a problem regarding the format for typing in addresses in input fields. In the pdf form, one field about street address was split into two parts: One field for street name and another for the house number in the street. Other fields in the form, however, required the user to type in street name and number in the same field. This inconsistency confused some of the users. Group 2 suggested a solution in which all address fields were of the same format, more specifically they designed for one input field containing both street name and number. As an extra feature this group also added a progress bar at the top of the layout to indicate the current state of the submission process.

Group 3 also proposed a wizard-based redesign. This group chose a top-down approach which made them emphasize a complete reordering of the workflow in the following steps:

1. Owner/Applicant information
2. Information about property
3. Type of construction work.

These steps are similar to the ones defined by Group 2, but the main theme for Group 3's design was simplicity for the citizen. For instance, they focused on letting office clerks decide whether or not a submitted application should be categorized as "permit application" or "notification" such that the citizen would not need to decide. This contrasts with the solutions suggested by groups 1 and 2, which suggested that the user (citizen) should decide.

Summary. From the overview of the design process, we see that the redesign strategies varied between top-down and bottom-up approaches and that the three groups addressed a different number of usability problems. The main themes of the redesign proposals also differed between the three groups, but all applied a wizard approach of three to four steps. The wizard steps of Group 2 and 3 were similar while Group 1 selected an alternative order and also designed an extra step. All steps in the redesign solutions deviated from the order in the original pdf form.

4.2   Problem Understanding

This subsection describes our findings on the developers' perception of the problems of the system. In the following we describe the numbers and categories of identified strengths and weaknesses and the collective list of these as prioritized by the five participants.

Categories of Strengths and Weaknesses. Using grounded theory [21] we identified a set of categories to describe and compare the contents of the perceived strengths and weaknesses before and after the redesign exercise. The identified categories are shown in the leftmost column of Table 1 which shows the number of mentioned strengths and weaknesses distributed according to these categories.

We see that the participants were able to identify 20 strengths in total before the redesign task and 13 after and 20 weaknesses in total before the group work and 20 after. Thus, the number of strengths perceived by the participants was considerably reduced after the redesign task, whereas the number of weaknesses remained the same.

Table 1. Number of strengths and weaknesses distributed according to identified categories. * denotes the categories with a change of at least 2 in either strength or weakness.

	Strengths before	Strengths after	Weaknesses before	Weaknesses after
Barcode	2	2		
Breadth	1			
Save	1			
Consistency		1		
Digital signature *	6	4	1	
Recognizability *	5	3		
Clarity *	2	2	5	1
Simplicity	1		1	
Instructions	1		5	4
Attachment	1	1	1	
Excess				1
Structure *				3
Terminology *			1	5
Visibility			2	1
Workflow			1	
Land register			2	1
Transparency *				3
Total	**20**	**13**	**20**	**20**

It is also interesting to note that the categories instructions, simplicity, breadth and save were mentioned as strengths before the exercise, but not after. Only a single new category emerged after (consistency).

We observed more shifts concerning perceived weaknesses compared to strengths. In Table 1 it is shown that three new categories (excess, structure and transparency) emerged after the redesign exercise, while four others disappeared compared to before (digital signature, simplicity, attachment, workflow).

For strengths, two categories were rated more than 2 higher after the exercise than before, and none were rated more than 2 lower after the exercises, while for weaknesses, three categories were rated more than 2 higher after the exercise than before, and one category was rated more than 2 lower after the exercises.

Based on the above observations we see that the redesign exercise lead the participants to change their perception about the system strengths, while for weaknesses it is more a change in type according to our findings from the usability evaluation.

Collective Strengths and Weaknesses. Table 2 shows the five strengths and weaknesses, which the participants collectively agreed on at the end of the workshop, in prioritized order.

For the five collective strengths it is interesting to note the connection to the result found in Table 1, where the participants initially perceived the categories of digital signature and recognisability as the foremost strengths but after the redesign exercise the excitement of these seemed reduced. The possible consequence of this may be what we see in Table 2 where digital signature is unmentioned and recognisability has the lowest priority of the five strengths.

We see a similar connection considering the collective list of five weaknesses in the categories instructions, excess, terminology, instructions and structure (in prioritized order). In Table 1 we see that instructions and terminology are the primary perceived weaknesses before and after the group work which correspond well to the priorities in Table 2. The two remaining categories of excess and structure were perceived important by the participants after the redesign exercise, which is also reflected in Table 2.

Thus, we see a connection in categories of strengths and weaknesses perceived after the exercise and the collective prioritized list.

Table 2. Five collective strengths and weaknesses (prioritized)

	Collective strengths	Collective weaknesses
1	Barcode useful for office clerks **[Barcode]**	Instructions provide no overview **[Instructions]**
2	Pdf form provides a final overview before submission **[Clarity]**	Many input fields seem unnecessary **[Excess]**
3	Pdf form provides an overview of requirements **[Clarity]**	Terminology in form difficult to understand **[Terminology]**
4	Provides ability to save temporarily **[Save]**	Required level of detail on provided information is unclear **[Instructions]**
5	Pdf form similar to paper version – well known to office clerks **[Recognisability]**	Layout of pdf form is not intuitive **[Structure]**

Strengths and Weaknesses after Reading the Usability Report. Table 3 shows the perceived strengths after reading the usability report. From this we see a total of 14 strengths, which corresponds well to the total of 13 found after the redesign task, see Table 1. Most of the categories after reading the report are the same as the strengths identified in Table 1. Recognisability has, however, decreased considerably, and two new categories; time and integration have emerged. We also see similarities to table 2 showing the list of collective strengths, of which all categories are represented in table 3. Thus, the number and types of strengths after reading the report correspond well to the findings identified previously.

Table 3. Perceived strengths after reading the usability report distributed according to identified categories

	Strengths before report	Weaknesses after report
Digital signature	5	1
Clarity	3	3
Recognizability *	1	
Barcode	1	
Save	1	
Time	1	
Integration *	2	
Structure		2
Terminology *		2
Instructions *		7
Visibility		1
Transparency *		1
User errors *		3
Functionality		1
Affordance		1
Total	**14**	**22**

Table 3 presents the perceived weaknesses after reading the usability report. The number of identified weaknesses is 22, which corresponds to the total of 20 identified after the group work, shown in [8]. Considering the categories observed after reading the report we see that the majority of these are the same as those identified after the redesign task and in the collective list of weaknesses shown in Table 2. The categories user errors, functionality and affordance, however, were not identified during the workshop and are new. Regarding the weaknesses we also see a strong connection to the observations done during the workshop.

4.3   Usefulness of Workshop and Usability Report

After reading the usability report we asked participants to anonymously respond to a survey asking questions about the usefulness of the workshop and the usability report. The majority of questions required participants to answer a five point Likert scale where 1 = Strongly disagree and 5 = Strongly agree.

Usefulness of Workshop. All participants rated the general usefulness of the work-shop as 5, which show clear indication of a positive perceived value.

We were also interested in examining the understandability of the presented usability problems before and after the redesign exercise, that is, whether or not the exercise helped them gain a more thorough understanding of the problems. Based on the presentation of the problems (just before the exercise) the average rating of the clarity was 4.6, which clearly indicates that the participants found the problem descriptions during the presentation to be understandable.

When asked if the redesign exercise provided a more clear understanding, the participants on average rated 3.2, which indicate that the exercise did not increase or decrease the clarity of the presented usability problems.

Usefulness of Usability Report. The usefulness of the report was rated as 4.8 on average. Although this rating is a bit lower than the workshop rating, we see a clear indication that participants also found the report valuable. We also asked participants to rate the understandability of problem descriptions in the report, which resulted in an average rating of 4.4. This result is also a bit lower compared to the workshop.

In addition we asked participants to openly comment on their experience in reading the report and all found the report positive. As an example one of the participants mentioned that "I think that the report is very good. It provides a good explanation of the approach and it works fine as an encyclopaedia of problems in the current system. The individual problems are easy to understand and it is very good that the critical issues are described in further detail".

Finally we asked participants to openly comment on both the workshop and the usability report. Four of these explicitly mentioned the workshop, where one answered that "The report combined with the workshop was very constructive because we discussed specific design solutions to overcome the problems" and another stated that "I hope that we will see more of this. It is very insightful to discuss different ideas on how to improve a system. It is also fun to disagree on, what the most important strengths and weaknesses are and then listening to the arguments".

5   Discussion

Our exploratory study with the redesign workshop originated from the experience that usability evaluation results and especially feedback have proved to have limited effects on software development in practice [5, 7, 15]. From an educational point of view, the transfer of usability evaluation knowledge seems to be ineffective and have very limited success.

In designing the workshop, we were inspired by Dewey's theory on education, which is seen as being constituted by transmission through communication. It reflects a sharing experience process until it becomes a common possession [4]. Dewey emphasizes that traditional teaching's concern with delivering knowledge need to be balanced with a much greater focus on the students' actual experiences and active learning [17].

We attempted to integrate cooperative and active learning through actual participation of both evaluators and developers in the process of conceptualizing the usability of the system and the redesigning activity. Thus, we explored how Dewey's theory on education can be combined with the idea that redesign proposals should be a key vehicle for providing feedback from a usability evaluation. It is interesting that all the developers rated the workshop very high, and their understanding of the problems identified in the usability evaluation clearly improved.

Dewey's educational theory focusses on learning by doing. But Dewey not only re-imagined the way that the learning process should take place, but also the role of the teacher in the learning process. The teacher should not stand at the front of the room doling out bits of information to be absorbed by passive students. Instead, the teacher's role should be that of facilitator and guide. Instead, the teacher should be a partner in the learning process, guiding students to independently discover meaning within the subject area. He expressed it this way: "Were all instructors to realize that the quality of mental process, not the production of correct answers, is the measure of educative growth something hardly less than a revolution in teaching would be worked."

In our study, the developers grew and improved their understanding of the usability problems that had been identified even if they did not produce the best overall solution. Yet they were able to contribute constructively to create redesign proposals and in particular to flesh out the concrete details of the overall pattern that was created by the usability specialists.

In our study, we had two groups of developers where one of them had process support from a usability specialist while the other only included developers. The experiences from the process and the redesign proposals created demonstrate very little difference between those two groups. Thus the inclusion of a usability specialist in one of the groups did not seem to make an important difference on the process. Group 1 and 2 both chose a low level bottom-up approach to redesign. The proposed designs evolved around three main themes, where Group 1 suggested the most technical advanced solution, while Group 2 focused on contextual help. We expected Group 1 to come up with a simpler and more pragmatic solution than the one they chose, since this would ease their workload on the upcoming system considerably. This indicates that they were dedicated in solving the usability problems and hereby to create an improved user interface.

After the workshop, the developers designed and implemented a new version of the system. This version was based on the overall ideas from Group 3, filled in with details from the redesigns created by Group 1 and 2. While the inclusion of a usability specialist in Group 2 made little difference compared to Group 1, the basic ideas in the solution from Group 3 was very useful as a basic pattern for the actual redesign of the system. Thus the influence from the usability specialists was more on the product and a pattern for that, than on the redesign process itself.

The aim of the workshop was to involve the developers actively in a collaborative process of redesigning the existing system and thereby improve the developers' understanding of the usability problems that had been identified. We measured the success in terms of the perceived strengths and weaknesses of the system as it was expressed by the developers. We observed a substantial reduction in the number of identified strengths after the redesign task. This shows that participants viewed the system in a more realistic perspective, which may have been caused by them improving their understanding of the usability problems through the active involvement in the redesign exercise.

We observed that the categories instructions, simplicity, breadth and save were mentioned as strengths before the exercise, but not after. This indicates that the participants have been influenced by the identified usability problems. Høegh et al.

[8] conducted a study with two developers, who were asked to list five strengths and weaknesses before and after reading a usability report. That study showed that the developers did not change their perceived strengths noticeably, which contrasts with our findings. This difference can be explained in terms of Dewey's theory on education because they only passively read the usability report.

Considering the perceived weaknesses we observed that participants identified the same number before and after the redesign exercise. This is a bit surprising since we saw a considerable change in the strengths before and after the redesign task. However, we observed considerable changes in the categories of clarity, structure, terminology and transparency. The categories digital signature, simplicity, attachment and workflow were identified as weaknesses before the exercise but not after, and we saw that participants who perceived these categories as problems shifted towards the new categories of structure, excess and terminology. Thus we see the participants being influenced by the group work in terms of perceived weaknesses. This corresponds to the findings of Høegh et al. [8], which show a developer completely altering his perceived weaknesses after reading the usability reports.

In our study, the developers had not received prior training in user interface or interaction design. It would be interesting to see if they could do better if they had been trained before the redesign process.

Training relates to the more general idea of qualifying barefoot practitioners in usability engineering. Bruun and Stage [27] have discussed this in relation to usability evaluation where they trained practitioners in that with very positive results. When software developers can be trained to conduct usability evaluations, it should be possible to achieve the same in redesign. This is important in practice, because the amount of usability specialists is limited, and many smaller development companies have no possibility of involving external specialists.

In this collaboration, a usability specialist may become a leader and facilitator of design, rather than the sole source of it. It is often argued that generating many alternatives is a key part of good design. In that case, it seems to be an advantage to have a facilitator for a larger group of barefoot practitioners rather than requiring this individual to be solely responsible for generating design ideas.

6   Conclusion

This paper has presented an exploratory study where a usability evaluation was followed by a redesign workshop. In this workshop, evaluators and developers worked together in an active collaborative learning process inspired from Dewey's educational theory. The aim of the workshop was that the developers should understand and try to resolve the identified usability problems. The workshop was a success in the sense that the developers' understanding of the problems with the system changed considerably, and they expressed a high level of satisfaction with the process. They did not produce the redesign proposal that eventually was implemented, but they were able to choose that as the best redesign, and they could fill in the details of this overall design pattern to arrive at a considerably improved system. The study indicates that usability specialist support to the redesign process is less important than having usability specialists generate a redesign pattern where the details can be filled in by the developers.

We have conducted an exploratory study. It is not possible to make any definite conclusions on this qualitative basis, but the study is useful for defining more quantitative hypotheses for a further study.

The basis for assessing the success of the workshop has been the developers' understanding of the strengths and weaknesses of the system and their statements about the process. It would be interesting with a follow-up study to assess the downstream utility of the workshop in the developers' work to eliminate the usability problems that have been identified and to measure the utility of the redesign proposals that were produced in the workshop.

References

1. Bailey, R.W., Allan, R.W., Raiello, P.: Usability Testing vs. Heuristic Evaluation: A Head-to-Head Comparison. In: Proc. Human Factors Society 36th Annual Meeting, pp. 409–413 (1992)
2. Bevan, N., Singhal, N., Werner, B., Degler, D., Wilson, C.: Formative Evaluation. Usability Body of Knowledge, http://www.usabilitybok.org/methods/formative-evaluation
3. Capra, M.G.: Comparing Usability Problem Identification and Description by Practitioners and Students. In: Proceedings of the Human Factors and Ergonomics Society 51st Annual Meeting, pp. 474–478. HFES, Santa Monica (2007)
4. Dewey, J.: Democracy and Education: an introduction to the philosophy of education (1916), http://en.wikisource.org/wiki/Democracy_and_Education
5. Dumas, J., Molich, R., Jefferies, R.: Describing Usability Problems: Are we sending the right message? Interactions 4, 24–29 (2004)
6. Hornbæk, K., Frøkjær, E.: Comparing usability problems and redesign propos-als as input to practical systems development. In: Proceedings of CHI 2005, pp. 391–400 (2005)
7. Hornbæk, K., Frøkjær, E.: What kind of usability-problem description are useful for developers? In: HFES 2006, pp. 2523–2527 (2006)
8. Høegh, R.T., Nielsen, C.M., Overgaard, M., Pedersen, M.B., Stage, J.: The Impact of Usability Reports and User Test Observations on Developers' Understanding of Usability Data: An Exploratory Study. International Journal of Human-Computer Interaction 21(2), 173–196 (2006)
9. Hvannberg, E.T., Law, E.L.-C., Lárusdóttir, M.K.: Heuristic evaluation: Com-paring ways of finding and reporting usability problems. Interacting with Computers 19(2), 225–240 (2007)
10. ISO, ISO 9241-11 Ergonomic Requirement for Office Work with Visual Display Terminals (VDTs) – part 11: Guidance on Usability. Switzerland, International Organization for Standardization (1998)
11. Jeffries, R.: Usability Problem Reports: helping Evaluators Communicate Effectively with Developers. In: Nielsen, J., Mack, R.L. (eds.) Usability Inspection Methods, pp. 273–294. John Wiley, New York (1994)
12. John, B.E., Marks, S.J.: Tracking the Effectiveness of Usability Evaluation Methods. Behaviour and Information Technology 16(4/5), 188–202 (1997)
13. John, B.E., Packer, H.: Learning and using the cognitive walkthrough method: a case study approach. In: Katz, I., Mack, R., Marks, L. (eds.) Proceedings of ACM CHI 1995 Conference on Human Factors in Computing Systems, pp. 429–436. ACM, New York (1995)

14. Lavery, D., Cockton, G., Atkinson, M.P.: Comparison of evaluation methods us-ing structured usability problem reports. Behaviour & Information Technology 16(4/5), 246–266 (1997)
15. Law, E.L.-C.: Evaluating the downstream utility of user tests and examining the developer effect: A case study. International Journal of Human-Computer Interaction 21(2), 147–172 (2006)
16. Mack, R., Montaniz, F.: Observing, predicting and analyzing usability problems. In: Nielsen, J., Mack, R.L. (eds.) Usability Inspection Methods, pp. 295–339. John Wiley and Sons, New York (1994)
17. Polito, T.: Educational Theory as Theory of Culture: A Vichian perspective on the educational theories of John Dewey and Kieran Egan. Educational Philosophy and Theory 37(4), 475–494 (2005)
18. Rubin, J.: Handbook of Usability Testing: How to Plan, Design, and Conduct Effective Tests. John Wiley & Sons, New York (1994)
19. Sawyer, P., Flanders, A., Wixon, D.: Making a Difference - The Impact of Inspections. In: Proc. CHI 1996, pp. 376–382. ACM Press (1996)
20. Smith, A., Dunckley, L.: Prototype Evaluation and Redesign: Structuring the Design Space through Contextual Techniques. Interacting with Computers 14, 821–843 (2002)
21. Strauss, A., Corbin, J.: Basics of qualitative research. Techniques and procedures for developing grounded theory, 2nd edn. Sage, Thousand Oaks (1998)
22. Uldall-Espersen, T., Frøkjær, E., Hornbæk, K.: Tracing Impact in a Usability Improvement Process. Interacting with Computers 20(1), 48–63 (2008)
23. Wixon, D.: Evaluating Usability Methods: Why the Current Literature Fails the Practitioner. Interactions 10(4), 29–34 (2003)
24. Hart, S.G.: Nasa-task load index (nasa-tlx); 20 years later. NASA-Ames Research (2006)
25. Hart, S.G., Staveland, L.E.: Developing the NASA-TLX (Task Load Index): Results of Empirical and Theoretical Research. Human Mental Workload. In: Hancock, P.A., Meshkati, N. (eds.) Human Mental Workload, pp. 239–250. North-Holland, Amsterdam (1998)
26. Kjeldskov, J., Skov, M.B., Stage, J.: Instant Data Analysis: Evaluating Usability in a Day. In: Proceedings of NordiCHI 2004, pp. 233–240. ACM (2004)
27. Bruun, A., Stage, J.: Barefoot Usability Evaluations. Behaviour and Information Technology (2014), doi: 10.1080/0144929X.2014.883552
28. Gothelf, J.: Lean UX. O'Reilly (2013)

An Autoethnographic Study of HCI Effort Estimation in Outsourced Software Development

Shalaka Dighe[1] and Anirudha Joshi[2]

[1] Tech Mahindra Ltd., India
`shalakad@techmahindra.com`
[2] IDC, IIT Bombay, India
`anirudha@iitb.ac.in`

Abstract. A fair amount of literature has been published concerning the gaps between HCI and software engineering. However, most of it tends to look at the effects of these gaps rather than their causes. We argue that the use of autoethnographic methods would help us in identifying the root causes of these gaps and can bring us closer to finding potential solutions. In this paper, we focus on issues associated with effort estimation for HCI activities in three projects in three typical engagement models for outsourced software development projects in a mainstream IT company in India, namely Fixed Price model, Mixed model, and Time & Material model. We found that the HCI practitioner needs to negotiate her position with several members of the team, both within the vendor and client organisations. At times, a foot-in-the-door project turns out to be a foot-in-the-mouth project. At other times, it leads to inefficiencies and imbalance of work load. The autoethnographic approach led to reflexive thinking by the HCI practitioner, helping her to develop a deeper understanding of all aspects of a problem, and bringing her closer to potential solutions in some cases. The paper also brings to light several aspects of autoethnography as a method, which can influence effort estimation of HCI activities for future projects.

1 Introduction

It has been more than three decades since Human Computer Interaction (HCI) has been recognized as an independent field of study. HCI has since then grown into a compelling discipline that asserts due consideration in the development of software. Software Engineering (SE) also recognizes the relevance of HCI methods in SE processes in their research. Nevertheless, there are major gaps in integrating HCI and SE in both theory and practice [1]. A review of SE literature reveals that there is still a lot to be desired with regards to references of HCI activities in SE processes, and both fields appear to be severely disjointed especially in the initial phases in the software development process [2] [3].

In practice, there is a substantial lack of mutual understanding among software engineers (SEs) and HCI practitioners, and research testimonies from their respective fields do not appear to strongly influence this interaction. The distance between

S. Sauer et al. (Eds.): HCSE 2014, LNCS 8742, pp. 19–35, 2014.
© IFIP International Federation for Information Processing 2014

the disciplines is perhaps the largest in context of outsourced software development projects; particularly if the teams are distributed and there are greater gaps of culture, time and distance between team members.

This research aims to identify issues related to entrenchment of HCI activities in SE practices in Indian organisations and their overseas counterparts wherever possible. The Indian Information Technology (IT) sector was born in 1968 and has seen an exponential growth to over 2.8 million people employed in this sector by 2012 [4]. It has also evolved from the initial era of staff augmentation services (also known as 'body shopping') to the current state of specialized software engineering and IT consulting. Most organisations work in an 'onsite-offshore' engagement model with the customers, where the 'onsite' employees, who are collocated with the customer, bring in a synergy with stakeholders, whereas the 'offshore' employees working from India help in building a cost advantage. Clearly, we are looking at a 'culture' that resides within these organisations, with the members of this culture sharing distinct experiences, behaviours, and even language.

Qualitative research with SEs and HCI practitioners to identify gaps in practice has been done though surveys [5] [6], but the root causes for the gaps seem to remain elusive. Perhaps these causes are rooted somewhere in the practical and sociological aspects of software development in practice, in the day-to-day interactions between people from different disciplines, regions and organisations, the process of their decision making, and their power structures. Perhaps surveys do not capture these intricacies sufficiently. Rönkkö has successfully used ethnographic approach to identify challenges in applying HCI methods in several SE projects, but the studies are either limited to singular projects, or in academic projects outside the environment of software organisations [7] [8].

Our research takes an autoethnographic approach to understand how software development works in practice; how small actions from day to day life have an unanticipated impact on a project in the longer term, how decisions get made, what role do the HCI practitioners, SEs and customers play, and what are the root causes that impede the integration of HCI activities in the development of software. We base our work in the context of mainstream IT industry in offshore software development.

In section 2 of this paper, we first summarize prior work done in the area of HCI-SE integration, autoethnography, and HCI effort estimation. Section 3 describes our study with respect to the research setting and the method. In section 4, we briefly describe three project stories that were written as an autoethnography and discuss our findings. Section 5 concludes our research and provides directions for future research in this area.

2   Prior Work

We discuss prior work in three major areas of our research, namely the gaps in HCI-SE integration,   autoethnography in organisational context, and HCI effort estimation.

2.1   Gaps in HCI and SE

HCI researchers have been extensively advocating inclusion of HCI practices in SE for more than three decades. Quantitative studies have shown that the better integration of HCI activities in SE processes leads to software that aligns better with its goals [9].

There have been attempts to integrate specific HCI methods [10] [11] [12] [13] and process models [14] [15] in software development with reasonable success. HCI practitioners have also achieved some success in implementing various User eXperience (UX) team models in software development organisations [16] [17]. Few qualitative case studies and first-person accounts of HCI practitioners through 'action research' of software projects [18] [19] have highlighted practical challenges in HCI-SE integration. And yet, studies do not show encouraging reports on the entrenchment of HCI in SE,   which is evident from the works of some HCI practitioners who have even proposed workarounds and shortcuts to handle these challenges [20] [21] [22] [23] with the view that 'something is better than nothing'.

A review of SE 'textbooks' reveals that any research in the area of HCI-SE integration has not permeated sufficiently in these books, and a clear-cut gap exists especially in the 'requirements' chapters [24] [25] [26]. However, considerable amount of scholarly research in SE discusses various methods to integrate HCI practices in SE. Text on requirements engineering as early as 1993 suggests the use of ethnographic techniques to inform software requirements [27].

In the next three paragraphs, we list the major obstacles in the integration of HCI practices in SE in the industry practice that are identified and summarized in three separate works [9] [18] [28]:

HCI practitioners are involved too late in the project and HCI activities are often included as an afterthought. SE managers think that their project cannot afford to spend time and efforts on usability. There is an overall reluctance to adopt HCI practices, and HCI practitioners are regarded as "nuisance", who get in the way of people who "really deliver" the project. Wherever HCI activities are included, they are not allotted sufficient time in the software development project plan. HCI practitioners are rarely involved in the requirements engineering stage, and software requirements are often over-specified by way of a description of the user interface rather than users' tasks or goals. Usability is considered and documented as a Non-Functional Requirement (NFR) in a software product. Porting projects, i.e. projects undertaken to 'port' the software to a newer technology platform, provide minimal input to HCI practitioners, as the requirements are simply copied from previous versions of the software. Usability is viewed as a 'window dressing' discipline, with focus only on style guides.

SEs and HCI practitioners do not share the same culture or perspective and do not understand the respective constraints under which each group has to operate. There seems to be a significant lack of communication between SEs and HCI practitioners, in spite of working together on the same project and from the same location. SEs and HCI practitioners use different names for similar activities and artefacts, often resulting in duplication of efforts and deliverables.

HCI techniques are relatively unknown, and are inaccessible to small and medium sized software development teams. Quite often SEs with little or no training in HCI are directly responsible for practicing and applying HCI methods in their organisations, making crucial HCI decisions without the benefit of usability knowledge. HCI activities do not get sufficient process support from software development organisations. Since inclusion of HCI activities is not a process improvement, but as a paradigm shift, organisational inertia inhibits the inclusion of HCI methods in their processes. Although HCI practitioners provide several iterations of design solutions, crucial design decisions are often taken by the client representatives.

Though the above gaps are qualitative in nature, most of these tend to describe the effect or the end result, and not the root cause of these gaps. Perhaps these researchers were not looking for the root causes, but intended to implement some specific HCI methods in an SE project, or the research methods that they were using to identify the root causes were not suitable.

One of the gaps that has not been investigated sufficiently, and that we believe has a significant early impact on the success of HCI activities in a project, is that of effort estimation. This is of particular importance in the context of outsourced software development projects.

2.2   Autoethnography

Since our research is directed to the practical and sociological aspects of software development, we use ethnographic studies of software engineering community and its practices as an exploratory method to identify the root causes behind the aforementioned gaps in HCI and SE.

Further, given that the first author of this paper works in a mainstream IT company in India, we choose autoethnography as a method to generate deeper insights. This company provides IT solutions to hundreds of customers across the world. This author has access to several projects in this company and hence enjoys a professional advantage for such a study.

Ethnography is a branch of anthropology dealing with scientific description of cultural phenomena through observation, participation and interpretation [29]. Ethnography is derived from Greek 'ethnos', meaning folk or people of the same race who share a distinctive culture, and 'grapho' meaning 'to write'. The word ethnography refers to both, the method and the result, the study and systematic recording of human cultures, and also a descriptive work produced from such research [30].

Ethnographic research methods include conversations, interviews and participant observation. While the first two are indistinguishable from other types of fieldwork, participant observation is a characteristic feature of ethnography. Diverse research techniques are employed here, including analysis of spoken discourses or narratives, collecting and interpreting artifacts, collecting oral and life history material. As a result, ethnographic work involves 'thick descriptions' of a cultural phenomena [31].

Participant observation is the core means of ethnographers to understand the world views of the culture of the researched community by not merely making observations, but also by participating. The term 'Participant Observation' consists of two conflicting or oxymoronic terms [32]. Participation indicates joining the activities, sharing experiences and emotions, contributing to discussions, and taking part in the very interactions that make up a social life. Observation implies an outsider watching and listening, not always taking part, recording the goings-on of the field and gathering other form of material evidence. In short, it entails trying to maintain some sort of dispassionate scientific objectivity. The tension between the two can be difficult to manage in practice. Clifford Geertz describes the participant observer's predicament as "a question of living multiplex life: sailing at once in several seas" [33].

Ethnography is an exploratory research. We use ethnography when we are not sure what research questions or even the categories of questions that we should ask. Focus and research questions emerge and evolve as the researcher learns about the studied practice. In organisational ethnography, it can be used as a comparative method – to make comparisons between the official and unofficial, or what should happen vs. what actually happens, and a comparison of formal vs. informal practices. For organisational ethnography, "the real voyage of discovery begins not with visiting new places but in seeing familiar landscapes with new eyes" [34].

When the ethnographer becomes a part of the people under study, she gains what is called the 'emic' perspective, which, as the insiders' point of view, is the heart of ethnographic research. She attempts to understand and accurately describe situations and behaviour, not objective reality [35]. When she stands back and tries to make sense of the observations, she acquires the 'etic' perspective, or the outsider's point of view, typically from the social scientific perspective of reality, or in the context of organisational ethnography, that of 'what should be'. The etic perspective has also been successfully achieved through collaboration with an academic researcher in organisational ethnography [36]. In software engineering organisations, ethnography has been the key method to inform the design of software for Computer Supported Collaborative Work (CSCW), as because of its unique ability to uncover the complexities of the social aspect of collaboration [37].

Ethnographic reflexivity occurs when the ethnographer looks at the methods and the ways of interpreting that she is applying while doing her field study. She needs to pay careful attention to how her own thinking, or maybe methods, is distorting the sociological phenomenon or biasing it [38].

Autoethnography is a specialised version of ethnography. It is a combination of autobiographical ethnography that interjects personal experience with field research, native anthropology where subjects study their own group, and ethnic autobiography that involves personal narratives [39]. As in case of ethnography, autoethnography is both a method and the product of that method. In autoethnography, the researcher "possesses the qualities of permanent self-identification through full internal membership of the researched community" [40], and hence it becomes most relevant in our research context. This method also suits the motivation of this research, since it not only invokes the autoethnographer to awaken to, respect, and make contact with her own questions and problems [41] but also to search for knowledge that can potentially bring about positive changes in the researcher's life [42].

Autoethnographic fieldwork relies on the researcher's personal documentation, including diaries, written communications and personal notes to capture the emotional and subjective aspects of the research. It is, of course, not practical to remember and make note of everything that happens in the researcher's daily life, and autoethnographers can write about important and remembered moments perceived to have significantly impacted the trajectory of subsequent events [42].

This study attempts to gain first-hand insights into the HCI practices in offshore software development from a social perspective, to gain comprehensive understanding of how HCI work is organized in SE processes and its implications to HCI as a profession. It throws light on the social aspects of how HCI activities are situated in the offshore SE context, and how they contribute to the effort estimation and scheduling of HCI activities in offshore software development.

Software development in the India takes place in complex environments that are geographically and culturally distributed, and involve people from various disciplines and cultures. Autoethnography facilitates a detailed account of the practice and situated activity of such a multifaceted environment. Since ethnography is not only about documenting facts, but also about interpretation of those facts, it allows us to view the happenings from a different lens. As a method, it has the unique ability to highlight the local rationalities of people's action and behaviour in the given context. As an exploratory method with constructivist approach, ethnography is most beneficial in under-researched areas. It is therefore relevant to use autoethnography in an attempt to understand the practical and sociological aspects of integration of HCI activities in SE.

2.3   HCI Effort Estimation

Per our understanding, no prior research has been done in the area of effort estimation of HCI activities in the outsourced software industry context. Perhaps this is because literature tends to be dominated by either university researchers or by independent HCI consultants, rather than by HCI practitioners in offshore software development organisations.

3   Our Study

The first author of this paper is a full-time employee of a large IT company in India. She has considerable exposure and experience both in SE practices and HCI methods, which provide her with 'unique adequacy', i.e. indigenous skills and knowledge to help her in making sense of the goings-on in the software development community, thus bringing in the emic. The second author is a full-time faculty member of a university, and though he has had interactions with the industry, he is very much an outsider to the industry. There are at least two levels of etic in our work. Firstly, both authors come from an HCI and design discipline which, in a sense, is still considered as 'outsider' to the mainstream software development work. Secondly, the second author is a further 'outsider' to the organisation being studied.

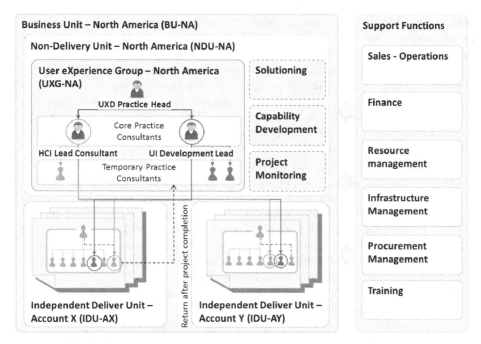

Fig. 1. Organisational structure showing placement of UXG team

The first author described the project stories as they happened in real life. Given her background, she at times did not question everything and took many events and happenings for granted. This is where the role of the second author came in wherein he questioned the current practices and showed them in a different light. Thus this research is a result of a co-produced autoethnography, where the autoethnographer collaborated with an academician to add richness to the interpretation.

3.1 Background

The company in question deals with IT solutions for 540 customers from 46 countries. The company follows an organisational structure of Business Units (BUs) based on the geographical location of the client. Each BU is treated as a separate entity with their own business targets, and contains several Independent software Delivery Units (IDUs) that are supported by Non-Delivery Units (NDUs) that consist of pre-sales and capability development practices.

The user experience practice in this company is called the User Experience Group (UXG) that employs about 100 people. This group is operational since year 2000 and is currently distributed in three BUs. The author of this paper heads the UXG practice of North America geography (UXG-NA), which currently consists of 30 team members (Fig.1). Of these, 17 are HCI practitioners and visual designers with under-graduate and graduate level qualifications in visual communication, interaction design, human factors engineering, computer science and graphic design, with experience ranging from 5 to 12 years in HCI. Several team members have additional certifications in usability, HCI and project management. The remaining team of 13 works in the UI development area with skills in UI technologies such as HTML/ CSS, Javscript, JQuery, Liferay, Flex. These developers are also sensitized towards HCI to an extent that they can interpret interactive prototypes and visual designs comfortably without the need for detailed design specifications. UXG members are geographically distributed in three cities in India and three cities in the USA. UXG-NA is a part of an NDU of a BU that deals with clients from USA and Canada.

UXG is involved in HCI design for various types of projects such as enterprise applications, customer self-service portals and customer support applications. UXG is also involved in pre-sales activities including preparing project proposals, effort estimation for the UX activities of a proposed project, and supporting proofs-of-concept (POCs). In 2013, the UXG-NA team has worked on over 50 projects and POCs. The UXG group and delivery team jointly prepare effort estimates for each project. Finance team quotes a 'dollar figure' to clients based on the effort estimates and the Sales Operations group deals with invoicing the clients.

Once a project is confirmed, an HCI practitioner is assigned to that project in a matrixed project organisation structure. Their direct reporting remains within UXG, but are assigned to work with the project manager as a part of the project team. If more than one person from UXG is assigned to the project, one of them is designated a UXG lead.

When they are not directly assigned to a client project, UXG members are assigned to a central 'practice' project in NDU, where they work on capability development and presales activities. A core team of HCI practitioners as lead consultants are a part of this practice project. These lead consultants from mentor and review the work of the HCI practitioners who are assigned to confirmed projects.

3.2   Method

The first author has been playing the role of an HCI practitioner, mentor and manager for UXG-NA for the past three years. She has been closely involved in the UXG projects from the proposal stages to the closure of UXG participation in the project. While working with her team on these projects, she has encountered several of the known gaps with HCI-SE integration that were discussed in the prior works section. It was felt that if she was to take steps to improve HCI-SE integration, merely identifying the existence and describing the nature of these gaps was not enough. It was necessary to seek a deeper understanding of the root causes of these issues. It was decided to use autoethnographic methods to understand the sociological and practical aspects underlying the causes of these gaps.

The first author started applying autoethnography techniques to her fieldwork and wrote a daily diary and several 'project stories' using her project notes, email communications, meeting notes, project documents, and organisational process documents. This paper refers to the project stories of three projects written between the five months of August 2013 and December 2013, which we believe represent three typical project engagement types in the Indian IT industry. The stories contained thick descriptions of the goings-on at the workplace, in relation to the project, including the autoethnographer's own thought process, perceptions and emotions, and interpretations of actions of her colleagues. Since Project B and C were already in progress when she started writing the diary, the initial parts of these stories were based on retrospective account of the events based on earlier emails, project notes, and the autoethnographer's memory.

These stories were further analysed by making sense of the data by bringing in the academic perspective into what really happened, using interpretations from previous works, which refers to the essential ethnographic technique of 'emic interpreted by the etic'. The original project stories are detailed descriptions of the way the project progressed, the organisation structure and roles of the project team, excerpts from communications, quotes from team meetings, excerpts from project artefacts, etc. that the autoethnographer perceived as 'what matters for HCI'. Further, the stories were written by the first author in the role of an autoethnographer, but the analysis was conducted by collaborating with the second author, whose academic background helped with the etic perspective in identifying issues and their causes in the light that were not viewed by the research community before. For the sake of this research paper, we abridged the project stories only in the context of our findings related to HCI effort estimation.

4   Findings and Discussion

To provide context to our findings we present a short description of the three representative project stories written as a part of the research. We further discuss our findings from these project stories in the way they influenced the project outcome.

4.1   Project Stories

The projects represent three typical types of commercial terms of engagement with customers in outsourced software development; the first is Fixed Price model, the second, a Mixed model, and the third, Time & Material model. These stories were written in a narrative format using a first person narrative 'I' in case of autoethnographer's individual actions and thoughts, and 'we' in case an additional UXG member was involved.

The Fixed Price (FP) model is typically used where the scope of work is clearly defined, making it possible to estimate the efforts required fairly accurately and thus charge the customer with an agreed fee for a well-defined scope of work. The Time & Material (T&M) billing is done using an agreed hourly rate based on consultants' time spent and other costs such as software and infrastructure. A Mixed model is used when consulting services are required for defining the scope of project work which, once defined, allows a more precise estimation of the efforts for subsequent design, development and testing activities. In this model, T&M billing is adopted for initial activities related to identifying scope and requirements, and a fixed fee is charged for the subsequent clearly defined scope of work. The FP and Mixed models are typically used when the vendor company is providing IT consulting services to the customer. However, when conducting business with IT divisions of large customer organisations having their own IT teams with their own program and project management, a T&M model is traditionally used for 'staff augmentation'. This is essentially 'filling up' vacant job positions within the customer organisations on contract basis, where monthly invoices are sent to the customer for each position as per T&M billing rates agreed upon in a Master Service Agreement (MSA) signed with the customer. The customer 'sponsor' often sends 'job descriptions', interviews candidates for these positions and issues work orders for start and end dates of the selected employees. These employees then either move to customer locations overseas or work from the customer's Offshore Development Centres (ODCs) which are secure offices connected to the customer's network but located in India within the IT company's premises.

Project A: UXG was asked by a senior member of the sales team to provide an FP estimate in about four hours with limited understanding of the scope as *"preparing wireframes/ HTML pages of an application consisting of 25 pages"* and to refer a requirements document prepared earlier by the presales team. This project arrived around the time the authors decided to write project stories as a part of autoethnographic research, and saw it as an opportunity to write the story as the project progressed. Hence this story does not contain any retrospective accounts. The said requirements document was an over-specification of the User Interface (UI) to an extent of a detailed description of the proposed UI, including description of links and controls to be provided on each page. We (UXG) interpreted the document from 'user tasks' perspective, made assumptions to arrive at a count and complexity of the probable tasks, and applied our standard estimation template to quote our efforts for HCI activities. Since we (UXG) had not worked with this customer before, we were urged by the sales leads to provide *"conservative"* estimates in order to get a *"foot-in-the-door"* to gain entry with this customer. The software development activities had already started, and since there was not enough time to invest in user studies, we had to completely rule out that activity from our estimates. Once the project started, the 'onsite' delivery lead asked us to *"produce screens"* without giving us any input on users' goals and task flows. Since the development estimates (also FP) were based on the said requirements document, we were asked not to digress from it and to refrain from proposing any design solution that would change the development effort. The software development team was required to review our design to ensure that we do not propose any design element that calls for a deviation in the development effort. However, the development team was occupied with their work, and our designs were taken to the customer representative for review without the development team's feedback on possible development scope changes. Due to limited initial input, our conceptual design was a far cry from the expectations of the customer representative, who had to spend time with us to explain to us the user goals and tasks. After ten days of deliberation, reviews and UI suggestions from the customer representative, our wireframe prototypes took shape, seemed to meet customer expectations and were signed off by the customer representative.

The wireframes were then passed on to the development team for implementation. That is when they realised that the development efforts would increase significantly if they were to use our wireframes. They raised a change request (CR) and quoted additional efforts to the customer for the changes. The customer was unable to procure additional funds due to lack of business justification, and consequently, we were asked to re-design the UI to match its description in the original requirements document. Our value-add was thus mostly limited to visual design as per the customer's brand guidelines. The delivery team perceived the resulting wastage of time and duplication of efforts as our fault, since apparently visual design was what was expected from us in the first place. Eventually, though a better design was produced and approved by the client representative, it was never implemented. Further, the project timeline was affected, and we left a bad impression with the customer as well as the delivery team.

Project B: UXG team of two HCI practitioners was already working on this project from the customer location in the USA for a year at the time we wrote this project story. The commercial engagement with the customer was on a Mixed Model basis. This was a greenfield project, i.e. a project which is independent of any constraints from prior software applications in terms of inherited technology, processes or functionalities. Since the scope was unknown at the requirements stage, the customer was charged on T&M basis for the HCI design activity. Subsequent visual design and development work was done on an FP basis. The customer had their own HCI team working on a part of this project. When additional scope was anticipated in the next releases, the delivery team proposed addition of UXG team members to work from offshore locations on T&M basis for working on the detailed design. Also, the customer's internal HCI team members were discontinued from this project for various political reasons, creating the need to add UXG team members on this project. Thus, a team of three additional HCI practitioners were added to the existing team for the new scope of work at the time we wrote this project story.

As per the client's information security mandate, these offshore HCI team members were required to work from the customer's ODC, having very strict security policies. The security controls included very limited internet access, restrictions on carrying books or mobile phones inside the ODC, and mailbox audits for possible violations.

As things turned out, the additional work that was anticipated was not enough to fully engage these three additional team members. The security policy restricted the installation of any software on the local machines and the offshore UXG team was required to work with software like Photoshop and Axure installed on remote desktops, resulting in severe loss of productivity of the offshore team. Mechanisms for file sharing between onsite and offshore team also proved to be tedious. The result was that the onsite team ended up doing most of the design and prototyping work and the offshore team was left with little or no work. Project delivery heads were unwilling to release them from the project, as it would mean loss of revenue in T&M mode. They also anticipated additional work in the near future, and were unwilling to let go of the team who were already familiar with the project, for fear that they may not be able to get the same team when additional work comes in. Eventually, one HCI designer left the organisation as he was left idle for too long. The customer also became aware of the lack of offshore productivity resulting in removal of one additional HCI practitioner.

Project C: Two HCI practitioners were working on this project for over a year on this program when we wrote this story. The customer belongs to the IT department within the client organisation. This was a porting project, where the new software was to have only a few additional features and functionality from a legacy application. All the team members involved in this project, including the program manager, were on staff augmentation (T&M) mode. A customer manager coordinated the activity of defining minor additional requirements and the scope for the next release. He planned the start date for each release, when the HCI activities started on the same date as development activity.

As per this delivery schedule, we allocated two HCI practitioners who started at the same time as the development and UI integration team. For the development team, however, the starting point for their work was the UI code, which was in fact the final deliverable of the UXG team. Since the developers' time was billed to the customer, they were required to produce evidence of their work and hence they demanded the UI code on day one. The UXG team was hard pressed on time to deliver the design and UI code in the first part of the release cycle. On the other hand, once the UI was delivered, the UXG team was left with very little support work till the end of the cycle. Conversely, the development team, having lost valuable time in the beginning of the phase, was overloaded at the end.

We recommended to the customer manager to stagger the start dates of UXG team and development team. However, from his perspective, each development cycle takes into account an approved budget for an approved scope of work, and he found it practically difficult to implement our suggestions. Therefore, this schedule continued for two cycles regardless of our recommendation. From the third cycle onwards, the UXG team members started to proactively utilize their idle time at the end of release to conduct HCI activities based on our 'gut feel' about the next logical scope for the fourth release. When scope was finalized for the fourth release, it turned out to be slightly different from our guess, but we were able to effectively use our design work with slight changes in the fourth release, thus getting a buy-in for our recommendation from the customer manager.

From the fourth release onwards, we were able to implement this staggering arrangement, which has now been running smoothly for the next three releases.

4.2   Discussions

Effort estimation and schedule of HCI activities in outsourced IT projects has not been discussed within HCI. Our study provided insights into this under-researched area from the perspective of causality.

Layers of Negotiations
HCI practitioners in outsourced software development companies have to deal with multiple layers of negotiation for their estimates and schedules, starting with sales teams, project delivery heads, development teams and then finally with the client. By the time we reach the client level, the effort estimates are reduced by 10 - 20% of the initial estimate. Our negotiations are not just limited to efforts, but also extend to the justification of proposed HCI activities affecting development timelines.

Foot-in-the-door Becomes Foot-in-the-Mouth

With *"conservative"* estimates for efforts as well as timelines, we are forced to cut down some crucial user-centred design activities, not only affecting the quality of our design output but also creating undesirable precedents for future engagements.

While trying to gain entry with a new customer, we tend to spend crucial time in the initial design stage in getting familiarized with the new organisation and new domain. Already pressured with a compressed estimate, this unavoidable activity is seen as wastage of time due to HCI practitioners' lack of domain expertise, creating a bad impression with the customer.

In case of Project A, the customer requested UXG involvement as an afterthought in an attempt to get a better UI which was perceived as a business opportunity by our sales team. However, since these events took place after development scope was finalized, slight deviation from the scope meant a Change Request in a Fixed Price project, triggering a change management process. This change request did not get budgetary approval due to insufficient business justification for the change, as the scope of work had never changed in the first place.

Effectively, the project did not benefit much from the HCI expertise, created a bad precedent and bad impression, and also failed to meet the original objective of getting foot-in-the-door with a new customer.

Over Estimation Leads to Under Performance and Inefficiency

Whereas in foot-in-the-door Fixed Price projects there is pressure on the UXG to minimise efforts put in the project and still make a good impression on the client, the pressure is in the opposite direction in case of a T&M project. Particularly for greenfield projects, with little clarity on project scope, project management literature suggests that it is safe for both the parties to sign in a T&M contract [43]. In case of large programs, as seen in Project B, the project management tends to over-estimate the human resources requirement, with a view to generating maximum revenue from the engagement.

This, coupled with an offshore software development scenario, the information security limitations, and the work environment in certain customer ODCs makes it difficult to utilize the full potential of offshore HCI practitioners, leading to inefficiency, employee dissatisfaction and attrition.

Relay Race Is Better Teamwork than Race against Time

Since HCI efforts are perceived as development activity, or at best, low level design activity, our project schedule is planned concurrently with the UI integration and backend development schedule. As seen in Project C, this resulted in unequal work distribution for the entire team during the development phase. The resulting work pressures amplified the lack of cooperation and co-ordination between software developers and HCI practitioners. When software development is iterative and the project plans to release multiple cycles, there is an opportunity to stagger the HCI and software development work. This approach is also the one used for HCI activities in agile software development projects, as suggested in literature on integration of HCI in Agile SE process [44] [45]. Staggering of start date for HCI activities in a project resulted in equal distribution of workload for both UXG and the software development teams leading to optimised resource utilisation. Instead of running a race against time, relaying design output in a staggered manner resulted in improved co-ordination amongst two teams, better work distribution, and effectively better output. However, current practices of organising such projects around features, makes it difficult to stagger the work in this manner. Though a desirable change was brought about through proactive and long-term involvement of the HCI practitioners in the particular case of Project C, such practices need generalisation and mainstreaming.

5   Conclusion

Our research led to a better understanding of effort estimation and scheduling of activities in the offshore software development context. We found that HCI practitioners have to continually deal with several layers of negotiations for estimating and scheduling HCI activities. In case of FP estimations, especially the foot-in-the-door mode led to cost cutting, insufficient HCI activities, time pressures, poor impressions, and poor quality of design output. The T&M estimation, on the other hand, allows sufficient time to conduct HCI activities leading to better quality of design output, but failed in terms of resource utilization for certain customers. In another case, better management and planning HCI in software development activities improved work distribution, cooperation and co-ordination amongst HCI and SE community working in T&M mode.

The issues related to HCI-SE integration literature in the context of industry practices have referred to the challenges that are faced by the HCI practitioners. Our findings provide deeper insights to the social situations and situated actions of individuals in the setting that led to some of these challenges for HCI effort estimation.

We found benefits in the use of autoethnography as a research method in providing deeper understanding of HCI projects in offshore SE environment. Previously, when the first author worked without the current research angle, she took some actions as 'given', as something 'that was always done' without giving them much thought. Collaborating with the academic co-author for analysing the project stories helped in comparing the 'what happened' against 'what should have happened' which she would have otherwise missed as 'what typically happens'. When she started thinking about her own actions as a part of the 'observing' in autoethnography, she may have affected her thoughts and actions reflexively. While this position is similar to that of a reflective practitioner [46], our work brings in the ethnographic element of the etic perspective to inform the reflections of the emic aspects.

In order to understand the perspectives and interpret the actions of others around her in the researched field, the first author gained renewed empathy with other disciplines, including software development teams, the sales teams (in Project A) as well as the client manager in (Project C).

However, the ethnographer found it extremely difficult to observe emotions, reactions and level of involvement in distributed teams, since a majority of communication takes place over teleconference and emails. We think that engaging in regular informal conversations outside of work related communications with co-workers, both from HCI and SE areas, can help in overcoming this limitation in future work. This level of insights into the rationale of individuals behind situated actions can allow deeper understanding of the causality of issues.

The use of autoethnography in outsourced software development industry from an HCI perspective can be extended towards identifying the root causes for several other gaps found prevalent in HCI-SE integration, the most pressing issues being the absence of HCI practices and practitioners in requirements engineering, lack of support from organisational processes, and perception of HCI activities as 'skin deep'.

References

[1] Seffah, M.C.: HCI, usability and software engineering integration: present and future, pp. 37–57. Springer (2005)

[2] Abran, Bourque, P.: SWEBOK: Guide to the software engineering Body of Knowledge. IEEE Computer Society (2004)

[3] Doerr, J., Opdahl, A.L.: Foundation for Software Quality

[4] NASSCOM, The IT-BPM Sector in India: Strategic Review 2013 (2013)

[5] Majid, R.A., Noor, N.L.M., Adnan, W.A.W.: Strengthening the HCI Approaches in the Software Development Process. Proceedings of World Academy of Science, Engineering and Technology (2012)

[6] Jerome, A., Kazman, R.: Surveying the Solitudes: An Investigation into the Relationships between Human Computer Interaction and Software Engineering in Practice. In: Seffah, A., Gulliksen, J., Desmarais, M.C. (eds.) Human-Centered Software Engineering - Integrating Usability in the Software Development Lifecycle. Springer (2005)

[7] Rönkkö, K.: Making methods work in software engineering: Method deployment-as a social achievement (2005)

[8] Rönkkö, K., Winter, J., Hellman, M.: Reporting user experience through usability within the telecommunications industry. In Proceedings of the 2008 International Workshop on Cooperative and Human Aspects of Software Engineering (2008)

[9] Joshi, N.: Integration of Human-Computer Interaction Activities in Software Engineering for Usability Goals Achievement. IIT Bombay (2011)

[10] Fischer, H.: Integrating usability engineering in the software development lifecycle based on international standards. In: Proceedings of the 4th ACM SIGCHI Symposium on Engineering Interactive Computing Systems (2012)

[11] Dupuy-Chessa, S., Mandran, N., Godet-Bar, G., Rieu, D.: A case study for improving a collaborative design process. In: Ralyté, J., Mirbel, I., Deneckère, R. (eds.) ME 2011. IFIP AICT, vol. 351, pp. 97–101. Springer, Heidelberg (2011)

[12] Leonardi, C., Sabatucci, L., Susi, A., Zancanaro, M.: Design as intercultural dialogue: Coupling human-centered design with requirement engineering methods. In: Campos, P., Graham, N., Jorge, J., Nunes, N., Palanque, P., Winckler, M. (eds.) INTERACT 2011, Part III. LNCS, vol. 6948, pp. 485–502. Springer, Heidelberg (2011)

[13] Al-Ani, B., Trainer, E., Ripley, R., Sarma, A., Van Der Hoek, A., Redmiles, D.: Continuous coordination within the context of cooperative and human aspects of software engineering. In: Proceedings of the 2008 International Workshop on Cooperative and Human Aspects of Software Engineering (2008)

[14] Memmel, T., Gundelsweiler, F., Reiterer, H.: CRUISER: A Cross-Discipline User Interface and Software Engineering Lifecycle. In: Jacko, J.A. (ed.) HCI 2007. LNCS, vol. 4550, pp. 174–183. Springer, Heidelberg (2007)

[15] Sousa, K.S., Furtado, E.: An approach to integrate HCI and SE in requirements engineering. In: Proc. of Interact 2003 Workshop on Closing the Gaps: Software Engineering and Human-Computer Interaction (2003)

[16] Gajendar, U., Johnson, C.: The inmates are still running the asylum: How to share a design vision with engineers. In: Marcus, A. (ed.) HCII 2011 and DUXU 2011, Part II. LNCS, vol. 6770, pp. 276–282. Springer, Heidelberg (2011)

[17] Nieters, J.E., Ivaturi, S., Dworman, G.: The internal consultancy model for strategic UXD relevance. In: CHI 2007 Extended Abstracts on Human Factors in Computing Systems (2007)

[18] Patton, J.: Hitting the target: adding interaction design to agile software development. In: OOPSLA 2002 Practitioners Reports (2002)

[19] Gulliksen, J., Göransson, B., Boivie, I., Blomkvist, S., Persson, J., Cajander, Å.: Key principles for user-centred systems design. Behaviour and Information Technology 22(6), 397–409 (2003)

[20] Bowles, Box, J.: Undercover User Experience Design. Pearson Education (2010)

[21] Krug, S.: Rocket surgery made easy: The do-it-yourself guide to finding and fixing usability problems. New Riders (2009)

[22] Khalayli, N., Nyhus, S., Hamnes, K., Terum, T.: Persona based rapid usability kick-off. In: CHI 2007 Extended Abstracts on Human Factors in Computing Systems (2007)

[23] Lin, L.-C., Lee, W.O.: UI toolkit for non-designers in the enterprise applications industry. In: CHI 2007 Extended Abstracts on Human Factors in Computing Systems (2007)

[24] Pressman, R.S.: Software Engineering - A Practitioner's Approach, 7th edn. McGraw-Hill (2010)

[25] Sommerville, I.: Software Engineering. International computer science series. Addison Wesley (2004)

[26] Lee, R.Y.: Software Engineering- A Hands-On Approach. Atlantis Press (2013)

[27] Sommerville, Rodden, T., Sawyer, P., Bentley, R., Twidale, M.: Integrating ethnography into the requirements engineering process. In: Proceedings of IEEE International Symposium on Requirements Engineering (1993)

[28] Seffah, A., Gulliksen, J., Desmarais, M.C.: Human-Centered Software Engineering-Integrating Usability in the Software Development Lifecycle, vol. 8. Springer (2005)

[29] Galman, S.C., Shane: The Lone Ethnographer - A Beginner's Guide to Ethnography. AltaMira Press (2007)

[30] Atkinson, P., Coffey, A., Delamont, S., Lofland, J., Lofland, L. (eds.): Handbook of Ethnography. Sage Publications Ltd., London (2001)

[31] Madden, R.: Being Ethnographic - A Guide to the Theory and Practice of Ethnography. Sage (2010)

[32] O'Reilly, K.: Key Concepts in Ethnography. Sage (2009)

[33] Geertz, C.: Works and Lives: The Anthropologist as Author. Stanford University Press (1988)

[34] Ybema, S., Yanow, D., Wels, H., Kamsteeg, F.: Organizational Ethnography - Studying the Complexity of Everyday Life. Sage Publications (2009)

[35] Hammersley, M., Atkinson, P.: Ethnography: Principles in practice. Routledge (2007)

[36] Kempster, S., Stewart, J., Parry, K.W.: Exploring co-produced autoethnography. Business Papers, p. 112 (2008)

[37] Shapiro: The limits of ethnography: combining social sciences for CSCW. In: Proceedings of the 1994 ACM Conference on Computer Supported Cooperative Work (1994)

[38] Davies, C.A.: Reflexive ethnography: A guide to researching selves and others. Routledge (2008)

[39] Reed-Danahay, D.E.: Auto/ethnography. Berg, New York (1997)

[40] Hayano, D.M.: Auto-ethnography: Paradigms, problems, and prospects. Human Organization 38(1), 99–104 (1979)

[41] Wall, S.: An autoethnography on learning about autoethnography. International Journal of Qualitative Methods 5(2), 146–160 (2008)

[42] Ellis, C., Adams, T.E., Bochner, A.P.: Autoethnography: an overview. In: Historical Social Research/Historische Sozialforschung, pp. 273–290 (2011)

[43] A Guide to the project Management Body of Knowledge (PMBoK Guide), 5th edn. Project Management Institute, Pennsylvania (2013)

[44] Joshi, Sarda, N., Tripathi, S.: Measuring effectiveness of HCI integration in software development processes. Journal of Systems and Software 83(11), 2045–2058 (2010)

[45] Beyer, H., Holtzblatt, K., Baker, L.: An agile customer-centered method: Rapid contextual design. In: Zannier, C., Erdogmus, H., Lindstrom, L. (eds.) XP/Agile Universe 2004. LNCS, vol. 3134, pp. 50–59. Springer, Heidelberg (2004)

[46] Schon, D.A.: The reflective practitioner: How professionals think in action (1984)

[47] Garfinkel, H., Sacks, H.: On Formal Structures of Practical Actions In Theoretical Sociology: Perspectives and Developments. In: McKinney, J., Tiryakian, E. (eds.) Appleton-Century-Crofts, New York (1970)

Bridging User Context and Design Models to Build Adaptive User Interfaces[*]

Mladjan Jovanovic[1], Dusan Starcevic[2], and Zoran Jovanovic[2]

[1] DISI, University of Trento, Italy
[2] School of Electrical Engineering, University of Belgrade, Serbia
mladjan.jovanovic@unitn.it, starcev@fon.rs, zoran@rcub.bg.ac.rs

Abstract. With respect to modeling the context of interaction, two different research communities consider the context from different viewpoints. The user-centered view which prevails in the HCI and the device-centered view which is dominant in the mobile and ubiquitous computing. Despite existing advances, context modeling and user interface (UI) design methods are still poorly integrated, making it difficult to use the contextual elements directly in UI design. This paper focuses on bringing user-related aspects of the interaction context in UI design. We propose a model-driven framework for the development of adaptive user interfaces. The framework describes the interaction context by integrating contextual factors from different context perspectives in a unison manner. Then it provides formal semantic relations between contextual and UI elements. The framework has been used in the data visualization domain, particularly in the design of the software instrument table for UAV (Unmanned Aerial Vehicle) that takes into account user context, namely human perceptual abilities.

Keywords: user interface design, user interface models, user context, user abilities, model-driven engineering.

1 Introduction

Trend to build UIs that look and behave according to the context of interaction is emerging [1]. This requires appropriate methods and techniques for formal integration of interaction context elements into UIs development and adaptation processes accordingly. While there are numerous efforts to integrate contextual data into UI design, they still suffer from a semantic gap between contextual and UI elements.

In our research, we aim to provide seamless formal integration of interaction context information into the UI design. Our work is based on a phenomenological view of the context [2] which advocates that humans create and modify the context during interaction. Likewise, we believe that humans perceive context as a feature of

---

[*] Research described in this paper is derived from the first author's previous work with the University of Belgrade, Serbia. We acknowledge EU FP7-PEOPLE 607062 ESSENCE Project.

S. Sauer et al. (Eds.): HCSE 2014, LNCS 8742, pp. 36–56, 2014.

interaction, rather than of objects or other people. This is important because the description of interaction context between humans and computers requires a clear definition of context. Based on existing developments, we propose a unified generic framework for designing UIs that provides formal specification of the interaction context in a way that it can be integrated in UI design. The framework includes an ontological and an architectural foundation that structure the development of adaptive UIs in a uniform way. In particular, our research has been concerned with:

- The design of the user-centered interaction model which integrates knowledge from a different context perspectives into a single unified view;
- Integration of the proposed model with the framework for development of adaptive UIs;
- Application of the proposed framework in adaptive UI design.

Next section briefly describes the previous research work devoted to user-related aspects of interaction context in the adaptive UI design. From that work we propose a generic approach to articulating and combining the interaction context and UI models in the space of Model Driven Engineering (MDE). The approach is fully supported by mainstream MDE technologies. Finally, the case study illustrates the approach considering human perception in designing visual UIs.

2   User Context Considerations in UI Design

If we consider interaction context, the UI design process typically becomes more complex since the number of situations (contexts) in which the system will operate increases. Early efforts to use interaction context in adaptive UI design can be found in work by Thevenin and Coutaz [3]. They have introduced the notion of UI plasticity to describe the ability of UI to adapt, or to be adapted, to the context of use while preserving usability. This brought Calvary et al. [4] to propose the theoretical framework for development of adaptive UIs, namely the CAMELEON reference framework. The aim of the framework is to combine all possible situation-optimized designs into a single, uniform design.

Based on seminal work of Calvary et al. [4], researchers and developers have introduced many implementations of the reference framework [5, 6, 7]. These approaches are mostly declarative and model-based relying on a number of models in describing different aspects of a UI. In the last decade, they have evolved in parallel with the aim of coping with the different challenges raised by the design of adaptive UIs in continuously changing technological settings and usage scenarios [5]. This initiated a large body of UI design methods producing productive models that can be automatically processed by computers. A number of different languages and tools was proposed, each focusing in specific aspect(s) of UI design [8]. Some of them are task-based, such as CTTE [9, 10] and HAMSTERS [11], while others work with multiple kinds of UI models such as UsiXML [7], MARIA [12] and CAP [13]. There are also approaches addressing development of interactive systems for a specific domain. Well-known example is the Petshop tool, based on a Petri net formalism, for designing UIs for safety-critical systems [14].

Analyzing the existing work from a usability perspective, we can see that the adaptation they perform is mainly device-oriented. If we consider user context, we can notice that the user is mainly modeled with logical activities it performs during interaction with the systems, i.e. various task notations [9, 10, 11, 15]. Existing approaches lack in providing formal specification of other user features (such as various abilities and skills) in a way that can be directly used in UI adaptation either in design-time or run-time or fits into UI development process. There are some attempts to describe and integrate user abilities [16], however, they are brought down to optimization problems.

With respect to the formal semantic connections between contextual and UI elements, existing approaches mostly aim at the utilization of context information built into UI design models to support the generation of user interfaces at runtime. The interconnection between contextual and UI elements is implicitly hidden within the UI model description and the interpretation is not made explicit.

3   Connecting Interaction Context and UI Elements

The proposed approach focuses on design; its current implementation does not support the automatic detection or recognition of contextual data, but rather complements to them. In this regard, we focus on:

- Formal specification of interaction context elements and
- Their integration in designing adaptive UIs.

To cope with the heterogeneity of interaction context elements and the lack of a specification to uniformly access and integrate these elements, we introduce a user-centered context interaction model. Using the model, we derive a generic framework for adaptive UIs. We propose a front-end architecture that complements with back-end architectures that may focus on the context acquisition and abstraction process.

In this section, we outline the technological foundation for building the framework. Thereafter we describe the unified interaction model and the generic UI development framework, respectively.

3.1   Technological Ground

In following paragraphs, we give a brief overview of software technologies we have used to design the models and the framework.

Modeling Language

In describing modeling framework, we extend standard UML with elements specific for adaptive UIs. The UML is mainly being used to communicate about the design of a software system. This makes the framework accessible to a wide range of software engineers from aspects of development tools and processes. The fact that all information is expressed in UML makes it easier to integrate the UI specification with the specification of the application functional core. Although there are UML extensions for UI modeling [17, 18, 19], they consider UI design process partially. UMLi [17] provides extensions for GUI design, while CUP [18] proposes UML-based task modeling notation using activities and states. Wisdom [19] is a UML proflile that describes high-level UI models at early stages of design.

UML Profile defines extensions to a reference UML metamodel with the purpose of adapting the metamodel to a specific platform or domain. The primary construct is the Stereotype, which is defined as part of a Profile. Stereotypes can be used to add constraints and properties (tagged values) to model elements. The profile provides UML constructs that describe particular domain. We have used the profile mechanism to create domain specific languages (DSL) for designing adaptive user interfaces.

Transformation Language

Model transformations represent the central operation for handling models in MDE. In our approach, we have opted for ATLAS Transformation Language [20] as the technology for UI model transformations based on the following arguments: an open-source software, the large user community, a solid developer support, a rich knowledge base of model transformation examples and projects, and a mature tool support. In addition, the technology provides dedicated support for UML model trans-formations. We have used ATL to design transformations between UI models on different abstraction levels that can be parameterized with various contextual factors contained in the interaction model.

3.2 The User-Centered Context Interaction Model

With respect to context representation, we adopted the canonical view of context that includes three components – the users, the devices and the environment [4]. However, the view contains elements at too high abstraction level to include in UI optimization at either design time or runtime. For this reason, we introduced the interaction model that serves as binding component and provides primitives that bridge semantic gap between UI elements and contextual elements (Figure 1). The interaction context enables us to describe context elements relevant to a particular user's interactions.

The generic interaction model describes common characteristics of contextual factors regardless of their specific manifestations.

Human model combines human abilities and preferences. Human abilities include various sensory, perceptual, cognitive and motor abilities. In describing human abili-ties we rely on the model that structures levels of human information processing. At the very basic level is sensation - a combination of biochemical and neurological events triggered by the stimulus of sensory organs. These sensory stimuli lead up to the level of perception where the signals are organized, analyzed and interpreted. Cognition is the eventual accretion of perceptual interpretations and past experiences leading up to intelligence and human actions. Preferences present subjective human characteristics that are tied to a particular domain, for example, preference to use specific communication channels (such as visual, voice or multimodal).

Devices are described with physical and logical properties, both connected to various stimuli they detect or produce, such as sound, light or pressure. Stimuli

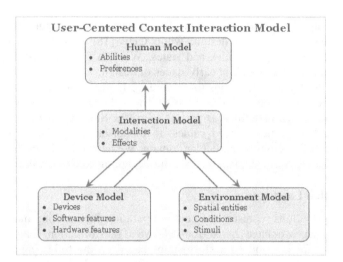

Fig. 1. High-level view on unified user-centered interaction model

are defined as physical signals in the environment with sensible properties, such as amplitude or frequency. In addition, environment model assumes various kinds of spaces in which interaction occurs (for example, room, vehicle or public space), as well as the existence of physical conditions that may influence the interaction (for example, sound and light conditions).

Interaction model is described using existing generic framework for modeling multimodal HCI [21]. Multimodal UIs combine natural human input modalities — such as speech, pen, touch, hand gestures, eye gaze, and head and body movements — in a coordinated manner with multimedia system output. In describing multimodal HCI, we consider UIs through modalities they employ. Modality is seen as a form of interaction designed to engage a number of human abilities. In this sense, it produces effects on humans or processes effects produced by humans. The idea is to describe UIs in terms of modalities that produce effects. Modalities can be simple or complex. Complex modality integrates other modalities to create simultaneous use of them, whereas simple modality presents a primitive form of interaction. Simple modalities can be input or output. An input modality transfers human output into a form suitable for device processing, while an output modality presents data to the user. Effects are abstract concepts and are closely related to human abilities. They are organized in five main categories: sensory, perceptual, linguistic, motor, and cognitive effects. Sensory effects describe processing of stimuli performed by human sensory apparatus. Perceptual effects are more complex effects that the human perceptual system obtains by analyzing data received from sensors, such as shape recognition, grouping, or highlighting. Motor effects describe human mechanical actions, such as hand movement. Linguistic effects are associated with human speech, listening, reading, and writing. Cognitive effects appear at a higher level of human information processing, such as memory processes or attention. More elaborate description of the UML multimodal HCI framework can be found elsewhere [21].

Following subsections describe the unified interaction model. In describing the model we focus on interaction model and user modeling.

Common Ground – Interaction Model

Interaction model is described using multimodal HCI design issues. In this way, we consider UIs through modalities they employ. Modality is seen as a form of interaction designed to engage a number of user capabilities. In other words, it produces effects on users or processes effects produced by users.

The basic idea behind the proposal is to model the UIs with modalities they use and associated effects. Next step is to connect these models to the user, device and environment descriptions [22]. The connections between contextual factors and UI elements are created on modality-specific (CUI) level. While we describe UIs with multimodal concepts, we introduce the term of contextual factor to describe concepts related to interaction semantics (Figure 2). UI element uses interaction modalities to engage specific human abilities. As the result of these engagements, various effects on users are generated. On the other side, human, environment and device entities specify contextual factors that act as filters for produced effects.

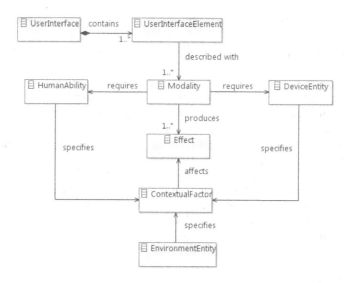

Fig. 2. Semantic relations between contextual and UI elements

Contextual factors can reduce or enhance usage of some effects from a user, device and environment perspectives (Figure 3).

In other words, contextual factors are associated with effects which they influence. This relation is described with the level in which some effects are available for a given contextual factor in terms of associated rating scale. The concept of a rating scale allows different types of evaluation. This way, we can precisely express the way contextual factors affect produced effects. Some relations can be described with a qualitative scale (for example, low, medium, high), while others can use quantitative scale from 0.0 to 1.0, or from 0 to 100 % with resolution of, for instance, 1%.

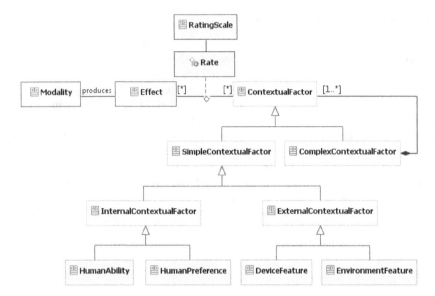

Fig. 3. Proposed approach to flexible definition of contextual factors described with UML Class Stereotypes

Contextual factors are classified into two categories – simple and complex. Simple contextual factors can be internal or external looking from the user viewpoint. Internal factors are further classified as human model elements, whereas external factors are organized as device and environment features. Internal factors describe the usage of effects from a human's perspective. External factors describe the way interaction environment and device characteristics influence the effects.

Proposed classification encapsulates information about a single piece of interaction context such as user ability or environment condition and provides a uniform interface for components that use the context. Moreover, it provides a flexible mechanism to design contextual factors of different complexities. In general, resulting factor can be a combination of user abilities, environment conditions and device properties.

Modeling User Abilities

With respect to formal specification of user-related aspects [23], the following principles are important for UI design:

- Architecture level to describe the user – We may focus on presentation details, or on the dialogue level expressing the order of user actions and responses;
- Level of abstraction to describe a user - We may have a concrete user model for a particular system design, or we may opt for a more generic model;
- Purpose of describing the user - We may create a formal description to be part of a running or system under design, or we may use the formal description to perform automated or hand analysis.

With respect to the principles above, appropriate user specification technique requires underlying ontology of human factors. The International Classification of

Functioning, Disability and Health (ICF) [24] proposed by the World Health Organization provides a comprehensive overview of many important functions of humans. It covers functioning from both an individual (such as various physiological and psychological functions) and social (such as communication issues and interpersonal relations) point of view. The ICF is a good candidate for describing all important user functionalities since it provides a detailed description of human functioning. Categories are the units of classification and are arranged hierarchically (e.g., the domain of Sensory Functions and Pain has nested categories such as Seeing Functions, Quality of Vision, and Light Sensitivity). The classification introduces generic qualifiers for measuring the extent or the magnitude of the functioning or disability for each class of human functions. In this respect, it has been used in the domain of personalized e-health systems [25]. The ICF is designed in a form of hierarchical textual ontology accessible through an online browser [26]. We have adapted and formalized the ICF ontology in a form of the UML profile.

Figure 4 shows basic ICF anatomy and function categories designed as UML Class stereotypes.

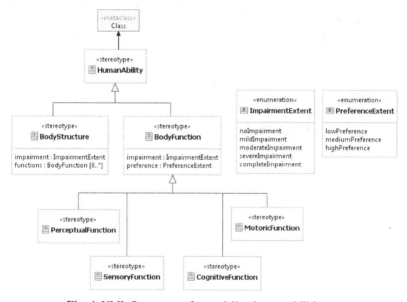

Fig. 4. UML Stereotypes for modeling human abilities

Specific categories are derived from these root elements. The measure of performance in human functioning is described with tagged value (ImpairmentExtent). These values are quantitative, expressed as a collection of distinct values in accordance with ICF. In order to express user individual preference for using particular human function, we have introduced additional attribute (tagged value) of enumerable type (PreferenceExtent). List of possible values of this type includes: *lowPreference*, *mediumPreference* and *highPreference*.

Generic concepts of modalities and effects are naturally connected to human functions described in ICF. This gives us formal mechanisms to describe humans' multimodal communication channels in a clear and flexible way.

4   The Framework

In this section we describe the UI development framework together with modeling extensions for designing UI models on different abstraction levels.

The community working on design of interactive systems has reached a general consensus in identifying several levels of abstraction by CAMELEON reference framework [4]. Connections between models from different abstraction levels are established through a sequence of model transformations.

Task model is provided for the end user's tasks. Modality independent model (Abstract UI) describes UI independently of any interaction modality and implementation. Modality specific model (Concrete UI) describes a potential UI after a particular interaction modality has been selected (for example visual, speech or multimodal). In existing framework, UI code (Final UI) is generated from modality specific level. At this point, we extend standard framework with additional abstraction level – platform specific UI model adapted to implementation technology as intermediate level between Concrete UI and Final UI. From this model the Final UI (the code) is generated. We notice that for given modality in Concrete UI (for example, List element in visual UI) a number of different implementation exists in different languages (including declarative, imperative or hybrid). On one hand, the model that captures the features of concrete technology allows us to better preserve UI interaction semantics contained in modality-specific model when decide to implement it. On the other hand, UI code generation from platform-specific model is easier and straightforward. This is especially important in case of more complex UIs such as ours.

In Figure 5 we describe the development space for the framework in which we connect interaction models with UI design models.

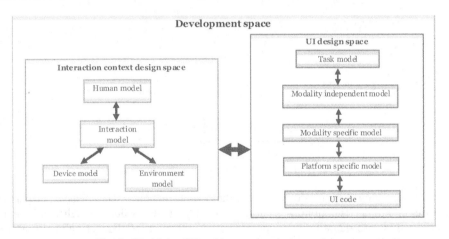

Fig. 5. Combining UI and interaction design spaces

In order to provide framework's tool support, we have developed customized extensions of Eclipse Modeling Framework (EMF), one of the most widely used UML tools, based on the described approach. UI designers can use proposed UML's semantic extensions to provide formal descriptions of interaction models and UI models. Developed tools incorporate descriptions of standard UI controls in terms of modalities and effects. The tools also automate UI design process since they include ATL libraries that perform transformations between UI models at different abstraction levels. These transformations are parameterized by interaction context models (taking and analysing them as additional input models). In addition, EMF provides mechanisms for describing object-oriented languages with UML models. We have used these mechanisms to design a platform-specific UML models adapted to a specific language, such as Java. Currently, the tools work with Java implementations of UIs.

4.1   Task Modeling

Figure 6 shows the basic set of UML stereotypes for task modeling.

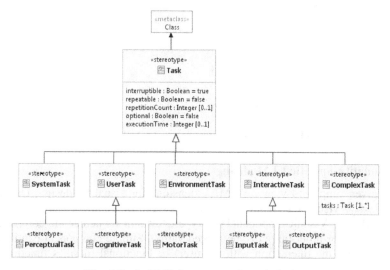

Fig. 6. Basic UML Stereotypes for task design

We consider the concept of a task in a broad sense. In this way, task can be system (connected to computer processing), user, environmental, interactive (input or output taking the computer as a reference point) and complex (integrates simpler ones). Depending on the level of information processing, user task can be perceptual, cognitive or motoric. In addition, each task is described with attributes saying whether it is interruptible, repeatable and optional, or containing information about execution time. We have introduced the ComplexTask type that enables designing composite tasks. In analogy with CTTE [9], we have also introduced stereotypes for modeling task relations as extensions of UML Association.

4.2   Modality-Independent UI Modeling

Figure 7 describes modeling extensions for description of abstract UI. AbstractUI-Component can be simple or grouping (serves as a container component). Interactive-Component realizes presentation aspects of the interface, as well as the interaction with the user. In this respect, it can be input or output. FunctionalComponent describes UI functionalities with the set of UIOperations and is associated with corresponding interactive component.

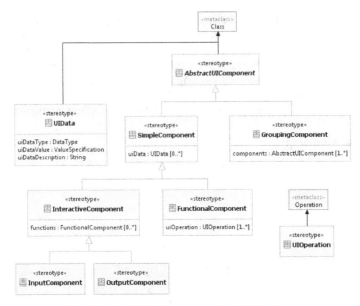

Fig. 7. Basic UML Stereotypes for AUI design

4.3   Modality-Specific UI Modeling

Figure 8 gives simplified view on UML extensions for visual UI design. Depending on complexity, visual UI component can be simple or complex (GroupingVisualComponent). The VisualComponentType type determines whether the component is an input, output or input-output (type tagged value). Simple component can be interactive (describes the interaction with the user) or functional (defines functionalities that enable the interaction).

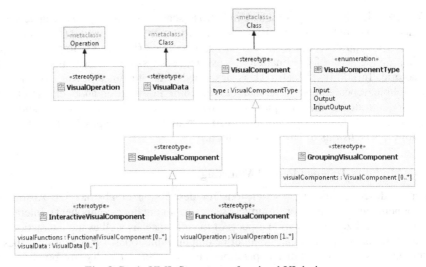

Fig. 8. Basic UML Stereotypes for visual UI design

4.4   Platform-Specific UI Modeling

Creating the platform specific model means to create UML model of a particular technology. Such a model can be built using a number of methods. EMF has so-called model importers that are able to construct UML models from XMI, XML Schema, or even Java annotated source code. We have used the model importer to describe Java Swing/AWT controls in UML. Figure 9 shows UML descriptions of common Java GUI controls.

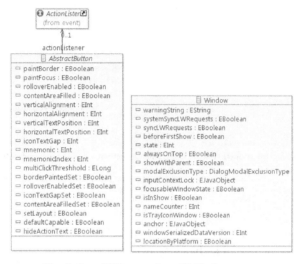

Fig. 9. Java GUI controls as UML classes

This model serves as the basis for UI code generation. We have developed code generators that transform platform-specific models into Java source code.

5   Case Study – Design for User Context

To improve usability of the UAV (Unmanned Aerial Vehicle) data visualization software tool [27, 28], we have used the framework for the design of adaptive software instrument tables that takes into account human perception. The table serves for tracking UAV flight parameters, as well as propulsion parameters. First, we describe user model used in adaptation, then we go through UI models on different abstraction levels.

5.1   User Context – Model of Human Abilities

The user is modeled with sensory, perceptual, cognitive and motoric abilities (Figure 10). *UAVOperatorProfile* is designed as InternalContextualFactor stereotype. It contains relevant human physiological and psychological functions expressed as corresponding ICF categories. Each function is designed as corresponding UML stereotype. Specific functions are organized as subcategories (nested classes) of the containing function. For example, specific eyesight functions, such as distant vision, near vision, visual field and light sensitivity, are contained in the *SeeingFunctions* class that is modeled as the *SeeingFunction* stereotype.

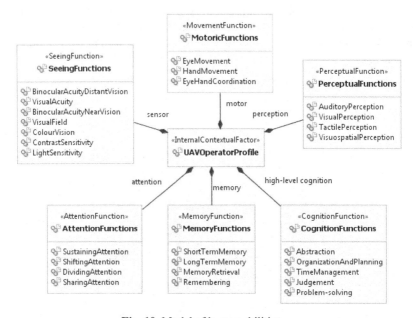

Fig. 10. Model of human abilities

Performance measure of each function is described with impairment extent and preference level designed as tagged values (attributes). On the other hand, these measures determine exploitation of the effects dependent on them. For the purpose of this paper, on the example of a specific instrument type (horizon instrument), we demonstrate instrument table design based on the analysis of impairment extent and preference level of using specific human function - visuospatial perception. Visuospatial perception is human perceptual function involved in distinction of the relative position of objects in the environment or in relation to oneself. The ability is important for the domain of interactive visualization dealing with a multidimensional set of data, such as the UAV data visualization platform.

5.2   Task Level

Analyzing existing types of tasks of a user responsible for UAV manning, we came to a common structure of a task concerned with aircraft flight parameter maintenance (Figure 11).

The task of UAV parameter maintenance is described as ComplexTask stereotype. It comprises two interactive tasks, an OutputTask stereotype of reading parameter's value and an InputTask stereotype of assigning parameter's value. The output task includes human tasks of parameter perception and parameter cognition, whereas the input task assumes the execution of human motoric action (such as voice or hand movement). Based on this generalized model, we have derived task models for maintaining various kinds of parameters, such as air speed and horizon. The task of reading the parameter's value is carried out using a specific instrument. On the other hand, the assignment of values is executed using manual steering console.

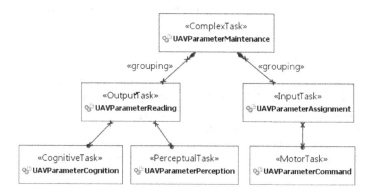

Fig. 11. Generalized task structure describing UAV parameter maintenance

5.3   Modality-Independent Level

Task model is transformed into an abstract UI model of instrument table, where each task is mapped to the corresponding abstract instrument. Figure 12 shows the model of abstract instrument that is independent of interaction modality.

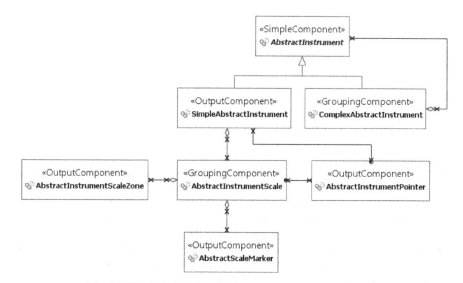

Fig. 12. Simplified abstract model of an aircraft instrument

An abstract instrument can be simple (designed as OutputComponent stereotype) or complex (designed as GroupingComponent stereotype). The complex type allows for definition of instruments that contain simpler ones. Simple instrument contains an instrument scale (designed as GroupingComponent stereotype) and scale pointer (designed as OutputComponent). The scale consists zones and markers. Zones enable presentation of critical value ranges for distinct parameters. Proposed approach to modeling instruments enables construction of generic instrument types with different structures and complexities.

5.4   Modality-Specific Level

This level combines different spaces for UI description, the UI space (Figure 13) and interaction context (Figure 14). Similar to abstract, visual instrument can be simple (designed as InteractiveVisualComponent stereotype) or complex (designed as GroupingVisualComponent stereotype). Simple instrument is further classified into common types of instruments that can be found in practice, such as counter instrument, angle counter instrument, gauge instrument and horizon instrument.

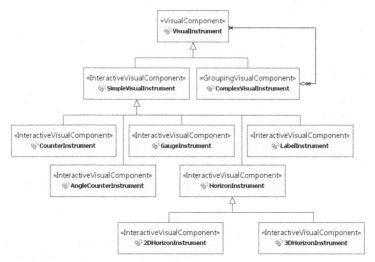

Fig. 13. Hierarchy of common visual instrument types described in terms of the UML Stereotypes

Figure 14 shows a simplified UML class diagram describing visual instrument as a complex modality together with associated effects using proposed UML modeling extensions [21]. The usage of these effects depends on related human functions contained in the model of human abilities (Figure 11). DynamicInstrumentPointer is modeled as a dynamic output modality consisting of StaticInstrumentPointers. Instrument pointer generates several perceptual effects: it is highlighted by its shape; orientation and motion. In addition, it employs slight eye movements.

InstrumentScale is designed as a complex modality consisted of scale zones and markers (both designed as static output modalites). *ScaleMarkers* add perceptual effects of highlighting by shape, size and color, whereas ScaleZones employ perceptual effects of highlighting by color and shape, and grouping by proximity. The VisualInstrument itself produces cognitive effects of sustained attention and short-term memory. In a similar way, we have designed derived types of instruments (from Figure 13). Some of them employ specific perceptual effects. For example, HorizonInstrument produces spatial perceptual effects such as *HighlightingByDepth*.

Table 1 illustrates concrete entities and their attributes considered when creating particular type of instrument on platform-specific level.

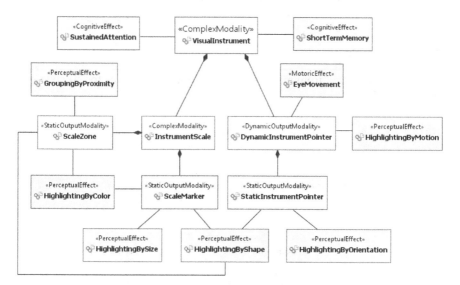

Fig. 14. Visual instrument described in terms of interaction concepts (modalities and effects)

Table 1. Elements of human perception and associated effects considered by transformation rule producing concrete instrument type

User context space		UI design space
Human Ability		**Perceptual Effects**
VisualPerception **VisuospatialPerception**		HighlightingByShape HighlightingBySize HighlightingByColor HighlightingByOrientation HighlightingByMotion GroupingByProximity **HighlightingByDepth**
Performance	**Preference**	**Rate**
noImpairment mildImpairment moderateImpairment severeImpairment completeImpairment	highPreference mediumPreference lowPreference	high medim low

The transformation rule takes two input elements – visual instrument (horizon) described in terms of modalities and effects (as shown in Figure 14), and model of human abilites (Figure 10). First, it performs mapping of the perceptual effects (*Highlighting By Depth*) to corresponding human functions (*VisuospatialPerception*). Analyzing performance and preference attributes for the function, it determines exploitation measure (rate) of related effects. Based on calculated ratings, it generates suitable horizon instrument model adapted to specific UI implementation technology (Figures 15).

5.5   Platform-Specific Level

This model is produced from modality-specific model and serves for UI code generation (Figure 15).

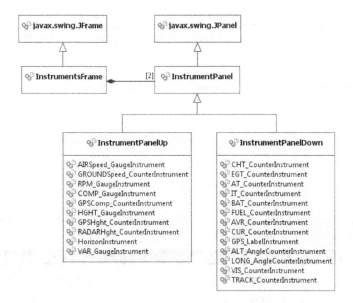

Fig. 15. Platform-specific software instrument table model

The platform-specific instrument table model comprises various types of visual instruments. The frame and panel component inherit corresponding Java Swing UML abstractions. Instruments are grouped according to their functions. The upper panel (*InstrumentPanelUp*) contains instruments for presentation of flight parameters, while the lower panel (*InstrumentPanelDown*) includes instruments for propulsion parameters.

Figure 16 shows the ATL rule that transforms UML visual horizon instrument from modality-specific level to platform-specific level (in this case adapted to Java platform).

```
rule Horizon2SwingHorizon extends VisualUIStereotypedClass {

from s : UML2!"uml::Class" in IN

(s.isHorizonComponent() and human.visuoSpatialPerception.isMediumToHigh())

  do {

    create3DSwingHorizon(s);

  }

}
```

Fig. 16. Simplified example of the ATL rule that produces platform-specific instrument

5.6   Implementation Level

Finally, we come to an executable UI level. Figure 17 shows different instances of software instrument table.

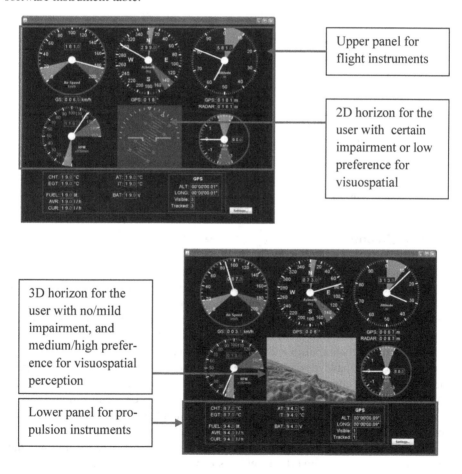

Fig. 17. Running prototypes of the software instrument table generated by analyzing human visuospatial perception

For clarity, we demonstrate the instrument table adaptation considering single instrument type – horizon instrument. The prototypes are produced from previous levels taking into account impairment extent and preference level of visuospatial perception for the concrete user. Accordingly, availability of corresponding perceptual effects is determined. Based on these, specific type of horizon instrument is created. In the first example, we have the user with certain impairment or low preference to use *Visuospatial Perception*. In this case, the availability of *HighlightingByDepth* effect is low and two-dimensional horizon instrument is created. The second example presents a three-dimensional horizon instrument for the user with no or mild impairment, and medium or high preference to engage *VisuospatialPerception*. In this case, the effect of *HighlightingByDepth* is exploited at medium or high level.

Figure 18. shows the ATL transformation rule that generates UI code from classes found in platform-specific model.

```
helper context UML2!"uml::Class" def : toCode() : String =
    self.visibilityStr +
    self.abstractStr +
    self.finalStr +
    'class ' + self.name + self.extendsClause() + self.implementsClause() +
    ' {\n' +
    self.nestedClassifier->iterate(e; acc : String = '' | acc + e.toCode()) +
    self.ownedAttribute->iterate(e; acc : String = '' | acc + e.toCode()) +
    self.ownedOperation->iterate(e; acc : String = '' | acc + e.toCode()) +
    '}\n\n';
```

Fig. 18. Fragment of the ATL code generation function

6   Conclusion

In this paper, we have proposed the model-driven framework for designing adaptive UIs. The main contribution of the approach is in defining formal mechanism for semantic integration of UI elements and interaction context elements. The mechanism is supported by the "Interaction Model" that brings together the human, device and environment contexts in terms of contextual factors. In turn, they can be used to adapt UI elements appropriately at multiple levels of abstraction.

To this end, we have designed a generic framework that provides developers means for designing adaptive UIs, as well as UML-compliant language that describes the framework. Our framework relies on standard adaptive UI architectures and lets developers use object-oriented design principles to construct and communicate domain models. Furthermore, it provides the set of abstractions - in the form of contextual factors - to formalize the description of communication between the user and the application. With our framework, developers can work with generic descriptions of UIs in terms of interaction elements, providing more flexible and more reusable solutions, suitable for a broader range of domains. High-level formal UI specifications could serve as a common ground for investigating both design and implementation concerns by design participants from different disciplines.

The framework was used to build adaptive user interfaces for data visualization domain in the context of human perceptual abilities. In order to evaluate the approach more thoroughly and to refine it, we plan to build different applications and tools based on the described framework including context perspectives other than human. The tools should facilitate the work of developers by providing appropriate visual development means.

References

1. Paternò, F.: User Interface Design Adaptation. In: Soegaard, M., Dam, R.F. (eds.) The Encyclopedia of Human-Computer Interaction, 2nd edn. The Interaction Design Foundation, Aarhus (2013)
2. Dourish, P.: What We Talk About When We Talk About Context. Personal and Ubiquitous Computing 8(1), 19–30 (2004)
3. Thevenin, D., Coutaz, J.: Plasticity of user interfaces: Framework and research agenda. In: INTERACT, pp. 110–117 (1999)
4. Calvary, G., Coutaz, J., Thevenin, D., Limbourg, Q., Bouillon, L., Vanderdonckt, J.: A unifying reference framework for multi-target user interfaces. Interacting with Computers 15(3), 289–308 (2003)
5. Coutaz, J.: User interface plasticity: model driven engineering to the limit! In: Proc. EICS 2010, pp. 1–8. ACM Press (2010)
6. Sottet, J.S., Calvary, G., Coutaz, J., Favre, J.M.: A model-driven engineering approach for the usability of plastic user interfaces. In: Gulliksen, J., Harning, M.B., van der Veer, G.C., Wesson, J. (eds.) EIS 2007. LNCS, vol. 4940, pp. 140–157. Springer, Heidelberg (2008)
7. Limbourg, Q., Vanderdonckt, J., Michotte, B., Bouillon, L., López-Jaquero, V.: USIXML: A language supporting multi-path development of user interfaces. In: Feige, U., Roth, J. (eds.) DSV-IS 2004 and EHCI 2004. LNCS, vol. 3425, pp. 200–220. Springer, Heidelberg (2005)
8. Jovanović, M., Starčević, D., Jovanović, Z.: Languages for model-driven development of user interfaces: The state of the art. The Yugoslav Journal of Operations Research 23(3), 327–341 (2013)
9. Mori, G., Paternò, F., Santoro, C.: CTTE: support for developing and analyzing task models for interactive system design. IEEE Trans. Soft. Eng. 28(8), 797–813 (2002)
10. Mori, G., Paternò, F., Santoro, C.: Design and Development of Multidevice User Interfaces through Multiple Logical Description. IEEE Trans. Soft. 30(8), 507–520 (2004)
11. Barboni, E., Ladry, J.F., Navarre, D., Palanque, P., Winckler, M.: Beyond modelling: an integrated environment supporting co-execution of tasks and systems models. In: Proc. EICS 2010, pp. 165–174. ACM Press (2010)
12. Paterno, F., Santoro, C., Spano, L.D.: MARIA: A universal, declarative, multiple abstraction-level language for service-oriented applications in ubiquitous environments. ACM TOCHI 16(4), paper no. 19 (2009)
13. Constantine, L.L.: Canonical abstract prototypes for abstract visual and interaction design. In: Jorge, J.A., Jardim Nunes, N., Falcão e Cunha, J. (eds.) DSV-IS 2003. LNCS, vol. 2844, pp. 1–15. Springer, Heidelberg (2003)

14. Navarre, D., Palanque, P., Ladry, J.F., Barboni, E.: A model-based user interface description technique dedicated to interactive systems addressing usability, reliability and scalability. ACM TOCHI 16(4), paper no. 18 (2009)
15. Paternò, F.: Model-Based Design of Interactive Applications. ACM Intelligence 11(4), 26–38 (2000)
16. Gajos, K., Weld, D., Wobbrock, J.: Automatically generating personalized user interfaces with Supple. Artificial Intelligence 174(12), 910–950 (2010)
17. Da Silva, P.P., Paton, N.W.: User interface modeling in UMLi. IEEE Software 20(4), 62–69 (2003)
18. Van den Bergh, J., Coninx, K.: Towards Modeling Context-Sensitive Interactive Applications: The Context-Sensitive User Interface Profile (CUP). In: Proc. ACM Soft. Vis. 2005, pp. 87–94. ACM Press (2005)
19. Nunes, N.J., Cunha, J.F.E.: Wisdom - A UML Based Architecture for Interactive Systems. In: Proc. Seventh Int. Conf. Design, Specification, and Verification of Interactive Systems, pp. 191–205 (2000)
20. Jouault, F., Allilaire, F., Bézivin, J., Kurtev, I.A.: A model transformation tool. Science of Computer Programming 72(1), 31–39 (2008)
21. Obrenovic, Z., Starcevic, D.: Modeling multimodal human-computer interaction. IEEE Computer 37(9), 65–72 (2004)
22. Jovanovic, M., Starcevic, D., Jovanovic, Z.: Formal specification of usability measures in model-driven development of context-sensitive user interfaces. In: Proceedings of the International Working Conference on Advanced Visual Interfaces, pp. 749–752. ACM (2012)
23. Jovanovic, M., Starcevic, D., Minovic, M., Stavljanin, V.: Motivation and multimodal interaction in model-driven educational game design. IEEE Transactions on Systems, Man and Cybernetics, Part A: Systems and Humans 41(4), 817–824 (2011)
24. Bruyere, S.M., VanLooy, S., Peterson, D.: The International Classification of Functioning, Disability and Health: Contemporary Literature Overview. Rehabilitation Psychology 50(2), 113–121 (2005)
25. Chittaro, L., Carchietti, E., De Marco, L., Zampa, A.: Personalized emergency medical assistance for disabled people. User Modeling and User-Adapted Interaction 21(4-5), 407–440 (2011)
26. World Health Organization (WHO): International Classification of Functioning, Disability and Health (ICF), http://www.who.int/classifications/icf/en/
27. Jovanovic, M., Starcevic, D.: Software Architecture for Ground Control Station for Unmanned Aerial Vehicle. In: Proc. Int. Conf on Computer Modeling and Simulation, pp. 284–288. IEEE Press (2008)
28. Jovanović, M., Starčević, D., Jovanović, Z.: Reusable Design of Data Visualization Software Architecture for Unmanned Aerial Vehicles. Journal of Aerospace Information Systems 11(6), 359–371 (2014)

Continuous Improvement in Agile Development Practice

The Case of Value and Non-Value Adding Activities

Marta Kristín Lárusdóttir[1], Åsa Cajander[2], and Michael Simader[3]

[1] Reykjavik University, Menntavegur 1, Reykjavik, Iceland
marta@ru.is
[2] Uppsala University, Lägerhyddsvägen 2, 751 05 Uppsala, Sweden
Asa.Cajander@it.uu.se
[3] Celum America Inc, 70 West Madison St.,
Suite, 1447, Chicago, IL 60602, USA
michael@simader.me

Abstract. Agile development has positive attitudes towards continuously improving work practices of IT professionals and the quality of the software. This study focuses on value adding activities such as user involvement and gathering metrics and non-value adding activities, such as correcting defects. Interviews were conducted with 10 IT professionals working with agile development in Iceland. Results show that IT professionals emphasise communication with users both through direct contact and using email, but they rarely use metrics to make improvements measurable. The most serious non-value adding activities are: partially done work, delays and defects. The core reason is that long lists of defects in the projects exist, which means that the software is partially done and the defects cause delays in the process. There are efforts to reduce non-value adding activities in the process, but IT professionals are still confronted with problems attributed to miscommunication and the impediments by the external environment.

1 Introduction

Software development is a complex task related to human, social and organizational factors, as well as technical factors [1]. It requires both plans as well as situated action [2] to be successful, and far too often the software built is hard to use [3]. There are several competing normative processes describing how software development should be done and these processes have changed as time goes by. In the 1990's more emphasis in software development was on delivering parts of the software to customers iteratively and incrementally than before, so time to market would be shorter [4]. Additionally, the software was getting more interactive with emergent requirements. In incremental software development the software requirements are divided into parts, which are implemented and a deliverable version of that part of the software is made [5]. The basic idea is that the IT professionals use the knowledge they gained in previous increments to improve the software being developed, but in the iterative development not much emphasis is on improving the process of the development.

S. Sauer et al. (Eds.): HCSE 2014, LNCS 8742, pp. 57–72, 2014.
© IFIP International Federation for Information Processing 2014

Agile software development has recently emerged as a popular iterative software development process and it focuses on communication and independent teamwork, as is stated in the principles behind the Agile manifesto [6]: "Build projects around motivated individuals. Give them the environment and support they need, and trust them to get the job done". Moreover, it is stated in the manifesto that continuous improvement of the process is recommended, as in this principle: "At regular intervals, the team reflects on how to become more effective, then tunes and adjusts its behavior accordingly." In the agile software development process Scrum this is done at the retrospective meetings, where the whole team discuss how to improve their work processes for the next weeks.

The practice of continuous improvement has been not much studied in research even though software developer's work with continuous improvement reveals what practitioners see as important in their practice and what kind of problems they address. Such research would also help researchers understand practitioners understanding of usability work as only one aspect of continuous improvement in software development. Hence, this paper describes an interview study identifying how continuous improvement is done in agile software development. We have analysed how the IT professionals involve customers and users to improve the software under development, what activities the IT professionals conduct for continuously improve their software development process and what measurements are made to measure the status of the improvements. Additionally we have analysed what non-value adding activities they describe according to seven categories of waste defined in Lean software development according to Poppendieck and Poppendieck [7]. Finally we discuss the main results from the interviews on continuous improvement in agile software development.

2   Background

In this section we first present agile software development (hereafter called Agile), and continuous improvement in Lean management as this has been used in order to elucidate the work with continuous improvement in Agile. We have chosen the concept waste from Lean since Agile has its roots in this process.

2.1   Agile Software Development

To improve the process of software development many processes have been suggested by IT professionals and researchers in the area [1]. In 2001 the Agile Manifesto was written by advocates of software development processes like eXtreme Programming, Scrum, Crystal and Feature Driven Development. Through the manifesto the term Agile Software Development was born [8]. In short the manifesto includes the following four key values: 1) Individuals and interactions over processes and tools; 2) Working software over comprehensive documentation; 3) Customer collaboration over contract negotiation and 4) Responding to change over following a plan.

Moreover, individuals and interpersonal communication between stakeholders are in the center of attention and the agile software development processes are iterative and incremental, hence it is possible to adapt to a changing environment and circumstances [6].

2.2   Continuous Improvement: Value Adding Activities

Lean management (hereafter referred to as Lean) is a holistic approach aiming at providing the right product in the correct amount of time at the right place with the right quality [9]. Lean is not a process but can be seen as as a set of principles [10]. In Lean management the focus is on continuously improving the process of working by defining and improving value adding activities such as customer involvement and minimising non-value activities called waste [11] in order for projects to become more efficient.

The main focus of customer involvement is to add value to the customers through making the software more usable for its users [12]. In theory customers or users could be involved in four human centred design activities: When understanding and specifying the context of use for the software, when specify the user requirements, when produce design solutions to meet these requirements and when evaluating the designs against requirements [12]. In practice customers are often involved when evaluating design solutions, but it is not as common to involve users when specifying requirements [13].

Typically thorough usability evaluation is conducted as seldom as twice a year, often by contracting an external usability expert despite of being highly rated by IT professionals as a value adding activity [14]. The main reason why thorough user evaluation is not conducted is lack of time in the Agile projects [14,15]. However, some user involvement activities, such as workshops, are typically used at least twice a year in Agile projects [14]. These activities are informal and therefore these fit better to the fundamental principles of Agile, which are speed and communication. Additionally producing incremental deliverables in short project periods is another popular and important Agile feature. One challenge for IT professionals working in Agile projects was maintaining the overall vision of the user perspective, despite of the Scrum tradition of slicing projects in smaller parts [16].

The main value adding factor reported in a paper describing a study on customer involvement activities was that activity should be planned, conducted and the results analysed [17]. The activities need to be conducted and the outcomes iterated for the usability of the software to be reasonable. The participants reported that the main constraints for choosing a particular activity were the stage of the project, availability of IT professionals and time. In one of the projects where the usability of the developed software was poor, the only customer involvement activity was evaluation. One of the main conclusions in the paper is that customers should be involved in all the four human-centred design activities [12].

2.3   Continuous Improvement: Non-value Adding Activities

Shingo has studied Lean for manufacturing and identified seven categories of waste in manufacturing: In-Progress Inventory; Over-Production; Extra Processing; Transportation; Motion; Waiting and Defects [18]. The work of Poppendieck and Poppendieck [7] presents a mapping of waste categories from Lean in manufacturing to waste in software development, and define the following seven categories of waste:

1. *Partially Done Work* is present when chunks of code are impeded somewhere in the process from the start of the work before they reach the state of being integrated, tested, documented and deployable. Partially done work can be diminished by dividing work into smaller chunks or iterations [7, p.74]. Middleton, Flaxel, and Cookson [19] describe that Partially Done Work delay the product from being deployed, therefore a continuous flow should be pursued. A high amount of requirements put into the system is mentioned as a typical example of a problems. Further examples for Partially Done Work are uncoded documentation, unsynchronized code, untested code, undocumented code and undeployed code [7, p.74].

2. *Extra Features* are features in the software that have no clear value for the customer, or features that do not support the accomplishment of the customer's current job [7, p.75]. Extra features are similar to over-production, which is deemed by Ohno [11] as the worst of the seven wastes. If the feature has no clear value it should not be developed.

3. *Relearning* is rediscovering forgotten knowledge. Therefore it is essential to create and preserve knowledge as part of a learning process. Further, it is crucial to utilize existing knowledge and experiences from employees [7, p.76].

4. *Handoffs* occur when knowledge is transferred from one colleague to another. With every single handoff some tacit knowledge is lost, because it is difficult to make tacit knowledge explicit. Poppendieck and Poppendieck [7] state that only 6% of the original knowledge is left after a chain of 4 handoffs. Therefore it is necessary to reduce handoffs in order to reduce waste [7, p.77].

5. *Task Switching* requires knowledge workers to reset their mind after each switch. This resetting is time consuming and therefore seen as waste. It is considered, that working on tasks ought to be kept to a minimum in order to reduce task switches [7, p.78].

6. *Delays* occur in many different situations. One of the most important types of delay is waiting for people in different areas. Developers make critical decision about every 15 minutes. These decisions can only be made, if the required information is present. Colocated teams with short iterations and regular feedback can provide developers with the information they need to make decisions without delay. Hence, knowledge needs to be available when and where it is needed [7, p.79].

7. *Defects* within the software cause numerous problems and may lead to customer dissatisfaction. The target should be to deploy or deliver the product with the lowest possible defect rate. Mistake proofing tests and the discovery of defects in early stages of the software development [7, p.80].

These seven types of waste were used as a basis for interviewing IT professionals in our study about non-value adding activities in their work practice.

3   Method

The qualitative study included 10 semi-structured interviews, all following the same structure asking for the experience and context of the informants within they organization. The introductory part was focussing on the experience of the informants and the applied processes to understand the context. Questions to the informants were directed to how the informants improve their software development process, how the involve customers and what non-value adding activities they conduct in relation to waste.

The interviews were conducted mostly on site of the informants' organizations. Two of the interviews were conducted at Reykjavik University. All interviews lasted for about 45 minutes and were all conducted in English. The researcher also took notes and recorded the interviews. All recorded interviews were transcribed verbatim, with slight modifications to make the text more readable, when filler words or phrases disrupted the structure of a sentence. Informants are presented as males despite their actual gender in this paper.

The companies were chosen by analysing data from the Statistics Iceland office [20] and the Icelandic chamber of commerce [21]. The focus was on companies selling business to business software, both bespoke software and off-the-shelf software. All the chosen companies use agile software development processes, and many used Scrum. Some of the companies have adapted the Scrum process to their own needs and/or also apply Lean Software Development principles.

The informants were found through recommendations within the chosen companies. All of which have several years of experience in the application of Agile, especially in Scrum, and worked also as members of the development teams. The roles of the informants vary from company to company. The informants were categorised in three roles: Director of development (3 informants), Head of development (4 informants) and Scrum managers (Product Owner and Scrum Master), (3 informants).

The data from the interviews were compiled, analyzed and assigned to categories. Interpretative phenomenological analysis as described in Silverman and Rapley [22, p.274] was applied to identify and generate themes and sub-themes. This was an iterative approach and the themes were refined with every transcript of the interviews, which results in the final themes and sub-themes. Notes and the assigned themes were directly put down on the printed transcripts. First themes were generated, which lead to an initial list of themes. The themes in this list were clustered, which resulted in a list of themes of connected areas. As the last step these themes were organized in a table consisting of themes and sub-themes.

4   Results on Value Adding Activities

The following results show how customers are involved in the process of software development to eliminate waste in the development, how organizations have implemented a continuous improvement process, how they utilize metrics to support this process and how they work with value adding activities.

4.1   Customer Involvement

Most of the informants shared a common desire for a high degree of customer involvement. The term customer refers to different stakeholders on the customer side including users. The informants describe that a close relationship can prevent from misunderstandings about the requirements. Most of the interviewees prefer direct communication on the phone or through emails to prevent misunderstandings and it is "more convenient to just pick up the phone". One informant reported about a loose relationship with the customer, which led to misunderstandings and a higher amount of later improvements, once the software had been delivered. This experience has made the company value a closer relationship with the customer.

Several informants reported that it is important that the customers formally agree to participate in the software development and that Scrum is integrated as a part of their organisational culture, as in this quote: "The customer needs to fit the Agile process in their environment. They must learn it and it is hard in the beginning." However, as stated in the quote the integration of Agile in the organisational cultures is not always easy. Some customers are not interested in working according to Scrum but prefer to use the waterfall way of thinking: "some customers want to stay with the plain and old-fashioned waterfall model, and this is reflected in the nature of the tenders". One result from the interviews is that it is difficult to work according the Agile if the customer organisation use another way of working: "It is difficult to be Agile in a non-Agile environment.".

Sometimes the development team have problems with receiving feedback from the customers, as the organisational culture was not based on feedback and continuous improvement work. The pace in Scrum teams is perceived to be quick compared to the customer organisation, and this becomes a problem: "We ask for feedback, but the answer comes a lot later."

One informant experience that using Agile actually was seen by the customer organisation as decreasing the contact with the customer since Scrum prescribes that the team meets the customer at the end of every sprint, and not during the sprint work. In Scrum this is prescribed in order to reduce distraction. However, it is interesting to note that the system developer interviewed did not agree with this, but saw Agile as a way of increasing the customer involvement in the process: "but in fact the service level is actually increasing".

One argument used for a good user contact was that the need for education becomes less if the customer is much involved in the systems development process. "Interesting side effects also are, after developing a big piece the training was basically nonexistent", because of the high customer involvement.

Results indicate that it might be easier to use Agile if the customer organisation is relatively small and has a flexible way of working. One informant complained about the process and the interaction with the customer was less Agile due to the acquisition by a large corporation, "We are less Agile today than before the acquisition". He said it was not possible anymore to involve the customers as much as before, even though that when "the customer invests the time, then this is really beneficial when it comes to waste" he commented.

4.2   Process for Value Adding Activities

Few of the informants reported that they have a well defined process for continuous improvement and that they follow this process strictly and most define continuous improvement work very loosely within the organization. This indicates the lack of awareness or even denial for problems within the development process in many organisation.

Several of the informants reported that they had not found a functioning process that supported their work with continuous improvement. Previous attempts to address working with continuous improvement was too tedious and time consuming: "it's a tedious process and the same old stories are addressed again and again. This lowered the motivation of the employees. This needs to be changed". The same happened in other organizations were continuous improvement used to be a part of the daily routine, "and nothing really changed, so the team members were not interested anymore. But we are trying to develop it again". One should note that the same informant reported about major problems when it comes to a mutual understanding of the requirements.

In one of the organizations there are different colors for different types of tasks, and among these tasks are improvement tasks "It's about improving the development process, solving root cause problems, if we are getting the same issue again and again". Some organisations had a very functioning routine for working with continuous improvement: "Every Friday after lunch, we only work on our company, we do not work for the customers, we work on improving our business". In one organisation a special improvement group maintains an improvement backlog, and everyone is invited to participate in this process. In one company there are retrospectives conducted on team level, but also on corporate level. There is a dedicated team, that tries to streamline those improvements, so teams can work together cross-functional.

4.3   Metrics

Results from our interviews show that metrics are rarely used to make improvements measurable. Making improvements measurable requires defined metrics to compare the state in the beginning and end. The respondents mostly have no metrics at all defined. This again indicates a certain lack of awareness for improvements. Those who have established metrics utilize them only on a high level, such as task traversing time as this is seen as the most important, as in this quote: "The most valuable metric, for instance in this Kanban thinking, is the lead time. How fast things flow through the pipeline". The ultimate goal, according to several informants, is to deliver code as quickly as possible.

They also pointed out that the definition of metrics is very difficult and to use numbers might be tricky as well. Some of the informants pointed to difficulties in defining the correct metrics, because "We are measuring finished story points in a sprint, but when a story with 15 points is not finished, it is passed to the next sprint, although most of its work happened in the current sprint. So the statistics are skewed". They also stated the problem of finding a correct definition of meaningful and useful metrics.

5   Analyzing Non-value Adding Activities

In this section we describe the results from the interviews which are analyzed according to the seven types of waste from Poppendieck and Poppendieck [7] since these denote non-value adding activities in a structured way.

5.1   Partially Done Work

It seemed as though the informants were not familiar with the concept of Partially Done Work, as they needed further explanations on the term in order to reply to the question. This indicates that they do not experience this type of waste regularly. A possible explanation can be found in the utilization of Agile, that inherently aim on reducing Partially Done Work, in order to deliver value fast by dividing the work load into smaller chunks to tackle this problem. Still, some informants mentioned that unfinished user stories were moved to the next sprint, but they did not seem to categorize that as partially done work.

Nine out of ten informants reported that unfinished features or non-fulfillment of requirements are the most common examples in the category Partially Done Work. Six informants described that testing is conducted by another person separately, therefore these informants finish the features partly, whereas four also test the software and thereby finish the development of that feature. All of the informants stated, that they use KANBAN like boards or status walls for better visibility of the status the work to be able to check if it is finished or not, e.g. one informant says: "We do visual management, so we have every ticket up on the wall".

Although the informants do not recognize a defect backlog as partially done work, 8 out of 10 maintain an inventory of defects, which is considered to be waste in the terms of partially done work by Poppendick and Poppendick [7]. One informant is aware of this type of non-value adding activities when he stated "It's an absolute waste to collect huge backlogs of defects that you review every 2 months and it's only the top 10% that's going to get ever implemented". He explained further, "We have a zero bug policy, although this is utopian, but we try at least."

It is interesting to note that even though, undocumented, untested or unfinished code is categorized as Partially Done Work in the theory from Poppendieck and

Poppendieck [7], the informants do not find these things problematic. Undocumented code is accepted since the Agile processes do not focus on documentation. Unfinished and undocumented code is also accepted according to the informants. Most developers choose a task or a user story, and make a running version of that requirement ready for testing.

5.2   Occurrence of Extra Features

Extra features occur in the informants' organizations. Some interviewees stated that they knew of this issue, whereas others claimed to exactly develop what is demanded by the customers. Only one informant stated to take the effort to analyze which features add value for the user in the productive system. They systematically remove them in succession, if there is no use for a particular functionality. For the rest, no real efforts were reported to estimate the value of a feature for the customer.

One informant did not see a problem with extra features, because even though they cannot charge this extra effort, "in the long run, we do not lose money with it, because of repeated business" and they want to live up to the expectations and even exceed them. Another informant appraised this issue similarly, "We learn from it and we profit from the knowledge we gain from it".

Reasons for extra features can often be found in miscommunication, and hence not knowing exactly what the customer demands. One informant has the problem of a "non-mutual understanding of what the users and what the business customers are actually asking for". In order to "keep the solution user friendly" one informant stated that they removed features and streamlined the solution. The same happens in another informant's organization. He explained: "it's a work system, there are people in there and there is no value having this feature in there when it's not used".

5.3   Relearning

Relearning is actually discovering forgotten knowledge, so the results are analyzed according to if the informants experience loss of knowledge and how the knowledge is preserved by documentation and communication in the team.

None of the informants responded that they would have a problem with the loss of knowledge within the development process. One informant stated, that about half of the development team left the company and this did not cause many problems, because "the application is tested, everything is tested and we use a high level language, so it's fairly easy to navigate through and also because everyone is telling everyone about everything."

The utilization of heavy-weight documentation is mainly used for contractual reasons, because it is requested by the customer. As one informant stated their customers would demand detailed documentation about the project, furthermore "The process is too partitioned; hence, documentation is needed, because there are so many people involved in the whole project development life-cycle". Some of the respondents maintain wiki pages and issue tracking systems for general documentation purposes, but they also emphasized that most of the knowledge is shared in an open communication process.

All of the respondents utilize daily stand-up meetings and encourage team members to communicate face-to-face to share knowledge within the team. Most of the informants facilitate KANBAN walls, e.g. one informant explains the advantages of this tool as follows, "So we have all the tickets up on the wall, and this makes all the tasks visible for everyone". In general the interviewees emphasize the open and respectful communication within the teams. One informant even reports about a social contract that is concluded among the team members as follows "Everyone is open minded about asking questions and giving feedback". As teams in Scrum are self-organizing, the teams decide what is important and needs to be written down and what not. The informant also highlights the level of respect and cooperativeness within the software development team when it comes to integrating new team members, "Everybody would be so helpful, it's really good to pick up speed with a new team member".

Some of the interviewees reported about rotation within the teams to distribute knowledge, like one informant stated, "it is helpful to be at least knowledgeable of each part of the code". One informant declined the involvement of experts within the team and reported that they tried to share knowledge as much as possible, by using e.g. pair-programming or team member rotation, whereas some informants think that experts are important and argue that the high complexity of products makes experts necessary. One informant states that experts might be distracted by other team-members as they are a valuable source of information and the single contact point.

5.4   Handoffs

The results show that there is a certain pattern regarding handoffs from one IT professional to another identifiable. The activities of the IT professionals could be grouped in three categories: a) Requirement elicitation; b) Development and c) Testing and Release. These three categories of activities occur in all of the informants' organizations and there are typically handoffs between these within the organizations. Typically the development process is described as one of our informants phrased it: 'One developer works on one task, for bigger tasks the work is divided into smaller tasks'.

The IT professionals developing bespoke software typically elicited requirement in collaboration with customer. The IT professionals developing off-the-shelf software maintain wish lists, which are compiled from requests by the customers. In general the user stories are developed by the developers themselves for describing the requirements and also tested by the same developers. One informant described the problem of losing knowledge when the requirements in form of user stories are handed to the developers, "There is probably a loss of information going on". He explained further this effect when saying: "because we sit in a really open space, so there are a lot of discussions going on". Another informant described handoffs as problematic in the requirements elicitation process and the delivery process, because the development team is embedded in a large corporation, which affects the communication with the customers, like he explained: "The customer is fairly isolated from the development". Additionally, he stated: "For me I think this is too partitioned, too waterfall. Especially, a lot of information is lost, when you have a totally separated team talking to the customer. So what is developed may have lost some context". Many informants stated that close relationship to the customer is beneficial when it comes to preserving knowledge.

One informant tries to tackle the problem of handoffs by delivering small parts of the software continuously: "It's a thinking of minimizing these handoffs and the costs of handoffs. So we have a deployment pipe all the way into operation". He also reported that having the same team working all the way from the kick-off meeting of the project to the operation eliminated a lot of waste. So a vital communication process within the team could counteract the loss of knowledge. The informants reported that there are basically no handoffs within the development activities, but there is an extra handoff when a separated testing team is involved. Some of the respondents also apply code-reviews to maintain a higher quality and support the communication process. This is technically not to be considered as a handoff, since knowledge is shared rather than transferred.

5.5   Task Switching

Because all informants use Scrum, an adapted Scrum process or Kanban, they all choose themselves which tasks to work on. One informant described this by saying: "The developer picks the task and then puts a sticky note on the board". Another informant describes this in a similar way: "It's the Agile and Lean principle of a pull system over push system, so the team pulls the tasks". The third informant describes how this is done in his team: "This happens in the daily stand-ups. Team members are self-organized and choose their tasks. We do not assign tasks. You commit to a task". One informant explained what all the other informants have in common, that is, that tasks are chosen accordingly to the priority by saying: "If you are a developer and you see the accepted tickets and there are three highly prioritized, so you pick one out of those three".

The informants agreed to that the limit to the number of tasks they are working on is just one task at a time, but this is not always possible due to many different reasons. Incoming defect reports can interrupt the development process, because defects need to be given a higher priority for some of the informants. Hence, when developers are working on defects they would have more task switching in their work. One informant explained this as follows: "Developers should work on one task at a time, but on the daily stand-ups they can choose more, because the planning period is 24 hours and they can finish more tasks within that period. Except if there are some defects coming in, that need attention, then the developer has to switch to that task". Two informants also explained that they needed to switch to solving a higher prioritized defect, if that was reported. In one organization a special role was introduced that is assigned to a particular team member every sprint cycle, which only handles defect reports. One informant explained that urgent customization requests from customers could interrupt a current task. One informant explained that this is disturbing for him, by saying: "If a developer needs to work on another ticket, the first task needs to be put on hold and then you can see how the hold queue is piling up. I think it's cumbersome to have many tickets or working on many things at the same time". Another informant explained that developers only work on one task at a time, but the method of pairing is used, so there might be more tickets assigned to one developer than he actually works on. The third informant pictured the situation in his organization as follows: "Ideally (we work on) one task, but in reality things tend to get a lot worse than that. So context switching is a problem, especially for certain team members that are very knowledgeable".

5.6   Delays

The informants reported different reasons for delays, but there are two main themes identifiable. First of all there is a blocking in the development process due to missing actions by an outer stakeholder. One informant explains it as follows: "We are not synchronized enough with them. They have to do something and then we have to wait and cannot move and then they have something done and then we have to go on. But within the department things run quite smoothly, I think". Miscommunication and a lack of clear responsibilities can be seen as a reason for these delays. One informant had a concise answer to prevent this from happening. He explains: "One of our tag lines is: Responsibility all the way. We are responsible for the value and this story has no value until this blocking is resolved, we have to finish it. So we are offering our help, call them, and make sure things happen".

One informant explains that poor software design and the resulting complexity delays the development process and it takes a while until the developer understands the problem and structure of the software. This leads to the next common problem, fixing defects. Many informants consider this as the main reason for delays. Also the testing process can hinder the release of a feature, like one of the informants explains: "In our case the main reason for delays was the testing process. The testing process took too long and then defects were found, which postponed the process". The informant suggested that more testers were involved in the development.

5.7   Defects

The informants handle defects similarly. In most of the organizations the defects are registered and prioritized in a backlog, and depending on the severity level, the defects are fixed right away or taken care of later. In some of the organizations the backlogs are assessed from time to time to evaluate the status of defect backlog, so if the defects had become invalid, they would be removed from the backlog. One informant described that there are three different levels of defects: "It depends where a defect is found in the cycle. When it's in development we do not log it and take care of it immediately. In the release stage we log the defect and fix it. If the defect was delivered to the customer, there is a strict change process implemented." Only one informant stated that they have a zero-bug policy, which is supported by automated testing and the continuous delivery approach. He also adds that zero bugs are utopian, but it reflects the attitude towards defects. Furthermore, issues grouped as defects could also be failure demands, which is something that needs attention and could have been avoided by setting the right actions in the very beginning. Failure demands evolve over the project period and need to be tracked and eradicated. Another informant explained that the high complexity within the system caused that it is more defect prone. So many defects were caused by a poor design in the very beginning. Informants also argued that defects interrupt their working pace.

In some organizations there was a special role introduced to handle defects. This role is reassigned to new developers every sprint, because this is a tedious work for developers, and it's positive for the individual's motivation to be only responsible for defects every couple of months. One informant explained: "Then the rest of the developers can focus only on stories and new features".

6   Discussion

In the following we discuss our results related to how IT professionals can continuously improve their way of working through value adding activities such as user involvement, better processes and metrics. Additionally we discuss our results on the non-value activities that IT professionals describe.

6.1   Discussions on Value Adding Activities

Our results show that many of the Agile projects have a close customer contact which concurs with the basic values in Agile [6]. The degree of contact is however perceived to be affected both by the size and the organisational culture of the customer organisation. According to the interviews the customer organisation needs to be flexible and able to deliver feedback and decisions at the same pace as the development project works, and this is not always the case.

One interesting finding is that several of the informants argue that formal agreements with the customer organisation regarding customer involvement are necessary. Since Agile is much based on motivation and close feedback [6], this does not concur with the basic value of the process.

It is interesting to note that Agile, as many other development processes, does not distinguish between the customer and the real user of the system. This blurs the aspects of real user involvement and makes them less visible.

Most companies in the interview study do not have a process for including value adding activities in their work, despite the fact that Agile has this explicit focus. Some explain this lack as caused by the tedious way in which previous attempt to include value adding activities. Others say that they do have a process, and that it is lightweight and adapted to the circumstances of Agile.

Agile does not give much detailed support, but is more a framework for systems development, and this results in lack of coherent methods such as methods for user involvement [23] and continuous improvement.

Our results show that metrics are rarely used for measuring in Agile. The only measurement mentioned in the interviews are measurements of speed and time. There were no measurements made of any quality aspects such as usability or user involvement. This concurs with other research on usability evaluations [13,14]. This situation might be caused by the basic value of speed in Scrum [6], but it might also be caused by the fact that it is difficult to measure other aspects than time related measurements [24]

One can wonder if one avenue forward to include usability work in organisations is measurement? Previous research on measuring usability and user experience have shown that such measurements have little or no influence on forthcoming decisions [25]. However, it is very possible that these results reflect the trends of that time and that the introduction of usability measurements would be more successful when included in systems development processes based on Lean values since measurement as such are a core value there.

When introducing measurements in organisation it is crucial that there are agreed success criteria, and it is difficult to establish evaluation criteria for social elements that are affected by the introduction of an IT system [1]. However, attempts have been made to use metrics in order to measure the establishment of user centred systems design [26] in organisations such as for example by Gulliksen et al. [27].

6.2   Discussion on Non-value Adding Activities

Our results show that the IT professionals are well aware of waste in their organizations and it seems as if they do not interfere with their ability to deliver fast. Yet, there are some types of waste that impede the development processes. Two categories were most dominant, defects in the software that often result in a partially done work and delays in the IT professionals' work due to lack of communication.

Most of the informants maintain defect backlogs, however, the informants do not perceive this collection of defects as a problem. This clearly contradicts the Lean Software Development principle "Build Quality In" [7], where they state that it is better to avoid defects in the beginning, than to test quality into the product in late stages. Maintaining a defect backlog leads to context switching, because developers are forced to choose more than one task at a time, depending on the prioritization. Most of the respondents referred to partially done work as working on defects and maintaining defect backlogs. The missing perception or negligence of this type of waste can lead to be highly ineffective. Some companies had introduced a special role to diminish these effects. It was described that a member of the development team handled these defects for a limited amount of time before this role was passed on to another person, because of its tedious character.

The lack of communication was the main factor for waste related to delays in the IT professionals work and producing functionality that the IT professionals regarded as extra features.The IT professionals needed good communication within the team and with the customer. Additionally the needed feedback from the customers or users in order to adapt to changing situations and deliver value fast. The following statement summarizes the main obstacles within the development process the best: "It is difficult to be Agile in a non-Agile environment." Even though Agile processes were applied (mostly Scrum), the customers and other stakeholders from the external environment are not used to collaborating in this Agile environment. This is mainly attributed to the disparity in the understanding of collaboration and communication between vendor and customer. Agile teams need a close collaboration and feedback from the customer in order to adapt to changing situations and deliver value fast. It seemed that customers are still more used to the traditional processes, e.g. waterfall model, where a different degree of communication is needed throughout the process. The customer needs to be educated to collaborate in an Agile environment. This lack of communication was the main factor for delays and extra features. The negligence of this issue leads might lead to major waste within the development process.

7   Conclusion

The results in this study on the value adding activity of involving users show that the IT professionals emphasise communication with user both through direct contact and using email to add value to the software development. However, some informants describe that it is not always easy to work according to agile processes with customer organisations that are not used to that way of working. The IT professionals rarely use metrics to make improvements or value adding activities measurable. The most serious non-value adding activities are categorised as: partially done work, delays and defects. The core reason is that there are long lists of defects in the projects, which means that the software is partially done and the defects cause delays in the process. Even though there are efforts to reduce non-value adding activities in the process, these organizations are still confronted with problems attributed to miscommunication and the impediments by the external environment.

References

1. Baxter, G., Sommerville, I.: Socio-technical systems: From design methods to systems engineering. Interacting with Computers 23(1), 4–17 (2011)
2. Suchman, L.: Plans and situated actions. Cambridge University, New York (1986)
3. Eason, K.: Changing perspectives on the organizational consequences of in-formation technology. Behaviour& Information Technology 20(5), 323–328 (2001)
4. Boehm, B.: A view of 20th and 21st century software engineering. In: Proceedings of the 28th International Conference on Software Engineering. ACM Press, Shanghai (2006)
5. Basili, V., Turner, J.: Iterative enhancement: A practical technique for software development. IEEE Transactions of Software Engineering, 390–396 (December 1975)
6. Beck, K., Beedle, M., van Bennekum, A., Cockburn, A., Cunningham, W., Fowler, M., et al.: Agile manifesto, http://agilemanifesto.org
7. Poppendieck, M., Poppendieck, T.: Implementing lean software development: From concept to cash, 3rd edn. Addison-Wesley Professional, New York (2007)
8. Williams, L.: What agile teams think of agile principles. Communication of the ACM 55(4) (2012)
9. Modig, N., Åhlström, P.: This is Lean – resolving the efficiency paradox. Bulls. Graphics AB, Halmstad (2012)
10. Kniberg, M., Henrik, S.: Kanban and scrum - making the most of both. C4Media Inc. (2010)
11. Ohno, T.: Toyota production system: Beyond large scale production. Productivity Press (1988)

12. International organisation for standardisation - ISO 9241-210:2010: Ergonomics of human-system interaction - Part 210: Human-centred design process for interactive systems, Switzerland(2010)
13. Lárusdóttir, M., Cajander, Å., & Gulliksen, J.: Informal feedback rather than performance measurements–user-centred evaluation in Scrum projects. Behaviour& Information Technology, 1–18 (2013) (ahead-of-print)
14. Jia, Y., Larusdottir, M.K., Cajander, Å.: The Usage of Usability Techniques in Scrum Projects. In: Winckler, M., Forbrig, P., Bernhaupt, R. (eds.) HCSE 2012. LNCS, vol. 7623, pp. 331–341. Springer, Heidelberg (2012)
15. Larusdottir, M.K., Bjarnadottir, E.R., Gulliksen, J.: The focus on usability in testing practices in industry. In: Forbrig, P., Paternó, F., Mark Pejtersen, A. (eds.) HCIS 2010. IFIP AICT, vol. 332, pp. 98–109. Springer, Heidelberg (2010)
16. Cajander, Å., Larusdottir, M., Gulliksen, J.: Existing but not Explicit - The User Perspective in Scrum Projects in Practice. In: Kotzé, P., Marsden, G., Lindgaard, G., Wesson, J., Winckler, M. (eds.) INTERACT 2013, Part III. LNCS, vol. 8119, pp. 762–779. Springer, Heidelberg (2013)
17. Bruno, V., Dick, M.: Making usability work in industry: An Australian practitioner perspective. In: Proceedings of the 19th Australasian Conference on Computer-Human Interaction: Entertaining User Interfaces. ACM Press, Adelaide (2007)
18. Shingo, S.: Study of toyoda production system from an industrial engineering viewpoint. Productivity Press (1982)
19. Middleton, P., Flaxel, A., Cookson, A.: Lean software management case study: Timberline inc. In: Baumeister, H., Marchesi, M., Holcombe, M. (eds.) XP 2005. LNCS, vol. 3556, pp. 1–9. Springer, Heidelberg (2005)
20. Statistics Iceland office, http://www.statice.is
21. Icelandic chamber of commerce, http://www.vi.is
22. Silverman, D., Rapley, T.: Qualitative research, vol. 3. SAGE Publications Ltd. (2011)
23. Salah, D., Paige, R., Cairns, P.: A Systematic Literature Review on Agile Development Processes and User Centred Design Integration (2011)
24. Jokela, T., Koivumaa, J., Pirkola, J., Salminen, P., Kantola, N.: Methods for quantitative usability requirements: a case study on the development of the user interface of a mobile phone. Personal and Ubiquitous Computing 10(6), 345–355 (2006)
25. Gulliksen, J., Cajander, Å., Eriksson, E.: Only Figures Matter?–If Measuring Usability and User Experience in Practice is Insanity or a Necessity. In: International Workshop on, vol. 91 (2008)
26. Gulliksen, J., Göransson, B., Boivie, I., Blomkvist, S., Persson, J., Cajander, Å.: Key principles for user-centred systems design. Behaviour and Information Technology 22(6), 397–409 (2003)
27. Gulliksen, J., Cajander, Å., Sandblad, B., Eriksson, E., Kavathatzopoulos, I.: User-Centred Systems Design as Organizational Change: A Longitudinal Action Research Project to Improve Usability and the Computerized Work Environment in a Public Authority. International Journal of Technology and Human Interaction (IJTHI) 5(3), 13–53 (2009)

Dynamic Interaction Plugins Deployment in Ambient Spaces

Bashar Altakrouri[1,2] and Andreas Schrader[1]

[1] Ambient Computing Group, Institute of Telematics
University of Luebeck, Luebeck, Germany
{altakrouri,schrader}@itm.uni-luebeck.de
https://www.itm.uni-luebeck.de/
[2] Graduate School for Computing in Medicine and Life Sciences,
University of Luebeck, Luebeck, Germany

Abstract. A large-scale dynamic runtime deployment of existing and future interaction techniques remains an enduring challenge for engineering real-world pervasive computing ecosystems (ambient spaces). The need for innovative engineering solutions to tackle this issue increases, due to the ever expanding landscape of novel natural interaction techniques proposed every year to enrich interactive eco-systems with multitouch gestures, motion gestures, full body in motion, etc. In this paper, we discuss the implementation of *Interaction Plugins* as a possible solution to address this challenge. The discussed approach enables interaction techniques to be constructed as standalone dynamically deployable objects in ambient spaces during runtime.

Keywords: Ambient Assisted Living, Natural User Interfaces, Kinetic Interactions, Dynamic Interaction Deployment, Sharing Interactions.

1 Introduction

The human computer interaction (HCI) research continues to enrich users' interactions with real-world pervasive ecosystems (ambient spaces), with an increasing interest in designing for the whole body in motion as part of the Natural User Interface (NUI) paradigm [9][10]. Various definitions of NUI can be found in the literature. Nonetheless, those definitions mostly refer to the user's natural abilities, practices, and activities to control interactive systems [11] and can be simplified to voice-based and kinetic-based interactions [15]. The later defines those interactions, which are mostly caused and characterized by motion and movement activities, ranging from pointing, clicking, grasping, walking, etc. [2]. Herein, we focus on motion-based interactions as a dominant subset of Kinetic-based interactions. This type of interaction has been adopted widely in various commercial domains and became accessible to the end user, ranging from gaming (e.g., motion-controlled active play by Microsoft Kinect[1] or the Wii system[2]),

---

[1] http://www.microsoft.com/en-us/kinectforwindows/,
latest access on 26.06.2014.
[2] http://www.nintendo.com/wii, latest access on 26.06.2014.

S. Sauer et al. (Eds.): HCSE 2014, LNCS 8742, pp. 73–89, 2014.

data browsing, navigation scenarios (e.g., tilting for scrolling photos as in iOS[3] and Android[4] devices) and many more.

Despite its success, the NUI paradigm poses a number of significant challenges to the design, engineering and deployment of NUI technologies, especially when considering a far more diverse and heterogenous user population, e.g., due to aging and demographic changes; unknown interaction context, due to increasing user mobility to unknown environmental settings at design time; and spontaneous construction of interactive environments in-situ at runtime. Thus the focus on isolated design of natural interface techniques will not be adequate in current and future ambient spaces, which rapidly experience increasing emergence of interconnected mobile devices, smart objects, and seamlessly integrated context-aware services.

In our previous work, we proposed a shift towards completely dynamic on-the-fly ensembles of interaction techniques at runtime. The Interaction Ensembles approach is defined as "Multiple interaction modalities (i.e., interaction plugins) from different devices are tailored at runtime to adapt the available interaction resources and possibilities to the user's physical abilities, needs, and context" [2]. This shift imposes new dissemination, deployment, and adaptation requirements for engineering interaction techniques and interactive systems for NUIs.

In this paper, we tackle some of the emerging deployment aspects of interaction in ambient spaces. We believe that the deployment of interaction in NUIs is a key player to enable a realistic adoption of NUIs in the design and engineering of interactive systems. The paper presents a detailed overview and a reference implementation for building and deploying interaction components for ambient spaces, called Interaction Plugins. We have previously defined an Interaction Plugin (IP) as "an executable component in ambient interactive systems that encapsulates a single natural interaction technique with a set of interaction tasks as input and delivers higher level interaction primitives to applications based on specific interaction semantics" [1][2]. While our previous work in [1][2] proposed the concept of IP on a high conceptual level, the work presented in this paper primarily describes a detailed description of this approach and the resulting implementation.

To the best of our knowledge, there is no research specifically targeted at community-based creation and sharing of encapsulated natural interaction techniques for ambient spaces. The Interaction Plugin approach is based on three main design characteristics, namely, matching users and natural physical context, precise and extensible natural interaction descriptions (human and machine readable), and flexible deployment of interactions at runtime [1].

Interaction Plugin approach fosters soft-wired (de-coupled) applications and devices in order to overcome the limitations of the static binding and to address one of the most challenging requirements in pervasive environments, namely the "come as you are" requirements. This approach matches calls from the HCI community to overcome various challenging issues for user interfaces in ambient

---

[3] http://www.apple.com/ios/, latest access on 26.06.2014.

[4] http://www.android.com/, latest access on 26.06.2014.

spaces. Pruvost et al. [12] noted that interaction environments are becoming increasingly heterogeneous and dynamic, hence they are no longer static and closed; the interaction context is becoming increasingly more complex; and, increasing adaptability is required for sustainable utility and usability.

We believe that investigating this approach is essential to understand some of the challenges for engineering interactive systems in ambient spaces and setting proper interaction dissemination guidelines, where interactions are becoming increasingly dynamic, adaptive and multi-modal. Our approach aims at avoiding mismatch problems between user's needs and device's offers by employing the best matching natural interaction techniques to the given context, hence the user independence (acceptability by permitting customizability) and usability qualities required by Wachs et al. [15] are inherently enhanced.

2   Background and Related Research

Reviewing HCI literature reveals an extensive effort in the area of traditional user interfaces adaptation in terms of context modeling, user modeling, automatic generation of interfaces, etc. Most of the well-established concepts mainly target the conventional Graphical User Interface (GUI) paradigm such as plasticity [3] and the WWHT framework [13]. Despite their strong relevance, most available adaptation approaches fail to satisfy four enduring challenges drawn from the natural characteristics of ambient environments, presented by Pruvost et al. [12]:

- Heterogeneity and Distributivity: The interaction eco-system contains a variety of interaction devices with various capabilities.
- Dynamic Media Mobility: Interaction capabilities are highly dynamic as interaction devices may join or leave the ambient space at anytime.
- User Mobility: The user mobility in ambient spaces challenges the interactive system attention to the user's interaction needs.

In addition, most adaptation approaches focus on interface issues such as information presentation but not the interaction per se. Pruvost et al. [12] clearly indicated that locking interaction devices in their own closed world is certainly an issue for interaction systems adaptability in ambient spaces. This closeness results into reducing the richness and unity of those interaction devices in various context scenarios. They also argued for highly adaptable user interfaces that preserve utility and usability across contexts. In their described adaptation vision, they have presented the concept of Off-the-shelf Interaction Objects, which are pre-implemented bundles of code, intended to be reused and composed at runtime. The objects aim to provide the necessary adaptation required for the interaction technique. While their vision is focused on the structural adaptation of user interfaces and the adaptation of a running dialogue, our work is more concerned with the sharing and deployment aspects of NUI, especially kinetic interactions. The Gestureworks Core[5], which is limited to multitouch interactions,

---

[5] http://gestureworks.com, accessed on 26.06.2014.

is one of the earliest multitouch gesture authoring solution for touch-enabled devices on a variety of platforms such as Flash; C++; and Java. Based on the GML (GML), the solution comes with a rich library of pre-built gestures and allows for new custom gestures and gesture sequences to be built by designers. For motion-based interactions, the OpenNI[6] is an open source SDK used for the development of 3D sensing applications and middleware libraries. The main targets of this framework include enhancing the natural interaction techniques development community; making it possible for developers to share ideas and problems; to share code with each other; and to address the complete development lifecycle by a standard 3D sensing framework.

Standalone deployable interaction components for NUIs are becoming essential needs for ambient spaces. To our best knowledge, the work presented in this paper is one of few HCI research efforts to tackle this problem. Interestingly, dynamic component integration has been a rich and yet challenging investigation aspect for the ubiquitous and pervasive computing research. The dynamic component integration approach enables software components to be discovered, downloaded, and integrated on-demand, as a means of adapting an application's behavior and enhancing its features [14]. This area of investigation has been recently successfully applied to mobile environments as in the Mobile USers In Ubiquitous Computing Environments (MUSIC) system that supports dynamic component integration on Android using OSGi (OSGi) containers [8]; the Context-Aware Machine learning Framework for Android (CAMF) that promotes plugin-based adaptation on Android [16]; and the Funf Open Sensing Framework[7] that promotes statically-linked context modeling plug-ins integration. More recently, the Dynamix framework [7] was introduced as an open plug-and-play context framework for Android.

3   STAGE Architecture and Implementation

Our current implementation utilizes the wide spread and adoption of mobile devices for rich personalization, customization, and context acquisition in ambient spaces. Hence, this work fosters the use of mobile devices as customized and personalized interaction hubs. In our implementation, called STAGE, we leverage Dynamix framework [7] as a mechanism for deploying natural interactions. Dynamix is used due to its unique capabilities and flexibility, especially related to dynamic discovery and deployment of suitable context plugins during runtime. Hence, it was feasible to adopt and extend context plugins for interactions. Although grounding the implementation on mobile devices may appear limiting from the first glance, the use of the mobile devices as a personalized interaction hub to facilitate interactions in ambient spaces provides various benefits in terms of personalization, decentralization, user control, and lightweight infrastructure. Figure 1 illustrates our underlying technical approach for implementing natural interaction techniques as deployable and shareable IPs, based

---

[6] http://www.openni.org, latest accessed on 26.06.2014.

[7] http://funf.org, latest access on 26.06.2014.

on the Dynamix framework on the Android platform. As intended, the Dynamix framework runs as a background service (Dynamix Service) and is situated between Dynamix enabled applications and the device's interaction resources (i.e., interaction devices).

The STAGE technical implementation appears mainly in two areas: first, the interaction application side; second, the context plugin side. Dynamix-enabled applications are standard Android applications with extra context modeling functionality provided by a local Dynamix Service. In STAGE implementation, two new components are introduced, namely the Interaction Manager and Ability Manager, to adjust the Dynamix framework to our needs. Additionally, Dynamix context plugins were adopted and extended in the IP implementation.

3.1 Context Modeling and Deployment with the Dynamix Framework

The Ambient Dynamix framework was first proposed as a rich framework for on-demand discovery and runtime integration of plugins for context acquisition (sensors) and modification (actuators) in wide-area mobile contexts. Interestingly, Dynamix features strong and flexible discovery and deployment of context plugins at runtime. The framework was successfully used to model and deploy context in different none-HCI related scenarios as in [5][6][4]. The two features are essential building blocks for the implementation of the Interaction Plugin concept. In fact, our work is the first to utilize and build on this framework for deploying interactions in ambient spaces. In this section, the most relevant internal components of the framework based on [7] will be described. The full specifications and more extensive discussion can be found in the Dynamix online portal[8].

Dynamix runs as a background service on Android-based devices, which allows multiple Dynamix-enabled applications to subscribe to Dynamix context events. Principally, a Dynamix-enabled application is a normal Android application that implements the necessary Dynamix API. Various context resources deliver raw sensor data to the framework, which are then modeled by Dynamix according to the available context plugins.

A context plugin is a standalone deployable OSGi container that allows for seamless runtime deployment (i.e., installation, uninstallation) according to the application needs. The flexibility of the Dynamix plugin's technical structure provided an adequate ground for our development of IP, as discussed lengthly in this section.

The OSGi Manager resides at the core of Dynamix implementation, which is build based on the Apache Felix OSGi. The manager is mainly dedicated for all plugins deployment actions, including the installation and un-installation of plugins from their OSGi containers. The OSGi framework allows for seamless integration of software units (called bundles) at runtime. Internally, the OSGi framework is composed of multiple layers responsible for bundle execution, bun-

---

[8] http://ambientdynamix.org, visited on 26.06.2014.

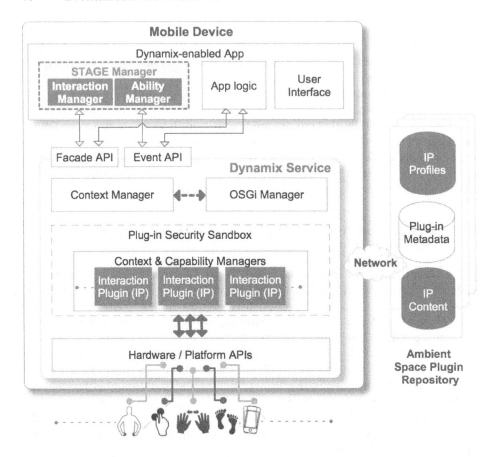

Fig. 1. A high-level overview - STAGE realization based on Dynamix (based on [1])

dle management, bundle life cycle, service and binding management, and security control. There are various communication aspects in Dynamix. We will focus, herein, only on the communication between plugins and applications. The communication between the Dynamix framework and Dynamix-enabled application is featured using the Facade and Event API. The Facade API controls all requests for context modeling support. Moreover, Dynamix currently uses POJO (Plain Old Java Objects) objects to encode the events shared between plugins and applications. The use of POJO objects allows both sides to work with Java objects, hence increasing the operability and reducing the programming and modeling load.

3.2   Implementing STAGE-Enabled Applications

Dynamix applications are designed to subscribe to dynamix and receive modeled context events. Those two features ease the implementation of context-based applications dramatically. Nonetheless, Dynamix-enabled applications are not fully adequate to the Interaction Plugin conceptual design. Hence, STAGE introduces two important extensions to the architecture, in order to facilitate the use of this framework for IPs, on the application and plugin levels. The changes and extensions are distinctly tinted (i.e., fully or partially shaded) in Figure 1. The STAGE components on the application side are further illustrated in Figure 2. STAGE-enabled applications contain the STAGE Manager (which contains the Interaction and Profile Managers) and the Interaction Profile Manifest (which encapsulates all necessary information about the required and relevant interaction capabilities by the application).

STAGE Interaction Manager. This class controls the activation of the available IP, based on the ability (the physical abilities required for the interaction e.g., major life activities), movement (the exact movements required for the interaction e.g., body part involved, type, and degree of movements), and interaction (the interaction semantic) profiles. The communication between the Interaction Manager and Dynamix service is facilitated using the Dynamix Facade API. Following the dynamix context plugin model, Interaction Plugins are tailored OSGi-based Bundles, which are loaded into the Dynamix embedded OSGi container at runtime. Once loaded and activated, an Interaction Plugin sends interaction encoded events to subscribed applications (as interaction primitive events) using POJO. Principally, Interaction Plugins are hosted in an Internet-based plugin repository, which in addition to the IP Bundle files, hosts the IP profiles and (optionally) additional related plugins.

In addition to the usual Dynamix context sensing tasks, IPs can be queried by the Interaction Manager to access the information encoded in the IP profiles. Currently, the Dynamix Service provides all plugin discovery services, plugin filtering based on the interaction requirements (interaction primitives required), and plugin installation support. Filtering and activating the available interaction plugins are currently handled by the Interaction Manager. The STAGE Interaction Manager is composed from the following components, as shown in Figure 2:

- *Subscription Manager* is responsible for communicating directly with the Dynamix facade API, in order to control and mange IP subscriptions;
- *Event Handler* consumes all Dynamix context events and filters all relevant Interaction Events;
- *Interaction Profile Builder* is responsible to serialize the content of the Interaction Profile Manifest into a runtime object;
- *Plugin Manager* keeps track of all accessible IPs and handles the status, subscription, plugin information, and discovery requests of all plugins;
- *Ensemble Engine* is responsible for monitoring interaction resources (i.e., IP) and build possible Interaction Ensembles adequate for the given context based on the application's required interaction capabilities, the available IP, and the user's physical ability profile; and
- *STAGE Interface Controller*: STAGE-enabled applications require to control the application's GUI elements according to the fired interaction primitives from the IP (once an interaction primitive is fired, the corresponding action on the interface is executed, e.g., a selection interaction primitive may be interpreted as a button press).

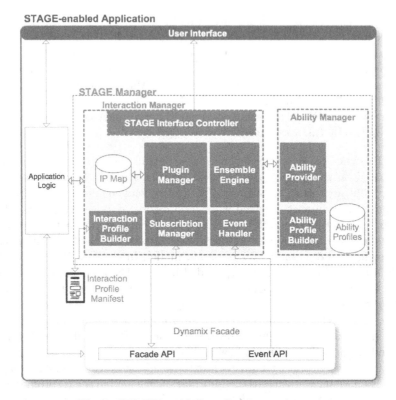

Fig. 2. STAGE-enabled application architecture

Ability Manager. This module is responsible for extracting the user's ability and disability qualities, based on the available Ability profile and Movement profile. Currently, both profiles are modeled and represented in tailored XML formats. This component is essentially split into the following modules:

- *Ability Profile Builder* is essentially an XML parser responsible to extract and serialize the content of the Ability Profile into a runtime object; and
- *Ability Provider* provides all necessary information regarding the required physical abilities for executing the interaction tasks adequately by the user.

Interaction Profile Manifest. This profile manifest captures the main interaction semantics including the interaction primitives such as pointing, selecting, dragging, etc. This is particularly important in ambient spaces because it provides indication on the main use of the interaction technique and its offerings. We are considering interaction profile as a prime key for interaction adaption and matching in ambient spaces. In ambient spaces, interaction profiles offer the needed manifestation for coupling interaction techniques with applications. Principally, it is used to in order to identify the required interaction capabilities for the application. The manifest file is constructed in XML format, and contains essentially the required interaction primitives. Figure 3 resembles a simple profile example (i.e., an application requires a selection interaction primitive).

```
 1  <?xml version="1.0" encoding="UTF-8"?>
 2  <appInteractionProfile>
 3      <primitives>
 4          <primitive>
 5              <type>de.itm.STAGE.nui.primitives.selection</type>
 6              <dynamixPluginDetails>
 7                  <pluginId></pluginId>
 8                  <dynamixPluginType>AUTONOMOUS</dynamixPluginType>
 9              </dynamixPluginDetails>
10          </primitive>
11      </primitives>
12  </appInteractionProfile>
```

Fig. 3. STAGE-enabled application architecture

STAGE-Enabled Application Interaction Sequence. The interaction sequence, shown in Figure 4, illustrates the communication steps between Dynamix and the STAGE Manager. The sequence illustrates the process of interaction requesting a certain IP, deploying IP in runtime, and delivering the event information to the requesting application. The Interaction Manager triggers and establishes the connection with the Dynamix framework. Upon connection, it receives all Dynamix related events as long as the Dynamix connection remains alive. For instance, the received events involve Dynamix activation events, deactivation events, and plugin installation events. Next, the Interaction Manager requests the ability profile from the Ability Manager. Moreover, it serializes the application's interaction profile, using its profile builder module.

The Interaction Manager requests Dynamix for all accessible plugins (i.e., those plugins available in its repository). Once the list is received, the Interaction Manager identifies all accessible IPs and ignores all other context plugins. Plugins that implement the required "InfoObject" datatype object proposed by STAGE are identified as IPs. Otherwise, the plugins are considered conventional Dynamix context plugins (i.e., not related to interactions). The "InfoObject" contains the essential Uniform Resource Identifiers (URIs) for the IP and its three profiles, which are used later for filtering adequate IP in a given context. Next, it configures the Interfaces Controller event listener, in order to allow the controller to utilize the detected events for controlling the interface controllers accordingly. Moreover, the Interaction Manager sends Dynamix subscription requests to the available IP. While getting accepted subscriptions, the manager requests the plugin's ability and interaction profiles in order to build a map of IP and physical abilities required for each. This information forms the core base for the Ensemble Manager's matching algorithm. Accordingly, the Interaction Manager requests the Interface Controller to activate those GUI elements that are possible to be controlled by the available interaction resources (i.e., IPs). Other GUI elements, not supported by the available interaction resources, are not activated for NUI interactions, but can be still used conventionally (using the conventional touch interface).

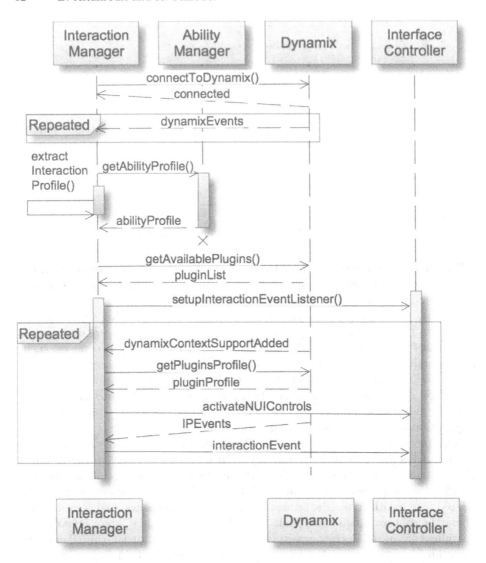

Fig. 4. Sequence Diagram for STAGE-enabled application

At the end of interaction sequence, the STAGE Manager is able to receive modeled interaction events from the various IPs. The triggered interaction primitives are then sent to the Interface Controller to perform the required interaction tasks. It is important to know that multiple plugins may deliver the same interaction primitive. In this case, the Ensemble Engine may decide on which plugin should be used according to the best match with the user's physical abilities (Ensemble Engine's matching algorithms are not covered in this paper due to the size limits).

3.3   Implementing Interaction Plugins

An IP is essentially an OSGi Bundle containing the plugin's logic and context acquisition code. In our case, Dynamix is responsible for handling the plugin's lifecycle, based on its embedded OSGi framework. Figure 5 illustrates the technical implementation of the IP. The distinctly tinted (i.e., fully or partially shaded) components in the diagram indicate the core STAGE components and extensions:

- *Context Acquisition & Modeling* module resembles the logic required to access the context provider and its raw context data. The raw context data resources may be local resources (i.e., running on the same device, for example a built-in orientation sensor) or remote sources (i.e., accessible ambient context providers available in an accessible ambient space, for example an external camera sensor);
- *STAGE Handler* is responsible to model the interaction events based on the received information from the previous module;
- *Plugin Factory* provides the required mechanisms for plugin instantiation (handled completely by Dynamix);
- *PluginRuntime* component contains the plugin's core lifecycle methods;
- *Profile Builder*, as part of the PluginRuntime component, is responsible for serializing and building the interaction, movement, and ability profiles associated with each IP. Those profiles are modeled as XML embedded in the plugin's file structure and accessible though the IPluginInfo object;

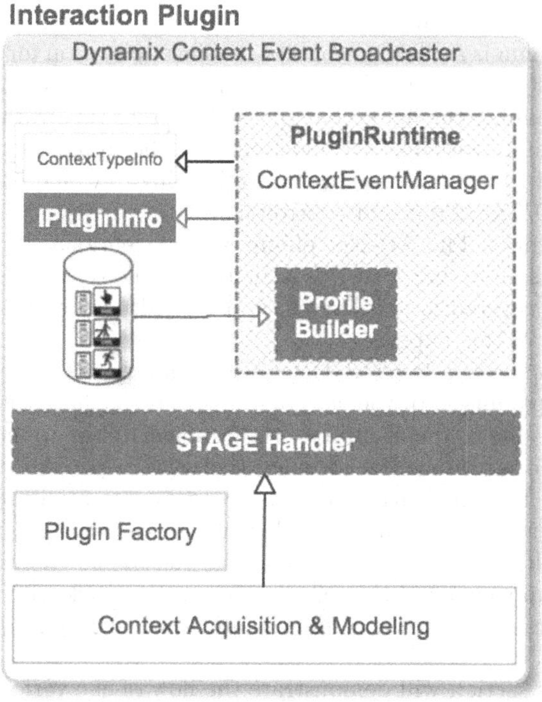

Fig. 5. IP internal architecture

- *ContextTypeInfo Objects* contains the plugin's supported datatypes. In our implementation, those context type objects are used as interaction primitive objects; and
- *IPluginInfo Object*, which is introduced as a new plugin information datatype and dedicated for the necessary movement, ability, and interaction profiles.

4   Examples and Scenarios

The practical benefits of IPs can be seen in an endless variety of showcases and scenarios. For instance, a person with limited arm rotation may take advantage of replacing the arm-based rotation IP exceeding a certain rotation degree with a foot-based rotation IP which utilizes an accelerometer sensor embedded in her smart sport shoes and wirelessly connected to her smartphone. Another example is allowing a person with total absence of three fingers due to an injury to interact with typical mobile operation systems, which often requires swipe gestures with three or more fingers. In such a case, one possible ensemble might comprise two IPs combining two fingers multitouch swipe with one foot-based motion swipe to replace the original three fingers swipe. In principle, the potential for building useful scenarios for interaction plugins and ensembles is only limited by the creativity of interface designers and engineers developing sensing devices in various forms and shapes to be used in future ambient scenarios. For further illustration, this section presents a full description of an interactive demonstration scenario, called the AmbientRoom, to showcase the dynamic aspects of dynamic interaction deployment at runtime.

The AmbientRoom is a STAGE-enabled mobile application for controlling the ambient lighting of smart rooms. The application provides three simple functionalities, namely dimming the light, changing light's color (i.e., rotate between the rainbow colors), and switching the light on/off. The application relies on our implementation of the Art-Net Light Controller plugin, which uses the Art-Net protocol to send DMX512 data for controlling lighting equipment over the Internet Protocol networks. The Art-Net plugin is a conventional Dynamix context plugin that acts as an actuator in this scenario, extensive discussion about this type of plugins is covered in [4]. Therefore, it should not be mixed with the IP concept discussed in this paper.

Because the application is STAGE-enabled, it adapts its interactivity to the user's physical capabilities. In the case of difficulties touching the interface controls with fingers (due to finger injury), the AmbientRoom application searches for alternative and adequate IPs allowing the user to perform the interaction tasks required by the application. In this scenario, the applications finds two motion-based interaction plugins for replacing the position (i.e., navigation) interaction task with a shaking IP (shaking the device for positioning the focus on the next GUI component) and the selection interaction task with an IP utilizing head movement respectively. Those plugins are found and dynamically deployed at runtime.

The rest of this section will demonstrate the flow of the various processes involved in this scenario. Once the application is started, the application will show the user with a disabled GUI presenting the application main functional capabilities, as in Figure 6 (1). These capabilities are initially looked or disabled until the required plugins are requested by the application and dynamically deployed and activated by dynamix. In this case, the application starts by requesting the Art-Net Light plugin. Once the plugin is found, downloaded, and activated successfully by Dynamix, the application GUI controls will be activated, as shown in Figure 6 (2).

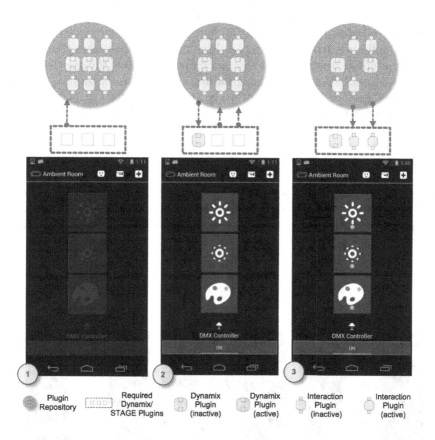

Fig. 6. AmbientRoom application (screenshots): (1) deactivated GUI controls; (2) activated GUI controls after Art-Net plugin runtime deployment; (3) GUI controls are marked after IPs runtime deployment

Next, the AmbientRoom application requests two motion-based IPs to enable users to interact with the application using two motion gestures. The first IP relies on the mobile device built-in accelerometer for detecting device shaking gesture to position the focus on the next button. The second IP relies on the Asus Xtion PRO LIVE[9] motion sensor for detecting head movements to select

---

[9] http://www.asus.com/Multimedia/Xtion_PRO_LIVE/, latest access on 26.06.2014.

(i.e., click) the selected button. Upon a successful deployment of the two plugins, the corresponding GUI control are marked with a green symbol to indicate the possibility to be controlled using motion gestures in addition to the conventional multitouch interface as shown in Figure 6 (3).

Figure 7 demonstrates the NUI style interactions with motion gestures enabled by the deployed IP. Figure 7 (1) shows the NUI-enabled buttons. Using the shaking gesture, the user positions the focus on the control of choice (each device shake will position the focus on the next button) as illustrated in Figure 7 (2). Using the head movement, the user is able to select (i.e., push) the button in focus as illustrated in Figure 7 (3).

Despite its limited scope, the AmbientRoom scenario illustrates the possibility to turn a mobile device into an interaction hub to enable the user to control ambient resources (i.e., lighting) using natural interactions techniques (i.e., different motion gestures). Most importantly, it demonstrates the potential and power of the soft wiring approach where interaction capabilities are deployed (as plugins) at runtime using the STAGE system.

5   Provisioning Interaction Plugins

Provisioning IP undergoes a number of phases as illustrated in Figure 8. In the first phase, the interaction techniques passes the usual design and implementation processes. In the second phase, the interaction developer (i.e., designer,

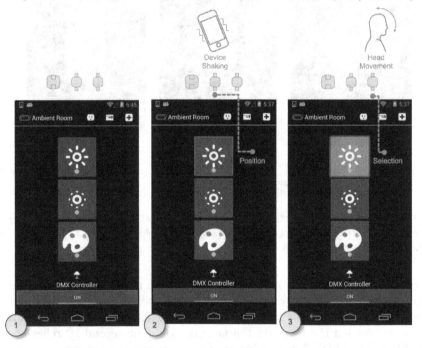

Fig. 7. AmbientRoom application NUI-enabled Interactions

Fig. 8. IP provisioning lifecycle

developer, or team) makes sure that the techniques satisfies the function and utility defined in the interaction design. In the third phase, the interaction developer should define the interaction's movement profile, based on an acceptable level of movement description; define the interaction's ability profile, based on the most important physical qualities that impact the interaction; and assign the interaction semantics, based on the envisioned utility of the technique. In the fourth phase, the interaction developer wraps the interaction's internal logic as a Dynamix plugin. In the fifth phase, the IP is published to an accessible repository. Dynamix supports two types of accessible plugin storage locations (file-system or network). Our implementation supports the later type as shown in Figure 1. The repository hosts the plugins OSGi bundles and the corresponding context plugin description XML documents.

6   Conclusions and Future Work

This paper argues that a large-scale dynamic runtime deployment of existing and future interaction techniques for Natural User Interfaces remains an enduring challenge for engineering interactive systems for ambient spaces. Only few research projects aim to target this problem in the context of HCI. In this paper, we have presented the architecture and implementation of the STAGE system, which enables interaction techniques to be constructed as standalone dynamically deployable objects (*Interaction Plugins*) for Android mobile platforms during runtime. The presented implementation is one of many possible ways to realize the proposed concept. Hence, the proposed implementation should not be necessarily considered as an ultimate implementation solution, instead the implementation aims to demonstrate and evaluate the feasibility of the approach. The current implementation utilizes the wide adoption of mobile devices for rich personalization, customization, and context acquisition in ambient spaces. Hence, this work fosters the use of mobile devices as customized and personalized interaction hubs. As future work continuation to this paper, we are working on an extended performance evaluation of the Interaction Plugins and rich feasibility tests by implementing a number of demonstration scenarios. We also aim at increasing the richness of Interaction Plugins and improving plugin's filtering and matching according to the user's physical context.

Acknowledgement. This work was partially supported by the Graduate School for Computing in Medicine and Life Sciences funded by Germany's Excellence Initiative [DFG GSC 235/1].

References

1. Altakrouri, B., Gröschner, J., Schrader, A.: Documenting natural interactions. In: CHI 2013 Extended Abstracts on Human Factors in Computing Systems, CHI EA 2013, pp. 1173–1178. ACM, New York (2013), http://doi.acm.org/10.1145/2468356.2468566
2. Altakrouri, B., Schrader, A.: Towards dynamic natural interaction ensembles. In: Devina Ramduny-Ellis, A.D., Gill, S. (eds.) Fourth International Workshop on Physicality (Physicality 2012) co-located with British HCI 2012 Conference, Birmingham, UK (September 2012)
3. Calvary, G., Coutaz, J., Thevenin, D.: Embedding plasticity in the development process of interactive systems. In: 6th ERCIM Workshop "User Interfaces for All". Also in HUC (Handheld and Ubiquitous Computing) First workshop on Resource Sensitive Mobile HCI, Conference on Handheld and Ubiquitous Computing, Florence, Italy (October 2000)
4. Carlson, D., Altakrouri, B., Schrader, A.: Ambientweb: Bridging the web's cyberphysical gap. In: 2012 3rd International Conference on the Internet of Things (IOT), Wuxi, China, pp. 1–8 (October 2012)
5. Carlson, D., Altakrouri, B., Schrader, A.: An ad-hoc smart gateway platform for the web of things. In: Green Computing and Communications (GreenCom), 2013 IEEE and Internet of Things (iThings/CPSCom), IEEE International Conference on and IEEE Cyber, Physical and Social Computing, Beijing, August 20-23, pp. 619–625 (2013)
6. Carlson, D., Altakrouri, B., Schrader, A.: Reinventing the share button for physical spaces. In: IEEE International Conference on Pervasive Computing and Communications Workshops (PERCOM Workshops), San Diego, California, USA, March 18-22, pp. 318–320 (2013)
7. Carlson, D., Schrader, A.: Dynamix: An open plug-and-play context framework for android. In: Proceedings of the 3rd International Conference on the Internet of Things (IoT2012), Wuxi, China (October 2012)
8. Consortium, I.M.: Óist-music: Context-aware self-adaptive platform for mobile applications (2010), http://ist-music.berlios.de
9. England, D.: Whole Body Interactions: An Introduction. In: England, D. (ed.) Whole Body Interaction, pp. 1–5. Springer London (2011)
10. Fogtmann, M.H., Fritsch, J., Kortbek, K.J.: Kinesthetic interaction: revealing the bodily potential in interaction design. In: Proceedings of the 20th Australasian Conference on Computer-Human Interaction: Designing for Habitus and Habitat, OZCHI 2008, pp. 89–96. ACM, New York (2008), http://doi.acm.org/10.1145/1517744.1517770
11. Iacolina, S., Lai, A., Soro, A., Scateni, R.: Natural interaction and computer graphics applications. In: Puppo, E., Brogni, A., Floriani, L.D. (eds.) Eurographics Italian Chapter Conference, pp. 141–146. Eurographics Association, Genova (2010), http://publications.crs4.it/pubdocs/2010/ILSS10
12. Pruvost, G., Heinroth, T., Bellik, Y., Minker, W.: User Interaction Adaptation within Ambient Environments. In: Next Generation Intelligent Environments: Ambient Adaptive Systems edn., ch. 5, pp. 153–194. Springer, Boston (2011)

13. Rousseau, C., Bellik, Y., Vernier, F., Bazalgette, D.: A framework for the intelligent multimodal presentation of information. Signal Process. 86(12), 3696–3713 (2006), http://dx.doi.org/10.1016/j.sigpro.2006.02.041
14. Schrader, A., Carlson, D.V., Busch, D.: Modular framework support for context-aware mobile cinema. Personal Ubiquitous Comput. 12(4), 299–306 (2008), http://dx.doi.org/10.1007/s00779-007-0151-6
15. Wachs, J.P., Kölsch, M., Stern, H., Edan, Y.: Vision-based hand-gesture applications. Commun. ACM 54, 60–71 (2011), http://doi.acm.org/10.1145/1897816.1897838
16. Wang, A.I., Ahmad, Q.K.: Camf - context-aware machine learning framework for android. In: Rey, M.D. (ed.) Iasted International Conference on Software Engineering and Applications, SEA, CA, USA, November 8-10 (2010)

Extending OpenUP to Conform
with the ISO Usability Maturity Model

Andrés Rodríguez

LIFIA, Facultad de Informática,
Universidad Nacional de La Plata, Argentina
andres.rodriguez@lifia.info.unlp.edu.ar

Abstract. Integrating practices and methods of Interaction Design and Usability into Software Engineering processes has posed some challenges. In this paper we extend a SE process to enable its instantiation as user centered in order to improve the usability level reachable by the final system. Also, we suggest a kind of a road map that enables software organizations to instantiate cumulative versions of this process to grow in their capability regarding the usability practices. The paper is organized in two parts. First, we describe de open source version of the Unified Process (OpenUP) and the ISO Usability Maturity Model (UMM-ISO) and present the results of an assessment made on the first to determine its conformity with the latter. In the second part we present an extension to OpenUP to fill the gaps discovered and report the highlights of an implementation of these contributions in a real project and the lessons learned.

Keywords: User Centered Design, Usability Maturity Model, OpenUP.

1   Introduction

Integrating practices and methods of usability and interaction design into the Software Engineering (SE) processes has posed some challenges. As Seffah has explained "the structure and techniques of Human Computer Interaction (HCI) are still relatively unknown, underutilized, hard-to-master and with little integration essential in software development teams" [1]. The magnitude of the integration effort is often wrongly minimized. Many developers still think that usability is affected only by the user interface. However, even early decisions on the software architecture may affect the usability a system can reach [2, 3]. If usability is considered as the result of the whole development process, its activities must be included throughout the process.

It has shown from HCI that there is a direct relationship between the level of usability that a product can reach and the use of a User Centered Design (UCD) process (there are many references on the topic, see for example [4, 5]). However, not all SE processes can become focused on user simply by making a few modifications. From SE, this topic has been recognized too (e.g. [6] for example) .

Another challenge deals with the improvement of processes that enable an organization grow in usability capabilities as predictable and controlled as in SE capabilities.

S. Sauer et al. (Eds.): HCSE 2014, LNCS 8742, pp. 90–107, 2014.
© IFIP International Federation for Information Processing 2014

Some model of capability and maturity in usability have been proposed trying to provide a basis for planners and process engineers to know what user centered activities to include in a particular project, as well as to assist those who wish to improve the whole process carried out by an organization.

Our work deals with these two challenges with the Usability Maturity Model presented in ISO Standards (UMM-ISO) as a base. First, we extend a SE process to enable its instantiation as a user centered one. Then, we suggest a kind of a road map that enables software organizations to grow in capability regarding the usability practices. The paper is organized in the following form. In Section 2 we contextualize our proposal analyzing related works. In Section 3, we describe the open source version of the Unified Process (OpenUP) and the UMM-ISO and present the results of an assessment made to determine the conformity of OpenUP with the UMM-ISO. In Section 4 we present the main contribution of this paper: an extension to OpenUP to fill the gaps discovered in Capability levels 1 to 3. Finally, we report the highlights of an implementation of these contributions and the lessons learned. Concluding remarks and further work needed are mentioned to close the paper.

2   Related Work

There have been several proposals to integrate HCI in SE processes. The common approach has been identifying some key HCI activities to be included a SE process to create a somewhat modified version.

Proposals for augmenting waterfall, agile or unified processes can be found in literature. For the waterfall cycle, can be mentioned for example the proposals of Costabile[7] and Joshi and Sarda (see [6]). Costabile augments de process including user and task analyzing, scenarios and User Interface (UI) specifications activities. She emphasizes on the evaluation as the central activity of a UCD process. Joshi and Sarda add several HCI activities at the Communication, Modeling and Construction phases.

The Unified Process (UP) has received different types of proposals for integrating HCI activities. Göransson[8] proposed a new discipline for RUP. After identifying identified some RUP characteristics that can be obstacles for implementing a UCD Process (centrality of architecture, prevalence of the use cases, usability activities concentrated only in the Elaboration phase) proposes a new discipline, Usability Design containing key elements from HCI and spanning the whole RUP lifecycle. Other proposals for RUP are the work by Krutchen[9], Heumann[10], Sousa and Furtado[11]. The first two, propose the inclusion of HCI models, activities and artifacts to the basic RUP (user experience model, prototypes and storyboards are the most important). Sousa and Furtado present the RUP for Interactive Systems (RUPi). It adapts the four RUP workflows. In the requirement workflow RUPi includes several modeling tasks and an explicit definition of usability requirements. In the Analysis and Design workflow a UI conceptual design and class model of UI are added. The Implementation workflow is increased with guidelines and in the Test workflow a strong focus is made on Usability evaluation.

The open source version of UP has received some contributions too. For example, the DSDM Consortium published the plugin OpenUP/DSDM[12] that adds specifics Business roles and assign them some responsibilities on tasks and work products: Executive sponsor, Visionary, Ambassador user, Advisor User. The goal of this plugin is to promote collaboration between business and technical communities during the project. In the same line, the Plugin Web Enabled UCD[13] is a proposal to augment UP as an UCD process for web development adding many new elements (11 new roles, 12 new work products and 6 new activities).

In the realm of agile methods, Beyer, Holtzblatt and Baker [14] describe a combination of the Rapid Contextual Design techniques [15] with a user stories based development process. Their proposal includes a separate UI design team as long as these skills are usually held by different people on the team. Nielsen[16] proposes a threefold integration between agile methods and usability field: perform usability activities in a few days, adopt a parallel track approach (where the UX[1] work is continuously done one step ahead of the implementation work) and make foundational user research going beyond feature development (ideally this should be conducted before a development project starts). Joshi[17] has proposed a similar integration: HCI activities hard to fit in a typical iteration should be done before the agile iterations begin, there must be a synchronization between software development iterations and HCI activities, the HCI team should closely coordinate with the software development team giving some "development support" to ensure that UI is implemented as close to its original intent as possible.

All these proposals show different ways of integrating the key HCI activities within SE processes. In some way or another the HCI elements that most contribute to the final usability according to Joshi and Sarda[18] are at the center of the different proposals (user modeling, UI prototyping, usability evaluation, collaborative work between HCI staff and development staff). Also an iterative cycle, user centered work is present at most of them. In our approach we try to extend these contributions on a side that has not been fully addressed in our opinion. In this paper, we are proposing a roadmap intended not only to help including HCI activities in a typical SE process but to provide a predictable way for improving that process and grow in HCI capability. We base our work on the concept of Capability Maturity Models, adopted in SE as a guide for process improvement.

3   OpenUP and the UMM-ISO

3.1   Open Source Unified Process (OpenUP)

OpenUP is the open source version of the Unified Process (UP) released as part of the Eclipse Process Framework (EPF) project[19] (an extensible set of framework, tools and sample content for authorship, configuration and publication of methods and processes). The EPF's metamodel is based on version 2.0 of the Software & Systems

---

[1]   UX stands for User eXperience.

Process Engineering Metamodel Specification (SPEM) by the Object Management Group OMG[20]. This framework includes definitions of method content and application delivery processes. The content is manifested through definitions of work products, roles, tasks and guidance. A relation between some work products (input, output), tasks and roles makes an Activity and a chain of activities build a Process. Finally, there is the concept of Practice: "an approach to solving one or several commonly occurring problems. Practices are intended as "chunks" of process for adoption, enablement, and configuration"[21]. Eleven practices are contained in the EPF Practices Library (EPL).

OpenUP presents itself as "a lean UP that applies iterative and incremental approaches within a structured lifecycle. OpenUP embraces a pragmatic, agile philosophy that focuses on the collaborative nature of software development". Its simplest version is OpenUP/Basic (a minimum, complete and extensible process oriented to work on projects of small and medium scale). OpenUP/Basic includes all the practices defined in the EPL, organized into two categories, Management practices (Iterative development, Risk-value lifecycle, Release planning, Whole team, Team change management) and Technical ones (Concurrent Testing, Continuous integration, Evolutionary architecture, Evolutionary design, Shared Vision, Test driven development, Use case driven development). Development lifecycle with OpenUP can be analyzed in three layers: a) personal effort is organized in micro-increments (short units of work typically measured in hours or a few days); b) team effort for delivering incremental value to stakeholders is organized in iterations (planned, time-boxed intervals typically measured in weeks); c) the project lifecycle is structured into four phases: Inception, Elaboration, Construction, and Transition (this provides stakeholders and team members with visibility and decision points throughout the project)[22]

3.2   The ISO Usability Maturity Model (UMM-ISO)

Different models have been proposed to drive process improvement in usability aspects (e.g., [23–28]). The UMM-ISO was presented in the report ISO TR18529 "Human-centered lifecycle process descriptions"[29]. The UMM-ISO attempts to provide a basis for planners to know what human centered activities include in a particular project, as well as to assist their improvement.

UMM-ISO's reference model is contained in ISO 15504 SPICE[30]. This model has two dimensions: processes and capabilities. Each process can be assessed with a degree of compliance on a scale of six Levels: incomplete, performed, managed, established, predictable, optimizing. The way to determine the Capability level in a process is to analyze which attributes of such process are checked according to the evidence collected. Each attribute is evaluated on a four ranges scale: unmet, partially achieved, widely reached, fully met.

Dimension of the Human Centered Development (HCD) Processes. Processes are described as practices that are required to implement for including system stakeholders and users during the whole lifecycle. Each process is described with purpose, success indicators, input work product and output work products. ISO TR18529 defines seven HCD process:

— HCD1.Ensure the HCD content systems strategy
— HCD2.Plan and manage the process
— HCD3.Specify the requirements of stakeholders and the organization
— HCD4.Understand and specify context of use
— HCD5.Produce design solutions,
— HCD6.Evaluate designs against requirements.
— HCD7.Introduce and operate the system

These seven processes can be grouped at three different levels of analysis: the organization (HCD1 and HCD7), the project technical development (HCD4, HCD3, HCD5 and HCD6) and its management and control (HCD2).

Dimension of Capability and Maturity Levels. To assess the capability level reached a number of desirable process attributes that has to be met in each HCD process. These attributes are cumulative, at every level of capability is expected that all attributes of the lower levels are achieved.

— Level 1: Performed. The degree to which output work products are produced from inputs work products through the enactment of the practices which comprise the process. There is one Process performance attribute to be assessed: "Ensure that base practices are performed to satisfy the purpose of the process".
— Level 2: Managed. The degree at which the process is managed to produce work products of acceptable quality within defined timescales and resource needs. The achievement is demonstrated assessing two kinds of attributes: Performance management (e.g., Identifying resource requirements to enable planning and tracking of the process, Plan the performance of the process by identifying the activities and the allocated resources according to the requirements, etc.) and Work product management (e.g., Identify requirements for the integrity and quality of the work products, Manage the configuration of work products to ensure their integrity)
— Level 3: Established. The established process ensures the deployment of a defined process based upon good SE principles. The evaluation will analyze the extent to which a given process is defined with an appropriate standard to contribute to the goals of the organization through definition of a standard process (e.g., Tailor the standard process, Implement the defined process) and through use of suitable, skilled human resources an process infrastructure (e.g., Define human resources competencies required, define process infrastructure requirements)

Level 0 (Incomplete) has no attributes to identify, while Levels 4 and 5 require an assessment on the organization beyond the scope of a particular project process (e.g., Process measurement attribute at Level 4: Define process goals and associated measures that support the business goals of the organization).

3.3   Assessment of OpenUP in the Light of the UMM-ISO

An assessment has been done to determine the capability profile of OpenUP in terms of UMM-ISO. The goal was not to find if OpenUP is fully compliant with UMM-ISO. It is clear that OpenUP is not a full UCD process so gaps with UMM ISO will be found. The assessment is used here as a structured approach to discover those gaps.

To collect evidence of achievement we use the complete specification of OpenUP/Basic 1.5.0.1[22]. Any item contained in that specification, either method or process, that enable us to interpret that it could satisfy some UMM-ISO attribute will be considered evidence enough of such capability. Assessment on levels 4 and 5 require evidence from the organization management practices beyond the specific development process used. That evidence cannot be got from the OpenUP specification, so the scope of our assessment is constrained to levels 1 to 3 of UMM-ISO.

The evaluation cycle is the following:

1. Take a UMM-ISO HCD process
2. Take a Level to assess. For each process attribute at the chosen level, analyze the OpenUP/Basic specification and look for content or processes which allow satisfying the attribute.
3. Determine the degree of achievement of the attribute in a ranking of 4 levels:
   (a) N (Not achieved): there is no evidence of the achievement (numeric score: 0)
   (b) P (Partial): implementing the activities included in OpenUP allows a partial achievement of the attribute (0 <= score <= 0.3)
   (c) L (Large): implementing the activities included in OpenUP allows a large achievement of the attribute (0.3 <= score <= 0.7)
   (d) F (Full): implementing the activities included in OpenUP allows a full achievement of the attribute (0.7 <= score <= 1)
4. In cases of doubt about the achievement between two levels for a particular practice, apply the benefit of the doubt and qualify in the higher level.
5. The process is repeated for the next attribute of the level.
6. The process is repeated for the next level, until there is no evidence of the preparation of any practice at this level or until reaching the upper limit established for the evaluation.
7. The cycle 2 to 6 repeats for the next HCD of UMM-ISO process

We use an evaluation form adapted from Earthy[31] (see Fig. 1). For each UMM-ISO attribute (column 1) we identify the OpenUP Practices including enough evidence to cover the attribute (column 2). Within each Practice we detail Process contents (Activities and Capability patterns, in column 3) and the Method contents (Roles, Artifacts, Tasks, in column 4) that allow that coverage. For each of the attributes of UMM-ISO the degree of achievement is recorded in the above-mentioned scale. Then we calculate the mean for all the attributes in a group (Process performance, Performance management, Product management, Process definition, Process resources definition). This mean set the achievement at that capability level for the HCD process.

UCD1. Ensure UCD contents in the systems strategy				
Practices and processes	Practices	Process contents	Method contents	Score
Level 1. Process performed				
AP1.1. Process performance attribute				
UCD.1.1 Represent stakeholders	Whole team. Shared vision. Release planning. UC Driven Development	Start the project. Identify and refine requirements	Define vision. Plan the project. Find and outline requirements	0,3
UCD.1.2 Analyze market	no evidence	no evidence	no evidence	0
UCD.1.3 Define and plan systems strategy	no evidence	no evidence	no evidence	0
UCD.1.4 Collect market answer	no evidence	no evidence	no evidence	0
UCD.1.5 Anayze user tendencies	no evidence	no evidence	no evidence	0
Combined score (DCU.1.1 to 1.5)				0,06
Combined score for the level				0,06
Level 2. Process managed				
AP2.1 Performance management attribute				
PM2.1.1 Identify resources requirements	Whole team. Shared vision. Release planning. UC driven development	Start the project. Identify and refine requierements	Define vision. Plan the project. Find and outline requirements	0,3
PM2.1.2 Plan	Whole team. Shared vision. Release plan	Start	vision. Plan the outline	

Fig. 1. Recording form (adapted from [31]). First column lists UMM ISO's attributes, the following three columns show evidence collected (Practice, Process and Method). Last column shows numeric score achieved for each row and the calculated mean for a group.

Results. Evidence collected shows that OpenUP/Basic doesn't achieve full coverage of any attribute for Levels 1 to 3. We measured a total of 156 attributes. Achievement was Partial in 76 cases, Large in 10 and Null in 70 attributes. The capability profile at three levels assessed is shown in Fig. 2. It is clear that the only areas that achieve some degree of conformity are the core (HCD2 and HCD3 to HCD6). Achievement is minimal on HCD1 and null for HCD7.

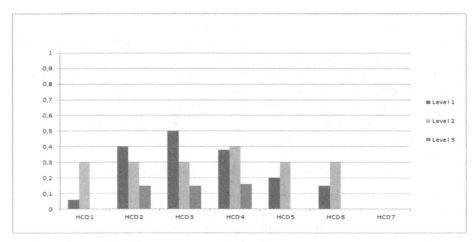

Fig. 2. UMM-ISO capability profile for configuration OpenUP/Basic. References: Range 0 to 0.3: Partial achievement, 0.3 to 0.7: Large achievement, 0.7 to 1: Full achievement.

The Management practices included in OpenUP contribute to show some evidence of achievement. However none of them qualify for an F or L. Only some method elements (or part thereof) could reach a partial achievement if they were carried out by staff members with background in HCI. Technical practices also exhibit a partial achievement (particularly, Shared Vision, Evolutionary architecture and Evolutionary design).

Use Case Driven Development could reach a greater achievement when staff members with HCI background are included. Specially, for identifying, specifying stakeholders, their tasks and contexts of use (however, this background is not a must by any role, just a suggestion in the Guideline "Staffing a Project").

In total, 10 attributes out a total of 156 has been assessed to a higher level using this "benefit of the doubt". For example, on HCD3 (Specifying requirements) OpenUP covers all attributes at Level 1. Three of them achieve a Large fulfillment. Practices like Shared Vision, Iterative development, Use Case Driven Development contribute to cover Performance attributes such as Clarify and document system goals, Assess risks to stakeholders, Generate the stakeholder and organizational requirements. However broader gaps are found for the other attributes. There is no evidence for a complete and detailed specification of stakeholders (Performance Attribute: Analyze stakeholders), nor is required taking into account the system context beyond the software (Attribute: Define the use of the system). Finally, OpenUP is too brief about quality in use goals (Attribute: Set quality in use objectives). Just one Guideline suggests 3 steps in order to identify key issues in usability, choose the right style to express requirements and write them. Assuming the scenario that staff members had enough HCI background we can give the benefit of the doubt and consider that OpenUP can reach Partial achievement on these attributes. Finally, a Large coverage at Level 1 for this HCD process is scored (mean=0.5).

Table 1. Score achieved at HCD2 at Level 1 and actions required to improve capability

HCD Processes and included activities	Score	LtoF	PtoL	NtoL
HCD2. Plan and manage the HCD process				
HCD2.1 Consult stakeholders	0.7	X		
HCD.2.2Identify and plan user involvement	0.7	X		
HCD.2.3 Select HC methods and techniques	0.3		X	
HCD.2.4 Ensure a HC approach within the project	0.3		X	
HCD.2.5Plan human-centred design activities	0.3		X	
HCD.2.6Manage human-centred activities	0.3		X	
HCD.2.7Champion human-centred approach	0.3		X	
HCD.2.8Provide support for HCD	0.3		X	

Actions to Fill the Gaps. Our proposal is to provide an OpenUP based development process that can reach Full compliance with UMM-ISO at the Level 1 and at least Large at Levels 2 and 3. In order to achieve a full capability profile at Level 1 three actions are to be taken on the OpenUP/Basic configuration:

— Take from Large to Full (LtoF): Add or modify method and process contents to fill the gap between the Large coverage to the Full one.
— Take from Partial to Large (PtoL): extend OpenUP/Basic processes that were assessed with a Partial coverage so they can reach at least the Large one.
— Take from Null to Large (NtoL): generate method and process contents to cover that HCD processes with no evidence of achievement by OpenUP/Basic.

HCD1 and HCD7 are almost not covered, so the actions there are mostly to include content lacking in OpenUP (NtoL). For the other processes, the coverage is incomplete too, but disparate. Table 1 and 2 show the actions required to improve capability at Level 1 for HCD2 to HCD6.

Table 2. Score achieved at HCD3-6 at Level 1 and actions required to improve capability

HCD Processes and included activities	Score	LtoF	PtoL	NtoL
HCD.3Specify the stakeholder and organisational requirements				
HCD3.1 Clarify and document system goals	0.7	X		
HCD.3.2 Analyse stakeholders	0.3		X	
HCD.3.3 Assess risk to stakeholders	0.7	X		
HCD.3.4Define the use of the system	0.3		X	
HCD.3.5Generate the stakeholder and organisational requirements	0.7	X		
HCD.3.6Set quality in use objectives	0.3		X	
HCD.4 Understand and specify the context of use				
HCD.4.1Identify and document user's tasks	0.7	X		
HCD.4.2Identify and document user attributes	0.3		X	
HCD.4.3Identify and document organis. envt.	0.3		X	
HCD.4.4Identify and document technical envt.	0.3		X	
HCD.4.5Identify and document physical envt.	0.3		X	
HCD.5Produce design solutions				
HCD.5.1Allocate functions	0.3		X	
HCD.5.2Produce composite task model				X
HCD.5.3Explore system design	0.7	X		
HCD.5.4Use existing knowledge to develop design solutions	0.3		X	
HCD.5.5Specify system and use				X
HCD.5.6Develop prototypes	0.3		X	
HCD.5.7Develop user training				X
HCD.5.8Develop user support				X
HCD.6 Evaluate designs against requirements				
HCD.6.1Specify and validate context of evaluation	0.3		X	
HCD.6.2Evaluate early prototypes in order to define the requirements for the system				X
HCD.6.3Evaluate prototypes to improve the design	0.3		X	
HCD.6.4Evaluate the system in order to check that the stakeholder and organisational requirements have been met	0.3		X	
HCD.6.5Evaluate the system in order to check that the required practice has been followed				X
HCD.6.6Evaluate the system in use to ensure that it continues to meet organisational and user needs				X

4   Extending OpenUP to Conform with the UMM-ISO

The EPL's guidelines offer two scenarios for extension that are useful in our case[21]:

- IF you need to add roles, tasks or work products that reflect a different approach, THEN create a new Practice including them and processes to articulate them
- IF you need to modify a current process by adding elements from other Practice, THEN customize an existing Configuration of Practices with the lacking elements.

Given these scenarios we propose to fill the gaps discovered with the following tasks:

1. **Adding new items to base practices.** All missing HCD contents included by the UMM-ISO should be incorporated in the Practices offered by EPL.
2. **Adding and modifying cross practice processes.** On Level 1 to ensure the convergence of the Evolutionary architecture, Evolutionary design and HCD. At levels 2 and 3, to include HCD process and product management.
3. **Using an alternative set of role assignments**, to set the responsibility for some processes to the new roles, in order to improve their human centeredness.

After doing these tasks, we add a new practice to the EPL: Practice User Centered Development and extend the OpenUP/Basic configuration generating three new process configurations.

4.1   The Practice User Centered Development (UCDev)[2]

This practice articulates the method elements (roles, tasks, work products and guidance) needed to instantiate a development process that actively involves all stakeholders during the whole cycle.

Roles. OpenUP/Basic offers three generic definitions relevant to UCD: Stakeholder, Analyst and Developer. However, their definitions do not ensure that necessary profiles and skills for carry out a UCD process can be met. Other UP or OpenUP extensions have already identified this problem and proposed adding new roles (e.g. [8, 12, 13]). In order to keep OpenUP with low level of bureaucracy and ceremony while including in the process the skills needed, we have identified six roles to be added: four Business actors (Sponsor, Domain Technical Leader, Users Representative, End User), an Analyst (UX Specialist), a Developer (UX Designer) and a Tester (UX Tester). Complete descriptions can be seen in [32].

Work Products. The first element that must be included explicitly is central in any iterative, user centered process: the user experience prototype in any of its versions [5],[33][18]. We also include other two artifacts with strong relations with prototypes:

---

[2]   Henceforth, we will use the term "User Centered" instead of "Human Centered" used in UMM-ISO. While both express the centrality of all those involved in the final system, User Centered is the preferred term by the HCI community.

the UX Storyboard and the Navigation map. The Storyboard will allow analyze the dynamic aspects of UX prototype, while the navigation map will leave clearly stable the relationship between all the Storyboards. The list of the new definitions of work products that we include in UCDev comprises: User model, Usability Goal, Task model, UX Concept, UX prototype, UX Storyboard, Navigation map and User and training document (details in [32])

Tasks. As for the Roles and Work Products, will use as background the UMM-ISO specifications, UCD literature and tasks definitions from configurations in the UP family (e.g., RUP[34], Agile Unified Process [35]). We have incorporated the following definitions of tasks:

— Tailor the UCD process
— Specify requirements and objectives of user experience
— Understand and specify the context of use
— Designing the user experience
— Components of interaction design
— Review the design of the user experience
— Preparing for usability testing
— Run usability tests
— Design and produce material training and user support
— Providing training and user support

Each Task is defined by: purpose, description and relations with other method elements and steps to be done. Some tasks also include specific guidelines. For example, the definition for *Task Specify requirements and UX goals* includes the following contents:

- Purpose (why including this task? What is its goal?):
    — To keep the focus on UX during the entire lifecycle giving developers concrete guides for developing and evaluating design solutions.
    — To set acceptance criteria for usability testing
- Relations (roles involved, input and output work products):
    — Roles: UX specialist (primary performer), Users representative, Technical domain leader, Analyst (additional performers)
    — Input: User model, Task model, Project goals
    — Output: Usability goals
- Steps (instructions for the performer, fully described in real specification)
    — Get information from available models
    — Identify and outline usability goals
    — Prioritize usability goals
    — Document usability goals
    — Review and get agreement on usability goals

The relations between all tasks included in UCDev and the UMM-ISO processes are shown in Fig. 3 (HCD processes organized in the figure as mentioned in Section 3.2)

Guidance. We propose the integration of two basic guidelines. The first one contains the definitions of the UCD processes. The other guide details the UMM-ISO levels. As a road map, both give guide the process engineer for the total or partial adoption of the practice and their inclusion in the development process.

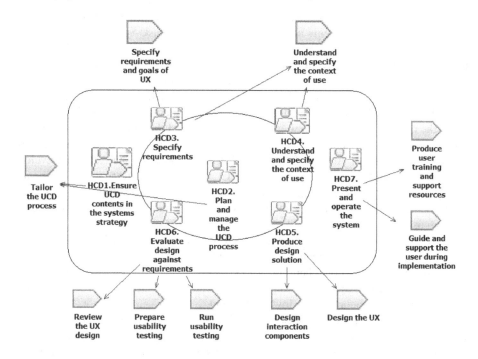

Fig. 3. Relations map between UCDev tasks and UMM-ISO processes

4.2   Three Method Configurations: OpenUP/UMM-ISO N[1,2,3]

We propose a scheme of three configurations that can be instantiated to achieve usability capability at UMM-ISO Level 1, 2 or 3. These configurations can be seen as incremental steps that guide for growing in usability capability in a predictable, structured way. Configuration for Level 1 (OpenUP/UMM-ISO N1) adds the new Practice UCDev to OpenUP/Basic. For levels 2 (managed) and 3 (established) we use the variability "extends" on previous level incorporating activities for process and work product management.

In the following descriptions, we use the four phases of UP (Inception, Elaboration, Construction and Transition) to show the customizations included.

OpenUP/UMM-ISO N1. The goal in the Inception phase is to understand the scope of the problem and the feasibility of a solution. The deployment process for a typical iteration of this phase in our configuration contains the same four core activities:

Start the project, Identify and refine requirements, Agree on the technical approach and Plan and manage the iteration.

Some changes are implemented to the interior of each activity. Our main contributions are in the Activities Start the Project and Agree on technical approach. In the first one we modified the tasks Develop technical vision and Plan the project. UCD roles are assigned and an extra step is included to Identify and Sketch Use Context. Usability related requirements are specified by the new task Specify UX Goals assigned to the UX specialist. So, this Task is developed in synchronized with Identify and outline requirements (from OpenUP/Basic specification) as long as outputs from one are inputs to the other. In the Activity Agree on technical approach we propose two simultaneous tasks: Outline the architecture (in OpenUP/Basic) and Outline UX (in UCDev), providing the team with an architecture that consider UX goals.

On the phase Elaboration (aiming to better understand the requirements of the system, create and establish a basis for the system architecture) we include the task Design the UX as part of Activity Develop architecture and UX. The Activity Develop Solution Increment includes two tasks from UCDev, Design interaction components and Review UX Design to ensure the inclusion of user issues from the early design. Finally, in the Activity Test solution other two tasks are added: Prepare usability tests and Run usability tests.

The third phase, Construction, starts when architecture has reached stability and focuses on implementing remainder requirements. Tasks Develop solution increment and Test solution are done here in a loop. Throughout this phase iterations the functionality will continue being implemented, tested and integrated. The phase can include one or more beta releases towards the end.

The final phase Transition focuses on deployment the software to users and ensuring that their expectations are met. However, in the basic version of OpenUP, the main objective of the phase is reduced to fine tune the functionality, performance and quality of the beta version of system generated at the end of the construction phase, excluding specific activities that are specific to the preparation of the deployment such as the final acceptance test or user support. To overcome this lack, we include the task Guide and give support to user during implementation (Practice UCDev). Also refine the extension of the activity: Test solution adding the User acceptance as a variant of usability testing.

OpenUP/UMM-ISO N2. In this level is necessary to identify attributes of process and work product management for UCD elements. In the first case, it is important to generate products of work within the established time and resource requirements. The configuration at this level is conceived as an extension of OpenUP/MMU-ISO N1. So, this level incrementally adds method and content items needed to meet those requirements. We need to ensure the use of Change and Configuration management practices and Quality control. OpenUP/Basic includes them with the Practice Iterative Development, we took it as a guide to extend these activities on UCD elements.

The main change happens in the task Plan the project from the Inception Phase. The original task from OpenUP/Basic includes the steps Establish a cohesive team, Estimate project size, Evaluate risks, Forecast project velocity, Outline project lifecycle, Establish costs and articulate value, Plan deployment. We add two additional steps: Plan the UX Quality (define a minimal plan for quality assurance on tasks and work products from UCDev) and Plan UX Change and Configuration management (set management politics for configuration management on UX work products). The tasks related to Iteration planning and management (Plan iteration, Manage Interaction, Assess results) are customized in the same line to ensure those plans are met. In the other phases, the Task Request Change allows to meet the management requirements on UCDev elements.

OpenUP/UMM-ISO N3. For the level 3 we need to ensure that the process configuration used in each project is adjusted to the specific situation and available resources as much as possible. The configuration for this Level is again built incrementally on the previous one.

We add the Task Tailor the UCD Process to the Activity Start the Project. The task's primary performer is obviously from Project manager, but roles form UCDev such as the Sponsor and Domain technical leader should be included as additional performers. The inputs are the development process as defined by OpenUP/UMM-ISO N2 and the two Guidelines HCD Processes Definitions and UMM-ISO specifications. The output is a customized configuration. Six steps are defined: Analyze the project, Determine adaptation effort, Develop specific content, Define lifecycle, Publish the process, Manage the process.

The task Assess results (in the four phases) adds the step Manage the process, to ensure that customizations are met as planned.

The Family of OpenUP/UMM-ISO Plugins. The EPF Composer[36] is a toolkit for engineers to implement and maintain software development processes. It provides the contents of the EPL and tools to select, customize, assemble and publish parts of this library as a specific process. We used the Composer to implement the extensions described before in plugins: a Practice Plugin that contains the definitions for Practice UCDev and three Configuration Plugins, one for each Capability Level to cover.

5   An Initial Implementation

The OpenUP extensions described were initially implemented during the development of a financial management system for the Argentine government. Here we briefly introduce some initial highlights of this experience in order to show the feasibility of implementing these extensions. A full assessment of this and other instantiations will be the goal of further works.

The project had been initially organized using a customized version of UP. The process was gradually adapted through the evaluation and selection of artifacts and activities using an iterative dynamic "evaluate-modify-implement". It was early detected the need to include and integrate UCD practices in the process. The system would be operated by many users working at geographically distributed agencies and it would replace a previous version that users were accustomed to for many years. So, in order to achieve acceptance and effective operation the impact of the change should be minimized and usability maximized.

First steps included hiring a usability expert and following the guidelines in the RUP Plugin for the UX. Storyboards modeled as UML class diagrams using stereotypes were implemented. These models represent the screen components, the logical data groups and data grids. Static screen content (field names, labels, titles, images, etc.) is not represented in this model because it relates only to the appearance of UI and has no implication in the system logic. The model was very complex for the system screens and presented a number of disadvantages: it required a long time for an analyst to generate, it was very difficult to be understood by designers and programmers, wasn't good for users validation, it didn't allow to easily deduce the UI prototype and finally it was difficult to set a general standards for creating similar screens (conspiring directly against one golden rule in usability). This solution also limited the participation of user representatives at the early stages of requirements elicitation and for the testing of built modules, generating delays and rework.

To circumvent these obstacles it was decided to adapt the process configuration to adhere to our OpenUP/UMM-ISO N1 including the contents of the Practice UCDev. Some roles were added, such as User Representative and UX Designer. The task of Analysts was enriched with new definitions to include specific work products for UCDev as more understandable Screen prototypes. In each phase of the process, there was the correspondent validation and testing with users as stated for UCDev and OpenUP/UMM-ISO N1. Over a period of a year the project run with the implementation of this level of configuration.

Good responses by users and successful achievement of project goals gained in the first year motivated the team to adapt the process to the second level of configuration. In the second year, the project configuration was again customized by adhering to our proposed OpenUP/UMM-ISO N2. Then method elements related to the change, configuration and quality management for usability artifacts and processes were included. The project continued on this configuration for a full second year.

5.1   Some Lessons Learned

After these implementations, we analyzed two sources of information to extract lessons from this experience. We get qualitative feedback from questionnaires to key members of team project. Also we collected evidence from project repository, where work products (plans, models, prototypes, testing reports, etc.) are versioned and stored. We sought for evidence supporting the feedback got from questionnaires. We found that adding the Practice UCDev and implementing configurations OpenUP/UMM-ISO N1 and N2 had the effect to improve the inclusion of UCD activities in the project and integrate usability tasks in the whole team.

Both initial and specified requirements and increment solutions could be validated by users during the complete process. Also, the UX expert wasn't seen anymore as an external auditor reviewing the designs made by other team members. It was understood that a set of practices and skills included in isolation and not framed in the whole process would not have the desired effectiveness in improving the usability of the final system.

It was possible to implement the practice in the project re-arranging available resources, with a few modifications of the process while running the project without significant deviations from the initial planning and with an increase in the degree of user acceptance.

The move to a higher level of capability was conducted in a non-traumatic and predictable way as long as before its starting it was clear what activities should change, what skills would be necessary to improve and what to expect from this new level of capability.

6   Concluding Remarks and Further Work

A proposal of using a capability maturity model as roadmap for the predictable and systematic improvement of usability processes is presented. In particular, we describe the maturity model in usability in the ISO standards, which identifies seven UCD processes and a scale of capability that includes six levels (from incomplete to optimizing). We take the Unified Process in its agile, open source version (OpenUP). After an assessment of it in the light of the UMM-ISO several shortcomings that cannot be covered just by modifying ad hoc some of their practices have been identified. In the first place, it is necessary to incorporate new roles usually not taken into account in the process of development to transform it into a user centered process. This implies not only engage stakeholders and end users, but add a new battery of skills and abilities in the project. Also, the way to make real UCD activities related to the UX must traverse the entire lifecycle. There is no way to guarantee good levels of usability in a product if all aspects of the quality of the use are reduced to the design of the user interface.

Our proposal has been to extend OpenUP so that it can be instantiated as a UCD process through two contributions. On the one hand, added the new practice UCDev to the EPL. This practice articulates specific method content items, their roles, tasks and work products, taking as a reference the life cycle proposed by the UMM-ISO. The second contribution is to extend the instantiation of OpenUP with three method configurations that allow reaching usability capability at levels 1, 2 or 3 in the UMM-ISO. In these configurations is articulated as practice with the rest of the framework to allow instantiations of the unified process which can conform to the UMM-ISO. These extensions have been implemented as plugins for the EPF to enable process engineers to implement them as is or customize them using the EPF Composer.

Further works will include extending the analytical work on others instantiations of OpenUP/UMM-ISO, full assessment of these instantiations and evaluate the feasibility of OpenUP extensions to reach the highest levels at UMM-ISO.

Acknowledgments. The author thanks to the team of Project eSidif (Ministry of Economy, Argentine) for the collaboration provided during the work reported here; also to the reviewers for their insightful comments to the first version of this paper.

References

1. Seffah, A., Gulliksen, J., Desmarais, M.C.: Human-Centered Software Engineering - Integrating Usability in the Development Process. Human-Computer Interaction Series. Springer-Verlag New York, Inc., Secaucus (2005)
2. Bass, L., John, B.E.: Supporting Usability Through Software Architecture. Computer (Long. Beach. Calif.) 34, 113–115 (2001)
3. Folmer, E., Bosch, J.: Case studies on Analyzing Software Architectures for Usability. In: EUROMICRO 2005: Proceedings of the 31st EUROMICRO Conference on Software Engineering and Advanced Applications, pp. 206–213. IEEE Computer Society, Washington, DC (2005)
4. Mayhew, D.J.: The usability engineering lifecycle: a practitioner's handbook for the user interface design. Academic Press, San Diego (1999)
5. Sharp, H., Rogers, Y., Preece, J.: Interaction Design: Beyond Human Computer Interaction. John Wiley & Sons (2007)
6. Joshi, A., Sarda, N.L., Tripathi, S.: Measuring effectiveness of HCI integration in software development processes. J. Syst. Softw. 83, 2045–2058 (2010)
7. Costabile, M.F.: Usability in the software life cycle. In: Chang, S. (ed.) Handbook of Software Engineering & Knowledge Engineering. Fundamentals, vol. 1, pp. 179–192. World Scientific Publishing Company (2001)
8. Göransson, B., Lif, M., Gulliksen, J.: Usability Design-Extending Rational Unified Process with a New Discipline. In: Jorge, J.A., Jardim Nunes, N., Falcão e Cunha, J. (eds.) DSV-IS 2003. LNCS, vol. 2844, pp. 316–330. Springer, Heidelberg (2003)
9. Kruchten, P., Ahlqvist, S., Bylund, S.: User interface design in the rational unified process. In: van Harmelen, M. (ed.) Object Modeling and User Interface Design. Designing Interactive Systems, pp. 161–196. Addison-Wesley Longman Publishing Co., Inc., Boston (2001)
10. Heumann, J.: User experience storyboards: Building better UIs with RUP , UML , and use cases. Ration. Edge. (2003)
11. Sousa, K.S., Furtado, E.: RUPi - A Unified Process that Integrates Human-Computer Interaction and Software Engineering. In: Kazman, R., Bass, L., Bosch, J. (eds.) ICSE Workshop on SE-HCI, pp. 41–48. IFIP (2003)
12. DSDM-Consortium: OpenUP/DSDM Plugin, http://process.osellus.com/sites/wiki/OpenUPDSDM/WikiPages/Home.aspx
13. IconATG: Web Enabled UCD v1.0, http://www.iconatg.com/iconprocess/plugins/web_enabled_ucd
14. Beyer, H., Holtzblatt, K., Baker, L.: An Agile Customer-Centered Method: Rapid Contextual Design. In: Zannier, C., Erdogmus, H., Lindstrom, L. (eds.) XP/Agile Universe 2004. LNCS, vol. 3134, pp. 50–59. Springer, Heidelberg (2004)
15. Holtzblatt, K., Wendell, J.B., Wood, S.: Rapid Contextual Design. A how to guide to key techniques for user centered design. Morgan Kaufmann, San Francisco (2005)
16. Nielsen, J.: Agile development projects and usability, http://www.nngroup.com/articles/agile-development-and-usability/
17. Joshi, A.: Index of Integration (IoI), http://www.idc.iitb.ac.in/~anirudha/ioi.htm
18. Joshi, A., Sarda, N.L.: Evaluating Relative Contributions of Various HCI Activities to Usability. In: Forbrig, P. (ed.) HCSE 2010. LNCS, vol. 6409, pp. 166–181. Springer, Heidelberg (2010)
19. Eclipse: Eclipse Process Framework Project (EPF), http://projects.eclipse.org/projects/technology.epf

20. OMG: Software & Systems Process Engineering Meta-Model Specification Version 2.0. (2008)
21. Eclipse: Eclipse Process Framework Practice Library (2008), http://epf.eclipse.org/wikis/mam/index.htm
22. Eclipse: OpenUP version 1.5.0.1, http://epf.eclipse.org/wikis/openup/
23. Nielsen, J.: Corporate usability maturity: stages 1-4. Nielsen Norman Group (2006)
24. Ehrlich, K., Rohn, J.A.: Cost justification of usability engineering: a vendors's perspective. In: Bias, R.G., Mayhew, D.J. (eds.) Cost-justifying Usability, pp. 73–110. Academic Press, Inc., Orlando (1994)
25. April, A., Coallier, F.: Trillium: a model for the assessment of telecom software system development and maintenance capability. In: Softw. Eng. Stand. Int. Symp., p. 175 (1995)
26. Schaffer, E.: Institutionalization of Usability: A Step-by-Step Guide. Addison Wesley Longman Publishing Co., Inc., Redwood City (2004)
27. Bevan, N., Claridge, N., Earthy, J., Kirakowski, J.: Proposed usability engineering assurance scheme (1998)
28. Jokela, T.: The KESSU Usability Design Process Model. Version 2.1 (2004)
29. ISO/IEC: 18529 Ergonomics of human system interaction. Human-centred lifecycle process descriptions (2000)
30. ISO/IEC: 15504 Information Technology and Software Process Assessment (2006)
31. Earthy, J.: Usability Maturity Model: Processes (1999)
32. Rodríguez, A.: OpenUP/MMU-ISO. Soporte para un proceso de desarrollo de software conforme al Modelo ISO de Madurez en Usabilidad (2011)
33. Gulliksen, J., Göransson, B., Boivie, I., Blomkvist, S., Persson, J., Cajander, A.: Key principles for user-centred systems design. Behav. Inf. Technol. 22, 397–409 (2003)
34. Krutchen, P.: The Rational Unified Process: an introduction. Addison Wesley, Reading (1998)
35. Ambler, S.: The Agile Unified Process (AUP), http://www.ambysoft.com/unifiedprocess/agileUP.html
36. Eclipse: EPF Composer 1.0 Architecture Overview, http://www.eclipse.org/epf/composer_architecture/

Integrating Agile Development Processes and User Centred Design- A Place for Usability Maturity Models?

Dina Salah, Richard Paige, and Paul Cairns

Department of Computer Science,
University of York, York, UK
{dm560,richard.paige,paul.cairns}@york.ac.uk

Abstract. The aim of this paper is to explore and evaluate the role that can be played by Usability Maturity Models (UMMs) in integrating agile processes and User Centred Design (UCD). UMMs can be utilised in Agile projects as a diagnostic tool to assess the extent to which UCD is systematically and consistently implemented and the extent of effective implementation of UCD in development projects. This paper investigated the suitability of Nielsen Corporate Usability Maturity Model for utilisation in the Agile domain in order to assess the organisation's UCD capability. It reported on applying Nielsen Model in five case studies that performed Agile and User Centred Design Integration (AUCDI) and utilising the model in assessing their usability maturity level. The results revealed the existence of a correlation between the success of AUCDI attempts and the AUCDI case study's usability maturity level. These results can have positive implications on AUCDI practice since practitioners who aim to achieve the integration can utilise Nielsen model to identify their strengths and weaknesses in regards to UCD related aspects and accordingly plan for improvement.

Keywords: Agile Software Development Processes, User Centred Design, Agile User Centred Design Integration, Usability Maturity Models, Maturity Models.

1 Introduction

Agile methods are lightweight software development methods that tackle perceived limitations of plan-driven methods via a compromise between absence of a process and excessive process [13]. Agile processes aim to deal with volatile requirements via discarding upfront, precisely defined plans. They are iterative and are used to develop software incrementally. Different Agile processes implement these ideas in different ways. All Agile processes share common values and principles, defined in the Agile Manifesto [1].

User Centred Design (UCD) is a set of techniques, methods, procedures and processes as well as a philosophy that places the user at the centre of the

S. Sauer et al. (Eds.): HCSE 2014, LNCS 8742, pp. 108–125, 2014.

development process in a meaningful, appropriate and rigourous ways [15,6]. The goal of applying UCD is to attempt to satisfy users via producing usable and understandable products that meet their needs and interests [6] in addition to their goals, context of use, abilities and limitations [2]. The usability of a product is the consequence of systematic UCD work that occurs throughout the development process and continues even after product release in order to enhance subsequent versions [6].

Maturity Models are normative [17] reference models that embrace the assumption of predictable evolution and change patterns. The main purpose of maturity models is to assess the current situation in order to evaluate the strengths and weaknesses and then prioritize and plan for improvement [17]. This is achieved via evolutionary successive stages or levels that signify step by step patterns of evolution and change designating the desirable or current organisational capabilities against a specific class of entities [28,14,25].

Improving the effectiveness of user-centred design in software development is a considerable challenge in many organisations. Usability Maturity Models (UMMs) were proposed to conduct a status-quo analysis of UCD. UMMs aim to assist organisations in conducting a systematic analysis that evaluates the strengths and weaknesses of the organisation in regards to UCD related aspects [19] and accordingly plan for improvement actions [21]. Usability Capabiliy is defined as

> A characteristic of a development organisation that determines its ability to consistently develop products with high and competitive level of usability [21].

This paper provides details of an exploratory study for the role that could be played by usability maturity models in the domain of integrating agile development processes and user centred design. The rest of this paper is structured as follows: section 2 provides a background on agile and user centred design integration. Section 3 discusses the research approach. Section 4 provides details of the utilisation of Nielsen Corporate Usability Maturity Model in five AUCDI Case Studies. Section 5 discusses the results and section 6 discusses the conclusion and future work.

2   Agile Development Processes and User Centred Design Integration

Agile development processes and User Centred Design integration have been gaining increased interest. This interest in AUCDI is arguably due to three reasons: first, the reported advantages of UCD on the developed software as it enables developers to understand the needs of the potential users of their software, and how their goals and activities can be best supported by the software thus leading to improved usability and user satisfaction. Second, none of the major Agile processes explicitly have guidance for how to develop usable software [23]. In addition, the interaction design role, usability, and user interface design in an Agile team is unclear and largely overlooked [5,3]. Furthermore, principles and practices for understanding and eliciting usability and user requirements and evaluating Agile systems for usability and UX are generally considerably deficient [23,22]. Third, there appear to be philosophical and principled differences between Agile methods and UCD in focus, evaluation method, culture and documentation that suggest that their integration will be fundamentally challenging.

Although Agile and User Centred Design Integration (AUCDI) research is growing, it has not yet exploited the potential of UMMs, which is strongly relevant to AUCDI practice. A systematic literature review [30] was conducted that included 71 papers on AUCDI that classified AUCDI studies according to the integration approach revealed eight different categories, non of which focused on utilization of UMMs. UMMs can be utilised in the Agile development projects as a diagnostic tool. They can assist in assessing the status quo to evaluate the extent to which UCD is systematically and consistently implemented as well as the extent of effective implementation of UCD in development projects. The results can help organisations identify their strengths and weaknesses in regards to UCD related aspects and accordingly plan for improvement actions.

Thus this study has two aims: first, to investigate the suitability of UMMs for utilisation in the context of Agile projects in order to assess the organisation's UCD capability and/or performance. Second, to investigate the relationship between the success of AUCDI attempts and usability maturity level.

3   Research Approach

This section provides details on the research approach that was used to achieve the research aims.

3.1   Comparative Study of Usability Maturity Models

The first step of this research involved conducting a comparative study of UMMs in order to choose one of those UMMs for utilisation in assessing the usability maturity level of case studies that integrated Agile development processes and UCD. To the best of our knowledge there exists eleven usability maturity models for which an overview will be provided below. The features, perspective of usability integration, maturity approaches, scope, and documentation of these models are diverse. An example of difference in scope is shown in the fact that some models focus on assessing the user centredness of the organisation whereas others focus on measuring the user centredness of projects. Moreover, the existing UMM literature is focused on presenting the structure of the models and the methods for performing the assessment rather than presenting empirical evaluation of these models [16,18].

Usability Maturity Models

1. **Nielsen Corporate Usability Maturity Model:** Nielsen Corporate Usability Maturity Model [26] was developed in 2006 by Jackob Nielsen. It is composed of 8 stages or maturity levels. It declares that as organisations' usability matures they typically progress through the same sequence of stages from initial hostility to widespread reliance on user research [26].

2. **Usability Maturity Model-Human Centredness Scale (UMM-HCS):** UMM-HCS [8] was developed in 1998 by the European INUSE project that focused on the assurance of interactive systems or web sites usability. UMM-HCS was derived from all significant existing UMMs. It embodies usability maturity via 6 maturity levels of a combination of attitude, technology, and management activities. UMM-HCS documentation includes an assessment recording form and its use is described [8].

3. **Trillium:** Trillium [4] is a process assessment approach for development of telecommunication products, developed in 1991 by Bell Canada. Trillium Model is based on (CMM) version 1.1. Although the model is extensively documented and published in the public domain, yet, it does not include methods on how to perform the assessment.

4. **Usability Leadership Maturity Model (ULMM):** Usability Leadership Maturity Model (ULMM) [10,12] was developed by IBM in the early 1990s as a means of benchmarking and improving the status of usability in software development projects. It examines organisations from three different aspects: organisation, skills, and processes. The model documentation that is available in the public domain is very limited and only two papers are available [10,12].

5. **Humanware Process Improvement (HPI):** Humanware Process Improvement was developed by Philips [11,24]. HPI includes 10 Key Process Areas (KPAs) which identify UI design practices and suggest how these can be incorporated in the product creation process [11]. HPI is based on the "Plan-Do-Check-Act" cycle and covers software and hardware aspects of products [24]. HPI provides a questionnaire as an assessment tool for self and full assessments [11].

6. **User Centred Design Maturity (UCDM):** User Centred Design Maturity (UCDM) [9] was developed at the University of Loughborough in the UK, initially as a tool for benchmarking information systems capability in the UK public sector. It has five capability areas, for example, "systems design", "project structure and goals" and maturity stages, and 15 foci of assessment [18].

7. **Usability Maturity Model-Processes (UMM-P):** UMM-P [7] was developed in the European INUSE project. It is intended to be used in the assessment and improvement of the human centred processes in system development. The model describes seven processes each defined by a set of base practices and associated work products. Examples of UMM-P processes are "Plan and manage the human-centred design process", and "Specify the user and organisational requirements". An assessment recording form is supplied and its use is described.

8. **KESSU:** KESSU [20] is an assessment model that was developed in a national research project at Oulu University in Finland. The main selling point of KESUU is that it examines the performance rather than the management aspects of user centred processes. KESSU includes seven processes of UCD including: identify user, context of use, determine user requirements, produce user task designs, produce interaction designs, usability feedback and usability verification [18].

9. **Procedures for Usability Engineering Process Assessment (DATech-UEPA):** DATech-UEPA was developed in Germany. The model has one main focus of assessment (usability engineering) and identifies three levels of maturity and 19 foci of assessment. The model is tailored for the assessment of manufacturing organisations and is documented in German as cited in [18].

10. **Human Centred Design-Process Capability Model (HCD-PCM Design and Visioning):** The HCD-PCM model was developed by Mitsubishi Research Institute, NTT Advanced Technology and Otaru University of Commerce in 2002. The model scope ranges over system life cycle processes such as processes from market visioning to system disposal process capability types. HCD-PCM model is composed of two models: one for visioning process and the other for design processes. The capability level for each of the visioning and the design process identifies five capability levels [18].

11. **Open Source Usability Maturity Model (OS-UMM):** OS-UMM [27] is a UMM for open source projects. It was developed by members from University of Western Ontario, Canada and Faculty of Information Technology, United Arab Emirates University. The OS-UMM model has five maturity levels. The proposed maturity scale has key usability factors, such as user requirements, user feedback, usability learning, user centred design methodologies, understandability, learnability, operability, attractiveness, usability bug reporting, usability testing, and documentation [27].

Table 1 provides a comparison for the maturity levels of the different UMMs. It indicates that the different UMMs vary in the number of maturity levels between eight (Nielsen Model) and three (DATech-UEPA).

Criteria for Comparing Usability Maturity Models

The following criteria were found relevant for the purposes of this work in order to compare the main characteristics of the different UMMs that are available in the public domain.

Lightweight: Since the chosen UMM will be utilized to assess the usability maturity level of each project, the model should be lightweight; it should require low overhead so as not to disrupt any Agile project schedule and low cost so as not to consume considerable time to perform the assessment or require additional personnel to conduct the assessment.

Detailed English Documentation: The model should provide detailed documentation that provides practitioners with detailed maturity model definition

Table 1. Maturity Levels of Usability Maturity Models

Nielsen	UMM-HCS	Trillium	UCDM	UMM-P	DATech-UEPA	HCD-PCM Design	HCD-PCM Vision-ing	OS-UMM
Hostility toward usability	Unrecognised	Unstructured	Uncertainty	Incomplete	Introduced	Do	Awake	Preliminary
Developer-centred usability	Recognised	Repeatable	Awakening	Performed	Reproducible Results	Plan	Know	Recognised
Skunk works usability	Considered	Defined	Enlightenment	Managed	Continuous Improvement	Control	Understand	Defined
Dedicated usability budget	Implemented	Managed	Wisdom	Established	–	Adapt	Infer	Streamlined
Managed usability	Integrated	Fully Integrated	Certainty	Predictable	–	Optimize	Create	Institutionalized
Systematic usability process	Institutionalized	–	–	Optimizing	–	–	–	–
Integrated user-centred design	–	–	–	–	–	–	–	–
User-driven corporation	–	–	–	–	–	–	–	–

and detailed descriptions of the assessment process. This detailed documentation will provide explicit guidance to practitioners to conduct self assessment, i.e., conduct the assessment on their own without the need for the presence of the model author. Moreover, since the available usability maturity/assessment models were developed in various countries, one of the criteria for choosing the usability maturity/assessment model is to be documented in English.

Domain Independent: Some UMMs are domain specific; i.e., they were created for specific domains like telecommunication or manufacturing. This implies that they focus on domain specific practices and cannot be utilized in other domains. Thus the model chosen should be domain independent; i.e., it should be suitable for utilisation in all organisations regardless of their domain of business.

Empirically Evaluated: The model should have been evaluated in empirical studies and iterated according to the results of these empirical evaluations.

The UMMs were examined using the criteria identified above and table 2 presents a summary of the results of the comparison between the different usability models according to the comparison criteria proposed earlier.

The UMM pursued is documented in English, has a detailed documentation, can be used irrespective of the organisation's domain (generic), is lightweight, and has been empirically evaluated.

These criteria led to the exclusion of a number of UMMs.

The language criteria led to the exclusion of DATech-UEPA, HCD-PCM Design and HCD-PCM Visioning since they were not documented in English. The detailed documentation criteria led to the exclusion of ULMM, HPI, UCDM, KESSU, and OS-UMM since they do not provide sufficient documentation to conduct the assessment in a self assessment form. However, this does not imply

Table 2. Criteria for Choosing a Usability Maturity Model

UMM Model	Language	Detailed Documenta-tion	Domain	Lightweight	Empirical Evaluation
Nielsen	English	Yes	Generic	Yes	No
UMM-HCS	English	Yes	Generic	Yes	Yes
Trillium	English	Yes	Telecommunication	No	Not published
ULMM	English	No	Generic	N/A	Not Published
HPI	English	No	Consumer Product Development	N/A	Not Published
UCDM	English	No	Information System Capability in UK Public Sector	N/A	Not Published
UMM-P	English	Yes	Generic	No	Yes
KESSU	English	No	Generic	N/A	Yes
DATech-UEPA	German	N/A	Manufacturing	N/A	N/A
HCD-PCM Design	Japanese	N/A	Generic	N/A	N/A
HCD-PCM Visioning	Japanese	N/A	Generic	N/A	N/A
OS-UMM	English	No	Open Source Projects	N/A	N/A

that they did not have extensive documentation, for example, KESSU is pub-lished in numerous papers, however, all these papers and documentation pro-vided a rather high level detail on the dimensions and processes rather than on the how to conduct the assessment. The domain criteria led to the exclusion of Trillium since it is domain specific as it is focused on the telecommunication in-dustry. The lightweight criteria led to the exclusion of UMM-P since the model is not lightweight and requires considerable time to be conducted which may disrupt any Agile project schedule and impose considerable cost as a result of consuming considerable time to perform the assessment.

In case of the lack of enough documentation or the lack of English documen-tation, it was hard to judge whether the model is lightweight or not. As a result "Not Applicable (N/A)" was used as an indication that it was not applicable to make an evaluation.

This left us with only two UMMs: Nielsen Corporate Usability Maturity Model and Usability Maturity Model-Human Centrdness Scale. Although Nielsen model was not empirically evaluated, yet it was decided to utilise both models in five AUCDI case studies in order to provide richer comparative analysis via two UMMs.

3.2   Choosing Five AUCDI Case Studies

The second step of the research approach involved choosing five case studies that integrated Agile development processes and user centred design and represented successful and unsuccessful AUCDI attempts

A candidate list of five academic researchers and industrial practitioners were selected. This list included authors who developed new AUCDI approaches and whose work on AUCDI was well received and highly referenced. The chosen case studies also reflect a "two tail" design [29] in which cases from both extremes (success and failure) are selected.

Interviewees were contacted via an email. All of the interviewees were professional usability practitioners whose job roles were: usability product manager, usability analyst, usability engineer, lead user experience designer, and team manager for user experience design. One interview was conducted per participant in which questions regarding Nielsen model were posed. At the beginning of the interview the interviewees were asked for their permission to record the interview and then the informed consent form was read and their consent on its terms was recorded. All interviewees agreed to record the interview. All interviews were transcribed in English. Each case study works in a different sort of software, however, all case studies implement Scrum. Four case studies represent successful integration attempts whereas one case study represent a failure integration attempt. The imbalance between the number of successful and unsuccessful case studies is attributed to the existence of publication bias since more positive results are published than negative results in the AUCDI domain as indicated by the results of a systematic literature review that was conducted on agile and user centred design integration [30].

For the sake of protecting the anonymity of participants, company names and some details on the projects will be withheld.

Case Study 1: The product developed in the first case study was a Software as a Service where high quality UX was crucial. The product developed an integration with a new ecommerce platform in order to allow sellers to sell their inventory to multiple ecommerce sites. The interviewee worked as a usability product manager, and was responsible for managing all the UX aspects of the project and designing the user interfaces. This project represented successful AUCDI attempt as declared by the author. This success occurred through utilising a variant of the Scrum methodology. The project had two peer product owners, one focused on usability and user experience and the other on the more conventional functions. The usability product owner took the lead in establishing a UX vision for the product along with a number of personas. The vision was realised in high level user goals, high level description of the UX with the product and a high level navigation model for the entire product.

Case Study 2: The second case study occurred at a leader company in the enterprise customer relationship management marketplace. The product developed was a second version of an approval process editor, the first version had very poor UX and users could not use the product as expected and there was poor adoption. Four years later it was subject to redesign. The interviewee worked as a usability analyst which involves being a dedicated UX researcher. This project represented successful AUCDI attempt as declared by the author. This occurred via first, introducing a new resource plan that reduced workload on UX team members and dedicated two hours per week by UX practitioners to assist Scrum teams that did not have assigned UX resources. Second, they introduced design transformations via moving to parallel development and design, working a release ahead, utilising interactive prototypes for usability testing, communication of designs to developers, and design studios. Third, using Rapid Iterative Test and Evaluation (RITE) for usability testing in all Agile projects.

Case Study 3: The third case study occurred at a home shopping network company. The product developed was a new system that facilitates show planning for a home shopping network. Show planners used the software in order to schedule shows, products to shows and hosts to shows. The interviewee worked as a lead UX designer, running a team with three designers. This case study represented successful AUCDI attempt as declared by the author. This success occurred through the use of a rapid process that allows designers, developers, and stakeholders to collaborate and explore design alternatives. This occurred via some common guidelines where participants produce several rough sketch designs, then attended a collaborative workshop to discuss each other's work. This was followed by merging ideas to one design concept with which to move forward. This process reportedly had several advantages, for example, facilitating role sharing and knowledge transfer, allowing rapid exploration of design alternatives, and fostering shared understanding of design vision.

Case Study 4: The fourth case study occurred at a leading software and services company in the asset performance management domain. The product developed was a touch screen kiosk system for mechanics in order to receive work orders and record the results of the repair. The interviewee worked as a usability engineer. This case study represented successful AUCDI attempt as declared by the author. This success occurred through the use of a development approach that draws from extreme programming and scenario based design. This approach has two separate and synchronized usability and development tracks and the usability engineer works one iteration ahead of the developers. The key design is represented in a set of mock-ups, scenarios, claims, and design goals that were used to support synchronization activities and help the usability engineer plan and run usability evaluations.

Case Study 5: The fifth case study occurred at an Internet infrastructure services company that enable and protect interactions across the world's voice, video, and data networks. In addition to domain name registration and resolution. This company is a leading provider of security related products, for example, SSL certificates, identity and authentication services and enterprise security management. The product developed was a redesign of an existing web site for a product that allowed customers to purchase and manage services on-line. The goal of the project was to increase sales and customer retention, and reduce the number of support calls by providing an improved UX during the purchase and product renewal processes. The interviewee worked as a manager of UX design team which was a central team serving the whole company. This case study represented unsuccessful AUCDI attempt as stated by the author. At the end of the release the project went into the beta phase and a major problem was discovered since the users were unable to complete their purchase successfully. The product did not satisfy its requirements of increasing sales and improving customer retention. This resulted in pulling the software back in order to fix it. The cause of this failure was attributed to a lack of communication among the cross functional team members due to geographical separation and unwillingness by the engineering team to collaborate with non engineering teams and as a result the product manager and the UX team were prevented from participating in the sprint planning and Scrums. This led the engineering team to interpret and implement the designs incorrectly. There was also a lack of iterative refinement of designs.

3.3   Utilising the Chosen UMM(s) in Five AUCDI Case Studies

The fourth step of the research approach involved utilising the chosen UMM(s)(Nielsen Model) in assessing the usability maturity level of five case studies that integrated Agile development processes and user centred design and represented successful and unsuccessful AUCDI attempts. This occurred via conducting a set of one to one, Skype interviews. A set of open ended questions were formulated and posed to interviewees to evaluate the achievement of different practices. The questions were formulated in a manner that is precise, unambiguous, and understandable to respondents.

Answers to interview questions were used in evaluating the usability maturity level of each case study and the results of each case study were compared with the achieved practices in the different usability maturity levels in order to determine the closest usability maturity level. Those results are reported in section 5 in table 4.

3.4   Synthesizing the Results of Utilisation of UMMs

The fifth step of the research approach involved synthesizing the results of utilisation of Nielsen Model in order to investigate the following: the existence of a relationship between the success of AUCDI attempts and usability maturity level and the suitability of UMMs for utilisation in assessing usability maturity in the context of Agile projects.

4   Utilising Nielsen Corporate Usability Maturity Model in AUCDI Case Studies

This section discusses the steps that were used in order to utilise Nielsen model in assessing the usability maturity level of the five AUCDI case studies introduced in section 3.2.

Maturity models as a design product can take various forms including: pure textual description, functioning of the maturity model, or instantiation as a software assessment tool [25]. The Nielsen model is a textual model that is composed of 8 maturity levels but is written primarily as a textual narrative and this form cannot be easily deployed for measuring usability maturity of an organisation. Accordingly, the model was carefully examined in order to transform its narrative form into a set of measurable dimensions and practices. Each dimension is composed of a number of practices. This examination resulted in a model that is composed of five dimensions and 24 practices as shown in table 3. These dimensions included: developers' attitude towards usability, management attitude towards usability, usability practitioners' role, usability methods and techniques, and strategic usability. Nielsen model describes each usability maturity level as a set of achieved practices. Thus 1 was used to signify an achieved practice and 0 was used to signify a non achieved practice in each usability maturity level. An identifier were given to each practice in order to assist with referring to it.

Table 3 reflects the dimensions, practices, and maturity levels involved in Nielsen model.

Table 3. Nielsen Corporate Usability Maturity Model Levels

Dimension	Practices	ID	1	2	3	4	5	6	7	8
Developers Attitude Towards Usability	Recognition of usability importance	A1.1	0	1	1	1	1	1	1	1
	Recognition of importance of understanding user needs	A1.2	0	1	1	1	1	1	1	1
	Developers not acting on behalf of users	A1.3	0	0	1	1	1	1	1	1
Management Attitude Towards Usability	Recognition of usability importance	B1.1	0	1	1	1	1	1	1	1
	Willingness to allocate funds for usability activities	B1.2	0	0	1	1	1	1	1	1
	Allocating funds for usability activities	B1.3	0	0	1	1	1	1	1	1
	Presence of dedicated funds for usability activities	B1.4	0	0	0	1	1	1	1	1
Usability Practitioners Role	Presence of internal usability practitioner	C1.1	0	0	0	1	1	1	1	1
	Presence of a usability team led by a usability manager	C1.2	0	0	0	0	1	1	1	1
Usability Methods and Techniques	Performing usability testing	D1.1	0	0	1	1	1	1	1	1
	Planning for usability	D1.2	0	0	0	1	1	1	1	1
	Presence of a dedicated usability lab	D1.3	0	0	0	0	1	1	1	1
	Utilising a usability reports archive to compile past usability findings	D1.4	0	0	0	0	1	1	1	1
	Performing early user research	D1.5	0	0	0	0	0	1	1	1
	Performing iterative design	D1.6	0	0	0	0	0	1	1	1
	Quantitative usability metrics can be used to track quality	D1.7	0	0	0	0	0	0	1	1
	Projects has defined usability goals	D1.8	0	0	0	0	0	0	1	1
Strategic Usability	Presence of a tracking process for user experience quality throughout design projects and across releases	E1.1	0	0	0	0	0	1	1	1
	Utilising user interface design standards or a centralised definition of preferred design patterns	E1.2	0	0	0	0	0	1	1	1
	Projects are prioritised according to the business value of their user experience	E1.3	0	0	0	0	0	1	1	1
	Recognition of the need for user centred design process	E1.4	0	0	0	0	0	1	1	1
	Usability data is employed to determine individual projects to be built	E1.5	0	0	0	0	0	0	1	1
	Concept of total user experience extend to other forms of customer interaction with the company	E1.6	0	0	0	0	0	0	0	1
	User research data is employed to determine overall direction and priorities	E1.7	0	0	0	0	0	0	0	1

5   Results

This section reports on applying Nielsen Corporate Usability Maturity Model in the five AUCDI case studies that were discussed in section 3.2 and utilising the model in assessing their usability maturity level.

Interviewees from case study 1, 2, 3, 4, 5 are referred to as PT1, PT2, PT3, PT4, and PT5 respectively. In order to protect the anonymity of participants,

Table 4. Case Study

Dimension	Practices	ID	CS1	CS2	CS3	CS4	CS5
	Recognition of usability importance	A1.1	1	1	1	1	0
Developers Attitude Towards Usability	Recognition of importance of understanding user needs	A1.2	1	1	1	1	0
	Developers not acting on behalf of users	A1.3	1	1	1	1	0
	Recognition of usability importance	B1.1	1	1	1	1	1
Management Attitude Towards Usability	Willingness to allocate funds for usability activities	B1.2	1	1	1	1	1
	Allocating funds for usability activities	B1.3	1	1	1	1	1
	Presence of dedicated funds for usability activities	B1.4	1	1	0	1	1
Usability Practitioners Role	Presence of internal usability practitioner	C1.1	1	1	1	1	1
	Presence of a usability team led by a usability manager	C1.2	0	1	1	0	1
	Performing usability testing	D1.1	1	1	1	1	0
	Planning for usability	D1.2	1	1	1	1	1
	Presence of a dedicated usability lab	D1.3	0	1	0	0	1
Usability Methods and Techniques	Utilising a usability reports archive to compile past usability findings	D1.4	1	1	1	1	1
	Performing early user research	D1.5	1	1	1	1	1
	Performing iterative design	D1.6	1	1	1	1	0
	Quantitative usability metrics can be used to track quality	D1.7	1	0	1	1	0
	Projects has defined usability goals	D1.8	1	1	1	1	0
	Presence of a tracking process for user experience quality throughout design projects and across releases	E1.1	0	1	0	0	0
Strategic Usability	Utilising user interface design standards or a centralised definition of preferred design patterns	E1.2	1	1	1	1	1
	Projects are prioritised according to the business value of their user experience	E1.3	0	-	0	0	0
	Recognition of the need for user centred design process	E1.4	1	1	1	1	1
	Usability data is employed to determine individual projects to be built	E1.5	1	1	1	1	1
	Concept of total user experience extend to other forms of customer interaction with the company	E1.6	0	1	0	1	0
	User research data is employed to determine overall direction and priorities	E1.7	0	1	1	1	0

the word "he" will be used to refer to all of them. Relevant interviewee quotes are included to illustrate the evaluations given to some of the assessed practices and these quotes are identified by the participant who said them. Case study 1, 2, 3, 4 and 5 will be referred to as CS1, CS2, CS3, CS4, and CS5 respectively.

Table 4 reflects the results of applying Nielsen model on CS1, CS2, CS3, CS4, and CS5. The following section discusses the findings from applying Nielsen Corporate Usability Maturity Model in five AUCDI case studies.

5.1   Maturity Level Evaluation of Case Studies via Nielsen Model

Table 4 reflects the results of maturity level evaluation of Nielsen model for CS1, CS2, CS3, CS4, and CS5. Table 4, column CS1, CS2, CS3, and CS4 shows that the closest maturity level that describe CS1, CS2, CS3, and CS4 is maturity levels 7, 8, 7-8,and 8 respectively. However, column CS5 shows that CS5 differed significantly from all maturity levels. Thus it was given a maturity level of "Unknown".

The exploratory study that was conducted via Nielsen capability maturity model aimed to investigate the existence of a relationship between the success of

AUCDI attempts and usability maturity level and the suitability of Nielsen Corporate Usability Maturity Model for utilisation in assessing usability maturity in the context of Agile projects.

Aim 1: Investigating the existence of a relationship between the success of AUCDI attempts and usability maturity level

This study revealed the existence of a correlation between the success of AUCDI attempts and AUCDI case study's usability maturity level. Successful AUCDI case studies all scored a usability maturity level that ranged from 7-8.

This result can have positive implications on AUCDI practice since practitioners who aim to achieve the integration can utilise Nielsen model before the start of their projects to assess their maturity level. In case of achieving a low maturity level then the different practices included in Nielsen model can be used as a checklist for areas that need to be improved.

It was not possible to determine the maturity level of CS5, an example of a failed AUCDI attempt as discussed in section 5.1. This was due to the wide difference between its achieved practices and any available maturity level. This difficulty of determining the maturity level of CS5 was due to the fact that it had low maturity for all practices related to developers' attitude dimension towards usability including: practice A1.1- "Recognition of usability importance", practice A1.2- "Recognition of importance of understanding user needs" and A1.3- "Developers acting on behalf of users". However, it had high maturity for all practices related to the dimensions related to management attitude towards usability, usability practitioners role, usability methods and some practices related to strategic usability. Nevertheless, due to developers' attitude towards usability all the management awareness, allocated funds, usability practitioners and strategic usability practices were not effectively utilised. Moreover, the lack of cooperation of the development team led to discarding a number of practices including: practices- D1.1 "Performing usability testing", D1.6- "Performing iterative design", D1.7- "Quantitative usability metrics can be used to track quality", D1.8- "Projects has defined usability goals". The lack of communication among the cross functional team members due to geographical separation and unwillingness by the engineering team to collaborate with non engineering teams resulted in preventing the product manager and the user experience team from participating in the sprint planning and scrums. This led the engineering team to interpret and implement the designs incorrectly and resulted in lack of iterative refinement of designs.

This implies that the existence of management acknowledgment of usability importance and providing necessary infrastructure for usability activities , i.e., dedicated usability labs, usability professionals, usability funds, usability tools, etc are all less important to project success than developers' attitude towards usability and how they communicate with usability practitioners.

Aim 2: Investigating whether Nielsen Corporate Usability Maturity Model is suitable for utilisation in assessing usability maturity in the context of Agile projects

Nielsen model was not initially developed for Agile software development processes, however, a number of criteria were set in order to investigate the suitability of Nielsen model for utilisation in assessing usability maturity in the context of Agile projects. These criteria involves the following:

CR1: The usability maturity model should not conflict with Agile values and principles

This criteria was set in order to maintain the agility of the development process in case of utilising Nielsen model. However, practice E1.1- "Presence of a tracking process for user experience quality throughout design projects and across releases" could pose a conflict with the Agile value of "Individuals and interactions over processes and tools". However, this practice also works in support of another Agile principle "Continuous attention to technical excellence and good design enhances agility" since the aim of practice E1.1 is to improve the quality of user experience across all products.

Thus it can be concluded that CR1 is satisfied by Nielsen model since the model does not conflict with Agile values and principles.

CR2: The usability maturity model should integrate UCD activities into the overall project plan and throughout the Agile development life cycle

The reason behind setting this criteria is that none of the major Agile processes explicitly include guidance for how to develop usable software [23]. In addition, the interaction design role, usability, and user interface design in an Agile team is unclear and largely overlooked [5,3]. Furthermore, principles and practices for understanding and eliciting usability and user requirements and evaluating Agile systems for usability and user experience are generally considerably deficient [23,22]. In general, it is not yet clear how to incorporate UCD into Agile processes without sacrificing the acknowledged benefits of each of these individual processes.

As a result, criteria CR2 was considered as a significant factor for judging the suitability of Nielsen model for utilisation in assessing usability maturity in the context of Agile projects since the main problem that faces the Agile domain regarding the integration is when to perform the different UCD activities and how to make them more lightweight in order to accommodate the Agile processes iterative and incremental nature.

Nielsen model includes a variety of UCD activities embodied in the following practices

- D1.1- Performing usability testing.
- D1.2- Planning for usability.
- D1.4- Utilising a usability reports archive to compile past usability findings.
- D1.5- Performing early user research.

- D1.6- Performing iterative design.
- D1.8- Projects has defined usability goals.

However, Nielsen model lacks details on the timing of applying practices D1.1, D1.2, D1.5, and D1.6. Although the model includes practice D1.2 that is focused on planning for usability, however no details were given on what this entails. Practice D1.2 does not clarify what is meant by planning for usability and whether it includes preparation for user research, usability testing or planning to integrate UCD activities into the software development life cycle or all of these issues collectively. Practice D1.4 is focused on utilising a usability reports archive to compile past usability findings, however, the practice does not discuss the form of this usability reports archive to clarify whether it is a lightweight or heavyweight form. Moreover, practice D1.4 focuses only on archiving (documenting) past usability findings without mentioning other aspects that are necessary for AUCDI and that need to be archived including: design rationale, source of requirements, results of user research, designs, expected delivery date of designs, etc that are all necessary in the context of Agile projects. Practice D1.5 is focused on performing early user research, however, it uses a generic term to refer to the timing of conducting user research (early), this can imply iteration 0 or sprint 0 in the Agile domain. Moreover, the practice is generic since it does not identify the activities that are involved in performing early user research including: identification of user groups, context of use, task analysis, etc. Practice D1.8 is focused on setting defined usability goals for projects yet the problem facing Agile teams is not to set usability goals but rather how to translate these goals into user stories or features in the product back log that can gain priority for execution in the tight Agile time lines and avoid marginalization.

Nielsen model is a generic model, i.e., it is not developed for a particular software development life cycle. As a result the model focus is on declaring the important practices for usability maturity rather than clarifying the timing, method or frequency for conducting these practices along the project plan or the phases of the product development life cycle. This is of specific importance in case of Agile development processes since significant part of the integration challenges are related to the iterative, incremental, tight time line nature of Agile development processes.

Thus it can be concluded that criteria CR1 is satisfied by Nielsen model since it does not conflict with Agile values and principle. However, criteria CR2 is not satisfied by Nielsen model since the model does not state clear timings and milestones along the Agile development life cycle for the inclusion of UCD activities into the overall project plan and all phases in the software development life cycle.

6   Conclusion and Future Work

This paper investigated the suitability of Nielsen Corporate Usability Maturity Model for utilisation in the Agile domain in order to assess the organisation's UCD capability. It reported on applying Nielsen Model in five case studies that integrated Agile development processes and user centred design and utilising the model in assessing their usability maturity level.

The investigation of the existence of a relationship between the success of AUCDI attempts and usability maturity level revealed the existence of a correlation between the success of AUCDI attempts and the AUCDI case study's usability maturity level since successful AUCDI case studies all scored a usability maturity level that ranged from 7-8. Whereas, with the failed AUCDI attempt, it was not possible to determine its maturity level and as a result it was given a maturity level of "Unknown".

Moreover, the investigation of the suitability of UMMs for utilisation in assessing usability maturity in the context of Agile projects gave an indication that the model does not conflict with Agile values and principles. However, although the model includes a variety of UCD activities, yet, it lacks details on the timing of applying the different practices along the Agile development life cycle iterations or sprints. This is of specific importance in case of Agile development processes as significant part of the integration challenges that faces Agile projects is related to the timing of performing the different UCD activities in order to accommodate the Agile processes' iterative and incremental nature.

Although the existence of a correlation between the success of AUCDI attempts and the AUCDI case study's usability maturity level result can have positive implications on AUCDI practice since practitioners who aim to achieve the integration can utilise Nielsen model before the start of their projects to assess their maturity level. In case of achieving a low maturity level then the different practices included in Nielsen model can be used as a checklist for areas that need to be improved. However, two issues are of concern: first, Nielsen model is a descriptive maturity model, thus it is limited to acting as a diagnostic tool rather than an improvement tool, so the model can assess the performance and pinpoint weak areas but the procedures of improvement of these areas are left to practitioners and are not tackled by the model. Second, the lack of timing for the different UCD activities can hinder the usefulness of the model since organisations can use it as a checklist of the UCD activities that need to be performed, however, when they initiate their software development process they will be more concerned with the timing and the lightweight method through which they can achieve the recommended UCD activities by Nielsen model.

Moreover, an open issue is the further AUCDI challenges that are specific to the Agile domain and that are not tackled in Nielsen model. These issues need to be taken into consideration by any researcher who considers developing a UMM in the context of Agile projects. AUCDI challenges that are not approached by Nielsen model are: practices regarding the communication, coordination and collaboration between UCD practitioners and Agile developers in order to synchronize and complete their work, practices related to design modularization and chunking, UCD practitioner workload, and maintaining communication between the customer and the development team [30]. Moreover, another issue that needs to be approached by the developers of UMMs for Agile development processes is the features and activities that should be played by some team roles including XP coach, and scrum master whose role can impact the integration process.

Future work will involve applying UMM-HCS model in the same five case studies that integrated Agile development processes and UCD and utilising the model in assessing their usability maturity level.

References

1. Beck, K.: Manifesto for Agile Software Developement (2000)
2. Blomkvist, S.: Towards a Model for Bridging Agile Development and User-Centered Design. In: Seffah, A., Gulliksen, J., Desmarais, M. (eds.) Human-Centered Software Engineering — Integrating Usability in the Software Development Lifecycle. Human–Computer Interaction Series, vol. 8, pp. 219–244. Springer Netherlands (2005)
3. Beyer, H., Holtzblatt, K., Baker, L.: An Agile Customer-Centered Method: Rapid Contextual Design. In: XP/AU (2004)
4. Coallier, F.: TRILLIUM: A Model for the Assessment of Telecom Product Development & Support Capability. Software Process Newsletter 2, 13–18 (1995)
5. Constantine, L.: Process Agility and Software Usability: Towards Lightweight Usage Centred Design (2001b)
6. Detweiler, M.: Managing UCD within Agile Projects. Interactions 14(3), 40–42 (2007)
7. Earthy, J.: Usability Maturity Model: Processes Version 2.3. Technical report, Llyod's Register, 71Fenchurch St, London,EC3M 4BS (2011)
8. Earthy, J.: Usability Maturity Model: Human Centredness Scale:INUSE Project Deliverable D5.1.4 (s) Version 1.2. Technical report, Llyod's Register, 71Fenchurch St, London,EC3M 4BS (1998)
9. Eason, Haker: User Centred Design Maturity. Internal Working Document. Technical report, Department of Human Sciences. Loughborough University (1997)
10. Flanagan, G., Rauch, T.: Usability Management Maturity, Part 1: Self Assessment: How Do You Stack Up? In: CHI 1995 Conference Companion (4) (1995)
11. Gupta, A.: Humanware Process Improvement Framework: Interfacing User Centred Design and the Product Creation Process at Philips. Position Paper Delivered at Human Centred Process Improvement Group (HCPIG) Meeting.Teddington, UK (1997)
12. Rauch, T., Flanagan, G.: Usability Management Maturity, Part 2: Usability Techniques - What Can You Do. In: CHI 1995 Conference Companion (1995)
13. Fowler, M.: The New Methodology (December 2005)
14. Gottschalk, P.: Maturity Levels for Interoperability in Digital Government. Government Information Quarterly 26, 75–81 (2009)
15. Gould, J., Lewis, C.: Designing for Usability: Key Principles and What Designers Think. Communications of ACM 28(3), 300–311 (1985)
16. Iivari, N., Jokela, T.: Evaluating a Usability Capability Assessment. In: Bomarius, F., Komi-Sirviö, S. (eds.) PROFES 2001. LNCS, vol. 2188, pp. 98–109. Springer, Heidelberg (2001)
17. Iversen, J., Nielsen, P.A., Norbjerg, J.: Situated Assessment of Problems in Software Development. ACM SIGMIS Database - Special Issue on Infomration Systems 30(2), 66–81 (1999)

18. Jokela, T., Siponen, M., Hirasawa, N., Earthy, J.: A Survey of Usability Capability Maturity Models: Implications for Practice and Research. Behaviour and Information Technology 25(3), 263–282 (2006)
19. Jokela, T., Abrahamsson, P.: Usability Assessment of an Extreme Programming Project: Close Co-operation with the Customer Does Not Equal to Good Usability. In: Bomarius, F., Iida, H. (eds.) PROFES 2004. LNCS, vol. 3009, pp. 393–407. Springer, Heidelberg (2004)
20. Jokela, T.: An Assessment Approach for User-Centred Design Processes. In: EUROSPI. Limerick Institute of Technology Press, Limerick (2001)
21. Jokela, T., Abrahamsson, P.: Modelling Usability Capability - Introducing the Dimensions. In: Bomarius, F., Oivo, M. (eds.) PROFES 2000. LNCS, vol. 1840, pp. 73–87. Springer, Heidelberg (2000)
22. Kane, D.: Finding a Place for Discount Usability Engineering in Agile Development: Throwing Down the Gauntlet. In: Proceedings of the Conference on Agile Development, ADC 2003. IEEE Computer Society, Washington, DC (2003)
23. Lee, J.C., McCrickard, S., Stevens, T.: Examining the Foundations of Agile Usability with eXtreme Scenario-Based Design. In: Agile Conference, pp. 3–10 (August 2009)
24. McClelland, I., Gelderen, T., Taylor, B., Hefley, B., Gupta, A.: Humanware Process Improvement - Institutionalising the Principles of User Centred Design
25. Mettler, T.: Maturity Assessment Models: A Design Science Research Approach. International Journal of Society Systems Science 3, 81–98 (2011)
26. Nielsen, J.: Jakon Neilsen's Alertbox: Corporate Usability Maturity:Stages, pp. 1–4 (2006)
27. Raza, A., Capretz, L.-F., Ahmed, F.: An Open Source Usability Maturity Model (OS-UMM). Computers in Human Behavior 28(4), 1109–1121 (2012)
28. Rosemann, M., de Bruin, T.: Towards a Business Process Management Maturity Model. In: European Conference on Information Systems, Regensburg. Germany (2005)
29. Yin, R.: Case Study Research: Design and Methods. Sage, Beverly Hills (2009)
30. Salah, D., Paige, R.F., Cairns, P.: A systematic literature review for agile development processes and user centred design integration. In: Proceedings of the 18th International Conference on Evaluation and Assessment in Software Engineering (EASE 2014), Article 5 , 10 pages. ACM, New York (2014), http://doi.acm.org/10.1145/2601248.2601276, doi:10.1145/2601248.2601276

LiLoLe—A Framework for Lifelong Learning
from Sensor Data Streams for Predictive User Modelling

Mirko Fetter and Tom Gross

Human-Computer Interaction Group, University of Bamberg, Germany
{firstname.lastname}@uni-bamberg.de

Abstract. Adaptation in context-aware ubiquitous environments and adaptive systems is becoming more and more complex. Adaptations need to take into account information from a plethora of heterogeneous sensors, while the adaptation decisions often imply personalised aspects and individual preferences, which are likely to change over time. We present a novel concept for lifelong learning from sensor data streams for predictive user modelling that is applicable in scenarios where simpler mechanisms that rely on pre-trained general models fall short. With the LiLoLe-Framework, we pursue an approach that allows ubiquitous systems to continuously learn from their users and adapt the system at the same time through stream-based active learning. This Framework can guide the development of context-aware or adaptive systems in form of an overall architecture.

Keywords: Lifelong Learning, User Modelling, Framework.

1   Introduction

Context-aware and adaptive systems promise to support users by allowing them to offload tasks to the system. For example context-aware ubiquitous environments automatically execute tasks for the users, by sensing properties about the current situation and inferring the users' needs based on learned models or specified rules. For simple forms of adaptation, such rules can be specified manually with the help of tools [25, 26]. For example the task of automatically muting the phone when arriving at a specific location such as a meeting room can be relatively easily described by a rule. More complex forms of adaptations often already require the application of machine learning algorithms, as a manual specification of rules would be too complex. For example, smartphones are able to distinguish different simple activities like walking, running, or bicycling through activity recognition based on accelerometer data [5] and thus they are able to adapt their user interface to the current activity of the user. In order to enable such devices to recognise specific activities, usually machine-learning classifiers are trained with labelled data collected from a number of users. However, even with these relatively simple machine-learning problems, the generalisability of the learned models to new users who are not part of the group that provided training data, is already a challenge. For example Biao and Intille [5] found that while some of the activities in their work could be identified well with "subject-independent training

S. Sauer et al. (Eds.): HCSE 2014, LNCS 8742, pp. 126–143, 2014.

data" some of the activities could be detected better with "subject-specific training data". In order to optimise general activity recognition models for individual users, a number of different approaches have been developed, which try to optimise general models to specific users [23, 35]. The reason for relying on general models, even if they perform worse, is that the final users are not bothered with the effort for training a system before using it.

However, adaptation decisions in ubiquitous environments and adaptive systems are becoming more and more complex, where such simplified approaches based on general models or their optimisation can be hardly applied. They often take a multiplicity of input factors like location, activities, social interactions, etc. that happen simultaneously in physical and electronic space. The input arrives from a plethora of heterogeneous sensors and the adaptation decisions often imply personalised aspects and individual preferences that also can change over time. An illustrative example is the scenario of mediating interruptions by predicting the interruptibility of users [10, 11, 17], where the data of numerous different sensors is brought together with personal interruptibility reports to predict the availability of a user for communication. In such scenarios, general models do not offer enough accuracy and thus fail to offer adequate adaptation support for various reasons, as reflected on by Fetter et al. [10]. In order to overcome such challenges the idea of lifelong learning systems for user modelling [18] was introduced. Thereby the approach is to collect labels for unobservable user states over a prolonged time span to continuously train an adaptive system. The underlying rationale is that the system continuously improves itself, and over time reduces the request for labels, unless novel situations are detected. Hence, lifelong learning aims at improving the prediction quality through learning personalised models while trying to keep the training effort for users low.

In the following we present the LiLoLe framework for lifelong learning from sensor data streams for predictive user modelling. The Framework can guide the development of context-aware or adaptive systems in form of an overall architecture. The Framework thereby provides a foundation for the research and development of systems that deliver more human-centred adaptations, by continuously learning from the user, while keeping the effort for the user low. In the remainder of the paper we motivate the LiLoLe-Framework based on the analysis of the requirements and a look at existing machine learning approaches and the related work. We give a detailed description of the framework and a reference implementation. Finally, we discuss the results of an experiment, which applied the reference implementation to a real world data set and thus is able to predict the availability of individuals for instant messaging (IM) based on 30 different sensors.

2   Background and Related Work

In the following we give an introduction to the background of our work, including work that motivated our approach, that is related to our approach, and such that is incorporated in our approach.

2.1   A Rationale for Learning Personal Models

While machine learning at first seems an ideal candidate for learning personalised user models, a number of challenges hinder its broad application. As discussed by Webb et al. [30], the main challenges are the need for a huge amount of labelled data for training and the fact that learned concepts may change over time (i.e., concept drift). In user modelling therefore mainly two approaches can be found [37]: content-based, and collaborative learning. In the first approach users' past behaviour is used, to make prediction about their personal future behaviour. In the second approach, the behaviour of a group of similar behaving people is used, to make predictions for an individual user. Yet, both approaches only work if the concept to be learned is not hidden for the learning system, but is available for *in-stream supervision* [18]. For example, for a media player the songs played by a user are observable. Accordingly, based on meta-information like artists and genre (content-based learning) or based on the similar musical taste of other users (collaborative learning), the media player is able to recommend new songs to the user on the basis of the kind of songs the user played before. However, in many cases in ubiquitous computing and context-aware systems the concepts to be learned are hidden from the system (e.g., the users' mood, interruptibility, activity), and labels need to be provided manually. Therefore, in most implementations, where data could not be learned from individual users, the data is collected from a smaller number of users and is used to build general models that later need to fit all users (e.g., in activity recognition, gesture recognition). From a human-centred computing perspective, such approaches do not account for the individual differences of users. Accordingly, often users are forced to adapt to the system instead of the systems adapting to them (e.g., perform an activity in such a way, that the system is able to detect it). Further, as recent work has shown, such general models are not feasible in more complex settings. For example, when Fetter et al. [10] examined the performance of general vs. personal models in the context of predicting Instant Messaging availability of nomadic users based on a number of sensors in mobile settings, they found several aspects that degraded the performance of general models such as: the learned concept (i.e., availability) is highly personalised, and the variation between users was accordingly high; some features that had high predictive power for an individual user had a limited predictive power for other users, and thus were discarded; and some features that worked well in the individual models even had contradictory information for other users when used in general models. Our approach accounts for these challenges.

2.2   Lifelong Learning Systems

Only few researchers so far investigated the feasibility of systems that are able to continuously learn personalised models of human situations and adapt the user interface. Kapoor and Horvitz [18] proposed the notion of lifelong learning, where a user trains a machine learning system over a prolonged period based on selective supervision using the experience sampling method (ESM) [16]. However, their approach only was applied in strictly controlled settings, where the knowledge about the feature space was clear in the beginning, and each feature was handcrafted upfront by the system designer. Accordingly this approach only partially adapted to new situations. With Subtle, Fogarty et al. [11] developed the concept of a toolkit to generate automatic sensor-based statistical models of human situations. The toolkit provided an extensible sensor library, although with a limited number of readily available sensors. It provided support for continuous learning, but only in form of an iterative batch mode, that did not combine the strength of online learning algorithms with selective supervision for choosing best instances to label. Further, it was based on automated feature construction and selection, but did not make use of online feature selection mechanisms, to cope with high dimensional data with a presumably sparse number of features with high predictive power.

While both approaches demonstrated the general feasibility of life-long learning adaptive systems, those ideas have not been further pursued. Though, for a human-centred assessment of these approaches, studies with real-users in real life situations are needed, measuring the users attitude towards such systems. The LıLoLe-Framework informs the design of life-long learning systems and promotes implementations, which are robust to deployments in different environments and situations, and thus can be the foundation of further human-centred evaluations.

2.3   Data Stream Mining and Active Learning

In the following, the two machine learning approaches that build the foundation of our lifelong learning approach are introduced: data stream mining, and active learning.

The research field of data stream mining is concerned with methods, algorithms, and tools for extracting knowledge from rapid and continuous streams of data. As the development of information and communication technologies make more and more data available (e.g., from sensor networks, network traffic, or human activity data), learning from data streams is an emerging field in the area of machine learning. The aim of the research is to develop new algorithms and approaches that can cope with the special characteristics and requirements of stream-based learning, discussed in the Data Stream Model by Babcock et al. [4] as well as in the work of Bifet [6], Aggarwal [1]), and Gama [12]. So, for example, the data needs to be processed in one-pass and only in small chunks as the amount of data is extremely large, arrives continuously and is potentially infinite [1, 4, 6, 12]. Further, the speed at which data arrives makes processing the data in real-time a prerequisite [4, 6, 12]. Also, a temporal order of the arriving data is not guaranteed [4, 6]. New algorithms furthermore need to be able to deal with temporal locality [2] (i.e., concept drift [31]), as the concepts underlying the data can change over time and thus make past data irrelevant of even contradictory. Finally, the algorithms need to be able to adapt the changing data structures and evolving feature space when old data sources are removed, new ones are added, previous potential features loose their discriminative power, and new features are becoming continually available [1, 4, 6, 12].

Active learning [27] is a recent approach to machine learning. As gathering labelled data mostly is expensive (i.e., causing user effort during the training phase), the idea of active learning is to allow the algorithm to choose the data from which it learns by requesting labels from an oracle (e.g., a human annotator) in form of a query. By using algorithms that only request labels for instances that are close to the decision boundary, the required number of labelled examples is significantly reduced. The main difference between various active learning approaches is the way the algorithms queries for labels. The literature [27] currently distinguishes between membership query synthesis, pool-based sampling, and stream-based selective sampling. While the first approach synthesises artificial examples based on the provided features and their range of values, the second evaluates the entire collection of unlabelled instances upfront to pick the most promising examples for the query. The last approach, stream-based selective sampling [3], sequentially evaluates the unlabelled instances. For each instance—based on a given querying strategy—the algorithms decides if a label provided by an oracle is likely to improve the overall model quality and accordingly presents a query to the oracle or not.

In the next section we discuss, how the two approaches play together, to support the implementation of a lifelong learning system.

3   A Concept for Lifelong Learning of Personalised User Models

Context-aware systems adapt to the users' preferences based on sensing the current context. Therefore they apply machine learning algorithms to the sensor data in form of previously learned models that were trained in a batch learning approach [12]. A sensor can be either a software or a hardware component used to capture data from the users' environment in the digital or physical realm. The underlying idea of batch learning is, that a certain amount of labelled data is available upfront and can be used to train a predictive model (e.g., a gesture recogniser). This trained model then can be applied to new data—with the primary assumption that the training and the new data is independent and identically distributed—in order to make inference on this data. However, the assumption that labelled training data is available at a given time and representative for future data may not hold in any case. When learning personalised user models for building adaptive systems, four influencing factors cause a demand a new machine learning approach:

- Firstly, preferences for context-aware adaptations are often highly personalised and accordingly labelled data is sparse. For example, privacy-based decisions like revealing the current location to others have been found to be personal decisions are influenced by various factors [9].
- Secondly, the data can often only be labelled by the individual and only in the moment when it is experienced; assigning labels later based on a presentation of collected sensor data to the user is often not feasible. For example, the question how interruptible a person was at a given point in time can hardly be answered retrospectively [18].
- Thirdly, the sensor data (like the labels) is highly personalised and grounded in the individual users' daily contexts, hence resulting in an individual evolving feature space based on a continuous sensor data stream. For example, if several people share the preference for muting their work phone when at home, the sensor data that allows localising a person as at home, is individually different (e.g., BSSID of the home network) [10].
- And finally, preferences and contexts can change over time. Accordingly mechanisms are needed, which allow forgetting previously learned concepts, or overwriting them with new concepts, and also allow learning new concepts in new contexts. For example, a changing class schedule after a term break could lead to new preferences for when a phone should be automatically muted.

Implementations of systems should take these factors into account, to provide user-centred adaptations in real-life contexts. In doing so, those systems should be clearly designed to reduce the overall effort for the user. That is, such systems should balance the training effort against the effort of manually adapting the system, and provide an optimised behaviour that greatly reduced the amount of work for the user.

3.1   Stream-Based Active Learning

Accordingly, to allow for lifelong learning of personalised user models, new machine learning approaches need to be utilised. We found that the characteristics of two machine learning approaches in their combination promise a solution, able to deal with the above constraints: active learning and data stream mining. As outlined before, active learning [27] departs from the premise that obtaining labelled data for supervised learning can sometimes be very expensive. Hence—instead of presenting a training set with labelled data to the algorithm upfront—the rational behind active learning is that an algorithm that is able to actively select the instances for which it requires labelling by an annotator performs equal or better with fewer labels needed. On the other side, data stream mining subsumes the ideas of learning from extremely large (potentially infinite) amounts of data that continuously arrive at great speed [13] with the possibility of variations in the learned concepts as well as in the underlying data structures. A combination of both, as theoretically explored by Zliobaite et al. [36], promises a solution to the requirements of learning personalised user models.

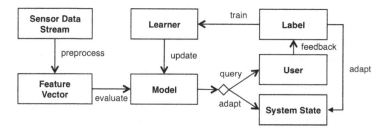

Fig. 1. Illustration of the basic principle of stream-based active learning from sensor data streams for lifelong learning

We therefore developed a concept, which utilises a combination of these approaches to enable *stream-based active learning* from sensor data streams, for lifelong learning of personalised user models. **Fig. 1** illustrates the underlying principle of our concept—forming the basis of LiLoLe-Framework.

In a ubiquitous environment, various sensors continuously monitor the users' contexts and activities, capture data from them, and provide this data in form of a sensor data stream. The arriving sensor data is pre-processed and converted to a feature vector that is processable by a machine learning algorithm. Based on this feature vector and a predictive model the system evaluates whether it is certain enough to adapt the system state and does so accordingly, or if it is uncertain continues training the predictive model. In the second case the user is queried by the system and gives feedback in form of a label. This label is used to train a learner to improve and update the predictive model and to directly adapt the system state.

3.2   An Application Scenario

For a more illustrative depiction of the principle we use a simplified, stripped-down scenario of a context-aware system that adapts the Instant Messaging availability status on a laptop computer based on the input of two sensors running on the computer: A *Wi-Fi-Sensor (WF)* and an *Application Focus-Sensor (AF)*. The *Wi-Fi-Sensor* sends a list of all nearby access-points (SSIDs and BSSIDs) together with the respective signal strength (RSSI) every 30 seconds, allowing conclusions on a user's whereabouts. The *Application Focus-Sensor* sends the name of the current application every time the user switches to a new application, allowing conclusions about the user's activity. Whenever a new sensor event arrives in the sensor stream, the application transforms this data into a feature vector and evaluates the data with a decision tree (i.e., the predictive model). When the laptop user starts working with a new application at a familiar location, the model might not be confident enough to adapt the IM status automatically. Accordingly the user is asked about the preferred current availability status in a dialog. The status is adapted based on the user's input, and an incremental training algorithm (e.g., Very Fast Decision Trees (VFDT)) is used to update the decision tree. The next time the user switches to this application at the same location, the status is automatically adapted. While this simplified illustration gives a basic idea of the framework, in order to be flexible and robust for various settings and applicable with current implementations of machine learning algorithms, a few extra steps have to be taken. In the following, we provide further details of the LiLoLE-Framework, starting with an overview that extends on the before discussed basic principle. We provide further details on the peculiarities when learning from streaming data in ubiquitous environments and how to integrate real-time feedback by end-users in form of active learning. Subsequently, we distil an algorithm for stream-based active learning from sensor events, which is the foundation of our framework. In the course of this paper we continuously refer to this scenario in form of examples for the different steps, algorithms and approaches.

4   The LILOLE-Framework

In the following overview of the LiLoLE-Framework (depicted in Fig. 2) we extend on the previously simplified conceptual model of the principle of stream-based active learning from sensor data streams by providing more details on the necessary steps and by proposing adequate methods for each of those steps.

We thereby concentrate on the transformation of the raw sensor data stream into a feature vector as well as the mechanisms of actively querying the user and training a predictive model. Finally, we derive an algorithm formalising the central steps.

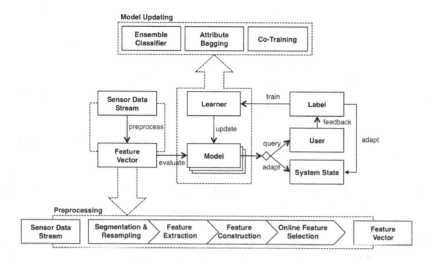

Fig. 2. Overview of the LiLoLe-Framework

4.1   Learning from Streaming Sensor Data

In order to learn from the sensor data stream, several steps need to be completed to preprocess the incoming stream of raw data into a feature vector that is processable by a machine learning algorithm. Each of these steps is now consecutively introduced:

Resampling & Segmentation. An incoming sensor data stream consists of a series of repeated measures from multiple sensors that basically can be understood as a multivariate time series (MTS). A MTS represents a series of observations over a time T where each observation at a given point in time t for a specific variables i is denoted. As each sensor can potentially send information at any given point in time, a first step is concerned with resampling the incoming sensor events to discrete timestamps. In our scenario where the WF-sensor was interval-based (i.e., sending an update every 30 seconds) and the AF-sensor is event-driven (i.e., sending an update only when a change occurred), there is a high possibility that for each point in time only data for one sensor is available (cf. Table 1). In order to further process this data, it is necessary to either upsample the data (e.g., through interpolation of the missing values) or downsample the data (e.g., by calculating the average over a sliding window) to a discrete time point resulting in a MTS with a fixed sample rate.

Table 1. Example of the sensor data stream from our scenario, showing that data from the interval-based WF-sensor and the event-driven AF-sensor can be available at different time points (x denotes an incoming sensor event at a given time t_n)

	t_1 (0s)	t_2 (11s)	t_3 (30s)	t_4(60s)	t_7(83s)
WF-sensor	x	-	x	x	-
AF-sensor	-	x	-	-	x

The right approaches and parameters for resampling should be chosen based on the application scenario and the data. The second step is to cut the MTS into discrete segments of finite length, as the data stream constantly grows, and the MTS cannot be processed in its whole. Again, different algorithms for segmenting time-series are available [19]. The application scenario and the expected data influence the selection of an appropriate algorithm. However, when apriori knowledge about the data is limited, a fixed-size sliding window for segmentation is often a valid first strategy.

Feature Extraction. After the data is resampled and segmented, it is ready to be processed by the feature engineering chain. Each incoming segment represents an example (i.e., instance) that is later presented to the predictive model to be classified and to eventually further train the system. Thereby, feature extraction is the first step [20]. The aim of the feature extraction process is to transform the raw sensor data into features that can be interpreted by the machine learning algorithms. This includes a transformation of the data into the data types the machine learning algorithms can process (i.e., numeric and nominal types [32]) and a reduction of the dimensionality to simple key-value pairs of attributes (i.e., features) with the aim to reduce the amount of irrelevant information. Coming back to our scenario, the WF-Sensor for each reading delivers a matrix listing the SSID, BSSID and RSSI of each nearby access-points (cf. Table 2).

Table 2. Example of one sensor event of the WF-sensor listing nearby access-points

SSID	BSSID	RSSI
UniXXXXXX	00:1F:45:97:E3:81	-54 dBm
eduroam	00:1F:45:97:E3:80	-51 dBm
eduroam	00:1F:45:97:E3:88	-62 dBm
MyNet	00:4F:81:05:0B:8A	-79 dBm

Based on this simple raw data, already a plenitude of features can be composed, as for example the following: The number of nearby access points (WF_Sensor_No=4) could indicate how dense the area around the users location is populated while a low average RSSI (WF_Sensor_Avg_RSSI=61,5) could indicate an outdoor usage. The absence, presence, or signal strength of an access point allows to infer the users whereabouts on different granularity levels. Different extractable features could tell that the user is on the University campus (WF_Sensor_SSID_ eduroam_Bool=true), near a specific lecture room (WF_Sensor_BSSID_001F4597E388_RSSI=62) or not at home (WF_Sensor_SSID_ HomeNet_Bool=false) when the history of sensor values is taken into account for feature extraction. The possible combinations are endless, while clearly not every combination does make sense (e.g., WF_Sensor_BSSID_ 001F4597E388_RSSI ="eduroam") and later can dilute the classification performance. While normally human domain experts guide the feature extraction process, in the case of our framework for lifelong learning, automatic strategies need to be found, as potentially new features are constantly arriving with each new sensor reading. Optimally, different strategies for feature extraction need to be combined here, that allow generating a rich representation of the sensor data. As exemplified above, this can happen through simple functions that calculate mean values from the sensor values, count the number of occurrences, etc. But also more sophisticated approaches such as Principal Component Analysis are conceivable as *FeatureExtractionStrategies*. If, in the end, not all extracted features meaningfully contribute to the classification result, simple filters or more powerful mechanisms for feature selection can remove those later.

Feature Construction. The next feature engineering step is concerned with creating additional features by discovering missing information about the relationship of individual features [20]. While these dependencies of features also can be of multifarious nature and only mechanisms for the automatic feature construction [21] can be taken into account, one aspect that becomes prevalent when using data streams is taking the factor time into account. So, instead of only using features from the last sensor reading, one promising strategy is to build features that take into account a period of time. Coming back to our scenario, features for the last 2, 5, or 15 minutes could be computed to provide additional information. By calculating the fraction of time a given feature was true they could indicate that somebody just arrived at a location in the last 2 minutes (WF_Sensor_SSID_eduroam_Bool_2m =0.2) or is focused on one application for longer (AF_Sensor_MSWord_Bool_15m =0.95). Other options for *FeatureConstructionStrategies* are calculating frequencies for Boolean values or the mean, standard deviation, etc. for numeric values.

Online Feature Selection. Feature Selection is the last step in the feature engineering [20] process. Hereby the aim is to reduce the dimensionality of the feature vector, as most classifier perform significantly better on data with a low number of features. The reduction of features is especially necessary, as our approach so far continuously increased the number of features through the strategies of feature extraction and feature construction. Normally, feature selection algorithms select the most predictive features and remove irrelevant and redundant features based on an evaluation process where all features are available upfront as well as labelled data as evaluation criteria. As both prerequisites are not given in our setting of stream-based active learning, special algorithms for online feature selection [29, 33, 34] need to be applied. Conclusively, the process of feature selection constantly can suggest different, improved combinations of features. As each new feature vector would require a new model to be trained, a *FeatureSelectionStrategy* also has to decide, when switching to a new feature vector—and hence to a new model—is beneficial for the overall performance. In the following, more details on how to deal with the resulting multiple models are provided.

4.2   Active Learning of User Preferences

Based on the previous steps, the framework is now able to provide the incoming sensor data as single instances with a fixed number of features to the predictive model for evaluation. Based on the update frequency of the sensors, and the chosen parameters for resampling and segmentation a new instance for evaluation is available in a fixed rhythm (e.g., every few seconds). Each time an instance arrives, an *ActiveLearningStrategy* decides whether it uses the instance for adaptation or whether it queries a label from the user. In order to provide an understanding of what a simple

ActiveLearningStrategy looks like, we use the example of the *Fixed Uncertainty Strategy* [36]. The *Fixed Uncertainty Strategy* provides the instance to the classifier (i.e., predictive model) in order to obtain a prediction. The strategy then compares the confidence value or the posterior probability of the classifier to a fixed threshold defined e.g. by the developer.. If the classifier is confident enough about the classification, the strategy performs the adaptation based on the classification result, otherwise the user is queried for a label. Of course, more sophisticated active learning strategies are needed, to allow building user-centred systems, not overburdening the user with the training effort. One illustrative example is the introduction of a simple upper-limit on the number of queries a strategy is allowed to pose to the user in a given time frame. Other strategies are decision-theoretic approaches as proposed by Kapoor et al. [16] and also strategies that simply detect novel situations, by applying clustering algorithm on the incoming data, as presented later in our implementation.

The presentation of the query to the user and the feedback by the user (i.e., provisioning of the label) also allows for different approaches. In GUI based systems, an experience sampling based approach [10, 16] is feasible, as exemplified for our scenario in Fig. 3. Of course depending on the application context, multifarious query and feedback mechanisms are conceivable, e.g., a vibration pattern of a smart watch could query the current interruptibility, allowing the user to simply respond by performing a gesture.

Fig. 3. Exemplary experience sampling dialog for our IM scenario

Depending on the provision of a label, the final step now is to update the model through training with the instance and corresponding label. As the training data arrives sequentially, only classification algorithms that allow for incremental learning can be applied in our framework. Examples for such algorithms are incremental decision trees like Hoeffding trees or Very Fast Decision Trees (VFDT), online variants of kernel learners like LASVM or more basic algorithms like an updateable Naïve Bayes classifier.

In respect to our setting that requires learning from data streams under the assumption of concept drift and feature evolution, additional steps need to be taken in the model updating process. As noted in an earlier step, foremost the application of a *FeatureSelectionStrategy* requires flexibility in the model updating process, as most algorithms cannot deal with instances represented by a changing combination of features (i.e., feature evolution). Accordingly, each time the *FeatureSelectionStrategy* suggests a new set of features also a new model needs to be trained. As this would require starting the learning process from scratch, three mechanisms (cf. Fig. 2) allow a smooth transition and preservation of the previously learned concepts. First, the use of ensemble classifiers [22, 24, 28] allows combining several models into one. When a classification is requested, different ensemble strategies (e.g., bagging or boosting) provide a weighted classification result, computed from the individual models. Ensemble approaches have been demonstrated to work well for learning from concept drifting data streams [22, 24, 28]. Second, attribute bagging [8] (also feature subset ensembles or random subspace method [15]) are specialised ensemble methods for learning from instances with different feature vectors, that can be fitted to tackle the challenges of dealing with an evolving feature space. Third, the application of co-training [7] in both cases allows to train new models separately, before they are added to an ensemble. Co-training simply uses the classification output of the current ensemble, to train new models, with new feature subsets, until a certain training criterion is met. This approach would allow training a new model for a specific period, before it is actively used for predictions in the ensemble.

4.3 An Algorithm for Stream-Based Active Learning

In the previous sections we described in detail our concept of the LiLoLE-Framework, and provided examples for the implementation including promising strategies and

---

Algorithm 1: Stream-based Active Learning from Sensor Data Streams

Input: strategy parameters, strategies
Output: o_t as output label for instance I_t
for each s_t - *incoming SensorEvent,* **do**
    resample s_t to discrete timestamps t' and add to resampled data stream
    segment resampled data stream into segments $S_{t'}=[s_{t'}, s_{t'-1}, s_{t'-2},... s_{t'-w}]$
    for each *FeatureConstructionStrategy(...)* **do**
        for each *FeatureExtractionStrategy(...)* **do**
            constructFeatures(extractFeatures(S_{t'}))
        end for
    end for
    build $I_{t'}$ – *instance* from Features
    if *FeatureSelectionStrategy (I_{t'},...)* = **true then**
        start a new classifier C_n with selected features
    end if
    for each $I_{t'}$ - *incoming instance,* **do**
        if *ActiveLearningStrategy(I_{t'},...)* = **true then**
            query the true label $a_{t'}$ of instance $I_{t'}$ from the user
            train ensemble E with $(I_{t'}; a_{t'})$
            return true label at' as output $o_{t'}$
        else
            classify $I_{t'}$ with ensemble E and obtain the predicted label $p_{t'}$
            return classification result $p_{t'}$ as output $o_{t'}$
        end if
        if C_n *exists* **then**
            co-train classifier C_n with $o_{t'}$
            if C_n *is trained* **then**
                add classifier C_n to Ensemble E
            end if
        end if
        adapt the system based on $o_{t'}$
    end for
end for

available algorithms. In order to provide a more formalised documentation of our approach, we propose the following algorithm for the stream-based active learning from sensor data streams to enable lifelong learning systems. In the next chapter we provide insights in an implementation and provide results of a simulation with real user data.

5   Implementation and Evaluation of the Framework

In order to put our approach into practise, we build a first reference implementation of our framework, and evaluated the feasibility of the approach in a simulation with real user data. The main aim was to test the end-to-end feasibility of our approach of stream-based active learning. As a basis for our implementation we used Sens-ation [14], an event-based platform for ubiquitous computing, that allows integrating sensors, inference engines (i.e., parameterisable inferencing mechanisms) and actuators. A visual editor for Sens-ation [26] allows us to easily connect sensors, inference engines and actuators in order to layout the event flow (cf. **Fig. 4**.1). We implemented a variety of the proposed strategies in form of parameterisable inference engines (IE) for Sens-ation, which could be configured in the editor (cf. **Fig. 4**.2). However, for some of the strategies we only provide naïve implementations, as the main focus at this state was on the general feasibility of the framework. For all machine learning algorithms, we used the WEKA toolkit [32].

For *Resampling* and *Segmentation* we implemented two separate IEs, each configurable to use one of various strategies. For resampling, we implemented one simple strategy called LastValueStrategy: each time a new sensor event arrives, the value is stored. Depending on a chosen push method, the stored last values for all sensors are either passed on to the next inference engine, each time a new senor event is incoming, or in a configurable time interval. For segmentation, we implemented a simple FixedWindowStrategy, with a configurable window size. While the IE for *feature construction* implements several of the mechanisms proposed above, the IE for *feature extractions* only extracts two simple features, which is the day of the week and the hour of the day. Finally, for the *online feature selection* (OFS), we implemented a naïve random strategy, that randomly selected a percentage of the features for the feature vector. While we were aware that this decision degrades the machine learning performance, the lack of implementations for OFS algorithms at this time in standard machine learning toolkits and the focus of the end-to-end feasibility did not allow for a different solution.

For the active learning IE we implemented two *ActiveLearningStrategies*:   a FixedUncertaintyStrategy with a configurable minimum and maximum threshold for the confidence value; a strategy based on the COWEB clustering algorithm that queries for labels, when changes in the underlying data are detected (ClusterStrategy). The IE for the model and the learner (i.e., classifier algorithm) provides the most flexibility by accepting WEKA command-line strings, for setting and configuring a classifier. Of course, the IE accepted only incremental classifiers, that is, all WEKA classifiers that implement the Interface UpdateableClassifier. Furthermore, the use of advanced strategies for model updating like ensemble classifiers and attribute bagging were not applicable, as we had no sophisticated mechanism for feature selection.

Finally, the adaptation mechanisms as well as the label query were implemented as Sens-ation actuators. For the adaptation we implemented two demonstrators: One was able to control the system volume of a PC, the other was able to adapt the Instant Messaging status. For the querying mechanisms, we implemented a simple, XML-configurable ESM-like dialog (cf. **Fig. 3**). The feedback of the user was passed back to the Sens-ation in form of a sensor event.

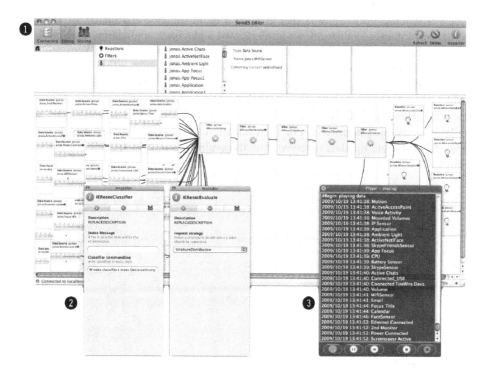

Fig. 4. Overview of our setup for the simulation, including the event flow in the visual editor (1) between sensors (white boxes with scale symbol at the left), inference engines (beige boxes with gear symbol in the centre) and actuators (lime boxes with light bulb symbol at the right); two inspector windows, each showing the parameters for an inference engine (2); and the sensor data player (3)

For the evaluation we relied on a dataset from previous work that assessed the predictability of availability for IM [10]. In average an accuracy of 81.35% was reached in this work for this dataset. It needs to be noted that these are the results of an offline, explorative machine learning approach, where step-by-step the best features, algorithms, and parameters where chosen by a human expert based on computational expensive grid search. Accordingly, this accuracy was not considered not as a benchmark but only as a guiding value for our current implementation, relying on naïve implementations and with near real-time constraints.

The data provided a variety of characteristics that deemed it an ordeal for our approach. The dataset, collected by four individuals consisted of several month of sensor data recorded on their laptop computers, together with two estimates of their own availability for IM every hour. 30 different sensors collected data such as nearby Bluetooth and Wi-Fi devices, running applications, connected USB devices, the presence of people, etc., with sampling rates between 30 and 150 seconds and in form of sensor events of varying dimensionality (i.e., sensors that only provide a single value per reading up to sensors that provide a multi-dimensional matrix of values). For the performance evaluation, we implemented a playback application (cf. **Fig. 4**.3), which read the data from the provided XML-dataset files and send it to Sens-ation—practically simulating events from live sensors. For the evaluation, the temporal information in the datasets was omitted, and the data was played back as fast as it could be read from the files. In Sens-ation, all incoming sensor data was pre-processed. However, of course only that data could be evaluated where a label was available as evaluation criteria. For the evaluation, a specially programmed actuator allowed to write out the data received from the evaluation inference engine.

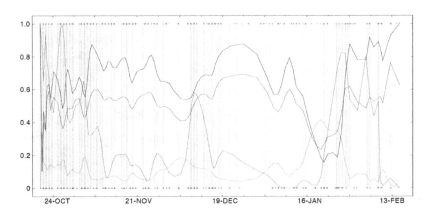

Fig. 5. Results of the NaïveBayesUpdateable classifier over time for one dataset. Each red and green cross marks the availability of a label in the data set, that was either predicted right (=1.0) or wrong (=0) by the classifier, whereby each vertical pink line shows a query for a label triggered by the *ActiveLearningStrategy*. The blue line shows the overall accuracy of the classifier over time. (Further: red line = confidence for real class; pink line = confidence for predicted class; green line = normalised absolute difference between real and predicted class).

As many existing metrics for measuring the performance of machine learning (e.g., accuracy, precision or recall) are of limited expressiveness for our setting of lifelong learning, we illustrate our results based on a trend chart over time. **Fig. 5** exemplary shows the results for the dataset of one user over a period of roughly four months (Oct. to Feb). The algorithm used for classification was an incremental Naïve Bayes implementation. A FixedUncertaintyStrategy was applied as the *ActiveLearning Strategy* with a minimum threshold of 0.6 for the confidence value—that is, if the confidence for a prediction falls below the 60% mark, a label is requested. The chart shows the accuracy of the classifier (blue line), quickly goes up and then dithers around 70% until in the last third—the weeks around New Year— it suddenly breaks down to 20% until it goes up again. This effect is likely caused through the occurrence of a concept or feature drift. In this specific case, probably due to a holiday break of the user that provided the data, which led to different circumstances, a different environment or different availability preferences for this period. Also clearly visible is how the number of queries for labels (vertical pink lines) triggered by the *ActiveLearningStrategy* goes down after an initial intense learning phase. And likewise, how the concept or feature drift around New Year, leads to a more intense training phase at the end of January. While the overall accuracy of the classifier does not reach a performance as demonstrated in [10]—where an average accuracy of 81.35% could be achieved in an offline evaluation with manually crafted feature sets and hand-picked algorithms—it is also true that our implementation does yet not fully exploit the full power of our proposed concept. As in most parts we relied on naïve implementations for the strategies, our main aims was to demonstrate the general feasibility of a lifelong learning system, based on our proposed conceptual framework. The integration of a real feature selection mechanism and the application of more advanced learners like kernel learners or tree ensembles are likely to boost the performance, leading to less queries and a higher accuracy—closer to that of the manual process in [10].

6   Conclusions and Future Work

We presented the LILoLE-Framework, a conceptual framework for lifelong learning from sensor data streams for predictive user modelling. The conceptual framework combines the strength of data stream mining and active learning, and thus allows building complex adaptive systems that learn from individual user over a prolonged period of time. We provided detailed insights in the necessary components and building blocks, as well as the underlying processes and data flow, which can guide the engineering process and architectures of similar systems. An end-to-end implementation, partially based on simple and naïve algorithm implementations, already proves that our system is able to learn form an evolving data stream and to adapt to concept drifts. In future work we will extend the number of implemented algorithm, and add more sophisticated mechanisms to the implementation, as already described in the concept.

Mainly, our implementation will ultimately allow us to assess more human-centred aspects of the approach of life-long learning. While previous work assessed the improvement of personal user models through life-long learning only theoretical through offline accuracy and performance measures, our implementation now allows to get real user feedback on the adaptation in field tests in real settings. This includes aspects like the adaptation quality or the satisfaction with the training effort, and allows researching and revealing further human-centred aspects.

Acknowledgments. We thank members of the CML, especially Jonas Pencke and David Wiesner.

References

[1] Aggarwal, C.: An Introduction to Data Streams. In: Aggarwal, C. (ed.) Data Streams - Models and Algorithms, pp. 1–8. Springer, Heidelberg (2007)

[2] Aggarwal, C.: Data Streams: An Overview and Scientific Applications. In: Gaber, M.M. (ed.) Scientific Data Mining and Knowledge Discovery - Principles and Foundations, pp. 377–397. Springer, Heidelberg (2010)

[3] Atlas, L.E., Cohn, D.A., Ladner, R.E.: Training Connectionist Networks with Queries and Selective Sampling. In: Neural Information Processing Systems, Denver, CO, USA, November 27-30, pp. 566–573. Morgan Kaufmann Publishers Inc., San Fransisco (1989)

[4] Babcock, B., Babu, S., Datar, M., Motwani, R., Widom, J.: Models and Issues in Data Stream Systems. In: Proc. of the Twenty-First ACM Symposium on Principles of Database Systems - PODS 2002, Madison, WI, USA, pp. 1–16. ACM Press, New York (2002)

[5] Bao, L., Intille, S.S.: Activity Recognition from User-Annotated Acceleration Data. In: Ferscha, A., Mattern, F. (eds.) PERVASIVE 2004. LNCS, vol. 3001, pp. 1–17. Springer, Heidelberg (2004)

[6] Bifet, A.: Adaptive Stream Mining - Pattern Learning and Mining from Evolving Data Streams. IOS Press, Amsterdam (2010)

[7] Blum, A., Mitchell, T.: Combining Labeled and Unlabeled Data with Co-training. In: Proc. of the 11th Annual Conference on Computational Learning Theory, COLT 1998, Madison, WI, USA, pp. 92–100. ACM Press, New York (1998)

[8] Bryll, R., Gutierrez-Osuna, R., Quek, F.: Attribute Bagging: Improving Accuracy of Classifier Ensembles by Using Random Feature Subsets. Pattern Recognition 36(6), 1291–1302 (2003)

[9] Consolvo, S., Smith, I.E., Matthews, T., LaMarca, A., Tabert, J., Powledge, P.: Location Disclosure to Social Relations: Why, When, & What People Want to Share. In: Proc. of the Conference on Human Factors in Computing Systems - CHI 2005, Portland, USA, April 2-7, pp. 81–90. ACM Press, New York (2005)

[10] Fetter, M., Seifert, J., Gross, T.: Predicting Selective Availability for Instant Messaging. In: Campos, P., Graham, N., Jorge, J., Nunes, N., Palanque, P., Winckler, M. (eds.) INTERACT 2011, Part III. LNCS, vol. 6948, pp. 503–520. Springer, Heidelberg (2011)

[11] Fogarty, J., Hudson, S.E., Akteson, C.G., Avrahami, D., Forlizzi, J., Kiesler, S., Lee, J.C., Yang, J.: Predicting Human Interruptibility with Sensors. ACM Transactions on Computer-Human Interaction (TOCHI) 12(1), 119–146 (2005)

[12] Gama, J.: Issues and Challenges in Learning from Data Streams. In: Kargupta, H., Han, J., Yu, P.S., Motwani, R., Kumar, V. (eds.) Next Generation of Data Mining. Chapman & Hall/CRC, Tailor & Francis Group, Boca Raton (2008)

[13] Gama, J., Rodriques, P.P.: Data Stream Processing. In: Gama, J., Gaber, M.M. (eds.) Learning from Data Streams - Processing Techniques in Sensor Networks, pp. 25–39. Springer, Heidelberg (2007)

[14] Gross, T., Egla, T., Marquardt, N.: Sensation: A Service-Oriented Platform for Developing Sensor-Based Infrastructures. IJIPT 1(3), 159–167 (2006)

[15] Ho, T.: The Random Subspace Method for Constructing Decision Forests. IEEE TPAMI 20(8), 832–844 (1998)

[16] Horvitz, E., Kapoor, A.: Experience Sampling for Building Predictive User Models: A Comparative Study. In: Proc. of the Conference on Human Factors in Computing Systems, CHI 2008, Florence, Italy, pp. 657–666. ACM Press, New York (2008)

[17] Horvitz, E., Koch, P., Apacible, J.: BusyBody: Creating and Fielding Personalized Models of the Cost of Interruption. In: Proc. of the 2004 ACM Conference on Computer Supported Cooperative Work, CSCW 2004, Chicago, Illinois, November 6-10, pp. 507–510. ACM Press, New York (2004)

[18] Kapoor, A., Horvitz, E.: Principles of Lifelong Learning for Predictive User Modeling. In: Conati, C., McCoy, K., Paliouras, G. (eds.) UM 2007. LNCS (LNAI), vol. 4511, pp. 37–46. Springer, Heidelberg (2007)

[19] Keogh, E., Selina, C., Hart, D., Pazzani, M.: Segmenting Time Series: A Survey and Novel Approach. In: Last, M., Kandel, A., Bunke, H. (eds.) Data Mining in Time Series Databases, pp. 1–22. World Scientific Publishing Co., Singapore (2003)

[20] Liu, H., Motoda, H. (eds.): Feature Extraction, Construction and Selection - A Data Mining Perspective. Kluwer Academic Publishers, Norwell (1998)

[21] Markovitch, S., Rosenstein, D.: Feature Generation Using General Constructor Functions. Machine Learning 49(1), 59–98 (2002)

[22] Opitz, D., Maclin, R.: Popular Ensemble Methods: An Empirical Study. Journal of Artificial Intelligence Research 11, 169–198 (1999)

[23] Reiss, A., Stricker, D.: Personalized Mobile Physical Activity Recognition. In: Proc. of the 2013 International Symposium on Wearable Computers - ISWC 2013, Zurich, Switzerland, September 9-12, pp. 25–28. ACM Press, New York (2013)

[24] Rokach, L.: Ensemble-based Classifiers. AI Review 33(1-2), 1–39 (2010)

[25] Salber, D., Dey, A.K., Abowd, G.D.: The Context Toolkit: Aiding the Development of Context-Enabled Applications. In: Proc. of the Conference on Human Factors in Computing Systems- CHI 1999, Pittsburgh, PA, USA, May 15-20, pp. 434–441. ACM Press, New York (1999)

[26] Schirmer, M., Gross, T.: CollaborationBus Aqua: Easy Cooperative Editing of Ubiquitous Environments. In: Proc. of the International Conference on Collaborative Technologies - CT 2010, Freiburg, Germany, July 26-28, pp. 77–84. IADIS Press (2010)

[27] Settles, B.: Active Learning. Morgan & Claypool Publishers, San Rafael (2012)

[28] Wang, H., Fan, W., Yu, P.S., Han, J.: Mining Concept-Drifting Data Streams Using Ensemble Classifiers. In: Proc. of the Ninth ACM International Conference on Knowledge Discovery and Data Mining - KDD 2003, Washington, D.C., USA, August 24-27, pp. 226–235. ACM Press, New York (2003)

[29] Wang, J., Zhao, P., Hoi, S.C.H., Jin, R.: Online Feature Selection and Its Applications. IEEE Transactions on Knowledge and Data Engineering (2013)

[30] Webb, G.I., Pazzani, M.J., Billsus, D.: Machine Learning for User Modeling. User Modeling and User-Adapted Interaction (UMUAI) 11(1-2), 19–29 (2001)

[31] Widmer, G., Kubat, M.: Learning in the Presence of Concept Drift and Hidden Contexts. Machine Learning 23(1), 69–101 (1996)

[32] Witten, I.H., Frank, E., Hall, M.A.: Data Mining: Practical Machine Learning Tools and Techniques. Morgan Kaufmann, San Francisco (2011)

[33] Wu, X., Yu, K., Ding, W., Wang, H., Zhu, X.: Online Feature Selection with Streaming Features. IEEE TPAMI 35(5), 1178–1192 (2013)

[34] Wu, X., Yu, K., Wang, H., Ding, W.: Online Streaming Feature Selection. In: Procedings of the 27th International Conference on Machine Learning, ICML 2010, Haifa, Israel, June 21-24, pp. 1159–1166. Omnipress, Madison (2010)

[35] Zhao, Z., Chen, Y., Liu, J., Shen, Z., Liu, M.: Cross-People Mobile-Phone Based Activity Recognition. In: Proc. of the Twenty-Second International Joint Conference on Artificial Intelligence, IJCAI 2011, Barcelona, Catalonia, Spain, pp. 2545–2550. AAAI Press, Menlo Park (2011)

[36] Žliobaitė, I.e., Bifet, A., Pfahringer, B., Holmes, G.: Active Learning with Evolving Streaming Data. In: Gunopulos, D., Hofmann, T., Malerba, D., Vazirgiannis, M. (eds.) ECML PKDD 2011, Part III. LNCS, vol. 6913, pp. 597–612. Springer, Heidelberg (2011)

[37] Zukerman, I., Albrecht, D.W.: Predictive Statistical Models for User Modeling. User Modeling and User-Adapted Interaction (UMUAI) 11(1-2), 5–18 (2001)

Rapid Task-Models Development Using Sub-models, Sub-routines and Generic Components

Peter Forbrig[1], Célia Martinie[2], Philippe Palanque[2],
Marco Winckler[2], and Racim Fahssi[2]

[1] University of Rostock, Department of Computer Science,
Albert Einstein Str. 21, Rostock, Germany
`peter.forbrig@uni-rostock.de`
[2] ICS-IRIT, University of Toulouse 3, 118, route de Narbonne
31062 Toulouse Cedex 9, France
`{martinie,palanque,winckler,fahssi}@irit.fr`

Abstract. Whilst task models are perceived as critical artifacts within User Centered Design methods, task models development is often considered as a re-source and time consuming activity. Structuring techniques can support han-dling issues such as reuse and scalability and can improve analysts' productivity and the overall quality of models. In this paper we propose (based on the nota-tion of the HAMSTERS project) several means to structure task models and present how they can be used in order to increase reusability and scalability in task models. Besides sub-models and sub-routines, generic components are de-scribed. These mechanisms are duly illustrated within a project for the ground segments of satellite missions. This paper shows, by example, how such ele-ments look like and how both readability and quality of models is improved by their use.

Keywords: Generic components, sub-models, sub-routines, task models.

1   Introduction

It is widely accepted that models help to explore and understand new domains by pro-viding insights into the domain at an abstract level, avoiding going too early into de-tails and supporting communication between the various stakeholders (by providing unambiguous descriptions). For designing interactive systems, task models are a valu-able source of knowledge as they represent large quantity of information related to user goals and to the activities to be carried out in order to reach those goals. Task models are particularly useful when describing complex activities for which informal descrip-tions (e.g. natural language text) are not manageable. Task models contain information that can be used to assess the complexity of activities in terms of number of actions to be performed, knowledge and skills required to carry out activities, information and objects required to accomplish tasks. By providing unambiguous descriptions, task models can be used to check the consistency of the information described and to detect modeling mistakes. Moreover, task models help analysts reason about activities, for example, about possible migration of tasks from the user to the system.

S. Sauer et al. (Eds.): HCSE 2014, LNCS 8742, pp. 144–163, 2014.

Despite all the advantages of task models, if the activities to be represented are complex, the resulting models might become complex too. Complexity in models is a recurrent problem with model-based approaches that might require significant availability of resources which is sometimes perceived as too much effort, too long to produce and not being cost effective enough. This might be true if every model has to be developed from scratch each time a new application is considered and if the modeling techniques are not equipped with adequate tool support. Moreover, beyond tool-support, model complexity is also a concern at the notation level.

In [15], a detailed argumentation is presented about the fact that abstraction and refinement of task models is not sufficient for handling large real world applications. For that two mechanisms were proposed (sub-models and sub-routines) to deal with complexity in task models. In the present paper we revisit these mechanisms and we propose a third one (component) that provides a powerful mean for reusing models parts. These three mechanisms are aimed at supporting rapid task-model development by structuring models and improving reuse of existing models. All these mechanisms are illustrated using the notation HAMSTERS which has been fully integrated in the eponym project and tool support [17]. These mechanisms can be used with other task model notations, but HAMSTERS already has them fully embedded. A full description of other objects (data, information, objects, knowledge...) in a HAMSTERS task model can be found in [16].

2   Three Mechanisms for Supporting Structuring and Reuse in Task Models

This section presents three mechanisms for structuring task models: sub-models, sub-routines and components.

2.1   Sub-models

Sub-models are based on the refinement/abstraction principle and make possible to define elementary reusable bricks in task models. A large task model can thus be decomposed into several duplications of elementary tasks (called sub-models). These sub-models can then be reused (as a kind of "copy") in various places of the same model and even in other models. Each time one of the attributes of these elementary sub-models is modified, the modification is reflected in all the other "copies" of the same sub-model.

Characteristics
While task notations propose reuse at the class level (an example of such a class being a "motor task type") the sub-model proposes reuse at the instance level. For example, if in a task model, a task "push button" appears many times (because moving the lever can be performed by users for reaching multiple goals, such as to change gears in a car to reduce or to increase velocity) the sub-model construct makes it possible to handle those instances altogether.

Advantages and Limitations

- The gathering of elementary tasks into a set of which all the elements can be manipulated at once. It reduces viscosity as changing one attribute of a task (e.g. name) is automatically reflected to the entire set it belongs to.
- Explicit representation of identical activities. The sub-models allow analysts to represent in an explicit manner the fact that several task models involve exactly the same elementary tasks.
- This mechanism does not provide support for reducing the size of the models.
- This mechanism provides support for reusing recurrent activities previously recorded. In a given domain (e.g. aeronautics) the activities of the operators are usually identified and codified. Sub-models make it easy to explicitly build a library of elementary tasks that can then be quickly reused while building models that correspond to interactions with new devices or systems.

Description in HAMSTERS

Fig. 1 illustrates sub-models in HAMSTERS (Fig. 2 b).depicts the task types available in the HAMSTERS notation). Copy tasks (such as the bottom left one "Push button" is the same sub model as the task with the same name under the disengage abstract

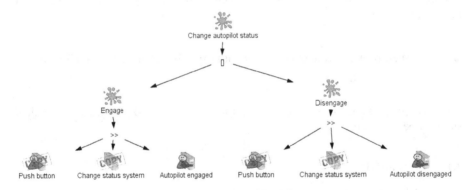

Fig. 1. Sub-models as copy tasks in HAMSTERS

Move the lever - Properties		
Properties		
description	Move the lever	
details		
criticity level	0	
optional	☐	
iterative	☐	
number of iteration	0	
type	INPUT	▼
position	1	
minimum execution time	0	
maximum execution time	0	
Subroutine	SubRoutineModel	
copyTask	☑	
inputports	0	
outputports	0	

Task type	Icons in HAMSTERS notation			
Abstract	Abstract task			
System	System task			
User	User task	Cognitive task	Perceptive task	Motor task
Interactive	Input task	Output task	Input Output task	

a)   b)

Fig. 2. a)Edition of a copy task in HAMSTERS, b)task types in HAMSTERS

task. All the properties of these two leaf tasks are shared and changing the type or name of one is immediately reflected on the other one. In HAMSTERS, "Copy" is an attribute of a task and it can be defined by selecting the checkbox "copy task" as shown in Fig. 2 a).

2.2   Sub-routines

Sub-routines are used to structure task models and to define information passing between task models. This mechanism is similar to procedure calls in programming languages and parameterization of the behavior is possible via input and output parameters.

Characteristics

The sub-routines aim at reusing a sub-tree in a task model. A group of tasks (represented as a tree) might have to be performed in multiple occasions with very little differences which are depending on some values and represented as pre and post conditions. The sub-routine makes it possible to describe recurring behaviors and to describe explicitly the parameters and how they influence the task model behavior.

Advantages and Limitations

- The grouping of a sub-tree of a task model into a sub-routine. It thus makes it possible to reuse the same sub-tree in one or several task models.
- The parameterization of a sub-tree by using parameters (both at input and output level) so that the sub-tree can represent a slightly different behavior. Input parameters are used as preconditions in some of the sub-tasks to describe conditional execution of tasks, while output parameters are used for describing different outcomes when tasks are executed.
- The identification of activities that operators perform in different contexts but are recurrent in their work (or the domain in which they operate). For instance, to report an incident each time it occurs might have a similar structure but it can appear as a sub-goal of another activity (monitoring the system for instance). In such case, incident reporting would not be a full task model but a sub-tree that has to be duplicated in every context where this activity has to be performed.
- This structuring mechanism reduces the models' size but, from the point of view of the HAMSTERS' user, it diminishes the global understanding of the model (the global hierarchical view is split into several models).
- Such structuring mechanism requires skills and knowledge in task engineering, in order to be able to select the sub-tree that should become a sub-routine and to be able to select and describe its parameters.

Description in HAMSTERS

A sub-routine is a group of activities that users perform several times possibly in different contexts which might exhibit different types of information flows. Fig. 3 provides the description of sub-routines. The icons for input and output parameters are filled if values are needed and computed. In the HAMSTERS CASE tool, the sub-routines are stored as task models but are gathered in the project tree under the same grouping called "subroutines" (see Fig. 9 a)). The task models are stored under the grouping called "Roles" because they specify the tasks related to a certain role.

Fig. 3. Representations of sub-routines in HAMSTERS

Fig. **4** describes how sub-routines can be called within a task model. That model describes tasks for a ground segment application that is currently used to monitor and to control the PICARD satellite that was launched in 2010 for solar observation. More details about the system are discussed in [15]. The model of Fig. **4** represents the fact that monitoring and controlling the PICARD system is an iterative task. Satellite monitoring and Failure detection and recovery are sub-routines with no input and output parameters. They can be executed in parallel and the second one is optional.

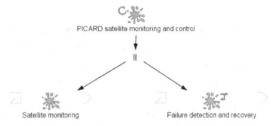

Fig. 4. Description of sub routines within a task model

Fig. **5** describes the content of a subroutine in HAMSTERS. That sub-routine called "IncidentReporting" has an input parameter (incidentLevel) and an output parameter (status). Within the task model the input parameter is used as a precondition (for instance if its value is "low" then the task LightReporting is performed). The output parameter "status" is set to "closed" when task "Register Incident is performed.

Fig. **6** presents the usage of input parameters in the sub-routines. Within the alternative tasks "Voltage failure" and "Signal failure" one can see that failure code must be an input parameter. Depending on its value VOLTAGE_FAILURE or

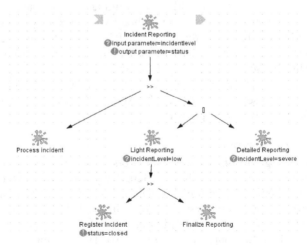

Fig. 5. Parameterization of a sub-routine

SIGNAL_FAILURE the corresponding sub-tree is executed. Both sub-trees have a very similar structure. There might be the chance to specify them with generic specifications. This will be explained within the following sub-section.

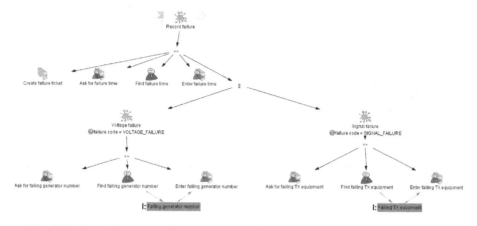

Fig. 6. Task model corresponding to the sub-routine "Record failure" (taken from [15])

Having a look at the graphical specification of the task "Record failure" (Fig. 6) one can see some further features offered by the HAMSTERS notation that have been introduced in [16]. The rectangles with an "I:" at their left describe the information required to perform the tasks that are connected to them. For example, the human task "Find failing generator number" produces the information "Failing generator number" which is then consumed by the interactive input task "Enter failing generator number".

2.3   Generic Components

The third mechanism for reuse is based on the notion of reusable components. The concept of sub-routines provides parameters for tuning the reuse of task models, but does not provide mechanisms for defining generic features of sub-models. Fig. 7 presents a generic task component that provides a general solution for both sub-trees of the tasks "Voltage failure" and "Signal failure" in Fig. **6**.

Characteristics
The goal of using generic components for task models is to allow for reuse of modeling efforts in a more general way than sub-routines.

Advantages and Limitations

- The grouping of a collection of sub-trees of task models into a component. It thus makes it possible to reuse similar sub-trees in one or several task models.
- Identification of repetitive activities within different contexts and context-dependent presentation of the models.
- Adaptation of the components can be performed based on the parameters during design time and during runtime.

- This structuring mechanism reduces the models' size but, from the point of view of the HAMSTERS' user, it diminishes the global understanding of the model (the global hierarchical view is split into several models).
- Such structuring mechanism requires skills and knowledge in task engineering, in order to be able to select the sub-tree that should become a generic component and to be able to select and describe its parameters.

Design time instantiation means that a designer of a new model uses generic components to build a new task model. Generic parameters are substituted and the resulting instances are inserted into the main model.

Description in HAMSTERS

The component of Fig. **7** is generic in such a way that names of sub-tasks and information (notation element tagged with an "I:" and representing information produced and/or required to accomplish a task [16]) are based on the generic parameters.

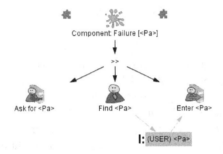

Fig. 7. Generic task component for "Failure"

This parameter can be substituted during design time, when a larger task model is built. It can also be substituted during runtime while executing the different parts of a model. In this case, a generic component instance is instantiated with the values of the generic parameters that are provided interactively.

Assuming that the generic parameter <Pa> gets the value "failing generator number" during design time, the task model of Fig. **8** is the result of building an instance of the task component of Fig. **7**.

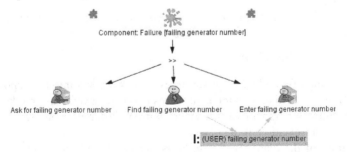

Fig. 8. Instance of component "Failure" with parameter value "failing generator number"

2.4   Patterns and Task Patterns

Patterns have a long history both in the area of software engineering (e.g. [11] for the definition of the Model-View-Controller pattern and [10] for the first collection of patterns). They have been reused from practice in the area of buildings architecture where they were introduced by C. Alexander et al. [2].

The essence of patterns is that they represent reusable solutions to a recurring type of problem. For instance, in the area of buildings, steps organized in groups are a pattern for making it possible for people to go from a level to another one (higher or lower).

This concept has already been applied to task analysis and even task modeling. In such case they are mainly used (as for software engineering) to define a generic solution to a given problem. Paternó et al. in [5] have proposed a pattern called "Multi-values input Task" where a set of iterative tasks are interrupted by a termination task. Such construction deserves the term of patterns as they are supposed to help the person in charge of modeling reuse this solution (a combination of the iterative operator with the interruption one) to describe users' tasks. Other approaches have also been proposed in [8], [9], [19] or [24] in order to provide reusable elements corresponding to solutions to recurring problems. The structuring mechanisms presented in this paper are of a different nature. Indeed, they are introduced for addressing scalability and modifiability of task models. Indeed, we don't present how they help modeling user tasks but instead how they can be used for structuring task models in order to ease their understanding, the modification and their reuse in other contexts. These two approaches (structuring mechanisms and patterns) are even orthogonal. Indeed, one could define design patterns without any structuring concepts (as in [19] for instance) or use structuring mechanisms for tasks models without addressing the aspect of patterns to solve recurring problems (as in [15] for instance). Of course, those two concepts could be integrated but this is beyond the scope of this paper.

3   Process of Identifying Reusable Components

Sub-models and sub-routines can be identified based on knowledge of the application domain. Sub-models are created for modification purposes mainly. This can be considered as grouping on the lexical level. On the contrary sub-routines can be considered as specifications at the level of semantics of the domain. They are used for structuring reoccurring activities with and without parameters related to functions or procedures.

Generic components of models are tools for reuse. They are on a different "direction" of abstraction. They or their instances can be on the one hand side part of sub-models or sub-routines. On the other hand they can contain sub-models and sub-routines.

From our point of view generic components can be considered to be specifications on the syntactic level. It seems to us that they only can be developed based on existing sub-models and sub-routines. This was at least the case in our project and is conform to the definition of design patterns in the object-oriented world.

Sub-models and sub-routines were already available while the task models for sa-tellite observation were designed. In this way those opportunities for reuse already found their way into the models. We did not find further opportunities for those lan-guage elements after reviewing the resulting models.

However, the idea of generic components was not available at the beginning of the project. The identification of reusable generic components was based on carefully stu-dies of the designed models. As a result several generic components were identified. Their instances had to be applicable at least at two different places of the task models.

At the beginning components with only one generic parameter were identified. Their instantiation was thought to be at design time. Later components with more parameters were specified that allowed more complex manipulations of task trees during instantiation.

The extension of the HAMSTERS environment by runtime instantiation of generic components was a result of intensive discussions after different complex components were specified. Short examples extracted from the case study of the controllers' activ-ities performed during the PICARD satellite mission and are presented in this paper.

4   The Three Structuring Mechanisms in the Hamsters Case Tool

This section presents how the structuring mechanisms can be used in the HAMSTERS CASE tool [12].

4.1   Editing

Creating a new component is performed the same way as creating a task model. The difference is that the file containing the description of the generic component belongs to the "Component" folder in the project tree (as illustrated in Fig. 9a)). When building a task model, a generic component can be added by a drag and drop of a "Component Task" from the Palette (Fig. 9b)).

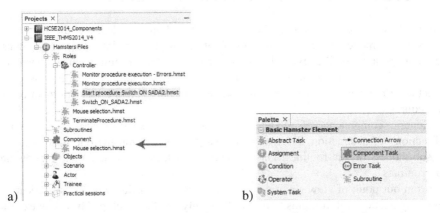

Fig. 9. a) Representation of the generic components directory in the project tree b) Representation of the palette in HAMSTERS

In order to instantiate a new instance of a component, the generic component task has to be selected and a right click has to be performed on this selection (illustrated in Fig. 10). After the pop-up menu displays, the user has to select the "Instantiate Component" item, which opens a dialog (illustrated in Fig. 11).

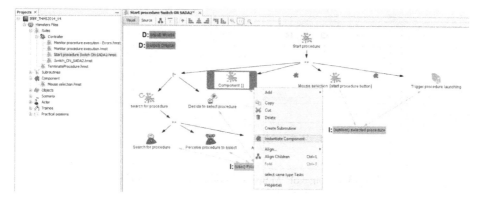

Fig. 10. Instantiation of a generic component

Fig. 11. Selection of the parameters for the instance of the generic component

This dialog window provides support to select the targeted generic component, and to enter the parameters. Once the "Instantiate" button has been pushed, a new instance is created (illustrated in Fig. 13) in the project tree (illustrated in Fig. 12).

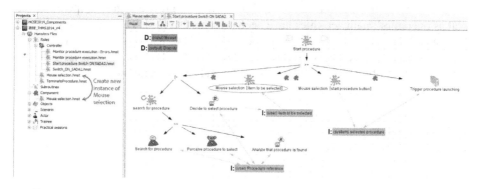

Fig. 12. New instance of the "Mouse selection" generic component in the current project

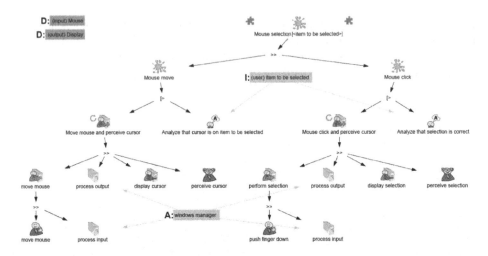

Fig. 13. Instance of "Mouse selection" generic component

4.2   Simulation

The HAMSTERS CASE tool provides support for executing task models. HAMSTERS provides support for editing and simulating task models related to collaborative activities [14]. Task models can be associated to roles and a main task model (corresponding to the highest goal in the hierarchy) has to be defined for each role in the project. The simulator executes all the task models referenced in each role's main task model as well as in its sub-models, sub-routines and generic components in a recursive way. Fig. 14 depicts the execution of a sub-routine and its generic components.

5   Case Study

This section presents a case study from space segments and aims at illustrating the various mechanisms introduced above. The context of ground segment operations as well as operators' main activities have been presented in [15]. This case study is used to compare the benefits of the use of the proposed mechanisms for structuring and reuse over large and complex task models. Fig. 15 presents a Bird's eye view on the task model of the PICARD satellite monitoring and control activities.

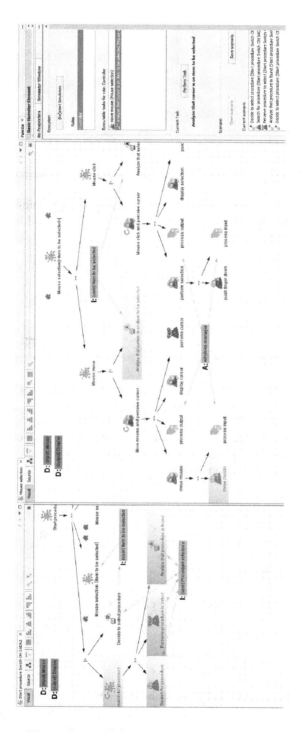

Fig. 14. Simulation of the models in HAMSTERS

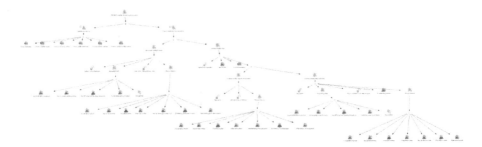

Fig. 15. Bird's eye view on the task model without structuring mechanisms

Assuming that the generic parameter <Pa> gets the value "failing Tx equipment" during design time, the task model of Fig. 16 is the result of building an instance of the task component of Fig. **7**.

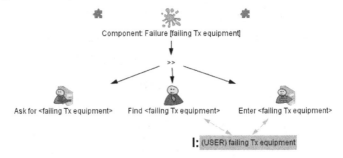

Fig. 16. Instance of component "Failure" with parameter value "failing Tx equipment"

The original model "Record failure" that is presented by Fig. **6** can be reformatted by using the introduced generic component (illustrated in Fig. 17). The generic component is applied and instantiated twice.

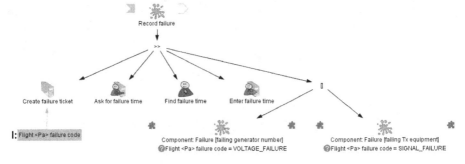

Fig. 17. Sub-routine "Record failure"

Avoiding Mistakes by Applying Components

Additional investigations of specified models within the PICARD project showed further opportunities of using generic components. It also demonstrated that such reusable elements can help to avoid modeling mistakes. Within the following model of sub-routine "Failure detection and recovery" in Fig. 19, another potential generic component was identified. However, slight differences of two sub-trees existed. The two related tasks are "Generator voltage issue" and "Communication failure 2nd try" (in Fig. 15). Indeed, there is a sub-task "Create failure token" that is part of the second task but not of the first one. Nevertheless, it came out that this sub-task was only forgotten to be modeled in the first case and should be added there as well.

By a detailed analysis it was realized that the differences were based on minor modeling mistakes and the identified potential component was applicable twice. In this way the careful studying of the possible application of reusable components helps to identify modeling problems as well. The generic component identified from the model in Fig. 19 is presented in Fig. 18. The rewritten model using the component is presented in Fig. 20.

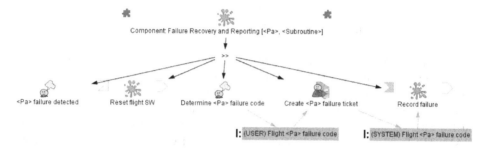

Fig. 18. Generic component "Failure Recovery and Reporting"

An instance of the specified reusable component "Failure Recovery and Reporting" with parameters *voltage* and *Reset flight SW* is presented in Fig. 19.

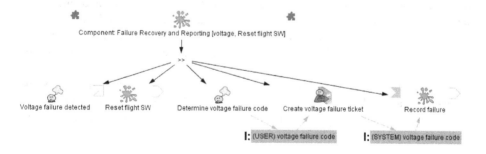

Fig. 19. Instance of component "Failure Recovery and Reporting"

The model presented in Fig. 20 is more compact than the previous version which was not using the generic component structuring mechanism.

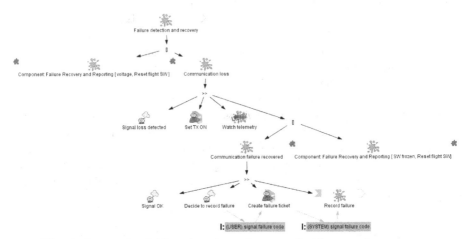

Fig. 20. Sub-routine "Failure detection and recovery" with usage of components

This approach provides support for avoiding the minor modeling mistake of missing out a specific task that is recurrent in the models. This can happen if a modeler has to specify the same type of sub-model several times.

In existing task modeling CASE tools there are no features for reusing models in such a way. We argue for implementing generic components in modeling tools like in HAMSTERS. The provided examples are represented with HAMSTERS. However, the discussed principles can be applied to different notations as well. The presented components are still very simple.

Runtime Instantiation

We already mentioned in section 4 the different options of generic component instantiation during design time and runtime. This is related to the different kinds of execution of decisions during design time or during runtime. In case of instantiating the above generic component during design time the contained decisions can already be executed.

However, a combined strategy could be used as well. For example, in Fig. 18, the parameter <Pa> could be instantiated with the value "voltage" and the parameter instantiation for <subroutine> could be postponed to runtime. In this way the value of the parameter <subroutine> has to be provided interactively during runtime.

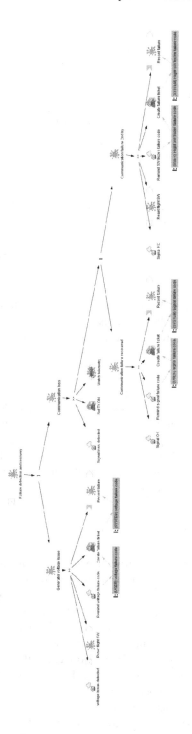

Fig. 21. Sub-routine "Failure detection and recovery"

Benefits and Concerns

This section summarizes quantitative and qualitative assessment of the proposed structuring approach.

Table 1. Quantitative comparison of the approach

Structuring methods	Number of tasks	Number of operators	Reduction percentage
Model without structuring mechanisms	59	13	Reference model for calculus
Sub-models and subroutines	45	13	24% less tasks than in model without structuring mechanisms
Structuring with sub-models, subroutines and components	35	7	41% less tasks and 46% less operators than in model without structuring mechanisms

Quantitative Analysis

Table 1 presents statistics about the size of models in terms of number of tasks and number of operators. It highlights the fact that the number of tasks to be edited highly decreases when using the proposed structuring mechanisms.

Qualitative Analysis

The case study shows that the proposed structuring mechanisms provide support for representing complex set of activities related to large scale systems. The components are reused several times in a set of models related to a project but they also can be inserted to a Palette of components and be reused from one project to other ones (as presented in section 4). However, such structuring mechanisms require skills and knowledge in task engineering in order to take in hand the modeling environment and to use the structuring mechanisms.

6   Related Work

This work is mainly focused on structuring mechanisms at notation level for dealing with complexity in large task models and for supporting reuse of task model elements. Structuring mechanisms should be adapted to the appropriate level of abstraction supported by the notation and its inner construct. For example, most of task model notations such as UAN [6], CTT [21], MAD [22] and AMBOSS [1] provide hierarchical task decomposition, which enforces the abstract/refinement mechanism for dealing with complex models [5]. They also include the operator iterative tasks (symbol T* in CTT) so that repetitive tasks can be drawn once even if they are executed many times in a row. That operator is mainly used for describing the behavioral aspect of the task but additionally makes it possible to significantly reduce the size of a model if such an operator was not available. Therefore, structuring mechanisms require appropriate support at the notation level to be fully support.

An important issue that must be considered when deciding the structure of task models is its potential for reuse [5]. The reuse of software artifacts has been the subject of research for many years in the software community and it has been proved that it might reduce time for development and cost, and increase the quality of software systems. In more recent years structuring mechanisms have been proposed to support the reuse of snippets of models such as use cases [4] and Petri Nets [13].

As far as task models are a concern, some tasks (such as login into systems) remain structurally similar even when reused in different applications. This feature has been introduced in notations like CTT [20] so that some generic tasks can be used as building blocks that can be integrated along the modeling process. Concerned by the reusability of tasks models, Gaffar et al. [9] have investigated structuring mechanisms around the notion of patterns to be used in task models. They propose a method and a tool to model generic task patterns as building blocks that can be instantiated and customized when modeling real-life socio-technical systems. One of the advantages of task patterns with respect to building blocks is the fact they provide more flexibility to adapt the specification to very specific needs. Nonetheless, all these solutions for reusing generic tasks and task patterns are limited to isolated models, lacking of a notational support to describe how such snippets of models are articulated once they are integrated into larger task models.

7   Summary and Outlook

This paper has presented three structuring mechanisms for notations dedicated to task modeling. These mechanisms are sub-models, sub-routines and generic task components. While the first two ones were already described in [16], the third one is new. It was developed while studying the models that were developed in the context of the PICARD case study for possibilities of reuse.

The specified generic task components helped to improve the readability of the models but also to improve their quality. It made it possible to avoid minor modeling mistakes. These mistakes could have been identified with reviewing methods of course as well.

We have shown how generic components can be used and how they can be instantiated during design time and during runtime. Both concepts are helpful for modeling and executing specifications. It is even possible to allow both strategies for one component. Some (not all) parameters can be instantiated during design time and the rest during runtime.

While this paper focuses on the HAMSTERS notation and tool, the presented ideas can be used within other task modeling frameworks.

Sub-models, sub-routines and generic task components structuring mechanisms provide support for managing complex and numerous tasks in all task modeling environments. In the context of safety-critical systems such elements are of primary importance as the resilience of the entire socio-technical system has to be assessed prior to deployment.

References

1. Amboss,   `http://wwwcs.uni-paderborn.de/cs/ag-szwillus/lehre/ws05_06/PG/PGAMBOSS`
2. Alexander, C., Ishikawa, S., Silverstein, M., Jacobson, M., Fiksdahl-King, I., Angel, S.: A pattern language: towns, buildings, construction. Oxford University Press (1977)
3. Barboni, E., Ladry, J.-F., Navarre, D., Palanque, P., Winckler, M.: Beyond modeling: an integrated environment supporting co-execution of tasks and systems models. In: Proc. of the 2nd ACM SIGCHI Symp. on Engineering Interactive Computing Systems (EICS 2010), pp. 165–174 (2010)
4. Bonilla-Morales, B., Crespo, S., Clunie, C.: Reuse of Use Cases Diagrams: An Approach based on Ontologies and Semantic Web Technologies. IJCSI 9(1(2) (January 2012) ISSN (Online): 1694-0814
5. Breedvelt, I., Paterno, F., Sereriins, C.: Reusable structures in task models. In: Harrison, M.D., Torres, J.C. (eds.) DSVIS 1997, pp. 251–265. Springer (1997)
6. Diaper, D., Stanton, N.A. (eds.): The Handbook of Task Analysis for Human-Computer Interaction, 650 p. Lawrence Erlbaum Associates (2004)
7. Dittmar, A.: More precise descriptions of temporal relations within task models. In: Paternó, F. (ed.) DSV-IS 2000. LNCS, vol. 1946, pp. 151–168. Springer, Heidelberg (2001)
8. Forbrig, P.: Interactions in Smart Environments and the Importance of Modelling. Romanian Journal of Human - Computer Interaction 5, 1–12 (2012)
9. Gaffar, A., Sinnig, D., Seffah, A., Forbrig, P.: Modeling patterns for task models. In: Proceedings of the 3rd Annual Conference on Task Models and Diagrams (TAMODIA 2004), pp. 99–104. ACM, New York (2004)
10. Gamma, E., Helm, R., Johnson, R., Vlissides, J.: Design Patterns: Elements of Object-oriented Software. Addison-Wesley (1995)
11. Goldberg, A., Robson, D.: Smalltalk-80: the Language and Its Implementations. Addison Wesley (1983)
12. HAMSTERS, `http://www.irit.fr/ICS/hamsters/`
13. Huber, P., Jensen, K., Shapiro, R.M.: Hierachies in Coloured Petri Nets. In: Rozenberg, G. (ed.) APN 1990. LNCS, vol. 483, pp. 313–341. Springer, Heidelberg (1991)
14. Martinie, C., Barboni, E., Navarre, D., Palanque, P., Fahssi, R., Poupart, E., Cubero-Castan, E.: Multi-Models-Based Engineering of Collaborative Systems: Application to Collision Avoidance Operations for Spacecrafts. In: Proc. EICS, pp. 45–55 (2014)
15. Martinie, C., Palanque, P., Winckler, M.: Structuring and Composition Mechanisms to Address Scalability Issues in Task Models. In: Campos, P., Graham, N., Jorge, J., Nunes, N., Palanque, P., Winckler, M. (eds.) INTERACT 2011, Part III. LNCS, vol. 6948, pp. 589–609. Springer, Heidelberg (2011)
16. Martinie, C., Palanque, P., Ragosta, M., Fahssi, R.: Extending Procedural Task Models by Explicit and Systematic Integration of Objects, Knowledge and Information. In: Proc. ECCE, articleno. 23, pp. 1–10 (2013)
17. Navarre, D., Paternó, F., Santoro, C., Feige, U.: A tool suite for integrating task and system models through scenarios. In: Johnson, C. (ed.) DSV-IS 2001. LNCS, vol. 2220, pp. 88–113. Springer, Heidelberg (2001)
18. Navarre, D., Palanque, P., Ladry, J., Barboni, E.: ICOs: A model-based user interface description technique dedicated to interactive systems addressing usability, reliability and scalability. ACM TOCHI 16(4), 1–56 (2009)

19. Palanque, P., Basnyat, S.: Task Patterns For Taking Into Account In An Efficient and SystematicWay Both Standard And Erroneous User Behaviours. In: IFIP 13.5 Working Conf. HESSD, pp. 109–130. Kluwer Academic Publishers (2004)
20. Paternò, F.: CTTE: An Environment for Analysis and Development of Task Models ofCooperative Applications. ACM CHI 2001 Extended Abstracts (2001)
21. Paternò, F., Mancini, C., Meniconi, S.: ConcurTaskTrees: A Diagrammatic Notation for Specifying Task Models. In: Proc. of Interact 1997, pp. 362–369. Chapman & Hall (1997)
22. Scapin, D.L.: K-MADe. In: COST294-MAUSE 3rd International Workshop, Review, Report and Refine Usability Evaluation Methods (R3 UEMs), Athens (March 5, 2007)
23. Sinnig, D., Wurdel, M., Forbrig, P., Chalin, P., Khendek, F.: Practical Extensions for Task Models. In: Winckler, M., Johnson, H. (eds.) TAMODIA 2007. LNCS, vol. 4849, pp. 42–55. Springer, Heidelberg (2007)
24. Zaki, M., Wurdel, M., Forbrig, P.: Pattern Driven Task Model Refinement. In: International Symposium on Distributed Computing and Artificial Intelligence, DCAI 2011, Salamanca, Spain, April 6-8 (2011)

To Trust or Not to Trust

Six Recommendations for System Feedback in a Dynamic Environment

Alexander G. Mirnig, Sandra Troesterer, Elke Beck, and Manfred Tscheligi

University of Salzburg, Salzburg, Austria
{firstname.lastname}@sbg.ac.at
http://icts.sbg.ac.at

Abstract. In today's rapidly developing Internet, the web sites and services end users see are more and more composed of multiple services, originating from many different providers in a dynamic way. This means that it can be difficult for the user to single out individual web services or service providers and consequently judge them regarding how much they trust them. So the question is how to communicate indicators of trustworthiness and provide adequate security feedback to the user in such a situation. Contemporary literature on trust design and security feedback is mostly focused on static web services and, therefore, only partially applicable to dynamic composite web services. We conducted two consecutive studies (a qualitative and a quantitative one) to answer the questions of how and when security feedback in dynamic web service environments should be provided and how it influences the user's trust in the system. The findings from the studies were then analyzed with regards to Riegelsberger and Sasse's ten principles for trust design [24]. The outcome we present in this paper is an adapted list of trust principles for dynamic systems.

Keywords: trust, automation, dynamic web services, feedback design.

1   Introduction: The User in A Dynamic Environment

As technology advances, the status quo of static web services is increasingly on the verge of being replaced by more dynamic solutions (e.g., Facebook's dynamic targeted advertising based on likes, etc. is probably one of the most well-known examples for this). The additional flexibility and convenience such a dynamic context can provide comes at the price of new privacy and security issues. These have to be tackled before a truly dynamic web can be regarded as a realistic alternative to today' still majorly static web services. A dynamic web platform is a framework for a multitude of web services which are presented to the web service end user, who comes into contact with only a very small part of the whole platform (see Figure 1 – service end users), in a dynamic way. The ANIKETOS project[1], which our research is based on, is one such attempt at providing a

---

[1] ANIKETOS (www.aniketos.eu) is an EU-funded project about ensuring trustworthiness and security in composite web services

S. Sauer et al. (Eds.): HCSE 2014, LNCS 8742, pp. 164–181, 2014.

platform for secure and trustworthy Internet services. The number of services presented to the user depends not only on the user's requirements, but also on whether or not the service is regarded as trustworthy by the platform. This is where the dynamic component comes into play, as the status of a certain web service might change due to an attack, a change of policies, etc. In such a case, the platform can adapt to these changes as they happen and replace the service with a different, more trusted one. Being in a dynamic environment means that service consumers will be interacting with applications based on a multitude of exchangeable service components that can adapt in an instant to changes in service availability, price, and security attributes. The security attributes and how well the system can handle them is ultimately what determines the success of such a system. With static and disconnected web services, a user might lose trust in the one web service they had a bad experience with. But if that one web service is part of a service platform, then the user might not only lose trust in the web service, but in the entire service platform the web service is part of. Thus, one bad apple could quite easily spoil the whole digital fruit basket, making it all the more important to ensure trust in the system at all times.

Currently it is not intended that the service end user is notified about any changes (recompositions) taking place "behind the user interface" by the platform developers, i.e., the replacement of a service component with a similar, but more secure and trustworthy one (see Figure 1 for an illustration of such a dynamic web service recomposition) is intended to occur without the end user ever noticing it. On one hand, this way of shaping what the user perceives has many benefits, e.g., to avoid annoying the users with uninteresting system

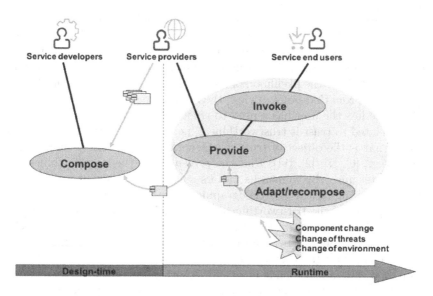

Fig. 1. The user in a dynamic composite web service environment (Image ©Per Håkon Meland)

information. On the other hand, the system remains a black box for the user and it is difficult for them to judge whether or not to trust it (e.g., to provide sensitive personal data). But even with such a system a complete secure internet experience cannot be guaranteed. So how should one deal with dynamic systems and their process (in)transparency for users and how does this affect the user's trust in the system? It needs to be clarified, which *parts* of the black box should be made visible to the user, so that they can make informed decisions whenever necessary, while still benefitting from the added convenience of automatic web service supply.

2   Trustworthy User Feedback Design

System transparency is an important topic in user interface design in general. In Johnston et al.'s [15] proposal of criteria for a positive HCI (Human Computer Interaction) and user experience applied in the area of security, "visibility of system status" is among these criteria. It is understood as "it is important for the user to be able to observe the security status of the internal operations." Studies have shown that system transparency affects how much trust a user puts into a system. For instance, the model for trust in automated systems of Hoff and Bashir [14] stresses the importance of design features for the user's perception of a system's performance, such as ease-of-use, transparency, and appearance. Therefore, designing for trust is an important issue ([26], [25]). Patrick et al. [21] define trust as "a positive expectation regarding the behaviour of someone or something in a situation that entails risk to the trusting party". Specifically for on-line trust, Corritore et al. [6] provide the following definition. Online-trust is "an attitude of confident expectation in an online situation of risk that one's vulnerabilities will not be exploited". Therefore, by this definition, trust is necessary only in situations of vulnerability and risk. Trust can be considered as a process with the goal of risk reduction, which is dynamic and develops over time ([7], [6]). Risk is "the likelihood of an undesirable outcome" (Deutsch, 1958, c.f. [6]), p.751). From that point of view, the higher the user's perception of being in control, the less the user has a need to trust.

Closely related to trust is trustworthiness, i.e., a characteristic of someone or something that is the object of trust [6]. Generally, there exist several hints in literature (e.g., [6], [7], [2], [11]) that the *perception* of the trustworthiness of a website is determined by numerous factors such as e.g., ease of navigation or freedom from grammatical and typographical errors. A further reason for different perceptions of the trustworthiness and security of a website is that there is a variety of different attitudes about privacy among Internet users. Ackerman et al. [1] differentiate between privacy fundamentalists, pragmatists, and marginally concerned Internet users. Further categorizations are provided by Sheehan et al. [27] and Berendt et al. [3]. Another important factor is acceptance, with the Technology Acceptance Model (TAM) [22] being one of the most influential and widely used explanatory models for explaining and measuring user/computer/technology acceptance.

All of these system- and user-related factors finally point towards the central problem of user feedback design, i.e., how to provide users with security-related information in an adequate way. Which *feedback* does the user require in order to be able to reasonably judge whether a certain service or website is trustworthy or not? Existing approaches on risk communication and security alert dialogs are manifold (e.g., [9], [4], [23], [29]). But their success is not undisputed – Raja et al. [23] summarize the situation well by stating that users do not pay attention to risk communications, that they do not read or simply ignore security warning texts, as the users often do not understand the messages, nor the options provided to them for responding to the warning. They are unaware of the risks or have an incorrect mental model of the risks. So a truly successful and widely applicable way to communicate trust-relevant information is still not an easy task with a uniform solution. Maurer et al. [17] have recently shown a very promising attempt at what they call a "semi-blocking" approach to help users identify fraudulent websites. Another interesting approach towards facilitating secure and trustworthy design is the work of Riegelsberger and Sasse [24]. They have put forward a comprehensive set of principles for trustworthy and usable design, that builds on a vast pool of research and puts it into a concise and comprehensible format.

To date, HCI research on system transparency and trust has mostly focused on automated systems (e.g., [14], [31]), recommender systems (e.g., [28]), and e-commerce systems (e.g., [6], [12]). Contemporary research on automation is mostly focused robotics and social computing (e.g., [13], [20]). In the ANIKETOS project, however, we were confronted with a different kind of system, namely a dynamic system of composite web services. A composite web service consists of several sub-services, and any of these services could be exchanged for another one at any time. So while the individual sub-services are more or less static individuals, the composite web service is the complete opposite and may change rapidly in composition in irregular intervals. Services in the ANIKETOS framework are modeled in a goal-oriented language [10] which depicts threats as their own entities. As Patrick et al. [21] state, "Any security system is only as secure as its weakest link. Invariably, because of their social nature (and because of their human nature), the weakest links are often humans." Therefore, it is not enough to design systems that are theoretically secure without taking the end users into account. It needs to be investigated, how end user feedback has to be implemented in such a framework, so that an appropriate level of security can be provided and communicated, while at the same time not inconveniencing the user.

It can be assumed that what is known about (static) trust design or trust design for automation of a different nature (recommender systems, anthropomorphic robots) might not completely hold for composite web services as well. Therefore, we decided to investigate this issue further and expand the status quo on security and trust design, both in general as well as for dynamic web services. Our goal was to expand what is known about trust and trustworthy design in familiar contexts, with the final aim of being able to derive recommendations for trust design in dynamic web systems that are grounded in an actual application Starting from the assumption that automated processes should not be completely invisible to the end user [14], we focused on the following areas in our research:

- Means of feedback provision about automated processes (behind the web interface) of a dynamic system to users
- Conditions under which such user feedback should be provided
- The effect of appropriate user feedback on the user's trust in and acceptance of a web service that is part of a dynamic system

We started with the first two of these and conducted an initial, qualitative interview study to collect information on user's needs and priorities regarding trust and system feedback in a web environment with dynamic composite services. Based on these findings we designed feedback prototypes along with concrete use scenarios for a final quantitative questionnaire study. There, we investigated trust and acceptance in both prototypes. As final step, we contrasted our findings regarding acceptance and trust influence of the feedback solutions in the scenarios with Riegelsberger and Sasse's principles for trust design.

3   Interview Study

In order to find out what information should be presented to the end-user and how it should be presented, we conducted an interview study with 8 participants (4 male, 4 female), aged between 24 and 40 (mean age 30 years). The subjects were recruited at our institution in Austria, out of a pool of about 45 possible subjects and all of them were external to the project. Each subject had a different professional background, to ensure a diversity of viewpoints. They were all frequent Internet users, i.e., seven participants used the Internet several times a day, and one several times a week for private purposes. Only one participant reported that they are always aware whether the website they are visiting is safe when surfing the Internet, and one participant that they do not care at all. All other participants reported that they only took care in specific cases, such as online banking, online shopping, entering contact data, entering credit card information, transmission of private data in general, when no choice is available concerning a specific website, or when information is only available on an insecure website. None of the participants were familiar with dynamic web services or details of the ANIKETOS project.

Each interview lasted between half an hour and an hour, was audio-recorded, conducted individually, and in German. The interview was set up in a way that the interviewee got an oral description of a possible scenario at the beginning of the interview, and the questions were posed in conjunction with this scenario. The participant had to imagine a vacation planning website, consisting of different web services, e.g., weather information, flight booking, hotel booking, and payment services. They were told that the website was controlled by a platform in the background that made sure that the services were trustworthy and secure, and that in case a threat was detected, the service would be substituted by another service that fulfilled the security requirements. This was illustrated with an example concerning credit card payment. Questions posed during the interview focused on how the subjects would want to be informed about such a service substitution, followed by questions about whether they would need that information and why they would need it. For the analysis the interviews were first transcribed. Then the individual statements were paraphrased in English and further summarized for each question.

3.1 Study Results

In the following we present the most relevant the results from the larger preliminary interview study, together with a summary of the overall implications for our further research at the end.

How Should the Information Be Provided? Whereas two participants suggested something like a pop-up window, other participants suggested a less obtrusive way, with the motivation that something like a pop-up window would probably scare them, or that they would think they have done something wrong. The message should not appear as a warning, but could be, e.g., a field at the bottom of the website which nicely explains the issue. One participant suggested to have no message at all, but that the website generally provides a statement in the sense "It is ensured that the most secure service is provided" and in case a change happens, it should be added that a new service is available or has been changed because it is ensured that the safest service is always available. Further information should be not provided directly, "only when one clicks on the message or a part of the message". Also the opportunity to click the window/field away if one is not interested should be given. All interviewees suggested visual feedback, expect for one participant who said they wanted to be informed, e.g., via telephone if there were harmful consequences (high financial damage) for them. The participants preferring a dynamic, situated information provision, e.g., a pop-up window, said that this should be shown to point out the urgency, or that it should show up before logging in, informing that there have been changes of services due to this and that, and whether one agrees to use it.

Which Information Should Be Provided? There was a general agreement among interviewees that information about which service was changed, and why it was changed, is relevant. However, the message should be kept short, and further information could be provided when clicking on a link for further information. Such further information could include a list of web services to choose from, or information about whether a web service was changed very often. Additionally, it was suggested that the message should contain information whether the user has been already affected in some way by the insecurity. One participant, however, mentioned that the feedback should not happen while they were in the middle of doing something, because this would disturb their workflow.

Which Information Do the Users Require in Order to Trust the Platform the Web Service Is Part of? One important issue which was raised in this regard is the reputation and popularity of the platform itself. It has to be made sure, that the platform is a certified platform and is secure and safe against phishing threats. Interviewees mentioned that the platform needs to gather reputation over time, and, therefore, information about which websites use the platform, and how this impacts their security, is relevant. Additionally, having the "big players", e.g., Amazon, or bank websites, visibly use the platform would increase user trust in it (or not, in case these big players themselves are untrustworthy in the user's eyes). Two interviewees also mentioned that the platform should provide a "seal of quality" that should be displayed on a protected website.

Conditions for (not) Notifying Users about Web Service Changes

Kind of web service (security relevance): Services that are related to the provision of personal data (credit card data, log-in data, personal email addresses) were generally seen as very security relevant and in case of an exchange of such services, end users prefer to be notified about the change. For less security relevant web services (e.g., weather information service), users do not seem to want further information about any related changes.

Visibility of changes for users: In case that any changes of web services cause additional changes that are visible for users, then users would like to be informed, because if another service appeared without information, they could get the impression that the website is not alright or has been hacked. Thus, in case of a "something is different" experience, users should be provided with an explanation for the change. In case of a change being unnoticeable to the user, one interviewee explicitly stated to prefer to not be informed about the change.

General trust or distrust in website: The general impression the website conveys to a user (trust or distrust in the website) also seems to affect their need for information about web service changes. If they generally trusted the website, they did not wish to be informed about service exchanges, whereas the opposite was true for websites they did not trust.

Change of data policy, contact person, web service functionality: Being informed about what happens to personal data once provided to the service, e.g., in case, when data are disclosed to 3rd parties, was of general importance to the interviewees. For some users it is also important to know who the contact person is in case something goes wrong during the use of a service. Finally, an exchange of web services may also lead to changed functionality, which affects the use of the service by the user. In such cases, the interviewees preferred to be informed about any changes regarding data policy, contact person, or web service functionality.

Existing negative consequences for users: In case of existing negative consequences for users due to a security flaw, users want to be informed about this flaw and any related security incidents with the web service(s) in question. One interviewee, for instance, mentioned that if there had been a security problem when they used a service, and the problem affected them personally, they wanted to get informed about it and about what they could do, e.g., to carefully check their credit card bills. Participants mentioned that when loosing confidence in one of the web services, this will also have a trust-reducing effect for any related web service within the application.

User contribution to security: Finally, some users are willing to contribute to security and want to be informed of opportunities to do so. One interviewee explained that when they can actively do something to improve the security of a service, e.g., to update their browser, then they want to be informed about these possibilities.

Overall, our primary finding was that, even in a dynamic environment, the users expect to receive feedback in the traditional and established ways. So as the logical next step in our research, we wanted to know whether this preference of traditional feedback still held true when actually put into practice. The interviews showed a clear tendency towards the need for feedback in cases where a change directly affected the user and potentially put them at risk. Risk and its influence on the desire for feedback is not a strictly binary affair [7], we wanted to take closer look at the *extent* to which risk influences the need for feedback. Based on our findings, we decided to examine two cases of risk for our follow-up research: (a) cases in which both the user's personal data and their money are at risk; and (b) cases in which only a user's personal data is at risk. Considering the dynamic environment and its high feedback potential, it was quite surprising to still see so many non-feedback related factors being mentioned. So It seems that appropriate and well-designed feedback might not be enough to ensure trust on its own. Although it can certainly maintain a certain level of trust, that trust likely has to be built up beforehand via other means.

Building on the results of the interview study, we decided to conduct a workshop involving only HCI and usability experts (all external to the project) to create low fidelity feedback design prototypes as examples for how feedback about dynamic web service recompositions might look like in practice. With these we would then prepare a final, quantitative study focused primarily on trust and acceptance. In the workshop, our general approach was to put the designers into the shoes of a particular user type via a persona[5]-like user description, and have them experience a certain scenario of an interaction with dynamically exchanged web services. To achieve this we decided to develop and make use of a user type description, more specifically a description of a privacy pragmatist (which is likely the numerically broadest user group [1]) according to Westin's General Privacy Concern Index [16]. To avoid characterising only a particular subgroup of security pragmatists and to keep the characterisation as broad as possible, we described the user type such that it could not be classified as a purely circumspect/wary [27] or identity concerned/profile averse [3] user respectively. The workshop participants, six in total, were divided into two groups, and each group was given the aforementioned user type description as well as a scenario. Both scenarios (an online payment and a forum post scenario) were designed in a way so that the recomposition component was initially invisible to the user. The outcome of the workshop were two paper prototypes designed to provide adequate feedback for both scenarios. These would then serve as the basis for the follow-up questionnaire study, in which we wanted to investigate, how the users would react to these scenarios and the prototype designs (i.e., whether these feedback solutions were perceived as adequate by them as well).

4   Questionnaire Study

The aim of the questionnaire[2] was to evaluate on a broader basis whether website users wanted feedback regarding service recomposition in scenarios of different risk (personal data vs. payment credentials) whether the provided feedback solutions are helpful in terms of acceptance of and trust in the website. Therefore, participants were given the textual description of the two scenarios in randomized order, followed by questions regarding the general use of the described website, general need for information about the occurring service recomposition, and items regarding acceptance of and overall trust in the website (based on existing questionnaires ([22], [18], [19]) and adapted for our purposes). In addition, participants were provided with an image of the corresponding feedback prototype for one of the scenarios developed in the workshop (see Figure 2 and Figure 3) with textual explanations of each step, before being asked to answer the questions. The scenarios were chosen randomly, so that each participant saw one scenario with the feedback solution, and the other one without in random order.The participants were then asked whether they would like to be informed about the service recomposition in the proposed manner. After that, they answered the 30 adapted trust and acceptance items (e.g., "The website is deceptive.", "I could imagine using this website", "The website is reliable", to name a few). We chose this approach in order to be able to compare acceptance and trust in the website when (1) no feedback about the service recomposition is given to cases in which (2) feedback about the service composition is provided. Our assumption was that providing feedback to the website user should raise the acceptance of and trust in the website, compared to the no-feedback condition. The language of the questionnaire was German.

The contained 38 questions in total, including demographic questions (age, gender, education), which were asked at the beginning. The items had to be answered on a 5-point Likert scale. Answering the questionnaire took about 10-15 minutes, and participants could win one of five Amazon vouchers worth 20 Euro as incentive. The questionnaire was distributed via several channels (student distribution list, Facebook, online portal of the Austrian National Student Union). In total, we received 101 completed questionnaires. The mean age of the

---

[2] Available at http://aniketos.icts.sbg.ac.at/questionnaire.html

participants was 26 years (SD=8.59); the youngest person was 18 and the oldest 65 years old. Female participants comprised 75%, while 25% were male. Some of the results that were gained from the online payment scenario questionnaire were discussed at a workshop at SOUPS 2013[30]. In the following sections we describe the scenarios and prototypes that were created in the design workshop, followed by the questionnaire results for each scenario.

4.1 Scenario 1: Online Payment

Data at risk: payment credentials. A web shop offers its customers the possibility to add several payment options as well as all the necessary information to complete a financial transaction to their customer profile. The user must then choose one as the default payment option and rank the remaining options according to his/her preference. At the time a purchase is made the system will automatically attempt to conclude the transaction via the default payment method. If this fails for any reason, the system will try again with the next in the list and so on, until it is either successful or has exhausted all available payment methods, all without any additional user input. In the case of a successful transaction, the user is not immediately notified of any failed attempts the system might have encountered internally. The reasons for failed payment attempts range from harmless (e.g., temporarily busy server) to severe (e.g., stolen credit card or malware infection). In this particular case, a payment is made and, after payment via the default option fails, successfully concluded via the second option. The prototype for the online payment scenario (see Figure 2) displays multiple animated progress bars (one for each payment method) upon the user confirming their purchase. If one payment method fails, the prototype would halt its respective progress bar, grey it out, and shift focus to the next method's progress bar, until payment succeeded. Once that happened, another window opens that informs the user of the successful transaction as well as any unsuccessful attempts. Each mention of an unsuccessful attempt would contain a link to wherever the user could find out more about the details as to why that particular attempt had been unsuccessful (e.g., to the credit card company's website).

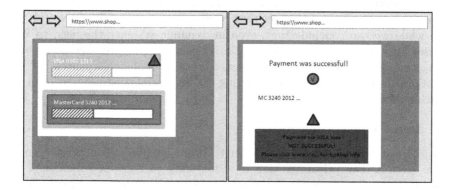

Fig. 2. Online payment scenario prototype excerpt

4.2   Scenario 1 Questionnaire Results

Generally, 14% of participants confirmed that they would use a website with automated payment transposition, whereas 37% indicated that they would rather not use such a website and 48% stated that they would not use it by any means. This high rejection seemed to further suggest that trust in such a system would have to be built in advance, as opposed to more traditional static services. In general, 78% of participants replied that they want to be informed in all cases about the payment transposition, 17% would prefer to be informed, and only 5% did not wish to be informed. This confirms our initial assumption that there is indeed a need for adequate feedback among a significant majority of all participants (i.e., the black box should not remain completely invisible to the user, even in a dynamic system).

Half of the participants were presented the feedback solution as described above and shown in figure 2 (the others did not receive this feedback). These participants were further asked whether they would want to be informed about the payment transposition in the presented way. More than a half of the participants (60%) replied that they wanted to be informed in this way while 40% would prefer another way. Comparing the feedback and the no-feedback condition, we could not find any significant differences regarding the acceptance of the website, independent of whether the participants were happy with the feedback solution ($t(76)=1.569$, n.s.) or not ($t(68)=-.420$, n.s.). For trust, we found different results. Participants who were satisfied with the feedback solution did indeed show significantly higher trust in the website when feedback was provided ($t(77)=2.546$, $p<.05$).

However, 40% would have preferred a different feedback solution. Here we also found no difference regarding trust in the website compared to the no-feedback condition ($t(68)=-.146$, n.s.). To account for that possibility we had included the possibility to comment on which feedback the participants would prefer. Approximately 40% were dissatisfied with the overly passive nature of the feedback solution. They wanted to be able to choose whether the system should try again with the second credit card or cancel the payment as a whole. Another 20% expressed that the red warning box at the end (see Figure 2) had frightened them too much. They had automatically associated it with errors, danger, and money loss – regardless of the fact that payment was eventually successful.

So while we can conclude that, even in dynamic systems, the need to keep the user informed *at all times* takes priority over convenience, the discrepancy between effective feedback and convenience is not to be underestimated and can potentially devastating effects, considering the low initial trust users seem to put in such systems.

4.3   Scenario 2: Forum Post

Data at risk: personal data. An Internet Forum is split into a private and a public section. The private section is visible only to registered members, the public section to everyone. In this particular scenario, a posting is made in the private section, containing personal details such as name, mailing address and phone number. During the time the post is written, but before it is submitted, owing to unfortunate circumstances the private section is switched to be visible to the public as well, so that at the time the user clicks "submit", the message is visible to everyone. The user notices this only a day later upon noticing that all sections of the forum are accessible without having logged in beforehand. We consciously chose a scenario in which the default configuration was sub-optimal in order to elicit when and how the user would want to be informed about and deal with such cases. The prototype from the forum post scenario (see Figure 3) notifies the user of the change in forum visibility directly via private message as well as via a notification in the system and privacy settings menu. Links to both sections are visible all the time (envelope and lightning bolt in the top frame) and superimposed with an exclamation mark whenever an important change occurs. In addition, the prototype featured a real-time warning system that worked similarly to an autocorrect function: It scans the text typed in for strings that look like addresses, telephone numbers, etc., highlights them and gives the user a brief warning that the information will be posted in a public section. In addition, the user also receives a brief recommendation on how to handle potentially sensitive data (e.g., "You might want to send this as a personal message instead."). Upon trying to send the message, the user receives another warning and is prompted to confirm that they want to send the message. They are presented with three options: send the message, delete it, or edit it. The button to edit the message is highlighted by default.

4.4   Scenario 2 Questionnaire Results

After being given the textual description of the scenario, participants were asked whether they would use the described website to post their contact details. Only 18% replied that they would use it, whereas 49% expressed that would rather not use it, and 33% that they would definitely not use it. An overwhelming majority (84%) wanted to be informed by all means if a change in the privacy

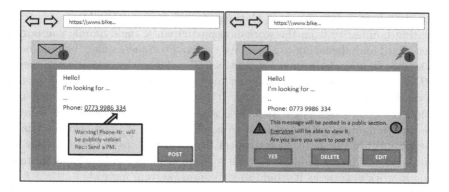

Fig. 3. Forum post scenario prototype excerpt

settings occurred, whereas 11% would rather be informed and only 3% were not interested in being informed at all. Once again, half of the participants were presented the feedback solution as described above and shown in figure 3, while the other half did not. Almost all of the participants (92%) presented with the feedback solution for this scenario, replied that they want to be informed in this way, while only 8% would have preferred another way. Here it was mentioned that some general hints and tips at the end with the possibility to confirm, cancel, or change would be better as it could be "exaggerated and disturbing if a warning appears at every underlined word". As opposed to scenario 1 we could find highly significant differences regarding acceptance $(t(99)=-3.67, p<.001)$ and trust $(t(99)=-9.20, p<.001)$ in the website depending on whether feedback was provided or not. Acceptance $(M=3.31, SD=.60)$ and trust $(M=3.40, SD=.65)$ were higher when feedback was given compared to when no feedback was given (acceptance: $M=2.90, SD=.53$; trust: $M=2.34, SD=.50$). We believe that this is due to the much higher satisfaction with the provided feedback solution as compared to scenario 1.

Summary. Regarding feedback modality, it seems that established ways of providing user feedback work and are understandable as well as acceptable in cases of dynamic web service exchanges. Furthermore, we can confirm that when high or medium risk is involved, the need for adequate and frequent feedback is higher than the desire for convenience, even in a dynamic system. Even so, a solution like the one in scenario 2 (potentially underlining every word was considered to be too much) shows that there is a fine line that separates what is necessary from what is too much.

It should be noted at this point, that when we designed the scenarios, we wanted to simulate a world in which dynamic web service systems were already part of a user's everyday web experience. We did this in order to gain more natural reactions and results that are less influenced by any sense of novelty of dynamic service transposition. So we took interactions we assumed everyone would be mostly familiar with (online payment and forum posting) and included a dynamic component. This also meant that the scenarios were only similar *in principle* to how a dynamic web platform would operate. While we succeeded in eliciting familiarity from the workshop participants, the dynamic component seemed weird and alienating to some. We received comments like "I would never use a service that works in such a strange way." or "But why does it work exactly like *this*? That seems very strange to me". Scenario 2 (forum post) seemed particularly unrealistic in this regard. It could furthermore be assumed that the high rejection rates (14% and 18%, respectively) of the feedback solution in the questionnaire study is at least somewhat due to the scenario description not being entirely adequate. In retrospect, it might have been better to put less emphasis on the user's familiarity with a given scenario and to focus more on making it work exactly as it would in a dynamic system instead.

The feedback solution for scenario 1 had a significantly positive effect on the user's trust in the system as opposed to when no feedback was given, but only when the way feedback was provided was accepted by the user. The same was true for scenario 2, except that we could not find a significant difference for participants who did not accept the feedback solution, due to the low number of participants who were dissatisfied with the feedback from scenario 2. Our finding, that adequate feedback does indeed increase trust in the platform, might not be very surprising on its own. However, automatisation and convenience are two of the main benefits of dynamic systems. So it is interesting to see a clear priority of feedback over convenience even here.

5   Discussion

In the following we discuss and analyze our results from the interview and questionnaire study, contrasting them (if applicable) with the principles for trust design developed by Riegelsberger and Sasse [24]. Our aim is to derive recommendations for security feedback and trust in dynamic websites and to point out, which particularities have to be considered in this specific context.

Trust Assessment: According to Riegelsberger and Sasse [24], a user's assessment of the trustworthiness of a website is always a secondary task to their primary goal, whichever that might be. The whole point of automation in a dynamic web system is to let the users focus on their primary tasks. The interviewee's preferences expressed during the interview studies seemed to emphasize that as soon as a user has to devote more effort to trust assessment than to their initial primary goal, the automated system loses its purpose and advantage over traditional systems. So establishing trust as well as providing adequate security becomes an even more difficult balancing act in the case of dynamic systems, as inadequate trustbuilding strategies and/or feedback solutions might lead to the system losing its main advantage. Hence, it should be kept in mind at all times when designing for a dynamic systems, that *trust assessment is a secondary task of primary importance.*

Risk: A dynamic service platform cannot remain a completely invisible black box once risk for the user is involved, or the user's uncertainty will increase, and their trust in the platform decrease as a consequence [8]. The results from the interview study showed a clear influence of risk on the desire for feedback among users, i.e., while our interviewees wanted to be informed, e.g., when financial risk was involved, they did not care about changes of weather services. The high rejection rates of both scenarios from the questionnaire study further suggest, that the benefits of dynamic services do not counteract the potential risk of personal data or even money loss. Although we also have to point out here, that the participants did not get any further information about the underlying system responsible for the web service recomposition, i.e., information in terms of a trust seal (as wished by some participants in the interview study) or information about its reputation was missing. Hence, we certainly had the worst case scenario here with the website user knowing nothing about the "security guard in the background", i.e., the trustee was "opaque" to the trustor.

Furthermore, a problem lies in the fact that a potential risk for the user might not always perceived as such. It is, therefore, further recommended that *feedback messages should contain information on the type of risk involved, in order to gain the user's understanding and their trust, but only if it is really warranted.* This goes hand in hand with the principle of "Trust requires risk and uncertainty" by Riegelsberger and Sasse.

Reliance: From both the interview and questionnaire studies we found that users have very low initial trust in a dynamic web service platform. This is certainly in part due to the fact that such services are not yet very widespread in today's Internet. Another factor that is likely a great influence here is what we like to call the "opaque trustee" phenomenon, as mentioned above. The interview study showed a desire of users to know who they are interacting with. So the users know of the fact that they are interacting with a multitude of services, but it cannot be expected of them to separately assess every single of these services with regard to its trustworthiness. However, if the user has had successful interactions with the system and its services, then the resulting reliance should take precedence over the unrealistic expectation of having to assess each potential web service's trustworthiness individually. So we suggest to go even further than Riegelsberger and Sasse's original principle "Support reliance, as well as trust", and argue that in dynamic systems, *reliance is fundamental for trust and reliance-fostering measures should be treated as important as (or perhaps even more important than) traditional trust building strategies.*

Feedback Density: Security feedback is a difficult balancing act of giving the user all the information necessary without annoying or frightening them. A high density of warning messages or similarly alarming feedback might easily intimidate a user and scare them off from using a certain web service. Nevertheless, the emphasis the design prototypes put on frequent and dense feedback, together with the relative success these feedback solutions had in the questionnaire study, suggests that in risk-involving cases the emphasis should clearly be put on informing and warning the user, with less regard for potential side effects. In dynamic systems *the user needs to be able to act immediately on any potential security issues.* This is only possible if these issues *are clearly perceived as such* by the user. However, one question remains at this point. Although most participants indicated in the questionnaire study that they wanted to be informed about the service recomposition by all means, further focus should be put on the active perception of such feedback over a longer period of time. As pointed out in section 2, after some time website users might get annoyed by these messages or just click them away without reading them. Furthermore, it still needs to be investigated how frequent web service recompositions, and with it frequent security feedback, would impact the overall trust in the website.

Choice and Control: When using a dynamic platform, the user is already delegating many of their choices to the platform. It is therefore very important that, when any event occurs that is important enough so that the user needs to know about it, the user is able to make a choice. The results of the questionnaire study clearly showed, that the feedback solution for the payment scenario was less preferred than the feedback solution for the posting scenario. In the former scenario, the users complained about not being given a choice (as opposed to the posting scenario) when the feedback was given, even though the scenario had allowed a multitude of choices via a user preference menu. This means that *the user needs to be able to make an active choice right as the feedback happens,* regardless of any other choices made by the user before that time. If the user perceives that they have no control at all even when risk is involved, they will not trust the platform. This goes hand in hand with the previous recommendation regarding the security feedback, in that a user will appreciate feedback that offers them to make a choice over being railroaded. From our findings we can only confirm this for cases in which risk is involved and, as a consequence, recommend this strategy to be applied only in such cases and not overload the user with information in low or no risk cases.

Color Coding: The perception of trust signals also depends on the situation the user is in at the time of interacting with the system. So if there is a multitude of situations a user of the system could potentially be in (e.g., using a payment service vs. reading a news site), then these differences must be accounted for. In our research we found that a high feedback density, with an emphasis of clearly warning the user, was acceptable over a more passive approach in risk-involving cases. However, a large number of participants from the questionnaire study was not satisfied with the feedback provided for the payment scenario. Apart from the problem of no choice mentioned above, many users had expressed dissatisfaction with the color coding, which had mainly adhered to common practices (red to warn the user, green to express everything works normally, etc.). However, when a web service recomposition happens, conflicting information has to be provided to the website user, i.e., that one service is secure and working, while the other is not. We conclude, that *it is better to avoid signal colors that connote danger or peril in cases of feedback in dynamic systems. In such cases, the warning should be communicated via the feedback text and not via its color.*

6   Conclusion and Future Work

We wanted to know how and under which conditions security feedback in dynamic web systems should be given and what its influence on user trust is. After a qualitative study, in which we explored these questions from a user perspective, we refined our findings in a final quantitative study. We matched our findings to the trust design principles laid out by Riegelsberger and Sasse [24] and were able to generate a concise list of recommendations for security feedback design in dynamic systems. This list shall serve as a reference for user-system trust design in HCI. There are still some unanswered issues that need to be investigated in the future. In our investigations, we focused on scenarios involving financial risk and the risk of losing personal data. While these rather medium to high risk cases are certainly the most important ones, we only gathered preliminary insights for low or no risk cases in the interview study and did not examine long-term security feedback effects in the subsequent study. More research with actual high-fidelity prototypes is needed for a more decisive answer on how feedback should be given in such cases. In the workshop for developing the feedback prototypes, we were working with a security pragmatist persona in order to cover the majority of Internet users. Although this is a good starting point, we believe that further research is needed on other (more extreme) user types. A one-for-all approach would be desirable, and we believe that shedding more light on the different particularities of certain user types, would help to refine and adapt security feedback in dynamic systems.

Acknowledgments. This work was funded by the European Union Seventh Framework Programme (FP7/2007-2013) under grant 257930 (ANIKETOS; see http://www.aniketos.eu/).

References

1. Ackerman, M.S., Cranor, L.F., Reagle Jr., J.: Privacy in E-Commerce: Examining User Scenarios and Privacy Preferences. In: Proc. 1st ACM Conf. on Electronic Commerce, pp. 1–8. ACM (1999)
2. Belanche, D., Casaló, L.V., Guinalíu, M.: How to make online public services trustworthy. Electronic Government, an International Journal 9(3), 291–308 (2012)
3. Berendt, B., Günther, O., Spiekermann, S.: Privacy in e-commerce: stated preferences vs. actual behavior. Commun. ACM 48(4), 101–106 (2005)
4. Bravo-Lillo, C., Cranor, L.F., Downs, J., Komanduri, S., Sleeper, M.: Improving computer security dialogs. In: Campos, P., Graham, N., Jorge, J., Nunes, N., Palanque, P., Winckler, M. (eds.) INTERACT 2011, Part IV. LNCS, vol. 6949, pp. 18–35. Springer, Heidelberg (2011)
5. Cooper, A., Reimann, R., Cronin, D.: About Face 3: CoThe Essentials of Interaction Design, pp. 75–108. John Wiley & Sons, Inc., New York (2007)
6. Corritore, C.L., Kracher, B., Wiedenbeck, S.: On-line trust: concepts, evolving themes, a model. Int. Journal of Human-Computer Studies 58(6), 737–758 (2003)
7. Diller, S., Lin, L., Tashjian, V.: The human-computer interaction handbook, pp. 1213–1225. L. Erlbaum Associates Inc., Hillsdale (2003)
8. Dzindolet, M., Peterson, S., Plmranky, R., Pierce, L., Beck, H.: The role of trust in automation reliance. Int J. Hum.-Comput. Stud. 58(6), 697–718 (2003)
9. Egelman, S., Cranor, L.F., Hong, J.: You've been warned: an empirical study of the effectiveness of web browser phishing warnings. In: Proc. SIGCHI Conf. on Human Factors in Computing Systems, CHI 2008, pp. 1065–1074. ACM, New York (2008)
10. Elahi, G., Yu, E.: A Goal Oriented Approach for Modeling and Analyzing Security Trade-Offs. In: Parent, C., Schewe, K.-D., Storey, V.C., Thalheim, B. (eds.) ER 2007. LNCS, vol. 4801, pp. 375–390. Springer, Heidelberg (2007)
11. Flavián, C., Guinalíu, M., Gurrea, R.: The role played by perceived usability, satisfaction and consumer trust on website loyalty. Information & Management 43(1), 1–14 (2006)
12. Friedman, B., Khan Jr., P.H., Howe, D.C.: Trust online. Commun. ACM 43(12), 34–40 (2000)
13. Glass, A., McGuinness, D.L., Wolverton, M.: Toward establishing trust in adaptive agents. In: Proc. 13th Int. Conf. on Intelligent User Interfaces, IUI 2008, pp. 227–236. ACM, New York (2008)

14. Hoff, K., Bashir, M.: A theoretical model for trust in automated systems. In: CHI 2013 Extended Abstracts on Human Factors in Computing Systems, CHI EA 2013, pp. 115–120. ACM, New York (2013)

15. Johnston, J., Eloff, J., Labuschagne, L.: Security and human computer interfaces. Computers & Security 22(8), 675–684 (2003)

16. Kumaraguru, P., Cranor, L.F.: Privacy indexes: A survey of Westin's studies. ISRI Technical Report (2005)

17. Maurer, M.E., De Luca, A., Kempe, S.: Using data type based security alert dialogs to raise online security awareness. In: Proc. SOUPS 2011, pp. 2:1–2:13. ACM, NY (2011)

18. Master, R., Jiang, X., Khasawneh, M.T., Bowling, S.R., Grimes, L., Gramopadhye, A.K., Melloy, B.J.: Measurement of trust over time in hybrid inspection systems: Research articles. Hum. Factor. Ergon. Manuf. 15(2), 177–196 (2005)

19. McKnight, D.H., Carter, M., Thatcher, J.B., Clay, P.F.: Trust in a specific technology: An investigation of its components and measures. ACM Trans. Manage. Inf. Syst. 2(2), 12:1–12:25 (2011)

20. Pak, R., Fink, N., Price, M., Bass, B., Sturre, L.: Decision support aids with anthropomorphic characteristics influence trust and performance in younger and older adults. Ergonomics 55(9), 1059–1072 (2012) PMID: 22799560

21. Patrick, A.S., Briggs, P., Marsh, S.: Designing systems that people will trust. In: Security and Usability. O'Reilly Media, Inc. (2005)

22. Pavlou, P.A.: Consumer acceptance of electronic commerce: Integrating trust and risk with the technology acceptance model. Int. J. Electron. Commerce 7(3), 101–134 (2003)

23. Raja, F., Hawkey, K., Hsu, S., Wang, K.L.C., Beznosov, K.: A brick wall, a locked door, and a bandit: a physical security metaphor for firewall warnings. In: Proc. SOUPS 2011, pp. 1:1–1:20. ACM, NY (2011)

24. Riegelsberger, J., Sasse, M.A.: Ignore these at your peril: Ten principles for trust design. In: 3rd International Conference on Trust and Trustworthy Computing, Trust 2010 (2010)

25. Riegelsberger, J., Sasse, M., McCarthy, J.: The mechanics of trust: A framework for research and design. International Journal of Human-Computer Studies 62(3), 381–422 (2005)

26. Riegelsberger, J., Sasse, M., McCarthy, J.: The researcher's dilemma: evaluating trust in computer-mediated communication. International Journal of Human-Computer Studies 58(6), 759–781 (2003)

27. Sheehan, K.B.: Toward a typology of internet users and online privacy concerns. The Information Society, 21–32 (2002)

28. Sinha, R., Swearingen, K.: The role of transparency in recommender systems. In: CHI 2002 Extended Abstracts on Human Factors in Computing Systems, CHI EA 2002, pp. 830–831. ACM, NY (2002)

29. Stoll, J., Tashman, C.S., Edwards, W.K., Spafford, K.: Sesame: informing user security decisions with system visualization. In: Proc. SIGCHI Conf. on Human Factors in Computing Systems, CHI 2008, pp. 1045–1054. ACM, NY (2008)

30. Raja, F., Hawkey, K., Hsu, S., Wang, K.L.C., Beznosov, K.: No choice, no trust? A Turn for the Worse: Trustbusters for User Interfaces. In: Workshop (SOUPS 2013) (2013), http://cups.cs.cmu.edu/soups/2013/trustbusters2013/No_Choice_no_Trust_Troesterer.pdf

31. Wang, L., Jamieson, G.A., Hollands, J.G.: Trust and reliance on an automated combat identification system. Human Factors: The Journal of the Human Factors and Ergonomics Society 51(3), 281–291 (2009)

Understanding End-User Development
of Context-Dependent Applications in Smartphones

Gabriella Lucci and Fabio Paternò

CNR-ISTI, HIIS Laboratory
Via Moruzzi 1, 56124 Pisa, Italy
{gabriella.lucci,fabio.paterno}@isti.cnr.it

Abstract. We are using our mobile devices in an increasing number of dynamic contexts, thus we need more and more context-dependent applications. However, only end users can know the most appropriate ways their applications should react to contextual events. In order to facilitate end user development of context-dependent applications in smartphones a first generation of mobile environments has been proposed in the market. In this work we analyse three such Android applications in terms of their ability to express the relevant concepts and their usability, also through a user study. We indicate some limitations of the current solutions and provide indications that can support future work for providing more effective results.

Keywords: End-User Development, Context-dependent Applications, Smartphones.

1 Introduction

In recent years we have witnessed the use of computers in an increasing number of dynamic contexts. The number and variety of users of computational devices and tasks are increasing [1]. Users' backgrounds can vary from management, engineering, construction, education, research, health, insurance, sales, administration or other areas. However, such users share a common requirement for software to support their common tasks, which may vary rapidly. With a different range of backgrounds, their software needs are diverse, complex, and require frequent modifications. On the other hand, slow software development cycles and the lack of domain knowledge on the part of software developers are limitations to addressing the requirements of different users. End-user development can help to mitigate this gap.

Lieberman et al. [2] defined End-User Development (EUD) as "a set of methods, techniques, and tools that allow users of software systems, who are acting as non-professional software developers, at some point to create, modify or extend a software artefact". The main EUD approaches have mainly considered the desktop platform and applications that are unable to adapt to the changing context of use. For example, desktop spreadsheets have been the most used EUD tools so far. Often, EUD approaches support users in composing and customizing sets of available basic elements

S. Sauer et al. (Eds.): HCSE 2014, LNCS 8742, pp. 182–198, 2014.

developed by programmers. Such basic elements are represented by and composed through intuitive metaphors, such as the jigsaw in which the basic elements correspond to the pieces to compose, or iconic data flow representations in which the icons correspond to the basic elements. HANDS [3] was an interesting contribution in investigating how to use HCI techniques to design a more usable programming system. It was a desktop environment exploiting an event-based language; the events considered were those related to application objects, while in this study we focus on how to indicate the reaction to events occurring in the context of use.

More recently, some EUD work has considered user mobility but in a limited manner. MIT App Inventor [4] is an EUD tool that allows users to create applications on the desktop to be executed on Android mobile devices, thus it still does not support development directly on the mobile device. MIT App Inventor expresses the application logic through OpenBlocks [5], where programming is performed by combining jigsaw pieces. Domain specific tools have also been developed targeting context-sensitive applications ranging from support for a set of template applications for tourism [6], domain-related content management to support guided tours [7], up to an EUD environment using concepts such as event-based rules and workflow rules [8].

More generally, desktop EUD environments lack the advantages of enabling end-users to create applications opportunistically in mobile scenarios. Recent advances in smartphones have enabled the creation of mobile EUD environments. Contributions for mobile EUD address: easy parameter contextualization for mobile applications, as in Tasker [9] (one of the Android apps considered in the study presented in the following); frameworks to support mobile authoring and execution, as in Puzzle [10]; creation of UIs through sketching or by adding interactive techniques in the touch screen [11].

The evolution of EUD for mobile applications is particularly important because users' mobility and the usage of smaller screens drive the need for context-awareness. However, the research in this field is currently at an early stage. Floch [12] describes the initial design of a city guide that can be tailored by end-users in order to include information from different service providers according to the visitor's position and visiting purpose. Our aim is to reach a better understanding of the requirements that should be satisfied by general end-users development environments that also offer the possibility to specify how the interactive application should behave according to the context of use. A first contribution in this direction has been recently put forward [13] but it has only considered practical trigger-action programming in the smart home by using the IFTTT ("If This Then That") Web environment, which still requires some technical knowledge greater than that of average persons.

More precisely, in the study that we present, we have considered three Android apps, which aim to support even user without programming knowledge to define their context-dependent applications that exploit the smartphones' sensors and capabilities. We have conducted an analysis of the three environments from two viewpoints: expressiveness (to what extent they support the relevant concepts) and usability (for which a user study has been carried out). We conclude with some indications drawn from this study that can inform future work.

2   The Considered EUD Environments for Smartphones

We focused our study on smartphone environments that allow non-professional developers to create context-dependent applications. For this purpose we found three Android Apps: Tasker, Locale[1], and Atooma[2] that provide different solutions. In this section we briefly describe each of them in order to better understand the analysis reported in next sections. It is worth noting that they provide three different solutions for supporting specifications of context-dependent applications according to the event / condition / action model. In general terms, an *event* is something that happens at a given time. Elementary events occurring in the interactive application or in the context of use, or a composition of such events. A *condition* is a specific constraint that should be satisfied, it can refer to something that happened before or some state condition. An *action* is the description of how the interactive application should change in order to perform the requested adaptation. In Section 3 we provide a more detailed analysis of the expressiveness of each environment.

2.1   Tasker

Tasker is derived from the evolution of an application designed to customize the capabilities of Palm OS handhelds available since 2007 and known as APT. The development of Tasker started in 2009, and then was expanded to extend the functionality of APT, and make it compatible with Android devices. At the end of the same year Tasker was awarded third place in the Android Developer Challenge 2. Tasker is available at a cost of 2.99 Euros and currently the number of its downloads is in the range 100000-500000.

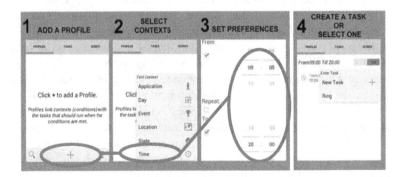

Fig. 1. Example of Tasker User Interface

In Tasker an application is called a profile. In order to develop an application the user can freely choose to start with the definition of either the triggering condition

---

[1] http://www.twofortyfouram.com
[2] https://play.google.com/store/apps/details?id=com.atooma&hl=it

(which is called context) or the actions (grouped in tasks). Unlike other solutions, in Tasker when a context type is selected for specifying a condition, then it is no longer available for another use within the current application (profile). A Tasker profile can contain up to four conditions. In addition, Tasker provides some specific functionalities to better handle the elements. For example, it supports an invert functionality that changes the state of an element (e.g. wifi active with this function becomes wifi deactivated). Figure 1 shows the initial steps in creating a context-dependent application in Tasker. The user starts a profile, and indicates first the type of context (Time in the example) and then specifies the corresponding parameters (in this case from 9:00 to 20:00).

Tasker requires that when users specify a condition then they have to immediately indicate one or more corresponding actions. If an additional condition is to be added, then at the end of the profile creation the condition specified firstly should be selected, followed by the Add button in order to indicate the additional condition.

As shown in Figure 1, at first the Tasks and Scenes tabs are also available. Tasks allows users to identify a set of actions that can be associated to a condition later on, while Scenes allows users to personalize some user interface elements that can be used to trigger a task. Tasker also allows users to specify what should happen when a condition is no longer satisfied. A further feature is the use of variables that allows users to indicate actions for unknown data in advance, for example to visualize in a notification the current state of a connection or to send an SMS when a call is missed.

2.2   Atooma

Atooma stems from the work of a young startup. Its first appearance was in September 2012, when the application became available on the Android Market and can be downloaded free. At the Mobile World Congress in 2013, Atooma won the Mobile Premier Award competition, obtaining first place among more than a thousand concurrent applications. To date, the number of downloads of the app is between 100,000 and 500,000.

Atooma represents the condition/action model using the IF ... DO ... representation through circular representations to indicate the relevant categories and elements. Figure 2 shows how to specify with Atooma whether the battery level is less than 20%. It requires four steps, one to select the category of the condition (mobile), next the type (battery), then the attribute (level), and lastly the corresponding value (less than 20%).

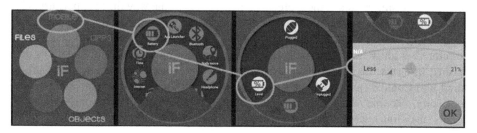

Fig. 2. Example of Atooma User Interface

In Atooma an application can contain up to five conditions (even of the same type) and up to five actions. It is also possible to share the Atooma applications with other users.

2.3   Locale

Unlikely Atooma, Locale is not a free application but can be purchased for 7 euro and 99 cents. Its release took place in 2008, and the number of installations is in the range of 50,000 / 100,000.

The main feature is its extensibility. The application in fact has a limited number of integrated elements but allows users to extend its functionality through the use of more than 400 Plugins downloaded from the Android Market (free or pay-for). The process of creating a Situation is not sequential: the user can arbitrarily decide the selection order of the elements because the interface is designed to show simultaneously (i.e. on the same screen) buttons for adding conditions and actions (in this environment they are called Settings), as shown in Figure 3.

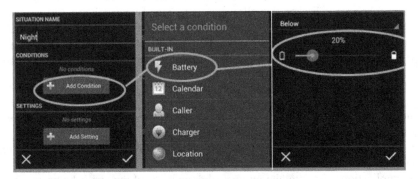

Fig. 3. Example of Locale User Interface

In Locale there is no maximum number of conditions to include in a Situation. It is also possible to specify actions to perform when no condition is satisfied.

2.4   Android Applications: A First Comparison

Even if we have introduced three applications for the same platform (Android Smartphones) with similar goals, there are some differences in the way they support users in achieving them. In general, they use slightly different vocabularies for the same concepts: application, event, action. In Atooma an application is called Atooma and is structured in an IF and a DO part. Locale supports the development of situations described in terms of Conditions and Settings. Tasker is used to create profiles structured into Contexts and associated Actions. In terms of number of events and actions to specify, Atooma limits them to a maximum of five for both; Tasker only limits the events (max four), while Locale does not specify any limit.

In terms of the development process, Atooma is completely sequential: developers have first to indicate the conditions and then the actions. In Locale it is not sequential and developers can freely choose to specify situations and settings in any order. Tasker is semi-sequential in the sense that the starting point can be either the condition or the action, but if a condition is specified then the corresponding actions must be indicated. Atooma and Tasker also support the sharing of the small context-dependent applications created. Tasker also allows the specification of exit tasks, which are actions to perform when the condition associated with the current rule is no longer verified. In addition, Tasker also supports the possibility to specify an execution order among rules that are triggered at the same time.

The support of logical operators in the conditions definition is rather limited: Tasker supports the specification of the NOT operator through the INVERT element (e.g. it is possible to specify conditions such as "the Bluetooth is not connected"), while Locale allows users to indicate OR conditions.

3   Expressiveness

In order to analyse the expressiveness of the environments in terms of their ability to support users to specify the relevant concepts, we have focused on the triggers that they allow users to indicate and the corresponding effects. Indeed, the three environments differ in terms of how they model what can be specified (events and actions). For example, right at the beginning Atooma asks users to select from four main macrocategories, Locale provides a list of conditions with some possible parameters, which can be extended through plugins, while Tasker structures the selectable events and conditions in terms of six Contexts. If we gather the elements that all three environments provide for both parts we can obtain a structure as indicated in Figure 4. Note that what can be specified in terms of conditions is similar to what can be specified in terms of actions, but there are also some differences: conditions can also depend on locations, while actions can also generate alerts.

Figure 4 shows which application supports each element by adding their initials (A for Atooma, L for Locale, and T for Tasker). It is possible to note that the three applications support only partially overlapping sets of elements. Figure 5 indicates how many triggers and actions can be specified through each environment. While Locale supports the two aspects in a balanced manner, Atooma supports more events than actions, and Tasker more action than events.

We can also analyse more in detail what they support with the following diagrams, one for the triggers and one for the actions. Tasker has the greatest expressiveness (more than double Locale's) and a number of actions that can be expressed (108) greater than the triggers (83). These numbers are to be attributed to the abundance of support in almost all categories. Figure 6 and 7 show that Tasker has a number of features always greater than or equal to Atooma and Locale, with the exception of the Applications (triggers and actions) and Connections (triggers) categories.

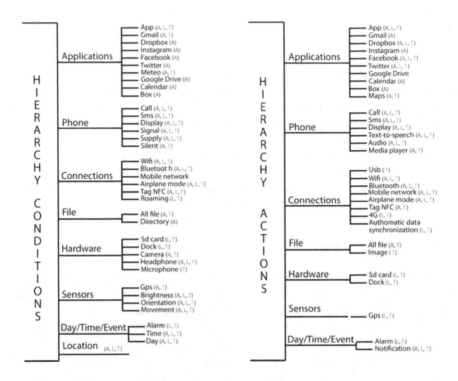

Fig. 4. List of all elements managed by the three environments collectively

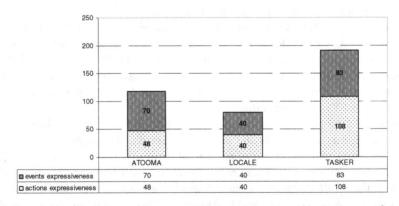

	ATOOMA	LOCALE	TASKER
events expressiveness	70	40	83
actions expressiveness	48	40	108

Fig. 5. Quantitative comparison of the concepts that can be expressed in the three environments

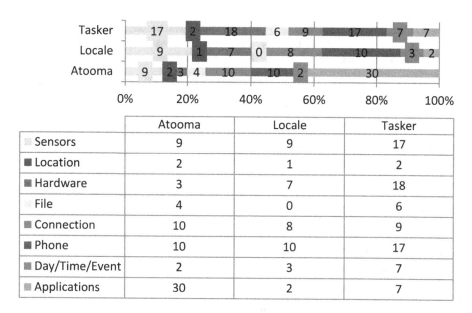

	Atooma	Locale	Tasker
Sensors	9	9	17
■ Location	2	1	2
■ Hardware	3	7	18
File	4	0	6
■ Connection	10	8	9
■ Phone	10	10	17
■ Day/Time/Event	2	3	7
■ Applications	30	2	7

Fig. 6. Comparison of triggers (event / conditions) supported by type

In Atooma the number of expressible conditions (70) is greater than the actions (48). Its expressiveness result is influenced mainly by the large number of features in the Applications category, but also by those of the Connections, Telephone and Sensors categories. The Applications and Telephone categories appear to be the most significant also as regards the functionality of the actions. In general, the ability to directly access the status and information of some of the applications installed on the device (including social networking applications, such as Facebook and Twitter) significantly increases the total value of its expressiveness.

In both triggers and actions, Locale results to have the same number of expressible functionalities (40) and, of the three environments, is the one that has the lowest total expressiveness. On a total of 80 features, 58 are obtained through plugins and this makes it even clearer how few elements are directly integrated into the environment. The presence of plugins, especially numerous in the Phone category, but also in the Sensors and Connections categories, allows the environment to significantly increase its degree of expressiveness, severely limited by the low number of features found in the Applications category and the inability to set conditions that relate to the File category.

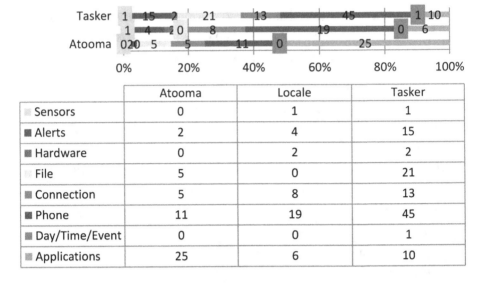

Fig. 7. Comparison of actions supported by type

	Atooma	Locale	Tasker
Sensors	0	1	1
Alerts	2	4	15
Hardware	0	2	2
File	5	0	21
Connection	5	8	13
Phone	11	19	45
Day/Time/Event	0	0	1
Applications	25	6	10

4   Usability

In order to analyse the usability of the three environments we have carried out a user test with 18 users with some familiarity in the use of interactive applications on mobile devices though without any expertise in the field of computer programming. Each participant was asked to perform two tasks of increasing difficulty on all three Android apps. To avoid that users being influenced by the order in which they used the applications, the 18 participants were divided into six groups; each one associated with one possible combination in the order of using the three applications.

Before starting the test, each user filled out an anonymous questionnaire aimed at understanding the level of familiarity with mobile devices and their personal attitudes. As we shall see in the following sections, for each of the environment considered, the test was divided into three consecutive parts: a first training phase, a subsequent phase of tasks execution, carried out by using the think aloud technique and recorded in audiovisual format, and a questionnaire. Once finished, the users' general impressions have been collected in a final questionnaire in which it was required to make judgments on a 1 to 5 scale regarding the three overall applications tested, and provide any comments.

The final stage of the evaluation was carried out by analyzing the quantitative data (number of users who completed the tasks, performance time, etc. ..) and qualitative information (comments, suggestions, etc. ..) contained in records and collected through questionnaires.

The versions of the applications used in the test were: version 1.2.6 for Atooma, version 5.0 for Locale, and   version   4.2 for Tasker.

4.1   Training

Before running the test, a short learning phase was necessary in order to allow the users to understand the purpose of the test and the general functioning of the three Android environments. The learning phase was composed of three steps:

1. Brief verbal explanation of the conditions / actions model implemented by the context sensitive applications.
2. A video tutorial that shows the creation of the following mini-application example:

  - From 8 to 18 hours (condition)
  - If the battery level falls below 20% (event)
  - Show me a notification with a message such as "low battery" (action)

3. Two minutes of free use of the application in question to become familiar with its interface.

4.2   Tasks

Once they finished the learning phase, the users were asked to perform two tasks consecutively using the interfaces just introduced. As mentioned before, the order in which the environments have been proposed to the users depended on the group to which they were assigned in order to balance the learning effect. The two tasks were always accomplished in ascending order of difficulty for each environment. The first was to specify an application composed of one event and one action, the second application included an event, a condition and two actions, in particular they were:

1. When I'm home (condition) -> Activate Bluetooth (action)

2. When I insert earphones (event), if the device is oriented vertically (condition) -> launch the application " Tuneln Radio" - installed in the device   (Action 1) and decrease the brightness of the screen (Action 2).

The users were asked to think aloud during the task performance, and their interactions with the three interfaces were recorded by using the Android app SCR Screen Recorder in order to collect further data (quantitative and qualitative) on which to perform the evaluation. The quantitative data we obtained include:

- the average time to perform the task
- the number of users who performed the task correctly
- the number of users who failed the task
- the number of suggestions offered to complete the tasks.

A person familiar with the environments was always present during the test sessions. Such person also provided suggestions, when requested. The suggestions were divided according to the type of difficulty encountered:

- serious misunderstanding of the trigger / actions model or complete misinterpretation of the application interface (in terms of the correspondence between conditions and actions and their logical structure, and how to obtain it in the environment). Such suggestions were associated with unsuccessful task performance because without them the users would not have been able to complete their tasks.

- medium, they were linked to poor interpretation of items and categories (they needed suggestions related how to understand the contents of the possible contexts and categories).
- negligible, if related to language difficulties (English translation of terms unknown to the user).

4.3   Users

The participants were 18 (8 females),   their age was between 19 and 35 (average was 26). The majority of them (15 out of 18) possessed an Android device and used various kinds of interactive applications more than 5 times per day.

The messaging application WhatsApp was found to be the most utilized; 16 out of 18 users said to use it on a daily basis. Facebook was in second place (12 users), followed by applications for browsing and e-mail, in particular Google browser (12 users) and GMail (8 users). The mobile applications used by the fewest participants were Youtube, Messenger, Instagram, weather applications, geolocalization and navigation applications such as FourSquare and Google Maps.

4.4   Task Performance

Considering both the first and the second task performance (which means a total of 36 tasks for each environment), the applications that yielded the greatest and the lowest number of successful task performance were respectively Atooma (32, or 88.8%), and Tasker (28, i.e. 77.8%). Locale is between these two values (30, 83.3 %).

The suggestions of medium entity, which derived from misunderstandings related to the interface (misinterpretations of the elements, the content of the categories, etc. ..), are significant for our purposes, as they allow us to understand which types of representations were unclear.

One participant who requested the medium suggestion was performing the second task proposed by the Tasker environment and was highly uncertain about the function of Contexts. With Tasker, creating a mini-application starts in fact from the choice of one of the six Contexts offered (Application, Location, Time, Day, State, Event). The difference between the roles of the State and Event contexts made it more difficult for the user to find the condition corresponding to the insertion of the earphones. He was therefore advised to focus on the type of condition to be set, abstracting the meaning and trying to identify which of the two contexts could contain the required functionality. After about a minute the user was able to understand that the element of interest was to be found in the State context, since the coupling of the earphones refers to the state of that particular hardware device.

As mentioned before, all serious misunderstanding suggestions were provided when the user did not understand the mechanism conditions / actions or, to be more precise, in cases where because of this misunderstanding users failed to grasp the overall functioning of the application interface and therefore entered an action in place of a condition or vice versa. Thus, without such help the users were not able to complete the task, so they were associated with task failures.

In some cases, even when the users were able to perform a task successfully, their navigation within the application interface followed incorrect paths, a problem which was then corrected autonomously during the course of the test.

Atooma

There were three unsuccessful performances of the first task with Atooma (one user received support to complete and two did not complete the task correctly). In an attempt to set the condition for localization (when at home), two users selected the GPS element, setting it to ON, rather than using the Location attribute. In the questionnaire the two users commented on the error stating that their device requires activation before you can indicate a GPS location.

As for the second task, the main mistake in navigation was related to the setting of the actions, and concerned finding the Radio application to open upon insertion of the earphones. Almost all the users looked for it within the macrocategory Apps, since the label gave them the idea of being able to access all the applications installed on the phone.

Locale

For the first task there was an error in which the user selected a wrong action (notification instead of Bluetooth). For the second task, five users selected the item Screen Orientation Up, thinking that it was equivalent to the condition "if the device is in a vertical position." The error was to proceed immediately to the Orientation element, in an attempt to set the condition on the vertical position of the device.

Tasker

For the first task three users made the same mistake: they set the Bluetooth Voice attribute (instead of Bluetooth), after having found it in the Settings category (rather than in the NET category). Even users who were able to perform the task had some initial concerns about which was the category in which to find the Bluetooth element, and therefore explored most of the categories relying more on reading the labels of the elements rather than the criteria of the logical categorization.

4.5   Performance Times

In the calculation of the average performance times we have considered only the tasks that were performed successfully.

First Task

With Locale the mean time of the first task execution was about half than Atooma. We can therefore easily infer that, as regards the performance of the first task, Locale was found to be more intuitive and understandable. In Atooma and Tasker the number of task successes and failures is absolutely identical (15 and 3). Comparing the respective average times, however, the average time for the execution of the first task with Tasker (3'50") was almost a minute longer than Atooma (2'52"). The time difference derives essentially from the fact that Tasker has a much higher number of categories and items than Atooma. Users spent more time searching the attributes necessary to complete the task and, in some cases, the abundance of categories meant that they committed errors whose correction increased the execution time of the task. In particular, twelve users were not able to immediately identify the NET category, which included the Bluetooth element, but explored almost all the categories (especially the Phone and Settings categories).

While the minimum time in Atooma (1'27'') and Tasker (1'21'') is similar, the difference between their respective maximum time is around a minute (5'41'' vs 6'44''). Locale shows the most interesting results: it not only has a smaller number of errors and a lower average execution time (1'29'') than the other applications, but also the minimum (0'42'') and maximum (3'24'') times are much lower than those obtained with the other environments. Locale results to have the smallest value (0'42'') also with regard to the standard deviation vs Atooma (1'17') and Tasker (1'34''). This means that the differences between the times taken by participants to successfully perform the first task was not very high and that users were able to complete the task using roughly the same amount of time. In contrast, the standard deviation of Tasker and Atooma are much higher than that of Locale, showing extreme variability in the times achieved by the users.

Second Task

In the second task, the application that required less average execution time was once again Locale (3'35'') followed by Atooma (4'00'') and Tasker (5'14''). The difference between the average time between the latter two even in this case is about one minute. The fact that Locale has obtained the lowest average times in both the first and the second task is due to the greater simplicity of its internal structure. The elements of conditions and actions are grouped into a well-defined, compact set of categories, each one with a few parameters, and this feature makes it easier to search for the relevant element.

Regarding the minimum and maximum times, those of Locale (2'29'' and 5'34'') appear once again to be lower than those of the other applications, but unlike the first task, in this case the difference between the minimum and maximum times of Atooma and Tasker is much wider: Tasker min time (3'15'') is almost a minute higher than Atooma (2'44''), while the maximum time (10'27'') exceeds it by almost five minutes (5'45''). The maximum time obtained with Tasker is a clear indication of how complex is to specify more structured adaptation rules through it, also for the abundance of categories for selecting an element.

The data related to the standard deviation of the times in the second task are in line with those achieved in the first task, but reveal additional information. The fact that the standard deviation of Locale is lower in the first than in the second task (0'53'') suggests that its value increases with the number of conditions and actions to be set. Atooma, on the contrary, obtained a standard deviation lower in the second (1'01'') as compared to the first task and this suggests that, although the number of conditions and actions to be selected was greater, the execution time depended mainly on the user's familiarity with the interface.

The difference between the standard deviation for Atooma and Tasker is greatly increased in the second task. Tasker proves once again to be the application with the most variation in execution times (1'43''), mainly due to the time spent navigating between available contexts and categories.

4.6   Discussion

The analysis of the data collected from the test allows us to obtain useful information on which to base our conclusions on the design of the considered environments, and formulate hypotheses for improvements.

Atooma obtained the highest number of successful performances (88.8 %) and the sum of the average execution times of the two tasks was 6 minutes and 52 seconds. The two main mistakes in the first task involved the setting of the current location because users did not notice the presence of the Position element and they immediately headed to the GPS element. This oversight is mainly due to the users being accustomed to dealing with the localization settings of their Android devices requiring prior activation of the sensor.

Among the most frequent navigation errors there was a tendency to think that the opening of the Radio application could be done through the APPS category, rather than the Mobile. However, exploration of the Atooma interface, which was for many users enjoyable and fun, meant that users were able to correct their errors independently and without too much difficulty.

Here are some of the considerations expressed by the users:

"The logical mechanism is very simple " ;
" The graphics are intuitive and the dial reminds me of the old phones ";
" IF and DO are easy to understand, the display is clear, you are aware of what you are doing " ;
" Once you understand, the mechanism is simple to use and visually intuitive" ;
" There are not too many categories and they are well organized ."

The criticisms to the interface were as follows :

"The dial can be confusing because there are a lot of elements in the Mobile category, the dial hides some of them and it is difficult to understand that the hidden elements are more numerous than expected" ;
and again: *"it is easy to use but the spinning dial hides elements and raises the doubt whether there are further elements in that category ."*
"The only flaw is that the elements with icons are not in alphabetical order";
" The colours of the major categories are too bright and distracting."

Of the 18 users, 50% said they had received a high level of satisfaction from the use of the application; 33.3% an average satisfaction level, and 16.6% a very high level of satisfaction. The icons and bright colours of the application were particularly appreciated.

Locale scored a good overall percentage of successes (83.3%) and to successfully complete the two tasks users employed an overall average of 5 minutes and 4 seconds. There was no need for serious suggestions. This indicates that the application interface appeared so simple to use that users did not need to ask for external aid. Indeed, the error committed by the users who failed the task (we refer to the second proposed task) was to think that Screen Up corresponded to a vertical position. An oversight which, as users explained, was derived from the fact that inside the Orientation category that was the only sensible choice. Locale, as evidenced by its level of expressiveness, has a limited number of features, especially if we consider only those integrated into the application and not provided by the appropriate plugin.

The comments were mostly positive about Locale :

" *There is a clearer distinction between conditions and settings* " ;
" *The button to add conditions and settings is on the same screen, there is the confirmation button and then the items are listed for easy identification* " ;
"*All the elements are in sight because you select from a list* " ;
"*It has an intuitive interface because the structure is simple and it is not possible to get lost* " ;
"*The elements are arranged in a list with colour icons whose level differs greatly*" ;

55.5% of users expressed a high degree of satisfaction; 16.6% an average level and 27.7% a very high level of satisfaction. Locale was positively assessed also for the size and contrast of the icons on the dark background of its interface, which were immediately visible. All 18 users stated that they would recommend it to anyone using the app for its extreme ease of use.

Tasker obtained a total of 77.8% of successful performance, the lowest percentage. The overall mean time to carry out the two tasks was 9 minutes and 4 seconds. There was a need for four main suggestions and three users carried out errors. Such errors were caused by a misinterpretation of the categories. In particular, the three users in question were highly uncertain about which category contained the Bluetooth element.

What created the most problems to the users was the high number of categories, with many elements within them often represented with the same icon; the presence of Contexts (States and Events) with doubtful meaning; and unclear limitations on how to specify sequence of events/conditions and actions. Indeed, in Tasker after indicating one event it was not possible to immediately specify further events but users had then to indicate the corresponding actions and only afterwards could add further events.

The positive comments on the Tasker interface were limited:

" *Not very simple and intuitive, however, it is highly functional and well categorized*";
" *Fairly intuitive .*"

Users provided more negative opinions :

"*The difficulty is not so much the functions but the whole program*" ;
" *Having to put the action immediately after the first condition makes it difficult to use* " ;

"It was difficult because it is not clear that I have first to set a condition and after the actions; if I had a profile already created by another person I would not understand anything " ;
" The graphics are poor and do not facilitate the use of the app " ;
" There are many categories and the elements have the same icon as the parent category " ;

Various users (38.8 %) said they had received an average satisfaction after testing the application; 22.2% , however, expressed a low level of satisfaction. 11.1 % said they were frustrated by the use of the app (level of satisfaction very poor), the same number, on the contrary, said they got a high degree of satisfaction . 16.6%   gave a very high level of satisfaction.

Eight of the respondents (44.4%) also indicated that, because of the complexity of Tasker due to the huge amount of categories and items, they would not recommend the application to a friend. All others indicated that they would recommend it to friends only with a minimum of technological experience.

The last question was about which environment the user would use. 44.4% of users chose Locale, 33.3% of them Atooma and only 22.2%, attracted by the expressive potential of Tasker, chose it even at the expense of ease of use.

5   Conclusions and Future Work

This study has provided useful insights on the main features that an environment for end-user development of context-sensitive applications should have. One first issue is associated with the lack of consistent terminology, each environment provides different names for similar concepts, which does not help users to immediately understand them.

We have seen how the most expressive environment (Tasker) is also the one that was found most difficult to use (highest performance time, error numbers, and unsuccessful performance numbers). This provides some interesting indications of the conflict between expressiveness and usability. Thus, there is a need for novel solutions that are able to support high expressiveness as well as usability. It is clear that with the increasing number of categories for grouping the relevant concepts, there is also an increasing risk of misunderstandings unless familiar classifications, icons and metaphors are proposed to represent and manage such concepts. In addition, it is important to improve the user experience in this type of environment, since too much effort in learning and understanding the relevant concepts discourages its use.

The elements that can characterise a novel solution able to improve the user experience in authoring end user development of context dependent applications include: the choice of elements terms and icons immediately understandable without ambiguity; since there are many possible elements they should be structured according to intuitive logical categories that match the mental representation of mobile users; the ordering in specifying events, conditions, and actions should be flexible without artificial constraints; usability should not be at the expense of expressiveness, thus it should be important to still allow users to easily indicate flexible events, conditions and related actions in which the elements can be composed according to various logical and temporal operators, without any particular limitation on the number of events and actions to compose.

Future work will be dedicated to better understanding how users classify the concepts that characterise context-dependent applications using a card sorting technique, and then to design a new environment for smartphone able to take into account user mental models and support the possibility of specifying context-dependent applications through an expressive language, such as the AAL-DL (Advanced Adaptation Logic Description Language) [14],   in such a way to allow even end-users to exploit it.

References

1. Scaffidi, C., Shaw, M., Myers, B.: Estimating the Numbers of End Users and End User Programmers. In: VL-HCC 2005 - IEEE Symposium on Visual Languages and Human-Centric Computing, Dallas, TX, USA, September 21-24, pp. 207–214 (2005)
2. Lieberman, H., Paternò, F., Klann, M., Wulf, V.: End-user development: An emerging paradigm. In: Lieberman, H., Paternò, F., Wulf, V. (eds.) End-user Development. Human-Computer Interaction Series, pp. 1–8. Springer (2006)
3. Pane, J., Myers, B., Miller, L.: Using HCI techniques to Design a More Usable Programming System. In: Proceedings IEEE HCC 2002, pp. 198–206 (2002)
4. http://appinventor.mit.edu
5. http://education.mit.edu/openblocks
6. Ghiani, G., Paternò, F., Spano, L.D.: Cicero Designer: An Environment for End-User Development of Multi-Device Museum Guides. In: Pipek, V., Rosson, M.B., de Ruyter, B., Wulf, V. (eds.) IS-EUD 2009. LNCS, vol. 5435, pp. 265–274. Springer, Heidelberg (2009)
7. Celentano, A., Maurizio, M.: An End-User Oriented Building Pattern for Interactive Art Guides. In: Costabile, M., Dittrich, Y., Fischer, G., Piccinno, A. (eds.) IS-EUD 2011. LNCS, vol. 6654, pp. 187–202. Springer, Heidelberg (2011)
8. Realinho, V., Romão, T., Dias, A.: An event-driven workflow framework to develop context-aware mobile applications. In: Proceedings of the 11th International Conference on Mobile and Ubiquitous Multimedia (MUM 2012), Article 22 , 10 pages. ACM, New York (2012)
9. http://tasker.dinglisch.net
10. Danado, J., Paternò, F.: Puzzle: A visual-based environment for end user development in touch-based mobile phones. In: Winckler, M., Forbrig, P., Bernhaupt, R. (eds.) HCSE 2012. LNCS, vol. 7623, pp. 199–216. Springer, Heidelberg (2012)
11. Seifert, J., Pfleging, B., Bahamóndez, E., Hermes, M., Rukzio, E., Schmidt, A.: Mobidev: a tool for creating apps on mobile phones. In: Proceedings of the 13th International Conference on Human Computer Interaction with Mobile Devices and Services (MobileHCI 2011), pp. 109–112. ACM, New York (2011)
12. Floch, J.: A Framework for User-Tailored City Exploration. In: Piccinno, A. (ed.) IS-EUD 2011. LNCS, vol. 6654, pp. 239–244. Springer, Heidelberg (2011)
13. Ur, B., McManus, E., Ho, M.P.Y., Littman, M.L.: Practical trigger-action programming in the smart home. In: CHI 2014, pp. 803–812 (2014)
14. Paternò, F., Santoro, C., Spano, D.: SerenoaEU Project, AAL-DL: Semantics. Syntaxes and Stylistics (2013)

Usability Engineering in the Wild:
How Do Practitioners Integrate Usability
Engineering in Software Development?

Nis Bornoe and Jan Stage

Aalborg University
Aalborg, Denmark
{nis,jans}@cs.aau.dk

Abstract. It has been argued that too much research on usability engineering is incoherent with the processes, and settings being the realities for practitioners. In this paper we want to extend the existing knowledge about usability engineering in the wild. Through 12 semi-structured interviews we wanted to get an understanding of how usability is perceived, and practiced in reality. We found that our participants primarily focus on upfront work to support the design, and implementation process. They implement usability engineering through informal evaluations, and by following a set of local de facto standards. We want to extend the existing body of knowledge about usability engineering in practice, to support the development of methods aimed at practitioners.

Keywords: Usability, usability engineering, user experience (UX), software development, agile development, usability practitioners.

1   Introduction

Developers have recognized usability as a crucial factor towards developing usable software [6, 11, 19]. Yet reaching this goal has shown not to be straightforward because usability engineering not is an exact discipline [7, 25], is occurring in interplay with interaction design [3, 11, 28] and software development methods [5, 7, 18, 23, 27] and usability can be difficult to describe in words [7, 10, 11]. Further, the innovation of technology and possibilities of user interaction has dramatically increased, classic post-design evaluation focused and measured upon efficiency and ease of task performance is too limited in today's software development [3]. Recently more qualities have been added to user-centered design. Usability is generally associated with *learnability*, *efficiency*, *memorability*, *errors* and *satisfaction* [22] but notable the introduction of *User experience* (UX) has extended the instrumental values of usability to also include hedonic qualities [2].

   When it comes to conducting usability engineering in practice, it has been argued that too much research on usability engineering is incoherent with the processes, and settings being the realities for practitioners [14, 29]. Method validation and studies are often taking place under controlled settings [12] leaving out the factor, that realities

S. Sauer et al. (Eds.): HCSE 2014, LNCS 8742, pp. 199–216, 2014.
© IFIP International Federation for Information Processing 2014

are very varied, and development processes are taking place under very different constraints [14, 21]. Studies about real settings are mainly surveys and case studies, it's suggested that more research takes place in an industrial setting [6] to understand the working context of usability engineering [10], and focusing research on concepts that can be implemented into a practical setting [15, 24].

Our overall research question is: *"How do practitioners perceive and integrate usability engineering in software development?"*

Through semi-structured interviews with 12 practitioners we have built on existing research by investigating practical usability engineering. In this paper we use *practitioner* as an umbrella term for both usability/UX designers and developers.

In the remaining part of the paper we will: summarize related literature (Section 2), provide an overview of our research method (Section 3), present our findings (Section 4), discuss our findings in relation to the related literature and suggest implications for supporting practitioners (Section 5) and finally make a conclusion (Section 6).

2   Literature Review

In this section we will summarize related literature about: 1) *usability engineering in practice*, 2) *obstacles for deploying practical usability engineering*, 3) *the interplay between usability engineering and agile software development* and 4) *new design complexity and challenges*.

A survey showed that software development organizations find usability to be an important part of software development, yet a gap exists between intentions and realities of conducting usability engineering. The importance of usability evaluation is perceived to be less of usability requirements [6]. A study found practitioners on one side expressing value in user-centered design, yet they found difficulties explicating what good usability was, some saw it as a feeling not easily documentable [7].

Several studies have investigated how usability engineering is conducted in practice. Software development organizations do consider usability an essential requirement, but in reality usability engineering is rarely conducted thoroughly [6]. Usability practitioners rarely follow a systematically approach when conducting evaluations [17, 24], for example, they conduct informal user studies [13, 17], and usability evaluations are analyzed informal [24] and according to lightweight and home-brewed approaches [9]. As a result the quality of usability evaluations is often questionable [20, 21]. Lárusdóttir *et al.* report that informal evaluations mainly are conducted to understand context of use and user requirements, and to support design [17]. Furniss and Blandford found that implicit usability expertise is developed through years of practice. This results in *'pre-done' thinking* that can be reused from project to project. Sometimes this experience was saved and shared throughout the organization. They also report that in general lightweight documentation and communication was appreciated because of a fast-paced setting [10]. Regarding methodology, qualitative approaches are more used than quantitative [17, 21, 28] and time constraints is an influential factor when choosing a method [21].

Significant obstacles for deploying usability evaluations in software development organizations have been found to be resource requirements, recruiting participants [19, 21], missing knowledge and competences, problems with developers neglecting usability perspectives [1, 19], establishing credibility in usability engineering [8, 10, 11], organizational factors [11, 16], for example, often it's not clear who influence the impact of usability [7], and terminology in practical usability is somewhat fuzzy [10, 11]. Documenting user perspectives and usability goals have been found difficult because there are no quality requirements to compare against [7]. Solving identified usability problems is also a challenge [11, 29], for example, it can be complicated to provide design suggestions in complex domains [4, 8]. As development projects are different and include specific constraints and limitations it's not possible to design general methods that apply to all projects [10, 12, 14].

Several studies have investigated the interplay between new development process paradigms based on agile development, and different forms of user-centered design, usability engineering and UX work. The widespread of agility in software development is changing the demands, and dynamics in how usability engineering is conducted [23], as software development takes place in a *fast-paced* environment [9, 27]. Practical problems of effective interplay between design and development has been pointed out by several studies [5, 7, 11, 14, 26, 27]. The challenge is mainly in the difference on how agile approaches, and designing considers, and deals with development projects. Agile approaches are incremental and design needs to keep a holistic view of the entire application [5, 17, 18]. For example, the method *Scrum* is geared towards completing functionality leaving out UX [5] and usability work [7]. A case study showed that conducting usability evaluations in this kind of environment was challenging because only chunks of the design would be completed at a time, making it impossible to evaluate the workflow of a design [27]. Cajander and colleagues found that the limited documentation in agile development, also applied to usability engineering. This made it difficult to document the overall vision of a system and design. Another challenge is measuring quality of usability when no usability quality requirements are stated. As a result all of the above can lead to vague consideration of users, and user involvement [7].

Designing has become more complex, as it's encompassing broader topics on top of making software useable in a specified context of use. Qualities are not only based on task efficiency but also on symbolic and aesthetics [2]. Recent studies indicate that usability, UX, and other design approaches, are used and blended together [16, 26]. Two case studies describe how usability was not considered a standalone discipline. Rather they both considered usability, UX and user-centered design loosely under the same umbrella with no strict lines in between [5, 27]. Designing for complex domains [8] and a wide variety of users in all sorts of contexts, have introduced a set of new challenges. For example, studying in situ is not straightforward since, especially non-work related activities tend to be a lot less defined and happens in many contexts [3].

3   Method

We here describe the: *study design*, *procedure*, *participants*, and *data analysis*.

Study Design: we conducted 12 semi-structured interviews with representatives from 12 different Danish software development organizations. Semi-structured interviews were chosen because this form offers flexibility while still maintaining a structure that makes it possible to systematically compare the interviews, and cover the essential topics. We only recruited participants employed by individual organizations, and did not include participants working as consultants. This was to keep a focus on development within the organization, as part of a team, and not on consulting work. During the initial phase we conducted a pilot study that served several purposes: 1) to test and adjust the interview guide, 2) to better be able to decide which specific profiles would be relevant, and 3) to locate topics of interest. Based on the pilot study changes were made to the interview guide. Two participants did not meet our final selection criteria and have not been included in this study.

Participants: Table 1 provides an overview of our participants. Table 2 provides an overview of the organizations. The participants will be referred to as P(1-12).

Table 1. Overview of the participants. AP means academy professional.

Participant	Role	Education	Industry experience
P1	Designer	M.Sc., IT	12 years
P2	Developer/Designer	Autodidact	16 years
P3	Developer	B.Sc., CS	8 years
P4	Designer	M.Sc., IT	4 years
P5	Developer/Project manager	AP, CS	11 years
P6	Designer/Project manager	Autodidact	8 years
P7	Designer	M.Sc., IT	2 years
P8	Designer	PhD, HCI	3 years
P9	Project manager	M.A, Media	8 years
P10	Chief product officer	PhD, CS	8 years
P11	Chief product officer	M.Sc., Eng.	26 years
P12	Chief product officer	AP, Design	14 years

Table 2. Overview of the organizations. P1-12 corresponds to O1-12.

Org.	Empl.	Primary expertise	Dev. Method
O1	~640	Human resource SW	Informal Scrum.
O2	10	Web-based SW, public, private sector	Informal agile dev.
O3	~60	Web-based SW, public sector	Scrum
O4	4	Web-based SW and apps	Informal agile dev.
O5	10	eCommerce module SW	Informal Scrum
O6	10	One specific web-based mobile solution	Informal Scrum
O7	~120	SW to the healthcare sector	Informal Scrum
O8	~240	SW for mobile devices	Informal Scrum
O9	~50	Web-based eCommerce SW	Informal Scrum
O10	~35	SW to the healthcare sector	Customized Scrum
O11	10	Web-based SW, public sector	Informal Scrum
O12	15	Web-based eCommerce SW	Informal Scrum, Waterfall model

Procedure: all interviews were conducted in Danish and lasted about 40 minutes each. Each interview was divided into two main categories. The first category was related to the type of products being developed and how the development process was organized. The second category was about usability engineering. Here the questions were centered on how usability was defined, and what purpose usability played during the software development phase. Based on recent experiences the participants were asked how usability engineering was conducted in practice. By having the participants talk about recent experiences, we hoped to get concordant stories, and a broader understanding of the development process, that could reveal more about how usability in reality is being conducted and perceived.

Data Analysis: we started out by getting a broad view of the data and locating general and niche topics. This process already started during the data collection, and served, as the foundation for the post data collection analysis. In an iterative process we first went through all interviews, and decided on several labels related to the topics initially found. We then extracted representative quotes from the interviews related to the topics and labels. During an iterative process the authors divided the quotes into groupings. This resulted in a set of groupings that we finally merged resulting in five general categories that reflect the subcategories in section 4. The translation of quotes from Danish to English has resulted in minor changes to the wording and formulation.

4   Conducting Usability Engineering in the Wild

Here we present our findings divided into five different subsections: 4.1) How practitioners understand usability and UX, 4.2) How practitioners set usability objectives, 4.3) How practitioners conduct usability in practice and set local de facto standards, 4.4) How practitioners combine design and development and 4.5) How practitioners report usability problems and act upon these problems.

4.1   Practitioners Understanding of Usability

In the following we present how our participants understood the concept of usability and implemented it into the design process. As recent literature indicates that usability engineering is conducted proactively and closely with other qualities, in particular UX qualities [5, 27], we asked our participants how they would describe usability, about the relation to other design qualities, and how usability engineering was implemented.

Usability is seen as being narrowed down to individual functionality and task completion leaving out a more holistic view.

"For me usability is focusing on the feature without considering the context of use." (P10)

UX was found interesting because it formalizes a set of factors not included in usability, but yet very real when designing.

"It's not just about how easy it is to click a button, it's also about trying to understand the context which the user operates within." (P9)

Usability is not to be replaced by UX. Even that the perceiving and practice of usability engineering has changed over time, usability engineering is still considered important for quality. Rather usability and UX are different and supporting approaches towards the same goal, as a participant noted:

"[Usability and UX] are two sides of the same coin." (P4)

Indicating that usability is reached through a holistic design view, rather than pointing out problems through post design evaluation. We found a clear mutual dependency between usability and UX principles, as the design activities are intervened. P4 noted that that:

"Interaction design facilitates usability." (P4)

From a classic focus on finding usability problems, usability engineering is a mean for reaching and justifying design solutions. Usability factors are to be used proactive just as UX mainly is. A participant explained the following about the role of usability and the interplay with UX:

"For me usability is just one of these areas of competence you must master to create good UX." (P1)

Proactive approaches towards actively considering usability was a main activity. Rather than focusing on the usability of features, the focus is on making design decisions from scratch that are focused on the flow of a process. When talking about interface design a participant explained the general philosophy when designing:

"Give them an interface that reflects the business process." (P4)

Especially during the initial design phase, the principles of UX seem to support designers, as UX is more geared towards a holistic design. In contrast usability engineering is focusing on more narrow design aspects. By itself usability is seen, as a set of principles used when filling out, and detailing a design frame.

"We conduct workshops where we look at traditional usability values, well, it changes during the project, so early in the project we focus a lot on user experience. When we get further along it's more about getting the usability tuned..." (P10)

This participant further elaborated how usability was used for *design tuning*. When the concept is in place, usability engineering is used to make this design solid.

"We start out with a relative low fidelity. It's all about getting the concept in place. Once we have coded the first prototypes, we hope we have been thoroughly enough during the design phase, so the focus can be on optimization, and less on the concept. Of course we can have missed some essential aspects, but this should only happen on rare occasions." (P10)

Practical challenges hold back the process of actual product evaluation, especially when to evaluate, and what to evaluate. As the objectives and needed outcome is quite different during the different stages of development, it's not possible to conduct the same type of evaluations on mockups, and running prototypes. A participant mentioned that his organizations simply isn't ready for this process:

"The basic problem is that we would want users to test in as realistic a system as possible and that is difficult before it's finished. I do not think we have reached a level where it makes sense to have users testing on mockups of screens or drawings." (P3)

Especially the challenge of evaluating, and testing software during development was pointed out, as something highly unplanned. Rather a common approach was based on trial and error. Design and development would be based on what seemed plausible, and based on experience (more about this approach in section 4.3). The outcome would then be tested in some kind of production form.

"We are trying to come up with something that makes sense based on previous experience from the field, and then we try it out in the wild." (P5)

Ambiguous concepts such as usability and UX were found resource demanding, and tough to thoroughly evaluate during the early design phases. What the designers and developers found reasonable, and how they perceive the usability and UX of a product can turn out to be considerable different from what the users perceive in production settings.

"Sometimes it is necessary that we actually release it into production and get some experience. Especially when it comes to the user experience we might very well say: 'hey, the users perceived the usability and user experience different from what we expected and intended with our design. It was not quite the way the users actually used it.'" (P10)

In summary we learned that usability was considered, as part of the overall design strategy, as opposed to a single process task, and used as a vague term often mixed with other concepts. UX was often mentioned, also this concept would be used in a vague manner. By vague we mean that the objectives and purposes were not clear, and the participants did not rely on a theoretical background, besides the classic five usability goals. Rather it was about a *good feeling* when designing. This made it difficult for the participants to explain what usability and UX meant, and how they were implemented into the process. From the interviews we have learned that the usability engineering methods presented in HCI research have little in common with practice. Yet it's clear that practitioners do informal work based on this research.

4.2 Setting a Foundation for Design

In this section we present how our participants explained usability, and prepared a design. Studies report that setting usability goals was found to be a challenge because practitioners, found it difficult to set requirements that can be compared against [7, 14]. We asked our participants about how they collected domain knowledge, prepared a project and set usability goals.

Especially the benefits of usability engineering can be difficult to explain, and document. For example, providing measurements of the value of conducting a series of usability evaluations, or other kinds of usability engineering, is tough to make explicable, and credible as a participant noted:

"...how does one get usability included into business cases so that they are credible higher up in the system?" (P10)

Instead of focusing on explaining the benefits of usability engineering one approach was to use measurements based on the purpose of the software. For example, a participant specializing in optimizing eCommerce software could show results of increased sales with optimized websites.

Another approach was to give a simple tangible explanation of the initial steps taken to reach a solution. This made the process understandable, and provided essential information, used as foundation of the software design:

"I usually explain the steps of the UX process, I go through during a software development project, to make sure that usability is achieved. In the beginning you have business goal clarification: What is it the business wants to achieve with this? What is their purpose? Whom are they developing to? What problem is it they want to solve?" (P8)

User/customer input was not found to be helpful during initial stages as our participants reported that users need something concrete to relate to.

"We are experiencing that our customers find it incredibly difficult to explain what works. They just don't know until they see it, and it makes sense, so we have difficulty using customer input when designing something new. Customer input is actually only useful when we have the first version ready. Then they can relate to it." (P5)

The customers can explain their business flow and overall vision for IT aided tasks, not the form or concept they are looking for. While providing needed input, part of the design challenge is to sort and analyze user input.

"I do not believe the user is necessarily the best designer. I believe design is a profession that is about taking input, and then come up with something that is more brilliant than you could have thought of yourself, and the user can rarely come up with the best solution." (P10)

Dealing with stakeholders can be an obstacle in the process as they might focus on influencing the development through being part of the process and design phase. The challenge is getting the needed input from the stakeholders, while avoiding digging too much into form and concept.

"You meet with the customer and find out what it is they actually want [...] it will probably be a while before you can turn customers, developers, project managers and all stakeholders in fact, to think the opposite or reverse of what they think now. " (P2)

In addition obtaining domain knowledge was a step towards problem domain analysis, as this is the part where it's possible to really get an understanding of challenges, and what to solve.

"...part of designing for usability is to generally understand how people use artifacts [...] Another thing equally important is to have sufficient domain knowledge, so you know what matters, and what doesn't matter for the users in relation to the tasks, they have to solve on a daily basis. It's about investigating where the shoe pinches." (P8)

Domain knowledge was gained through different means such as: phone calls with stakeholders and users, user observations and conversations, learning current IT-systems and processes, and through workshops. This supported several layers in the design process, including information about what problem to solve, the context of use and the users. Domain knowledge makes it easier to exploit user input, as both input sources enlighten from different perspectives. Gaining domain knowledge was a challenge. Firstly, the participants needed access to sources. Practically difficulties such as scheduling with users and discussing the right subjects occurred. Secondly, getting an understanding of a domain can be very time consuming.

Clear measurements for comparing usability goals afterwards was not used, despite some participants seeing this coming in the future:

"We have not actually worked with standard metrics [...] it could well be that we come to a point where we say: 'well it's these metrics', but at the moment we say: 'now we have been through a series of reviews, now we think only trifles are left'. That is what we set as our quality, but we have not systematized at this point." (P10)

Despite having usability goals and using these for setting visions, these visions would not be systematic followed up.

In summary we found that usability not is easily explicable. As a result it's difficult to justify and make creditable. User input and domain knowledge are mutual dependencies. The participants are highly domain knowledge driven when preparing a design. Domain knowledge was useful during initial stages. User input was helpful for adjustments, feedback and visions. The participants would set usability visions, but none used clear goals or measurements.

4.3   Usability Engineering in Practice

Here we present how our participants conducted usability engineering. Studies have pointed out, that implementing theory into practice is challenging due to the constraints, and limitations of practical settings [5, 7, 14, 26, 27]. This leads to informal evaluations [9, 10, 13, 17, 24]. We asked our participants to explain how they conducted usability engineering, if they involved users, and how they aimed at securing usability goals. We focus on two aspects: *informal and ad-hoc evaluations* and *local de facto standards as usability engineering*.

Informal and Ad-Hoc Evaluations

Several studies have pointed out that usability engineering is conducted informal and ad-hoc [6, 9, 13, 17, 24]. This approach is also confirmed by this study. This study also shows, that a trend was to use formative approaches. Summative approaches were rarely used, and when used, they were used as secondary evaluation approaches.

During development the teams need ongoing feedback, especially about specific features. Feedback would be gathered instant, for example, by asking a colleague to try out a feature, or get feedback on a certain design idea. A P2 explained how instant feedback was gained:

"...we have been running around with our cell phones and shown our colleagues the best solution we have found. We give people the cell phone, and a simple task, for example: 'find the menu...'" (P2)

This would generate instant informal feedback that could be acted upon immediately. P2 further explained how the team could setup quickly arranged evaluation sessions:

"...sometimes we conducted an evaluation ourselves. We recruited parents and friends, who really not understood anything, and asked them to find a specific thing, or place on the site. We wrote down some points about how they felt about various things, such as menu structure, search queries, structure of articles and stuff." (P2)

Finding users for evaluations is time consuming, especially finding relevant users. On top of that, evaluation sessions have to be arranged, and appropriate evaluation activities needs to be planned. This informal ad-hoc approach was considered a shortcut that, despite not being ideal, still could help the developers setting a course. P2 considered his own activities during development as part of an ongoing evaluation:

"...I sit and test things. At least the first time, I see how they work on different devices. [...] When I cut things into pieces of HTML and JavaScript, I'm also testing too to see, how things work, and often I make changes to how things work." (P2)

Especially when it comes to small projects this was common. With a strict deadline, a small team and limited usability engineering experience and knowledge, this lightweight made approach made sense because it was very practical, and did not slow down the implementation.

In one case this was taken to the extreme, as the usability goal was simply: if the software tester did not have any complaints, and the users could use the system, the evaluation was successful.

"...if the tester can understand to test the program, and the users can figure out how to use it, then it's good enough. We have never made usability tests similar to what one does in a usability lab..." (P11)

The teams all worked in very practical manners and needed practical explicit feedback they could act upon.

"When we release a feature into the wild, it's based on our own ideas, and understanding. Afterwards we listen to the customers' reaction, and see if they can figure out how to use it." (P5)

In a practical setting this approach was found to be productive. As we will get into later, our participants did not complete formal and detailed analyses of usability factors, and therefor preferred to try out ideas in a trial and error concept.

In summary, when diving into what informal and ad-hoc means, we found that our participants did not follow a clear plan, or organized planed approached. They would need ongoing feedback, especially about specific features and ideas that cheap, easy, and fast could be reported to the developers and implemented.

Local De Facto Standards as Usability Engineering

We found that the individual organizations had built up a body of principles and standards for individual software types. They would use this body more or less for each relevant project. Here local de facto standards were used as a low budget, and easy achievable strategy for reaching usability goals.

Most design and evaluation was conducted somewhat unsystematically, yet the practitioners had made up their own systematic design rules, they would keep on following during development. This type of usability engineering relied on expertise, experience, and gained knowledge about *what works*, by following good practices, and reuse standards. For example, P2 explained how best practices were buildup over time, and used as a set of principles, when designing websites. This included adding certain elements, and placing them in a certain order.

"...unspoken rules regarding how such a website should look like, for example, pressing the logo should bring the user back to the front page. Such de facto standards should not be changed otherwise people get confused. [...] It's like the red button on the TV remote control. You can move things around on the site all you want, but there are some rules that should always be followed. For example, the search box should be up at the top, so it's easy to reach." (P2)

An organization developing web-based software did not explicit work with usability. Usability engineering was implicit in the form of a set of design decisions:

"...we have made some design decisions that permeates an entire system portfolio [...] when you create a new page, it makes no sense, to begin a major usability discussion with yourself, or with each other, because the whole drill is about getting it to look like the other pages." (P11)

As this organization did not conduct usability engineering, the set of design rules was seen as an effective, fast and cheap approach towards usability engineering. This simple formalization was tangible in an organization with low usability expertise.

A participant developing eCommerce solutions explained, that a lot of research has been conducted when it comes to, what converts into a sale. They would base their development on this research, because it made no sense to keep reinventing the wheel. Instead they relied on best practice models. As a secondary activity they experimented with new ideas to keep building a knowledge base about what works.

"We have made an analysis of how a web shop converts the best. Our design is based on a set of best practice models. For example, we know that a certain percentage of users expect the shopping cart to have a certain placement..." (P12)

In summary we found that these local de facto standards were based on accepted principles, and by harvesting the fruit of gained experience. As the companies each had specializations in certain software types, it was easy, fast and useful, to keep following the same principles.

4.4 Reporting and Acting Upon Usability Problems

In this section we present how our participants documented, and dealt with identified usability problems. It has been reported, that it can be complex and difficult finding consensus about, and solving identified usability problems [8, 29]. We asked our participants how they identified, reported, classified, and solved usability problems.

A common approach to judge the severity of a problem, and later finding a solution, was through discussion among colleagues. Who makes the decision can be quite different from organization to organization. Different roles will make the final decision, such as project managers, business development or a salesperson. At other organizations it's up to the developers and designers.

"...during the small tests we sit down and look at what users have written, and if they all agree. For example, if the placement of the search field, or the left menu doesn't make sense, we'll just step in, and change it right away. Perhaps the project manager will send an e-mail to the customer." (P2)

Overall our participants did not engage in systematically classifications, but this participant explained how they systematically would classify problems. What is interesting, is that they have the classification divided into two phases:

"We look into potential consequences of different problems and add different labels to the problems: Is it about speed? Is it about consistency? Is it about outright failure or risk of error? Earlier in the process, we categorize into other labels. Here it's about looking into different needs. For example, is this specific need something we will go for? Is it something significant that will improve the solution? Is it nice to have? Or is it something that we should take into consideration in the future?" (P10)

A participant explained how they changed the form of documentation from usability problem list, to other formats that are stored in the developer backlog:

"...initially [...] we compiled reports with long lists of usability problems. Now we instead write user stories, or bug reports in line with other system requirements. They are added into our back log, and will be prioritized, and dealt with along with all other requirements of the system." (P3)

Problems with no obvious solution were, as a first step, brought up for internal discussion. In addition inspiration was sought both abstract, as a thought process:

"Inspiration comes by letting a whole lot of input run through your mind... (P5),

and more specific by looking into existing technology and solutions:

"I bring examples of the technology: 'Here is an example of technology or code [...] that's how others have solved it. [...] They have done it. This web shop is running like this.' [...] It is easier to communicate when they can relate to something." (P7)

Several developers explained how they often would be stuck in a dilemma, about choosing between imperfect solutions to a problem. Generally *discussion* was the keyword. This was realized in anything from informally discussing with colleagues, or organized by meeting in workshops to discuss, and review suggested solutions.

"...those people assigned to come up with a solution to the problem will present the solution and get some critic. They will then continue with iterations until we believe, we have an acceptable compromise." (P10)

In the end it's about acting, and we found the teams were driven by trial and error.

"Internally we can discuss issues to death, but we're not getting any smarter than we are right now, so it makes more sense getting the feature released as is." (P5)

This requires the teams to make a decision, which often is a compromise, and then come up with a solution, that at least fulfill the feature requirement.

"...now we develop something that works, so at least it doesn't break. We must accept that there are circumstances, under which it doesn't function well." (P9)

In other cases the root of the problem might not relate to the design, but to other factors. For example, the business model, or the customer might want, or expect the users to behave in a certain way. In one example, a customer wanted a system for selling e-tickets for travelling. However, several travel routes that seemed logical from the users perspectives, were not allowed due to the customer's business model, this lead to confusion. Another example is information that could support the user, but due to security or other reasons, wasn't accessible during the user interaction.

"You can not solve this solely through interface design. When the users are stuck, you can only try to help them continuing the process, for example, by providing a more meaningful error message with an explanation." (P8)

In summary we found that reporting of usability problems was done in a wide variety, with the common denominator being lightweight. This happened in the form of simple notes, presentations, workshops and user stories. Instead of documentation, an ongoing communication was the primary force. This fits into the light hierarchies, the fast pace of the projects, and because this approach made it possible to act upon problems, and potential problems during the process. Complex problem solving is done through discussion, and inspiration from how others have solved similar problems. The business or system logic can be a constraint, forcing less desirable solutions.

4.5   The Interplay between Usability Engineering and Software Development

In this section we present how our participants mixed design including usability engineering with the development process. This interplay has been found not to be straightforward [5, 7, 18, 26, 27]. We asked our participants about the interplay between usability engineering, UX design, and agile development, and challenges about implementing a design.

All organizations followed some form of agile approach. This highly impacted the design phase, and the usability engineering. Design and development in practice is very much about taking decisions, and not least settling on compromises. Certain elements of a piece of software have to work. Functions have to be able to do what they are supposed to do, even when they might not do it well.

" *All projects run into challenges because there are certain features that cannot be finished, suddenly it meets reality...*" (P9)

Designing is an ongoing iterative task, and obstacles during the implementation phase is a guarantee. Some examples of problems were: designs that practically could not be implemented as thought by the designer, for example, an input field that wasn't designed to handle the right type of input, an interface not being able to display specific information, users having troubles using the software, and change is legislation forcing the developers to accommodating new laws and regulations.

Here is the iterative nature of agile development not only an advantage to the developers, but also to all involved in the design.

"There are always things along the way you did not consider during the initial stages, and you now have to take these short comings into account as they arise." (P8)

The iterative process makes it possible to quickly implement changes and revisions. P8 furthered elaborated that:

"The strength of the agile process is, that it's possible to quickly respond to changes, and things you learn along the way, and you are not tied to a requirement specification. Therefore, I am engaging in the development process, so I can make on the spot decisions about the things that have not been thought about." (P8)

As has been reported in the past, a key problem is how to include design work with sprints in agile development. This is also a challenge faced by our participants, and is somewhat opposite to the statement above.

"We have had some challenges in getting the interplay between the agile development, and the usability evaluation to run smoothly." (P3)

This is related to keeping the vision/holistic view of the design and the sprints of agile approaches. A problem pointed out when using an agile approach, is that the focus during sprints can become very narrow.

"We have challenges with Scrum [...] by chopping a project into so many little bits, the focus has moved away from what is being developed, such as ensuring the overall usability of the product, towards achieving delivery of the parts committed to in the sprint [...] To some extend Scrum can become focused about deliverables, rather than aiming at developing as perfect a product as possible [...] we had some challenges ensuring that people are dedicated to the feature being developed, even if it is spread over several sprints, while working under the time constraints of a sprint." (P10)

In summary we found that, an agile approach is a double-edged sword. It allows dynamics between the designers and developers, and makes it possible to implement changes, as part of the process, and changes are always needed. On the other side the focus on sprint completion can become the main factor, with the result that the developers lose track of the holistic view of the software. This occurs because projects are divided, or *chopped* into many parts.

5   Discussion

We here discuss four different aspects of the findings.

5.1   The Merging of Interaction Design and Usability Engineering

Interestingly not a single participant mainly included classic post evaluation usability engineering. Usability engineering was always mentioned in association with UX and interaction design. Gulliksen and colleagues note that:

"You can only design your way to usability, hence, the usability professional must design—i.e. generate interaction design solutions in terms of e.g. concepts, structures, contents and navigation." [11]

To our participants interaction design was the leading force, and usability engineering an *add-on* supporting, tuning and justifying the design choices. 11 of the participants were using interaction design as the driving force for the development. One participant did not conduct interaction design, and very limited usability engineering. All were orientated towards problem solving. Here interaction design adds explicit value in the form of designs of functionality that can be implemented. With 'pure' usability engineering a design is needed before it's possible to evaluate, and the outcome of usability engineering towards product development can be limited. A common part of the interaction design process, was evaluating design ideas. This both generated feedback related to the interaction design and usability.

5.2   Perceived Quality of Usability Engineering

Studies have reported that usability engineering is being neglected due to missing perceived quality, and the mindset of developers [1, 11]. We did not find the same skepticism in our study. We believe the organizations have realized that usability engineering is worth including, even that the amount of usability engineering varied a lot. Because of tight deadlines, the practitioners are forced to deliver, as a minimum, something that at least works, even when the solution is not optimal. By combining interaction design and usability engineering, the organizations not only have the hurdle of fixing problems but also proactively receive important input that is helpful during the development process.

A *Good Feeling*: Studies have mentioned that usability is considered a *good feeling* hard to document [7, 11]. We also found that our participants had difficulties explaining what makes usability engineering, and interaction design successful. We looked into what is meant by a *good feeling*. Based in using well-known principles and standards, mixed with relying heavily on experience and routines reflected in the local de facto standards, the participants had built up a body of knowledge to implicit facilitate interaction design. We believe this body, by Furniss and Blandford described as *'pre-done' thinking* [10], is essentially the *good feeling*. Further, several participants gained new knowledge through blogs, forums and by exchanging experiences at different venues. We also see this knowledge exchange, as part of what forms the *good feeling*.

5.3   Design Goals and Quality Measurements

Usability was a requirement in nearly all projects developed by our participants, yet defining the objectives for usability quality is quite a different story. This was found to be highly challenging, and is clearly a main obstacle for more explicit and systematic usability engineering. Our participants mainly conducted bottom up designs. We believe this is a reason why setting clear usability objectives are not done. The exception being that the local de facto standards to some extent can be classified as usability goals.

Informal and Ad Hoc Evaluations: Several studies have reported informal and ad hoc evaluations as frequently used [6, 9, 13, 17, 24]. Our participants often engaged in informal and ad-hoc evaluations. Besides running into the same practical problems as described in the related literature, they also had no clear plan, of what to evaluate, and why to evaluate. Further, the need for ongoing input for development is also a reason why, especially the small teams, would conduct on the spot evaluations. It's too resource demanding and troublesome setting up formal evaluations, when feedback is needed immediately. To deal with the ongoing flow on minor unexpected problems with the interaction design and usability, these informal studies were used to test, and shape functionality in the works.

5.4   Implications for Supporting Practitioners

Furniss and Blandford argues that to provide value the usability component must be flexible enough to fit into a wide variety of practical constraints and limits [10]. Based on both the related literature and the findings presented in this paper we agree. We here point out three specific implications, we find to have potential for supporting practitioners. The common dominators are flexibility, and options for customization.

Scale for Prioritizing Different User Needs: As P10 mentioned in section 4.4, his organization used the following scale when prioritizing different user needs:

"...is this specific need something we will go for? Is it something significant that will improve the solution? Is it nice to have? Or is it something that we should take into consideration in the future?" (P10)

The principles of this scale reminds a lot, of the classic scale used for rating the severity of usability problems in the form: *minor*, *moderate* and *severe*. We support the idea of such straightforward scales. They are easy to understand, learn, and can be used by teams consisting of people, with a wide variety of backgrounds and roles. It could be interesting to further develop this scale, and evaluate it in a production setting. We speculate that such a scale could be used for structuring, and facilitating initial discussions, about which features to include in a prototype. We also speculate, that similar scales could be used to facilitate decision-making during other phases.

Facilitating Workshops: We found that workshops were used during several phases in the projects. This included gathering domain knowledge, presenting designs to customers, evaluating designs, and internally in the organizations to present usability problems, and when discussing potential solutions. A recent study found that workshops are a popular approach [13]. We find that especially workshops were popular because it's a dynamic approach, allowing customizations to many different purposes. We also found that practitioners had problems using workshop sessions optimal. This was especially true when including users, because the practitioners experienced problems both running the right activities, and directing the users towards providing relevant feedback. Here we see potential for better optimizing an already poplar method. For example, Bruun and Stage showed how focused redesign workshops supported developers to *look forward,* and focus on overcoming current system limitations, when solving usability problems [4]. P5 mentioned that:

"Internally we can discuss issues to death, but we're not getting any smarter than we are right now..." (P5)

Based on the practices presented in this study, along with the example above, we see workshop facilitation as a promising approach for supporting practitioners.

Local De Facto Standards as Local Interaction Design Patterns: Juristo and collogues proposed making patterns similar to design patterns known from software development, to support the design and development team [15]. Furniss and Blandford found that designers would develop implicit expertise through years of practice. This results in *'pre-done' thinking* that can be reused. They further point out that it's assumed that the goal of usability is to improve systems rather than identifying usability problems. Therefor it's concluded that effective communication of experience and knowledge, is essential [10]. As we found that local de facto standards are highly used, and seem to support the practitioners, we see potential in systemizing this. This could be methods for documenting, sharing, and communicating these local de facto standards within the organization. Such activities could be an approach towards building up a corpus of local design patterns. Potentially such standards can also support setting usability goals that can be used during evaluation, as there will be something to measure against.

6   Conclusion

Through 12 semi-structured interviews, we investigated our initial research question:

"How do practitioners perceive and integrate usability engineering in software development?"

We found that practical usability engineering is highly driven by local de facto standards, and most work related to usability engineering is informal and lightweight. This includes: setting goals, including users, evaluating, and reporting usability problems. Usability engineering is mixed together with other concepts such as UX and interaction design.

A large majority of the development projects are completed within weeks to a few months. Especially this factor is central, as such fast-paced environments do not leave much time for traditional usability evaluations. The participants need ongoing feedback that can be acted upon during development. They see usability engineering as part of interaction design, and interaction design needs to support developers developing functionality. Especially the local de facto standards were seen as an efficient approach towards creating solid designs fast.

When it comes to using an agile development framework, we found that this was a doubled-edge sword. An agile development environment allows dynamics between the designers and developers, and makes it possible to implement changes, as part of the process. On the other side the focus on sprint completion can become the main factor, with the result that the developers focus less on usability perspectives.

An obstacle listed in the literature review was missing expertise. In this study we found, that an example of this missing expertise is how to effectively use different usability engineering methods. For example, conducting workshops with users could be a challenge. The reason being that it could be difficult running the right activities and getting the needed output from such sessions.

This study was limited to Danish software development organizations. They mainly developed standalone and web-based applications intended for desk and laptops, and they all worked within some type of agile development framework. Therefor these findings do not extend to all organizations and projects.

Based on the findings presented in this paper and together with the related literature we see potential for further investigating, how the implications for supporting practitioners can be further developed, and evaluated in a practical setting.

References

1. Bak, J.O., Nguyen, K., Risgaard, P., Stage, J.: Obstacles to usability evaluation in practice: a survey of software development organizations. In: Proceedings of the 5th Nordic Conference on Human-computer Interaction: Building Bridges, pp. 23–32. ACM, New York (2008)
2. Bargas-Avila, J.A., Hornbæk, K.: Old wine in new bottles or novel challenges: a critical analysis of empirical studies of user experience. In: Proceedings of the SIGCHI Conference on Human Factors in Computing Systems, pp. 2689–2698. ACM, New York (2011)
3. Bødker, S., Sundblad, Y.: Usability and interaction design – new challenges for the Scandinavian tradition. Behav. Inf. Technol. 27(4), 293–300 (2008)
4. Bruun, A., Jensen, J.J., Skov, M.B., Stage, J.: Active Collaborative Learning: Supporting Software Developers in Creating Redesign Proposals. In: Sauer, S., et al. (eds.) HCSE 2014. LNCS, vol. 8742, pp. 1–18. Springer, Heidelberg (2014)
5. Budwig, M., Jeong, S., Kelkar, K.: When user experience met agile: a case study. In: CHI 2009 Extended Abstracts on Human Factors in Computing Systems, pp. 3075–3084. ACM, New York (2009)
6. Bygstad, B., Ghinea, G., Brevik, E.: Software development methods and usability: Perspectives from a survey in the software industry in Norway. Interact. with Comput. 20(3), 375–385 (2008)
7. Cajander, Å., Larusdottir, M., Gulliksen, J.: Existing but Not Explicit - The User Perspective in Scrum Projects in Practice. In: Kotzé, P., Marsden, G., Lindgaard, G., Wesson, J., Winckler, M. (eds.) INTERACT 2013, Part III. LNCS, vol. 8119, pp. 762–779. Springer, Heidelberg (2013)
8. Chilana, P.K., Wobbrock, J.O., Ko, A.J.: Understanding Usability Practices in Complex Domains. In: Proceedings of the SIGCHI Conference on Human Factors in Computing Systems, pp. 2337–2346. ACM, New York (2010)
9. Følstad, A., Law, E., Hornbæk, K.: Analysis in practical usability evaluation: a survey study. In: Proceedings of the 2012 ACM Annual Conference on Human Factors in Computing Systems, pp. 2127–2136. ACM, New York (2012)

10. Furniss, D., Blandford, A., Curzon, P.: Usability Work in Professional Website Design: Insights from Practitioners' Perspectives. In: Law, E.-C., Hvannberg, E., Cockton, G. (eds.) Maturing Usability SE- 7, pp. 144–167. Springer London (2008)
11. Gulliksen, J., Boivie, I., Göransson, B.: Usability professionals—current practices and future development. Interact. with Comput. 18(4), 568–600 (2006)
12. Hornbæk, K.: Dogmas in the assessment of usability evaluation methods. Behav. Inf. Technol. 29(1), 97–111 (2010)
13. Jia, Y., Larusdottir, M., Cajander, Å.: The Usage of Usability Techniques in Scrum Projects. In: Winckler, M., Forbrig, P., Bernhaupt, R. (eds.) HCSE 2012. LNCS, vol. 7623, pp. 331–341. Springer, Heidelberg (2012)
14. Jokela, T., Koivumaa, J., Pirkola, J., Salminen, P., Kantola, N.: Methods for Quantitative Usability Requirements: A Case Study on the Development of the User Interface of a Mobile Phone. Pers. Ubiquitous Comput. 10(6), 345–355 (2006)
15. Juristo, N., Moreno, A.M., Sanchez-Segura, M.-I.: Analysing the impact of usability on software design. J. Syst. Softw. 80(9), 1506–1516 (2007)
16. Kuusinen, K., Mikkonen, T., Pakarinen, S.: Agile user experience development in a large software organization: Good expertise but limited impact. In: Winckler, M., Forbrig, P., Bernhaupt, R. (eds.) HCSE 2012. LNCS, vol. 7623, pp. 94–111. Springer, Heidelberg (2012)
17. Lárusdóttir, M., Cajander, Å., Gulliksen, J.: Informal feedback rather than performance measurements – user-centred evaluation in Scrum projects. Behav. Inf. Technol. (2013)
18. Lee, J.C., Scott McCrickard, D.: Towards Extreme(ly) Usable Software: Exploring Tensions Between Usability and Agile Software Development. In: Agile Conference (AGILE) 2007, pp. 59–71 (2007)
19. Lizano, F., Sandoval, M.M., Bruun, A., Stage, J.: Is Usability Evaluation Important: The Perspective of Novice Software Developers. In: The 27th International BCS Human Computer Interaction Conference (HCI 2013) (2013)
20. Molich, R.: The Quest for Quality: Usability Testing Assessment. In: Proceedings of the 11th Danish Human-Computer Interaction Research Symposium, pp. 56–59 (2011)
21. Monahan, K., Lahteenmaki, M., McDonald, S., Cockton, G.: An Investigation into the Use of Field Methods in the Design and Evaluation of Interactive Systems. In: Proceedings of the 22Nd British HCI Group Annual Conference on People and Computers: Culture, Creativity, Interaction, vol. 1, pp. 99–108. British Computer Society, Swinton (2008)
22. Nielsen, J.: Usability engineering. Morgan Kaufmann (1993)
23. Nielsen, L., Madsen, S.: The Usability Expert's Fear of Agility: An Empirical Study of Global Trends and Emerging Practices. In: Proceedings of the 7th Nordic Conference on Human-Computer Interaction: Making Sense Through Design, pp. 261–264. ACM, New York (2012)
24. Nørgaard, M., Hornbæk, K.: What do usability evaluators do in practice?: an explorative study of think-aloud testing. In: Proceedings of the 6th Conference on Designing Interactive Systems, pp. 209–218. ACM, New York (2006)
25. Seffah, A., Metzker, E.: The obstacles and myths of usability and software engineering. Commun. ACM 47(12), 71–76 (2004)
26. Da Silva, T., Martin, A., Maurer, F., Silveira, M.: User-Centered Design and Agile Methods: A Systematic Review. In: Agile Conference (AGILE), pp. 77–86 (2011)
27. Sy, D.: Adapting usability investigations for agile user-centered design. J. usability Stud. 2(3), 112–132 (2007)
28. Venturi, G., Troost, J., Jokela, T.: People, Organizations, and Processes: An Inquiry into the Adoption of User-Centered Design in Industry. Int. J. Hum. Comput. Interact. 21(2), 219–238 (2006)
29. Wixon, D.: Evaluating Usability Methods: Why the Current Literature Fails the Practitioner. Interactions 10(4), 28–34 (2003)

Usage-Based Automatic Detection of Usability Smells

Patrick Harms and Jens Grabowski

Institute of Computer Science, University of Göttingen,
Göttingen, Germany
{harms,grabowski}@cs.uni-goettingen.de
http://swe.informatik.uni-goettingen.de

Abstract. With an increasing number of supported devices, usability evaluation of websites becomes a laborious task. Therefore, usability evaluation should be automated as far as possible. In this paper, we present a summative method for automated usability evaluation of websites. The approach records user actions and transforms them into task trees. The task trees are then checked for usability smells to identify potential usability issues. The approach was applied in two case studies and shows promising results in the identification of four types of usability smells.

Keywords: task trees, usage-based, automatic usability evaluation.

1 Introduction

Usability engineering is important to develop high quality websites [1]. But a fully-fledged application of traditional usability evaluation methods like user-oriented usability tests applied for several devices for displaying websites requires a high effort [2]. Therefore, in the recent years usability evaluation strives for automation and, hence, cost reduction.

In this paper, we present a new method for automated detection of indicators for usability issues, so called usability smells, based on recorded user actions on websites. The user actions are first transformed into task trees using a methodology proposed by us in [3]. Then, we scan the task trees for patterns of usability smells. As a result, our approach generates a list of detected usability smells. For each smell, it provides details about the user tasks and actions that are related to the smell, as well as the elements of the websites (e.g., links and buttons) that are involved. Our method detects four different types of usability smells. We show in this paper, how the smells are detected and clarify if our approach can be used to automatically detect usability issues.

The paper is structured as follows. First, we introduce the terminology and basic concepts used throughout the paper in Section 2. Then, we describe the detection of usability smells using the generated task trees in Section 3. Afterwards, we depict the validation of our approach in two case studies in Section 4 and discuss the respective results in Section 5. Finally, we compare our approach with related work in Section 6 and conclude on our findings with potential for future work in Section 7.

S. Sauer et al. (Eds.): HCSE 2014, LNCS 8742, pp. 217–234, 2014.

2   Background

Usability is the result of executing tasks with *effectiveness, efficiency,* and *satisfaction* [4]. It is influenced by the *usage context* which comprises the tasks to be executed, the physical environment, and the users performing the tasks. In this paper we consider the usability of websites and, hence, users of websites and the tasks they execute.

A *usability issue* is a problem that occurs during the usage of a website and decreases one or more of the factors effectiveness, efficiency, and satisfaction for a specific usage context. The problems can be caused by the design of the website, the functionality, the performance, and other aspects. As an example, a login process of a website can be inefficient (usability issue) because users have a long navigation to the login mask (design).

As *usability smell*, we refer to exceptional user behavior that may indicate a usability issues. For example, if users typically require many actions to perform a login on a website (usability smell) this may indicate a usability issue with respect to inefficiency of the login process. A usability smell has a description and refers to potential usability issues reflected by the smell. Furthermore, the severity of a usability smell indicates the likelyhood that the smell actually identifies a usability issue.

The following terminology is based on [3]. A user utilizes a website by performing individual, atomic *actions*. Examples for actions are a click on a button or typing text into a text field. The set of all actions executable on a website is the bounded set A. Users combine a subset of actions $B \subseteq A$ to execute a specific *task* on a website. For example, to perform the task of logging in on a website, a user combines the actions of typing his name and his password into two text fields and clicking on a confirmation button. Users can further combine tasks and actions to perform higher level tasks. For example, for performing the task of submitting a transaction on a bank website, a user performs the *subtask* of logging in on the website, the subtask for submitting the transaction, and a final action to log out by clicking on a button. We refer to the set of all tasks that can be performed on a website as the set T.

A task $t \in T$ has an ordered list of children $C_t = c_1 \dots c_n$ where each child is either an action or another task $(c_i \in (A \cup T))$. Furthermore, a task defines the execution order of its children using temporal relationships [5]. Our approach is based on the task tree generation mechanism proposed in [3], which generates the temporal relationships *sequence* and *iteration*. In case of a sequence, a task has one or more children and they are executed in their respective order. In case of an iteration, a task has exactly one child which is executed zero or more times. We refer to tasks with a temporal relationship sequence simply as sequence and to tasks with a temporal relationship iteration simply as iteration.

A task is never directly or indirectly its own child. But a single task or an action can be a child of more than one parent task. With these constraints being applied, tasks form a directed acyclic graph. For simplification, this structure is usually represented as a tree by doubling the representation of tasks occurring several times. Therefore, the directed acyclic graph is called a *task tree*. The leaf

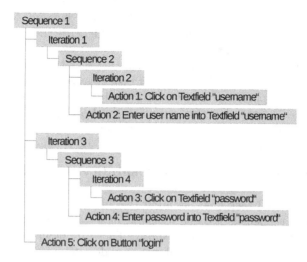

Fig. 1. Example for a task tree of a login process on a website

nodes of a task tree are the actions a user performs to complete the root task of the task tree. The intermediate nodes in the task tree divide the root task into a logical execution order of subtasks and actions.

An example for a task tree is shown in Figure 1. It represents a login process on a website. The actions are the leaf nodes. The temporal relationships of the tasks define the order in which the children have to be performed. The task (Sequence 1) starts with an iteration (Iteration 1) of a sequence (Sequence 2) for entering the user name. The user can click on the respective text field (Action 1) several times (Iteration 2). The entering of the password is modeled accordingly (Iteration 3). The overall task (Sequence 1) is completed after the user entered the user name and the password and clicks on the login button (Action 5).

The execution of an action a by a user is called an *action instance* a'. The execution of a task t is called a *task instance* t'. A task instance t' is an ordered list of action instances $a'_1 \ldots a'_n$ defining the order in which the contained action instances were executed. We define $|t'|$ as the number of action instances executed in the task instance t'. A task instance must adhere to the task that was executed, i.e., the action instances and their order must match the allowed combination of actions defined by the task, its tree structure, and the temporal relationships. A task t is a representation for the set of all its instances. Therefore, we use the notation $t' \in t$ to indicate that t' is an instance of t. Furthermore, $|t|$ is the number of all instances of t.

Task and action instances contain detailed information about the task execution. For example, an action instance has a time stamp ts indicating when the action was executed. For two action instances a'_i and a'_j, we define the function $\Delta ts(a'_i, a'_j)$ that returns the time difference in milliseconds between the two action instances. Let a'_1 be the first action instance of a task instance t' and a'_n be the last action instance of t'. Then $\Delta ts(a_1', a_n')$ is a measure for the execution time of t'. The smaller the execution time, the higher is the efficiency of t' and, hence, the usability of the task execution.

In [3], we describe an approach for generating task trees based on recordings of user actions on websites. The resulting task trees contain only sequences and iterations that were performed by the users and that, therefore, represent actual user behavior. We extended this approach to also dump the instances of the detected tasks in the way they were executed by the users.

3   Automated Usage-Based Usability Smell Detection

Using the generated task trees as input, we identify usability smells. We currently consider the smells *missing feedback*, *important tasks*, *required inefficient actions*, and *high website element distance*. These are described in the following subsections. For each usability smell, we provide a foundation, a description of the expected user behavior, and a description of our expectations towards the generated task trees. Furthermore, we describe the detection of the smells based on the generated task trees as well as a measure for their severity. For most smells, we also provide an example.

3.1   Usability Smell: Missing Feedback

Foundation. When utilizing a websites, users require feedback for the actions they perform [6,7,8,9]. Otherwise, they are not sure if the action has any effect and if it is processed by the system.

Expected User Behavior. Users repeat an action, if they don't see any feedback. For example, if users click on the login button during a login process and nothing visible happens, they click the same button again. Users may repeat this action even more than twice until they see some feedback.

Expected Occurrence in Generated Task Trees. Repeated actions lead to iterations in the task trees. But not all iterations of actions indicate the smell. For example, a user may repeatedly scroll a page. Therefore, we consider only a subset of iterations of actions which covers iterations of clicks on buttons and links.

Users may accidentally perform a click twice. Furthermore, they may perform a click a second time after a long period of time. For example, they may click on a download link and click the same link again to download the same file a second time. Therefore, we consider repetitions of actions as indicator of missing feedback only if they occurred within a specific time frame. This time frame may not span a full iteration of actions. For example, a user may have clicked a download link for a file three times. The first two times belong to the time frame, the third not. Therefore we consider only subsequences of repeated actions.

Let t' be an instance of an iteration of an action a and $a'_1 \ldots a'_{|t'|}$ are the repeated executions of a. For each pair of action instances (a'_i, a'_j) where $1 \leq i < j \leq |t'|$, we calculate $\Delta ts(a'_i, a'_j)$. We consider an iteration of actions only, if for at least one of its instances the time difference $\Delta ts(a'_i, a'_j)$ is larger or equal to 1,000 and smaller or equal to 15,000. This means, we consider only repetitions of actions performed in a time frame of 1 to 15 seconds. All other repetitions are considered accidental multiple clicks or multiple clicks for some reason.

Detection. We filter the tasks for iterations of actions. We then consider the instances of each iteration. For each instance, we calculate a measure for the missing feedback. For this, we first subdivide the list of repeated actions $a'_1 \ldots a'_{|t'|}$ into subsequences $subseq_{i,j} = a'_i \ldots a'_j$ where $1 \leq i < j \leq |t'|$ and for which $1,000 \leq \Delta ts(a'_i, a'_j) \leq 15,000$. We choose these subsequences as large as possible and non-overlapping. For this, we scan the list of repeated actions for the first subsequence matching the criterion and for which $\Delta ts(a'_i, a'_j)$ is maximized but still smaller or equal to 15,000. We then search for the next subsequences starting with action instance a'_{j+1}. We repeat this searching until we find no further subsequence matching the criterion. The result of this process is a list of subsequences $subseq_{i_1,j_1} \ldots subseq_{i_k,j_k}$ where k is the number of disjunctive subsequences. For the missing feedback measure of an iteration instance, we define a function $mf(t')$ as follows:

$$mf(t') = \begin{cases} \sum\limits_{subseq_{i,j}} (\Delta ts(a'_i, a'_j) \cdot (j-i)) & |subseq_{i_1,j_1} \ldots subseq_{i_k,j_k}| > 0 \\ 0 & |subseq_{i_1,j_1} \ldots subseq_{i_k,j_k}| = 0 \end{cases} \tag{1}$$

Through this calculation, the missing feedback measure increases with the time the user waits for repeated clicks and the number of repetitions. If the user clicks very often, the missing feedback measure increases accordingly. For each iteration of actions t, we then calculate the average missing feedback for all instances as follows:

$$mf(t) = \frac{1}{|t|} \sum_{t' \in t} mf(t') \tag{2}$$

Severity. The average missing feedback measure defines the severity of the usability smell. The usability smell is considered present if $mf(t)$ of an iteration is greater than 50ms.

Example. An example for a smelling iteration representing missing feedback is shown in Figure 2a). Iteration 1 has 3 instances. The first instance has a repetition of Action 1 (Click on Button "OK"). Based on the time stamps of the action instances, Δts for this instance was calculated to be 3000ms. For the three instances, $mf(t)$ evaluates to 1000ms. As this value is higher than 50ms, the usability smell missing feedback is present.

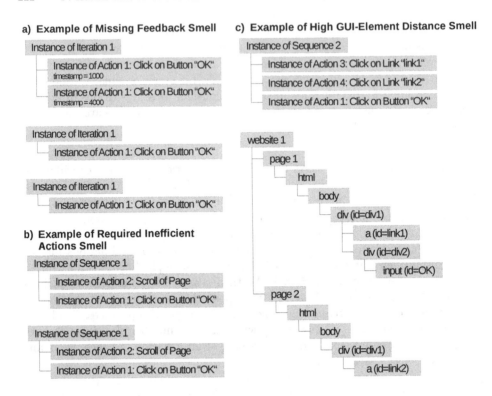

Fig. 2. Examples of smelling tasks

3.2 Usability Smell: Important Task

Foundation. Tasks performed regularly should be executed with a minimal number of actions [10,11]. If applicable, the tasks can be supported by automation, e.g., using macros.

Expected User Behavior. If users perform a task regularly, they execute always the same or similar actions.

Expected Occurrence in Generated Task Trees. Regularly performed user tasks are reflected as nodes in the generated task trees.

Detection. The task trees were generated based on the ordered set of recorded action instances RA. We search the task tree for tasks being executed most often, i.e., covering most of the recorded action instances $ra \in RA$. We only consider sequences as only sequences represent common combinations of actions and other tasks. For each sequence t, we calculate the number of all action instances covered by all instances $t' \in t$ and divide it by the number of all recorded action instances. Through this, we get the ratio

$$r(t) = \frac{1}{|RA|} \sum_{t' \in t} |t'_i| \qquad (3)$$

of action instances covered by instances of sequence t with respect to all recorded action instances. The higher this ratio, the more actions are executed in the context of task t. Therefore, the number of actions executed for task t should be minimized or automated for improving the usability.

Severity. We use the ratio $r(t)$ as indicator for the severity of the detected usability smell. The smell is considered present, if a task covers at least one percent of the recorded actions, i.e., $r(t) \geq 0.01$.

3.3   Usability Smell: Required Inefficient Actions

Foundation. Some actions are known to have no or minimal effect for fulfilling a task but also do not prevent its completion [12]. For example, when filling out a form, vertical scrolling may be required to reach the next element of the form to be filled out but does not semantically advance the process. We call such actions *inefficient actions*. The number of inefficient actions should be minimized to increase the users efficiency.

Expected User Behavior. Users perform inefficient actions during the normal usage of a website. In the case an inefficient action is required to fulfill a task, users will perform it when required.

Expected Occurrence in Generated Task Trees. As the task trees are generated based on all recorded actions, they will include inefficient actions. If an inefficient action is required at a specific point in the execution of a task, the generated task trees include this action accordingly.

Detection. For each task t, we calculate the average ratio of inefficient actions $ria(t)$. For this, we first consider each instance $t' \in t$ and determine the number of instances of inefficient actions $ia(t')$. As inefficient action, we currently consider vertical and horizontal scrolling of single panels and whole pages. Then, we calculate the average inefficient action ratio as

$$ria(t) = \frac{1}{|t|} \sum_{t' \in t} \frac{ia(t')}{|t'|} \qquad (4)$$

Severity. The higher $ria(t)$, the higher is the likelyhood of task t to have a usability issue with respect to inefficiency. Therefore, $ria(t)$ is the severity of the usability smell. We consider this smell present, if $ria(t) \geq 0.1$, i.e., more than 10% of the action instances covered by instances of a task are inefficient actions.

Example. An example for the smell is shown in Figure 2b). Here, Sequence 1 has two instances. Both instances have two action instances of which one is inefficient (the scroll action). For Sequence 1, $ria(t) = \frac{1}{2}(\frac{1}{2} + \frac{1}{2})$ and evaluates to 0.5 indicating a usability smell with a high severity.

3.4 Usability Smell: High Website Element Distance

Foundation. The elements of a website required for executing a task, such as buttons and text fields, should be as colocated as possible to ensure an efficient task execution [10].

Expected User Behavior. Users utilize website elements in the order that best fits the task they use the website for.

Expected Occurrence in Generated Task Trees. The task trees show the order of website element usage.

Detection. A website consists of several pages. A page may be subdivided by several panels. Several pages may contain elements that are semantically identical. For example, all pages of a website have a menu with identical structure and menu items. We consider two distinct website elements identical if they serve the same purpose on different pages, such as a menu item. We consider two website elements close to each other, if they are on the same page in the same panel. Two website elements are less close to each other, if they are on the same page but in different panels. Furthermore, two website elements have a high distance if they belong to different pages and do not serve the same purpose. Based on this, we define a measure for the distance $d(e_1, e_2)$ of two website elements e_1 and e_2 as follows:

$$d(e_1, e_2) = \begin{cases} 0.0 & e_1 \text{ and } e_2 \text{ are identical or have the same purpose} \\ 0.2 & e_1 \text{ and } e_2 \text{ belong to the same panel} \\ 0.5 & e_1 \text{ and } e_2 \text{ belong to the same page} \\ 0.75 & e_1 \text{ and } e_2 \text{ belong to the same website} \\ 1.0 & e_1 \text{ and } e_2 \text{ belong to different websites} \end{cases} \tag{5}$$

As a panel in a page, we only consider Hyper-Text Markup Language (HTML) *div* elements as they are nowadays mostly used for structuring pages. Div elements can contain nested div elements. Furthermore, they may be freely positioned on a page using, e.g., Cascading Style Sheets (CSS). Therefore, the nesting of div elements in the HTML source code of a page is no indicator for the actual positioning on a rendered page. Hence, we consider two website elements in the same panel only if their direct parent div element is the same.

For detecting the smell, we apply the distance measure $d(e_1, e_2)$ as follows. We only consider sequences as only sequences represent common combinations of actions and, hence, website elements. For each sequence instance $t' \in t$, we determine an ordered list of website elements in the order they were used in the sequence instance. We remove from this list the website elements used for inefficient actions (see Section 3.3) as these are not semantically required for completing a task. The result is the ordered list $E(t') = e_1 \ldots e_n$ of website elements used in t'. For each subsequent pair of $E(t')$, we calculate the distances $d(e_{i-1}, e_i)$ and sum them up to the cumulative distance between all website elements used in t'. Furthermore, we determine the number of distances, which is $|E(t')| - 1$. For the whole sequence t, we sum up the cumulative distances of all sequence instances $t' \in t$ and divide it by the sum of all distances. This results in the measure $gd(t)$ which represents the average distance between two subsequently used website elements for sequence t.

$$gd(t) = \frac{\sum_{t' \in t} \sum_{i=2}^{|E(t')|} d(e_{i-1}, e_i)}{\sum_{t' \in t} (|E(t')| - 1)} \tag{6}$$

Severity. $gd(t)$ is the severity of the usability smell. We consider this smell present if $gd(t)$ for a sequence is higher than 0.5, i.e., if in average two subsequently used website elements are not on the same page.

Example. An example for the smell is shown in Figure 2c). The tree on the top is an instance of a sequence called "Sequence 2". The tree on the bottom represents the structure of the corresponding website (root node). The website has 2 pages (children of the root node) which consist of several HTML tags and their respective structuring (all other nodes). An HTML tag may have an id to differentiate two HTML tags having the same name.

The instance of Sequence 2 consists of three action instances. The action instances utilize $|E(t')| = 3$ elements of two different pages of the website: first "link1" on the first page, then "link2" on the second page, and finally button "OK" on the first page again. The cumulative distance of the website elements for this instance is 1.5 and the number of distances is 2. As this is the single instance of Sequence 2, the resulting distance measure for Sequence 2 is $gd(t) = \frac{1.5}{2}$. This value is greater than 0.5 and, therefore, a usability smell is present.

4   Case Studies

We implemented our approach based on the tool suite for Automatic Quality Engineering of Event-driven Software (AutoQUEST) [13]. In addition to others, AutoQUEST allows recording user actions for different platforms. We utilized AutoQUEST's ability to record user actions on websites. For this, each page of a website must include a JavaScript provided by AutoQUEST. The recorded action instances are sent to a dedicated AutoQUEST server which stores them intermediately. Afterwards, they are fed into AutoQUEST for further processing.

AutoQUEST provides the mechanism for generating task trees based on recorded user actions which we described in [3]. As explained in Section 2, we extended this mechanism with the ability to generate task instances. Furthermore, we implemented the detection of the usability smells described in the previous section. Finally, we used this implementation in two case studies.

4.1   Description of the Case Studies

In the first case study, we applied our approach on the website of our research group [14] at the University of Göttingen. This website offers information about the members of our research group (e.g., contact information), details and materials of lectures we offer to students, as well as details of our research including publication lists. Members of the research group can login on the website to edit the content. The website offers 18 different types of pages. As type of page, we consider several pages having the same structure. For example, all details pages with information about the group members have the same structure and, therefore, are of the same page type.

The website is based on a content management system in which we integrated AutoQUEST's mechanism for recording user actions. As a result, we recorded 33,690 action instances over a period of 8.5 months. The task tree generation generated 1,847 tasks of which 1,431 were sequences and 416 were iterations. Further details of the case study can be found in Table 1.

Table 1. Facts of the case studies

	Case Study 1 Website of Research Group	Case Study 2 Application Portal
Page types	18	35 (21 application part, 8 review part, 6 shared)
Recording period	8.5 months	4.5 months
Start	July 2013	October 2013
End	March 2014	March 2014
Recorded actions	33,690	241,306
Generated tasks	1,847	10,634
Sequences	1,431	9,530
Iterations	416	1,104

In the second case study, we applied our approach on a master studies application portal on our university. This portal is subdivided into two major parts. The first part allows student applicants to apply for master studies at our university. In a wizard based fashion, applicants are asked to enter their personal data and information about previous studies and achievements. At the end of the wizard, they get an overview of the entered data in which they are asked to upload their CV, a photo and certificates, e.g., about former studies. In the second part of the portal, a reviewer team can verify the applications and accept or reject them including entering reasons. The portal offers a login mechanism including functions for registration and changing the password.

The application portal is based on a content management system in which we integrated AutoQUEST's mechanism for recording user actions. As a result, we recorded 241,306 action instances over a period of 4.5 months. The task tree generation generated 10,634 tasks of which 9,530 were sequences and 1,104 were iterations. Further details of the case study can be found in Table 1.

The number of reported usability smells in both case studies and their distribution to the different smell types is shown in Table 2. Our approach reported 5,900 smells of which 1,464 were found in the first, and 4,436 were found in the second case study. These were too many to be interpreted manually. Furthermore, many findings referred to tasks that cover only a small set of recorded action instances or that were executed only seldom. Hence, we considered these smells as less valuable. Therefore, we performed a preselection of the detected smells based on a measure for the importance of the tasks for which the smells were found. Similar to the respective smell, we considered a task more important, the more recorded action instances it covers. We selected a variable percentage q of tasks that cover the most recorded action instances and being, therefore, most important. Then we selected only those smells that referred to the selected tasks. We adjusted q so that for both case studies at most 100 smells resulted from the selection. Setting q to 5%, i.e., selecting only smells for those 5% of tasks that cover most of the recorded action instances, resulted in 96 detected smells for the first case study and 75 smells for the second case study.

Table 2. Smells detected in the case studies

	Case Study 1 Website of Research Group			Case Study 2 Application Portal		
	all	redundant	true positive	all	redundant	true positive
Detected smells	1,464	275		4,436	985	
Missing feedback	52	0		39	0	
Important task	19	10		13	4	
Inefficient actions	959	199		3,772	878	
High distance	434	66		612	103	
Considered smells	96	30	83	75	22	64
Missing feedback	12	0	11	9	0	6
Important task	19	10	10	13	4	11
Inefficient actions	54	17	51	51	18	47
High distance	11	3	11	2	0	0

In both case studies, several smells of the same type were reported for a task and also for one or more of its children. We call these reports *redundant findings*. We considered them as a hint to better analyze the cause of a finding for a parent task. The number of redundant findings for each smell is shown in a dedicated column in Table 2.

4.2 Findings for the Smell Missing Feedback

The detection of missing feedback (Section 3.1) revealed 91 tasks with usability smells of which 52 were found in the first case study and 39 in the second. There were no redundant findings. Based on the filtering we considered 12 smells for the first case study and 9 for the second. The smells referred to the following repetitions of clicks:

- First case study
  - clicks on 9 links for navigating inside the website (e.g. the menu)
  - clicks on 2 links for navigating inside the publication list
  - clicks on 1 download link for a file
- Second case study
  - clicks on 6 links and buttons concerned with user registration and login
  - clicks on 2 buttons used for navigating back and forth in the wizard
  - clicks on 1 button used to download and view an uploaded file

4.3 Findings for the Smell Important Task

The detection of important tasks (Section 3.2) resulted in 32 tasks with 14 redundant findings. 19 smells with 10 redundant findings were found in the first case study and 13 smells with 4 redundant findings in the second. The filtering of the smells did not filter any of the detected smells. This is due to the fact, that the filter for the smells and the filter for important tasks use the same mechanism and that the filter for the smells is less restrictive. Therefore, we considered all found smells for this smell type. The smells referred to the following types of task, that overlap each other:

- First case study
  - 9 tasks that included at least one inefficient scrolling action
  - 6 tasks including the navigation via the menu of the website
  - 6 tasks concerned with the login process
  - 5 tasks for showing the overview and details of the lectures offered by our group
  - 4 tasks for showing details of our group members
  - 2 tasks for filtering the list of publications of our group
  - 2 tasks for showing details of our research in general
- Second case study
  - 2 tasks that included at least one inefficient scrolling action
  - 6 tasks representing the utilization of a date chooser in the wizard
  - 3 tasks concerned with the login process
  - 2 tasks for entering details about former studies
  - 1 task for navigating in the wizard
  - 1 task for uploading files

4.4   Findings for the Smell Required Inefficient Actions

The detection of required inefficient actions (Section 3.3) resulted in 4,731 findings of which 1,077 were redundant. 959 smells with 199 redundant findings were found in the first case study and 3,772 smells with 878 redundant findings in the second. The filtering of the smells reduced the amount of considered smells to 54 with 17 redundant findings in the first case study and 51 with 18 redundant findings in the second case study. The smells referred to the following types of tasks:

- First case study
  - 26 tasks including the usage of the menu
  - 19 tasks for showing the overview and details of the lectures offered by our group
  - 11 tasks for showing details of our group members
  - 9 tasks concerned with the login process
  - 7 tasks for filtering the list of publications of our group
  - 4 tasks for showing details of our research in general
  - 2 tasks for editing content
  - 1 tasks for showing news of our research group
- Second case study
  - 15 tasks for providing application details during the usage of the wizard
  - 12 tasks for uploading files
  - 7 tasks for showing details of a specific application on the reviewer part
  - 6 tasks concerned with the login process
  - 5 tasks for navigating in the wizard
  - 5 tasks representing the utilization of a date chooser in the wizard
  - 4 tasks for providing review details and rejection reasons on the reviewer part
  - 2 tasks for submitting and revoking an application

4.5   Findings for the Smell High Website Element Distance

The detection of high website element distances (Section 3.4) found 1,064 usability smells of which 169 were redundant. 435 smells with 66 redundant findings were found in the first case study and 612 smells with 103 redundant findings in the second. The filtering of the smells reduced the amount of considered smells to 11 with 3 redundant findings in the first case study and 2 with no redundant finding in the second case study. The smells referred to the following types of tasks:

- First case study
  - 10 tasks for showing the overview and details of the lectures offered by our group
  - 9 tasks including the usage of the menu
  - 3 tasks concerned with the login process
- Second case study
  - 1 task for navigating in the wizard
  - 1 task for showing details of a specific application on the reviewer part

5 Discussion

Our case studies show, that our approach finds usability smells. The number of detected smells that indicate true usability issues are listed in Table 2 in the "true positives" columns. To decide, which of the smells are true positives, we performed a manual check for each of the filtered smells. However, the severity of several found smells is rather low. This should be addressed by adjusting the lower boundary of the severity for each smell which must be exceeded to consider a finding. Furthermore, a ranking of the smells is required based on their severity.

The detection of missing feedback shows good results. We consider 17 of the 21 smells detected in both case studies as real usability issues. The findings for internal navigation on our research website are inline with our observations. During the recording period, our research website had a performance problem which may have caused users to click several times on the same link. We addressed this issue by adjusting the configuration of the content management system. We also consider the findings for the login process in the second case study as usability issues, as we also here experienced performance issues. The findings for the next and previous buttons in the wizard of the application portal are false positives as the users utilized these buttons subsequently to navigate between several wizard views. The findings of missing feedback for file downloads in both case studies could not be confirmed. The downloads were usually fast enough and the progress was indicated by the web browser. These findings may show, that the 1 and 15 seconds boundaries used in the smell detection require an adjustment.

The findings for important tasks are helpful in both case studies. We consider 21 of 32 as true positives. The other findings referred to tasks that included only one efficient action and, therefore, did not represent useful action combinations. Based on the findings for our research website, we saw findings for five tasks representing navigations from the start page via the list of lectures to details of a specific lecture. This shows that details of a specific lecture are often required. We now consider to put links to ongoing lectures to the start page to reduce the number of clicks required for accessing this information. The same applies to details of our group members and the login process. For the application portal, the usage of the date chooser is most important. Therefore, we consider to optimize it further to reduce the number of required actions.

The findings for required inefficient actions showed many redundant findings (35 of 105). However, the findings were helpful and we consider 98 of them as usability issues. The others are caused by the fact, that users vertically scrolled pages with a lot of information which are intended to be read or to display an overview. And vertical scrolling of pages while reading is not a usability issue. For our research website, we consider to restructure the pages so that the size of the top banner decreases on all pages but the start page. This would allow to move content of details pages to move upwards on the page. Furthermore, we consider to move the menu from the top of the page to the left and prevent its scrolling out of sight. Through this, we hope to reduce the number of required scrolling for navigating on the website and its details pages. For the application portal, especially the scrolling during the wizard usage was important. A wizard should break down a task into simple subtasks. The required scrolling indicates that still the subtasks are quite complex, require many website elements and, hence, much screen space. Therefore, we consider to check the wizard and the presented forms for their complexity. If required, we will further break down some subtask. Furthermore, scrolling after a file upload was important. This issue is caused by the fact that for a file upload, the current page reloads and starts at the top again. The users have to scroll the page to get to the next file to be uploaded. This issue was already tried to be addressed by adding a link on the top of the page allowing the automatic scrolling to the next file to be uploaded. But still, this is inefficient. Therefore, we propose to change the file uploads to make them possible without requiring scrolling.

The findings for high website element distances are mostly inline with the findings of other smells. We consider 11 of the 13 smells detected in both case studies as real usability issues. In the research website case study the findings showed that users have to navigate via several pages to reach details of a lecture or group member. Therefore, the website element distance is relatively high. Hence, these findings support, e.g., the findings for important tasks. The findings for the second case studies are not considered usability issues. Both findings represent required navigation between pages either for drill down in a large set of information (finding for the reviewer part) or for navigating in the wizard.

Our approach relies on a large number of recorded user actions. Otherwise, the task trees would not represent real user behavior. Therefore, the approach can only be applied on large data sets recorded over a long period of time. Based on the observations in the case studies, the validity of our results seems relatively high. We consider 147 of 171 detected usability smells as indicators for usability issues and, hence, as helpful findings. However, the validity should further be confirmed using other, established usability evaluation methods, e.g., usability tests with thinking aloud, in a comparative study. Furthermore, we should apply our approach in further case studies to determine if we obtain similar results. For example, we need to clarify if the minimum severity used for each smell is also adequate for smaller websites or websites with different structures.

6 Related Work

The term usability smells is similar to code smells introduced by Fowler [15]. Code smells are structures of source code being a hint for a required refactoring. Similarly, usability smells are usage patterns indicating required usability improvements.

Ivory and Hearst [16] introduced a categorization for usability evaluation methods with respect to automation. The categories are *capture*, *analysis*, and *critique*. Depending on the level of automation, an evaluation method is assigned to one or more of these categories. According to Ivory and Hearst, there are no methods yet covering all these categories at the same time. Our method spans all categories in that it records user actions (capture), transforms the recorded data into task trees representing actual user behavior (analysis), and automatically reasons on aspects of the websites usability (critique).

There are several methods that record users when utilizing a website and subsequently analyze the data to detect usability problems. Examples are Web-Hint [17], WebRemUsine [18,19], and ReModEl [20]. With respect to Ivory and Hearst [16], these methods belong to the groups capture and analysis. The methods compare recorded user actions with expected user behavior. The expected user behavior is either a recording of actions of an example session (WebHint) or a manually defined task model (WebRemUsine, ReModEl). The methods only show differences between expected and recorded user behavior. Therefore, they do not belong to Ivory and Hearsts critique category. In comparison to these methods, our approach does not consider expected user behavior. Instead, our approach assesses only real user behavior. This has the additional benefit that no wrong expectations on user behavior influence our analysis. Furthermore, our approach provides details about the location and causes of potential usability issues and does, therefore, belong to Ivory and Hearsts critique category.

John et al. [21] propose an approach to record user actions and generate Goals, Operators, Methods, and Selection Rules (GOMS) models based on them. The GOMS models are used to estimate the average efficiency of users for executing a specific task. In comparison to our approach, this method focuses on efficiency measurement and is only used for example sessions performed by an evaluator. Sessions of real users are not considered.

An approach that belongs to Ivory and Hearsts critique category is the Mental Model workbench (MeMo) [22] and its combination with the Multi-Access Service Platform (MASP) [23]. In this concept, a Graphical User Interface (GUI) is rendered and an analyzer tool, which simulates a user, evaluates which action is most likely to be chosen by the user in a specific state of the GUI. An extended and iterative version of this approach is proposed by Quade [24] where the evaluation also performs GUI adaptations for usability improvement. The goal is to iteratively design a GUI guiding users as good as possible in the execution of specific tasks. In contrast to our approach, this technique works at design time to improve a GUI under development. It does not consider real user behavior but simulates it. Furthermore, it requires predefined user tasks and does not expect users to apply a GUI for unexpected tasks.

7   Conclusion

In this paper, we presented an automated approach for detecting usability smells of websites based on recorded user actions. The detected types of usability smells are missing feedback, important tasks, required inefficient actions, and high website element distance. The approach was applied in two case studies. For all smell types, we gained helpful results but also some room for improvement. For example, the detected smells included redundant findings and false positives. As the majority of the detected smells that we considered in our analysis also indicated usability issues, we conclude that it is possible to detect usability issues using our approach.

In our future work, we plan to improve the described usability smell detection, e.g. to reduce the number of redundant findings. In this context, we will also perform detailed studies with different detection parameters such as the minimal severity that must be reached by a smell to be reported. Furthermore, we will perform studies for specific smell detections with adjusted algorithms to check whether a modified algorithm provides better results. For example, we plan to implement the high website element distances detection without excluding inefficient actions and compare the results with our current findings. Finally, we plan to implement more usability smell detections, e.g. to detect unused but prominently positioned website elements which may also require an improved task tree generation to allow for more sophisticated findings.

References

1. Sarodnick, F., Brau, H.: Methoden der Usability Evaluation: Wissenschaftliche Grundlagen und praktische Anwendung, 1st edn. Huber, Bern (2006)
2. Krug, S.: Web Usability: Rocket Surgery Made Easy. Addison-Wesley (2010)
3. Harms, P., Herbold, S., Grabowski, J.: Trace-based task tree generation. In: Proceedings of the Seventh International Conference on Advances in Computer-Human Interactions (ACHI 2014). XPS - Xpert Publishing Services (2014)
4. ISO 9241-11: Ergonomic requirements for office work with visual display terminals (VDTs) – Part 11: Guidance on usability (ISO 9241-11:1998), ISO (1998)
5. Paternò, F.: ConcurTaskTrees: An engineered approach to model-based design of interactive systems. In: The Handbook of Analysis for HumanComputer Interaction, pp. 1–18 (1999)
6. Polson, P.G., Lewis, C., Rieman, J., Wharton, C.: Cognitive walkthroughs: A method for theory-based evaluation of user interfaces. Int. J. Man-Mach. Stud. 36(5), 741–773 (1992)
7. Ferré, X., Juristo, N., Windl, H., Constantine, L.: Usability basics for software developers. IEEE Softw. 18(1), 22–29 (2001)
8. Norman, D.A.: The design of everyday things, 1st edn. Basic Books, New York (2002)
9. Balbo, S., Goschnick, S., Tong, D.: Leading Web Usability Evaluations to WAUTER. In: The Eleventh Australasian World Wide Web Conference. Gold Coast (2005)
10. Lecerof, A., Paternò, F.: Automatic support for usability evaluation. IEEE Trans. Softw. Eng. 24, 863–888 (1998)
11. Tidwell, J.: Designing Interfaces - Patterns for Effective Interaction Design. In: Treseler, M. (ed.), 2nd edn. Oreilly Series. O'Reilly Media, Incorporated (2010), http://books.google.de/books?id=5gvOU9XOfuOC
12. Patern, F., Piruzza, A., Santoro, C.: Remote usability analysis of multimodal information regarding user behaviour, pp. 15–22 (2005), http://giove.isti.cnr.it/attachments/publications/2005-A2-134.pdf
13. Herbold, S., Harms, P.: AutoQUEST - Automated Quality Engineering of Event-driven Software (March 2013)
14. Software Engineering for Distributed Systems Group. Software Engineering for Distributed Systems (2014), http://www.swe.informatik.uni-goettingen.de/ (retrieved: 4, 2014)

15. Fowler, M.: Refactoring: Improving the Design of Existing Code. Addison-Wesley, Boston (1999)
16. Ivory, M.Y., Hearst, M.A.: The state of the art in automating usability evaluation of user interfaces. ACM Comput. Surv. 33, 470–516 (2001), http://doi.acm.org/10.1145/503112.503114
17. Vargas, A., Weffers, H., da Rocha, H.V.: A method for remote and semi-automatic usability evaluation of web-based applications through users behavior analysis. In: Proceedings of the 7th International Conference on Methods and Techniques in Behavioral Research, MB 2010, pp. 19:1–19:5. ACM, New York (2010), http://doi.acm.org/10.1145/1931344.1931363
18. Paganelli, L., Paternò, F.: Tools for remote usability evaluation of web applications through browser logs and task models. Behavior Research Methods 35, 369–378 (2003)
19. Paternò, F., Russino, A., Santoro, C.: Remote evaluation of mobile applications. In: Winckler, M., Johnson, H., Palanque, P. (eds.) TAMODIA 2007. LNCS, vol. 4849, pp. 155–169. Springer, Heidelberg (2007)
20. Buchholz, G., Engel, J., Märtin, C., Propp, S.: Model-based usability evaluation – evaluation of tool support. In: Jacko, J.A. (ed.) HCI 2007. LNCS, vol. 4550, pp. 1043–1052. Springer, Heidelberg (2007)
21. John, B.E., Prevas, K., Salvucci, D.D., Koedinger, K.: Predictive human performance modeling made easy. In: Proceedings of the SIGCHI Conference on Human Factors in Computing Systems, CHI 2004, pp. 455–462. ACM, New York (2004)
22. Jameson, A., Mahr, A., Kruppa, M., Rieger, A., Schleicher, R.: Looking for unexpected consequences of interface design decisions: The memo workbench. In: Winckler, M., Johnson, H. (eds.) TAMODIA 2007. LNCS, vol. 4849, pp. 279–286. Springer, Heidelberg (2007)
23. Feuerstack, S., Blumendorf, M., Kern, M., Kruppa, M., Quade, M., Runge, M., Albayrak, Ş.: Automated usability evaluation during model-based interactive system development. In: Forbrig, P., Paternò, F. (eds.) HCSE/TAMODIA 2008. LNCS, vol. 5247, pp. 134–141. Springer, Heidelberg (2008)
24. Quade, M., Blumendorf, M., Albayrak, S.: Towards model-based runtime evaluation and adaptation of user interfaces. In: User Modeling and Adaptation for Daily Routines: Providing Assistance to People with Special and Specific Needs (2010)

Aspects of Human-Centred Design
in HCI with Older Adults: Experiences from the Field

Ana Correia de Barros, Sílvia Rêgo, and João Antunes

Fraunhofer Portugal AICOS, Porto, Portugal
{ana.barros,silvia.rego,joao.antunes}@fraunhofer.pt

Abstract. Common characteristics of older adults have led to the rise of recommendations to conduct user research and testing with this particular age
group. Even though guidelines exist regarding human-centred design with older
adults, there are not many reports on experiences with creating and maintaining
elderly user groups for design and research purposes. This paper reviews previous reports in the literature about user groups and adds i) results of qualitative
research about the experience of researchers who built their entire professional
experience with user groups of older adults, along with ii) the authors' own account of building and maintaining an elderly user group for years. The paper
provides recommendations for recruiting, maintaining and motivating elderly
user groups towards participation in HCI design and research activities, along
with suggestions of strategies to use during field work.

Keywords: Human-centred design, older adults, interviews, recommendations,
qualitative methods, user recruitment, user group.

1 Introduction

The World population is getting older. The Eurostat reports an inversion of the demographic pyramid and sharp ageing of the population in Europe until 2060 [1]. With
ageing, several impairments (e.g. sensorial, motor, and psychological) are likely to
come about which, in turn, may have effects on people's activities of daily living,
independence, or quality of life. Also rising is the array of Information and Communication Technologies (ICT), which are becoming increasingly sophisticated and hold
the promise of bringing health care into older adults' homes [2].

However, solutions designed to be used by this age group must take into account
natural ageing decline and the implications it may have on the interaction with ICT.
On the other hand, a thorough knowledge of people's needs, expectations and attitudes towards ICT is needed so that solutions being designed indeed meet end-users'
needs and are regarded by the latter as appealing.

In order to achieve this purpose, many authors agree, users must be invited to be
active participants in the design of these technologies [3]. Designers can only go so
far in trying to put themselves into users' shoes and the more distant the experiences
of end-users and those of designers, the more difficult the challenges become [4].

S. Sauer et al. (Eds.): HCSE 2014, LNCS 8742, pp. 235–242, 2014.

In the European Ambient Assisted Living Joint Programme, for instance, the involvement of end-users through end-user organisations is indeed mandatory[1].

While there are reports on how to conduct research activities or on how to set up test sessions with older adults, literature is scarce on the latter and scarcer on what is needed to create and maintain a user group for the purpose of human-centred design (HCD) activities that need to involve older adults, caregivers and other stakeholders. Nevertheless, there are research groups who have engaged in these activities and could share their experience with the community towards promoting the practice of HCD.

This paper i) gathers information from different sources regarding this matter, ii) reports experience from the field in building a user network of older adults, and iii) illustrates some points through statements provided by our centre's researchers about their experience and challenges in conducting HCD with older adults. The experiences from the field come from a user network of older adults and caregivers that we have created and maintained at our research centre since 2011–network *Colaborar*[2]. The network has been growing over time, having at one point reached 400 users, and has supported over 1000 HCD activities required by the manifold research projects at the centre, which is related to ICT solutions towards independent living in old age. Researchers' statements used along the paper were gathered during semi-structured interviews, the major outcomes of which are reported elsewhere [5].

2   Previous Work

Conducting research with and about older adults is challenging in different fields, namely in clinical research. Mody and co-workers [6] share methods for the effective recruitment and retention of older adults for research purposes. The methods target four main goals: *attaining a representative sample*, *promoting participation of older adults and other stakeholders in the research*, *assess feasibility in advance*, and *retain the participants in the particular study*.

Working with older adults in Human-Computer Interaction (HCI) requires specific care not only regarding design, but also regarding the process itself, and how one must prepare sessions, treat participants or deal with idiosyncrasies of the age group [7]. Rubin and Chisnell [7] have laid out recommendations to address these issues.

Lindsay and co-workers [8] have documented their experience, findings and methods extensively after using participatory design with older adults and people with specific impairments (e.g. dementia). They have developed their own method on top of 4 main challenges they identified from previous work, that were related to *focus and meeting structure*, *representation and taking action*, *ability to envision future concepts*, and *design beyond tasks* (p. 1201).

Gregor and Newell [9] have made the case for 'User sensitive inclusive design', an approach to allow and encourage designers to accommodate diversity within the group of 'older adults', which, the authors argue, is far from homogeneous. The authors

---

[1] http://www.aal-europe.eu/get-involved/who-can-apply/
[2] www.colaborar.fraunhofer.pt

claim that the approach allows overcoming the drawbacks found in traditional user-centred design (UCD) techniques, which are meant for more homogeneous groups.

Researchers from the Universities of Dundee, Abertay Dundee and Glasgow, amongst whom were A. F. Newell and Peter Gregor cited above, have concluded that traditional UCD methods used in HCI require some adaptations in order to be effectively used when working with and for older adults [10]. Through the UTOPIA project, the researchers have created a database of 160 individuals for research purposes and have outlined the methods used to efficiently elicit requirements about new technologies from older adults. The methods begin with the work towards the creation of a partnership with end-users and the maintenance of it throughout the research and design process.

Bringing end-users into the design team, a principle of participatory design, has long been praised within the Inclusive Design community. Julia Cassim, through her 'Design Challenges' [11], brings people with disabilities into design teams as design partners. Newell, Gregor, and Alm [12] have brought together not only older adults and designers, but have also fostered get-togethers of older adults where learning of new technologies happens on a peer-to-peer basis, and have reported the benefits of this approach in regards to older adults' engagement in the design activities.

There are different challenges related to participatory design [13] and different challenges related, in particular, to research and design with and for older adults [14]. Our previous work has listed an array of difficulties that 6 researchers (R1-R6) experienced when setting up and conducting usability tests with older adults [5]. These at times support, and at other times add points to existing literature on the creation and upkeep of an older adult user group. The examples outlined above seem to suggest that retention of older adults in a group is an activity that is built not only outside design/research activities, but indeed within the activities themselves. One such example is the theatre promoted by Newell [15].

3   Creating and Maintaining a User Network

The existing literature on creating and maintaining groups of older adult users usually reports efforts for a single design or research project. We will go over existing recommendations and add our own experiences from the field.

3.1   Recruiting Older Adults

The challenge begins with finding a large enough number of older adults to take part in the activities. Some authors suggest resorting to nursing homes, day-care centres, and clubs, amongst others. We have found that these are all viable options, although, as Mody and co-workers [6] point out, reaching out to older adults in nursing homes may pose severe challenges. To build a user network encompassing diversity, we should target as many different institutions as we can. It often happens that if we remain with a single type of institution, we will have a narrow age range.

Furthermore, when we study older adults, it is often the case that we are looking for specific chronic diseases or impairments. Our previous work has suggested that this is an important aspect for researchers [5]. The user network should be wide and diverse enough to secure participants with these specific characteristics.

In addition, researchers mentioned that in cases when they rely on information from staff at elder institutions where they go to conduct tests, or on the best of their own judgment, they might not get an adequate assessment of participants' cognitive abilities. Four participants [5] shared stories in which they realized that users were not able to conduct the tests already while the test was underway and at a time when there was no chance for them to turn back. In this context, reliable information regarding participants' particular abilities for the project at hand seems to be of paramount importance to researchers, as it helps avoiding stressful situations for both the practitioner and the older adult participant.

In order to set the terrain for future work, a previous screening should be made. This can be done by talking to the staff in the institutions and getting an idea of the type of group, and through a more formal screening using questionnaires for older adults to fill in with socio-demographic data, general health information or others that cover the specificities required for the tests or activities themselves. From our experience, it is also useful to take time to talk to each potential participant individually prior to conducting any screening, or even planning any activity. This helps us to understand the users, helps to create a relationship of trust and serves as an opportunity to explain to each potential participant what the user network is about.

During the initial contact with the institution it usually helps to mention other institutions in the area that are already part of the network, as it often happens that institutions know one another. In accordance with Eisma and co-workers' experience [10], we have also found that after the initial contact, and after formalizing the collaboration between the team and the end-user organization (i.e. a signed protocol), the first activity should take place within a short timeframe. Organizations of older adults are very much sought after. Therefore, it is advisable to maintain the contact, so that people do not suspect of researchers' intentions, nor forget about them. These activities may be design or research activities, but may very well be just a leisure activity with older adults.

3.2   Maintaining Relationships with the Group

It must be noted that, for the purpose of a user network that serves many different projects, a large number of older adults is required not only because of the sheer amount of design/research activities of each project, but also because practitioners should be careful not to convert them into a burden for the users in the group. Nevertheless, as going to meet the users is a recurrent activity in HCD, the designers/researchers come to learn through their experience about the groups, their idiosyncrasies, and routines. In day-care centres with which we work, older adults tend to strictly follow their routines and timetables, in particular regarding eating hours, as noted by one of our researchers. Learning about these may be useful for the design and research work [5], e.g.:

If you try to apply the questionnaires closer to tea time they talk much less, because they know it is tea time and must get on with it. (R2)

Rubin and Chisnell [7] alert to the fact that, when welcoming older adults to one's facilities, arrangements should be made for a second person accompanying the first. Our experience confirms this need. As visiting the research centre facilities is a new experience that many users in the network look forward to, we should try to give all an opportunity to come over for research purposes. If this is not possible, we can invite older adults over just to get to know the facilities and the team.

Following the same line of thought, the person in charge of the user network should make sure to keep a record of activities being carried out and the users involved, so as to spread the activities between the available older adults as much as possible. The person should manage the amount and type of activities each user takes part in and make sure that participating in the activities is not a burden for the participants. Users in our network often take notice and complain that they have been less called upon for activities than others in the same group.

The people in charge of managing the user network should also make sure to share the outcomes of the design and research with the users. This helps people understand their contribution and helps to maintain the relationship.

Throughout time we gather much information in video or photographs. These materials are useful to publicize the network and recruit new users. However, it is crucial that we talk individually to each person who can be identified in these materials, so as to gather their authorization to make these materials public in any way. This authorization is signed apart from the particular informed consent used by the research project.

As a result of keeping a strong relationship with older adults and staff at the institutions, introducing the test sessions or other kinds of design/research activities becomes easier to practitioners.

3.3 Training Researchers

However carefully the relationships with the institutions and the users in the network might be managed, two fundamental points are i) to support, prepare and train researchers to address older adult users in the network and ii) to periodically gather their insights about their contacts with older adults [5]. The excerpts illustrating some of the points that we will be making in the following two sections were gathered during qualitative research with researchers, reported elsewhere [5].

Support, Preparation and Training
Contrary to what one might think, the age gap may lead to difficulties in communication between two generations. Our young researchers have reported that, on their first contacts with older adults in their research, not only did they have to pay special attention to language they used so that complex concepts could be communicated in laymen's terms, but they also actually reported being a bit fearful, on the first encounters, of talking to older adults they did not know because they were not used to talking

to any older adults beyond their grandparents [5]. This is in line with the "cultural and experimental gap between researchers and older people" mentioned by Eisma and co-workers [10].

If for nothing else, working with and for older adults is a difficult line of work because of the emotional impact it can have on researchers. If contacts are frequent, researchers and users develop a relationship and older adults' personal problems, illnesses or death are likely to affect researchers. New team members need to be alerted and informed about this possibility and prepared to deal with these situations.

The case we are sharing in this paper is of a user network that needs to support multiple research projects. This means that, rather than dealing with the same group of researchers all the time, older adults in the network come to deal with a variety of researchers and a variety of research projects. In order to, on the one hand, support researchers in meeting the users for the first time and, on the other hand, to put users at ease, one person – the one in charge of managing the network, doing the recruitment, and so forth – will accompany researchers most of the times and introduce the activities. This person gives a face to the research centre and always bridges researchers and users. This person is also responsible for helping researchers plan ahead the time and resources they will need to conduct the various activities within their projects. Beyond that, this person is in charge of planning leisure activities (e.g. Christmas parties) and answering requests from the users or institutions in the network (e.g. demonstration of a particular project for an event). Other activities supporting the network are a website of its own, periodical newsletters or periodical dissemination of the network in specific fairs and events.

Researchers' Insights

Some of the users' reactions during user research or usability testing are completely unexpected to someone new to the field, but are part of everyday life for those working with the specific user group for a longer time. We have come to observe in time that there are some behaviour patterns within the network.

The experience (and tips) from more experienced researchers is useful to new researchers not only because it helps them plan ahead for some situations, but also deal in the moment with others. This, in turn will help make the best out of the research.

Researchers mentioned several examples of older adults' behaviour during the tests in regard to their own performance, their beliefs about themselves and their capabilities. Researchers commented that older adults in the network often felt they should try to help researchers out and even try to please or try not to look bad in front of researchers—a phenomenon which is documented in the literature concerning not only older adults, but participants in research as a whole [16].

Researchers furthermore comment that older adults they worked with tended to focus on the results of their performance, wanted to do well, and even sometimes regarded usability testing as a competition amongst test participants. In the following excerpt about the process for diary studies regarding games with older adults, the researcher illustrates this aspect of competition as well as the behaviour of older adults when trying to please the researchers:

I went to the same [day-care] *centre twice a week for a long time. (...) so I handed it* [diary] *over on a Tuesday, and when I got there on Thursday they would look at me, take out the little books and start filling them in, like "I didn't forget it, it's here, I'm doing it". (...) Sometimes they'd ask me if I could help them here and there (...)* (R3)

In the same testimony, the researcher continues with an illustration of a behaviour associated with older adults' performance, which another researcher also noticed to be common—that older adults in the network often asked for approval or for help during the tests:

But that was the other thing, they always assumed that I would be evaluating their results: if they'd done well, if they'd done poorly, and it's hard for one to explain that there's no good or bad, and that we just wanted to know which things they liked best. And they insist a lot on that "But did I do well? But did I do badly? How did I do? But is that right, but is that wrong?" (R3)

Nevertheless, there might often be unexpected behaviours, such as the one described by researcher R3 during a diary study:

Eventually I stopped asking [for the diaries] *because they said they had forgotten, didn't know where the books were anymore. One lady gave it to her grandson to do because she thought it was more fun for him.* (R3)

In order to face these challenges, all interviewed researchers referred to the importance of having a user network at their service and, more specifically, a person who knows the people in the network and who helps them manage all that is related to the involvement of older adults in HCD.

4 Discussion and Conclusions

The experiences from the field reported in this paper refer to a particular set of over 350 users within a particular socio-cultural setting and might not be applicable to other settings. Some of the lessons learned are, however, aligned with existing reports in the literature.

The paper provides a brief overview of literature reports on the use of HCD with older adults and on the issue of creating and maintaining a user group. It complements existing knowledge by adding the authors' experience in the field and researchers' accounts of their experience with conducting design and research activities with older adults. The contributions of the paper are particularly novel in that they share lessons learned, methods and strategies to recruit and maintain an older adult user network to serve a wide array of projects. In our case the user network is treated as a project in itself, with its own management. One main conclusion is that the project should have, at least, a dedicated person to handle the network and preferably, as is our case, it helps that user network is a project in itself with its own human resources, tasks and budget. This has proved to be helpful for the researchers.

Acknowledgments. The authors would like to express their gratitude to all the institutions, staff and users in the network (www.colaborar.fraunhofer.pt).

References

1. Directorate-General for Economic and Financial Affairs of the European Commission: The 2012 Ageing Report - Economic and Budgetary Projections for the 27 EU Member States (2010-2060). European Commission (2012)
2. Mykityshyn, A.L., Fisk, A.D., Rogers, W.A.: Learning to Use a Home Medical Device: Me-diating Age-Related Differences with Training. Human Factors 44(3), 354–364 (2002)
3. Rogers, W.A., Fisk, A.F., Mead, S.E., Walker, N., Cabrera, E.F.: Training Older Adults to Use Automatic Teller Machines. Human Factors 38, 425–433 (1996)
4. Nicolle, C.: USERfit - Design for All Methods and Tools. In: COST 219bis Seminar 'Human Aspects of Telecommunications for Disabled and Older People', Donostia-San Sebastián, Spain, June 11-12 (1999)
5. Correia de Barros, A., Leitão, R.: Young practitioners' challenges, experience and strategies in usability testing with older adults. In: Assistive Technology: From Research to Practice, AAATE 2013, pp. 787–792. IOS Press, Amsterdam (2013)
6. Mody, L., Miller, D.K., McGloin, J.M., Freeman, M., Marcantonio, E.R., Magaziner, J., Studenski, S.: Recruitment and Retention of Older Adults in Aging Research. Journal of the American Geriatrics Society 56(12), 2340–2348 (2009)
7. Rubin, J., Chisnell, A.L.: Handbook of Usability Testing: How to Plan, Design and Conduct Effective Tests. Wiley Publishing, Inc., Indianapolis (2008)
8. Lindsay, S., Jackson, D., Schofield, G., Olivier, P.: Engaging Older People Using Participatory Design. In: SIGCHI Conference on Human Factors in Computing Systems (CHI 2012), Austin, Texas, USA (2012)
9. Gregor, P., Newell, A.F.: Designing for Dynamic Diversity - Interfaces for Older People. In: The Fifth International ACM Conference on Assistive Technologies (ASSETS 2002), Edinburgh (2002)
10. Eisma, R., Dickinson, A., Goodman, J., Syme, A., Tiwari, L., Newell, A.F.: Early User Involvement in the Development of Information Technology-Related Products for Older People. Journal of Universal Access in the Information Society 3(2), 131–140 (2004)
11. Cassim, J.: Designing Effective User Interactions - Examples from the Challenge Workshops. In: 3rd Conference of the International Association for Universal Design IAUD, Hamamatsu, Japan (2010)
12. Newell, A.F., Gregor, P., Alm, N.: HCI for Older and Disabled People in the Queen Mother Research Centre at Dundee University, Scotland. In: CHI 2006 Extended Abstracts on Human Factors in Computing Systems (CHI EA 2006), Montréal, Québec, Canada (2006)
13. Vines, J., Clarke, R., Wright, P., McCarthy, J., Olivier, P.: Configuring Participation: On How We Involve People in Design. In: CHI 2013, Paris, France (2013)
14. Vines, J., Blythe, M., Lindsay, S., Dunphy, P., Monk, A., Olivier, P.: Questionable Concepts: Critique as a Resource for Designing with Eighty Somethings. In: CHI 2012, Austin, Texas, USA (2012)
15. Newell, A.F.: Design and the Digital Divide: Insights from 40 Years in Computer Support for Older and Disabled People. Morgan & Claypool (2011)
16. Bertrand, M., Mullainathan, S.: Do People Mean What They Say? Implications for Subjective Survey Data. The American Economic Review 91(2), 67–72 (2001)

CASSIS: A Modeling Language for Customizable User Interface Designs

Jan Van den Bergh and Karin Coninx

Hasselt University - tUL - iMinds
Expertise Centre for Digital Media
Wetenschapspark 2, 3590 Diepenbeek, Belgium
{firstname.lastname}@uhasselt.be

Abstract. Current user interface modeling languages usually focus on modeling a single user interface and have a fixed set of user interface components; adding another user interface component requires an extension of the language.

In this paper we present CASSIS, a concise language that supports creation of user interface components using models instead of language extensions. It also allows the specification of design-time and runtime user interface variations. The support for variations has been used to generate constraints for custom user interface components, to specify design patterns and design decisions. CASSIS has been used in several projects including a multi-disciplinary applied research project.

1 Introduction and Related Work

This paper introduces CASSIS, Context-Aware SyStem Interaction Specification, a tool supported language to model the interaction between humans, computing systems and their user interfaces. CASSIS contains generic constructs with a corresponding (graphical) notation to model user interfaces, events, related concepts and their interactions. The language has specific constructs that allow flexible, customizable reuse of models or parts thereof through the definition of custom types and templates or interaction patterns that can be bundled in a library. These libraries can later be imported in new projects.

CASSIS supports the specification of design options, design decisions (accept, reject, runtime option), which can be used to define the structure and behavior of the specified user interface and as well as the usage context of custom types.

Several languages have been defined that target modality-independent specification of user interfaces. Van den Bergh et al. [1] give a reasonable overview of several of these languages. In contrast to CASSIS, the languages in their overview all contain a fixed amount of user interface components. Their proposal, CAP3, defines four user interface components as part of the language and defines other user interface components in a library. They, however, do not specify how this functionality is realized. In contrast to CASSIS, CAP3 is completely focused on Canonical Abstract Prototypes and extensions thereof. It does not include

S. Sauer et al. (Eds.): HCSE 2014, LNCS 8742, pp. 243–250, 2014.

events, nor design options and has no possibility to define the structure of new components.

IFML beta 1[2] is a more recent proposal for an Object Management Group standard. It does support graphical specification of events, but has a fixed set of user interface components and no support for context-awareness. A preview of the final IFML standard[1] promises to include modules that allow to define reusable flows, but the concept differs from user interface components, now extensible through stereotypes. In contrast to CASSIS, IFML exclusively focuses on interaction flow and cannot be used to specify user interface structure.

UsiXML [7,15] consists of several submodels, including a modality-independent specification of user interfaces, a context model, a domain model and several other user interface related models. UsiXML has a fixed number of user interface components.

MARIA [11] is an XML-based language that allows specification of user interfaces at different levels of abstraction. Similar to UsiXML, MARIA supports a fixed number of user interface components and its dialog expressions are connected using CTT [8] operators and it can target multiple platforms.

CUP 2.0 [14] is a UML-profile [9] that allows the specification of context-aware user interfaces. It has a fixed number of user interface components. It defines the user interface structure and behavior using two different diagrams (class diagram and activity diagram). Context-awareness is supported within the activity diagram.

UIML [4] is an XML-based language that allows the definition of user interfaces based on custom user interface component vocabularies, which are linked to very generic parts. In contrast to CASSIS, parts do not contain any specific information regarding the properties of the user interface component. All properties are specific for a UIML vocabulary. Some implementations provide support for multiple platforms.

Design decisions, visual layout similar to concrete layout (both requested by UX practitioners in interviews) were not addressed in (these) model-based approaches at this level of abstraction. Similarly, visual specification of custom user interface components and patterns with custom icons including constraint generation, which allow the user to adapt the notation (a bit) to their specific domain, were not addressed.

2   CASSIS

CASSIS is a modeling language that is defined by a metamodel (a model that defines the structure of all CASSIS models), constraints and its concrete syntax.

This section introduces the metamodel as well as the graphical concrete syntax. This graphical syntax is not completely defined within the language itself. CASSIS supports the creation of libraries of components, concepts and events, which can specify their own icon. Constraints will be informally discussed.

---

[1] http://www.slideshare.net/mbrambil/ifml-omgftfreportsanta-claracadec2013

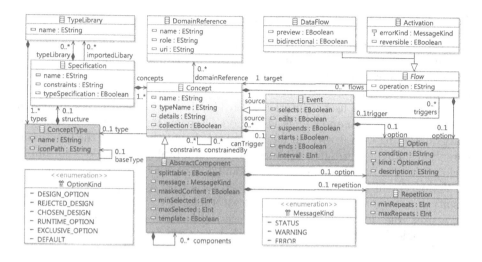

Fig. 1. The complete CASSIS metamodel

2.1 Metamodel

The CASSIS metamodel (Fig. 1) is defined using ECore [13, Chapter 5], which is part of the Eclipse Modeling Framework (EMF). It consists of twelf metaclasses (and two enumerations):

- *Concept, Event* and *AbstractComponent* define the core constructs of the language,
- *TypeLibrary, ConceptType* and *Specification* are used to enable the definition of system interaction, custom types, templates and patterns,
- *Flow, DataFlow* and *Activation* define the control and information flow,
- *Repetition* defines how many times an *AbstractComponent* can be present in a specific part of a user interface,
- *Option* defines conditional presence of *Event*s and *AbstractComponent*s, and,
- *DomainReference* allows to specify relations between the core constructs and constructs in other resources (models or other files).

Table 1. Possible option types and corresponding icons

?	DESIGN_OPTION	⚙	RUNTIME_OPTION
√	CHOSEN_DESIGN	⚙	DEFAULT
X	REJECTED_DESIGN	⚙	EXCLUSIVE_OPTION

2.2   Behavior of Interactive System

The behavior expressed by a CASSIS model is determined by events, flows and option-objects and how they connect to abstract components and concepts. For this discussion of a system's behavior specification by CASSIS, we consider only two states of a concept; active and inactive. Active components are components that are available to a user to interact with. This does not mean that for graphical user interfaces the component is visible on a screen. It means that a user can start interacting with it without having to first change the state of the functional core. E.g. changing a tab in a Ribbon interface or a tabbed dialog does not imply a change to the functional core. The meaning of active or inactive is undefined for a Concept in general. It can be defined on a case by case basis. Active for a software component could be defined as "there exists at least one instance"; for a user role, it could mean that a user with this role is logged in; or for a geographical location it could mean that its GPS location is recorded in a specific database.

Abstract components that are contained by the same component (or by no component at all) by default execute in parallel; users can interact with these components in any order and without having to complete interaction with any of them at any time. Users can even interact with several components at the same time. This corresponds to how users can interact with user interface components (widgets) contained in the same container (a window) when developers do not specify constraints between these components. This ensures that this part of the behavior coincides with what a developer might expect when using the visual syntax of CASSIS.

When one or more of the abstract components have an *Option* attached to them, this may impact this behavior; a *DEFAULT* option indicates the component that users can interact with first; it gets the default focus. There should only be one *DEFAULT* component within an abstract component. In Fig. 3, *Main Window* is the *DEFAULT* component. A *RUNTIME_OPTION* indicates that availability of the component is dependent on constraints that can be changed at runtime. Only one of all components with an *EXCLUSIVE_OPTION* Option can be active at any time. Which one this is, is determined by associated constraints. The remaining values for options have no impact on the behavior of the specified system other than static specification of the availability of components.

Three event attributes specify an effect on the source when they occur:

1. *starts*: the event never deactivates the source. When an activation relation connects the event with a *target* component, it starts in parallel.
2. *suspends*: when the source is connected through an *Activation* with a *target* component, the source is suspended until the corresponding activity *ends*. This may mean that other abstract components are activated before the originating abstract component is reactivated. When the target is the first screen of a wizard, the originating component is only reactivated after the whole wizard is completed (or canceled). When the event is not connected to an *Activation* the behavior is unspecified.
3. *ends*: the source of the event becomes inactive in all cases.

When none of the above attributes is true the source is only deactivated when the event is connected to an *Activation* whose *target* component does not have an ancestor in common with the originating component. We believe that the behavior that can be expressed using these event attributes and *Option* and *Repetition* is at least as powerful as using CTT operators as defined in [8].

2.3 Type Specification

A user can use a *ConceptType* to customize the meaning of a concept using a type *Specification*, which can be expressed in a dedicated diagram, as well as its appearance with a user-defined icon. To specify constraints on the application of the type to concepts, one should define the *structure* using a type specification. A type specification can contain manually specified *constraints*. Constraints can also be generated based on the *ConceptType*'s *structure*.

For all concepts the attribute values and associations are translated in errors or warnings. Using EGL [12] we generate EVL [5] to propose automated fixes for these constraints. Constraints for the inner structure are only generated for *template* components. When the template attribute of a component is false, its inner structure is considered as human documentation rather than constraints that should be validated by a tool.

Although all flows should originate from *Events*, it is not necessary to always specify these events if a concept type is applied to a *Concept* or *AbstractComponent*; When the event can be uniquely identified based on the type specification, the event does not have to be repeated on a *Concept* with this type specification. This significantly reduces the number of elements in a model (see Fig. 3).

2.4 Mobile City Guide

We use the mobile city guide presented by Degrandsart et al. [3] as a *specification exemplar* of a context-aware application. We present only the parts of the exemplar relevant for discussing the features of CASSIS.

The mobile city guide is an interactive application running on mobile devices (such as a smart phone or a tablet PC) that presents information about points of interest in the vicinity of the person carrying the device. The guide has two modes: a guided mode and a free walking mode. The free walking mode is considered to be more important for the users and only this mode will be implemented for the first version of the mobile guide (as indicated by the DEFAULT and RE-JECTED *Options* indicating design-time variations). To increase interactivity, the information is displayed when the user is approaching one of these points of interest. The presented information can be of various kinds: pictures, text, video, sound, etc. When approaching a point of interest, the application should quasi-instantaneously present a picture, a name and a small description and allow a user to request more information if necessary. Video and sound may be played on demand, depending on the availability of a connection to an external database and memory available on the device. The mobile city guide depends on network availability to play this video.

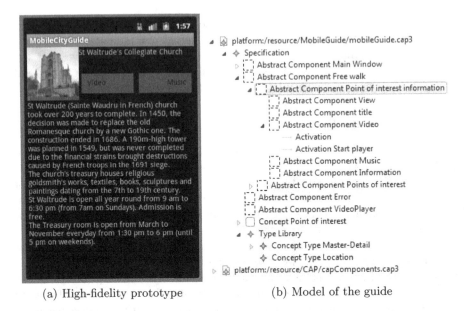

(a) High-fidelity prototype   (b) Model of the guide

Fig. 2. Mobile city guide: (a) screenshot of a prototype of the Point of interest information, and the corresponding part of the CASSIS model highlighted in (b)

Fig. 3 shows the graphical CASSIS specification of the mobile city guide. Fig. 2(b) shows the corresponding CASSIS model using a reflective EMF editor in Eclipse. The usage of the library of Canonical Abstract Prototypes components is shown on the last visible line in Fig. 2(b).

The mobile guide has three main parts: the *Main Window* (the start screen, as indicated by the *DEFAULT* option), an overview of all points of interest (*Free Walk*), and details about a Point of Interest (*Point of interest information*). A screenshot of the latter in a high-fidelity prototype is shown in Fig. 2(a). This screen is automatically shown when the user of the mobile guide is near a point of interest (*Activation* from *near Point of interest* to *Point of interest information*). The automated display of information is however dependent on user-configurable settings (*RUNTIME_OPTION*) at runtime. From this screen, the user can activate a video. As this video is downloaded over the network, this may cause an error when no network is available, modeled through a thick red *Activation* arrow to the *Error* message.

3   Assessment and Discussion

At several stages during its development CASSIS was discussed with interaction designers and user interface developers from industry and academia. These discussions formed the basis for major and minor revisions to CASSIS. Making these changes was greatly eased through tool support, which was created and frequently recreated using Eclipse EMF [13] and Epsilon [6].

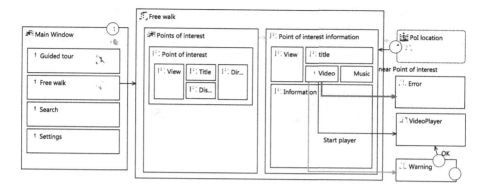

Fig. 3. Mobile city guide specification using CASSIS; the CAP library; *Free walk*, a master-detail template component; and a custom Location concept (Fig. 2(b), bottom)

The developed models had varying sizes. The largest model had over 100 model elements (excluding the Canonical Abstract Prototypes library used to create the model). It was successfully used to discuss the structure and behavior of a context-aware mobile application, targeting professional caregivers for people with dementia, with academic and industrial partners in an applied research project[2]. The people involved in the discussion included 4 persons with a software development and software engineering background, a cognitive scientist and a designer. The fact that the screens were presented within their interaction context, meant that the discussion was not only focused on the structure, but also on the behavior of the designed application. The ability of the supporting tool to hide the details of structures nested within a component was also helpful to focus the discussion on a particular part of the interface.

Proof-of-concept tool support for CASSIS has been realized using Eclipse EMF [13], and a subset of the Epsilon [6] tools. This tool support allows the specification of CASSIS models and diagrams, the generation and validation of constraints of concept type *structures* as well as the generation of Android layout specifications, including the corresponding Java code from a CASSIS model, such as that in Fig. 2(b) and the associated diagram (Fig. 3).

4   Conclusions

This paper introduced CASSIS, a tool-supported modeling language that supports customizable user interface designs. We believe that CASSIS tackles an important issue in user interface system research [10]; it supports system interaction specification in an adaptable manner. This allows a user interface design and engineering team to more effectively communicate about the specification.

---

[2] http://www.iminds.be/en/projects/2014/03/05/atom.

CASSIS was used to specify the interaction with a mobile city guide, including both design-time and runtime variation points. We were able to generate all layouts of this mobile city guide from the presented model and diagram. Generation of interactive prototypes from CASSIS models can be future work.

Acknowledgments This work was partly supported by FWO project Transforming human interface designs via model driven engineering (G. 0296.08). Master thesis students Jochem Vanderheiden and Yves Bottelbergs contributed to the tool support.

References

1. Van den Bergh, J., Luyten, K., Coninx, K.: Cap3: context-sensitive abstract user interface specification. In: EICS 2011, pp. 31–40. ACM, New York (2011)
2. Bongio, A., Brambilla, M., Butti, S., Comai, A., Ferronato, P., Fraternali, P., Kling, W., Molteni, E.: Interaction Flow Modeling Language (IFML) Version 0.2.3 (6 2012), OMG Doc. Nr.: ifml/2012-08-20
3. Degrandsart, S., Demeyer, S., Van den Bergh, J., Mens, T.: A transformation-based approach to context-aware modelling. Software & Systems Modeling 13, 191–208 (2014), http://dx.doi.org/10.1007/s10270-012-0239-y
4. Helms, J., Schaefer, R., Luyten, K., Vanderdonckt, J., Vermeulen, J., Abrams, M. (eds.): User Interface Markup Language (UIML) Version 4.0. OASIS (January 2008)
5. Kolovos, D., Paige, R., Polack, F.: Detecting and repairing inconsistencies across heterogeneous models. In: ICST, pp. 356–364. IEEE (2008)
6. Kolovos, D., Rose, L., Page, R.: The Epsilon Book. Web (2011), http://www.eclipse.org/gmt/epsilon
7. Limbourg, Q., Vanderdonckt, J.: UsiXML: A User Interface Description Language Supporting Multiple Levels of Independence. In: Engineering Advanced Web Applications. Rinton Press (December 2004)
8. Mori, G., Paternò, F., Santoro, C.: CTTE: support for developing and analyzing task models for interactive system design. IEEE Trans. Software Eng. 28(8), 797–813 (2002)
9. Object Management Group: UML 2.2 Superstructure Specification (February 2009)
10. Olsen Jr., D.R.: Evaluating user interface systems research. In: UIST 2007, pp. 251–258. ACM (2007), http://doi.acm.org/10.1145/1294211.1294256
11. Paternò, F., Santoro, C., Spano, L.D.: Maria: A universal, declarative, multiple abstraction-level language for service-oriented applications in ubiquitous environments. ACM Trans. Comput.-Hum. Interact. 16(4) (2009)
12. Rose, L.M., Paige, R., Kolovos, D.S., Polack, F.A.: The epsilon generation language. In: Schieferdecker, I., Hartman, A. (eds.) ECMDA-FA 2008. LNCS, vol. 5095, pp. 1–16. Springer, Heidelberg (2008), http://dx.doi.org/10.1007/978-3-540-69100-6_1
13. Steinberg, D., Budinsky, F., Paternostro, M., Merks, E.: EMF: Eclipse Modeling Framework 2.0, 2nd edn. Addison-Wesley Professional (2009)
14. Van den Bergh, J., Coninx, K.: CUP 2.0: High-level modeling of context-sensitive interactive applications. In: Wang, J., Whittle, J., Harel, D., Reggio, G. (eds.) MoDELS 2006. LNCS, vol. 4199, pp. 140–154. Springer, Heidelberg (2006)
15. Vanderdonckt, J., Beuvens, F., Melchior, J., Tesoriero, R. (eds.): USer Interface eXtensible Markup Language (UsiXML). UCL (February 2012)

Creating and Using Personas in Software Development: Experiences from Practice

Jane Billestrup[1], Jan Stage[1], Anders Bruun[1], Lene Nielsen[2], and Kira S. Nielsen[2]

[1] Aalborg University, Department of Computer Science, 9220 Aalborg East, Denmark
[2] IT University of Copenhagen, 2300 Copenhagen S, Denmark
{jane,jans,bruun}@cs.aau.dk, {lene,kist}@itu.dk

Abstract. Personas is a technique that supports designing and engineering interactive systems with the focus on the end-users. This paper reports from a case study, where we interviewed four software developers about their usage of personas in software development practice. The purpose of was to identify the practices of personas development in the software development industry. How the respondents perceive personas and its use does not always correlate with what is described as best practice in the literature. We found that practitioners are not using personas as stated in the literature but are developing their own practices both in regards to when and how personas are created.

Keywords: Personas, software development practice, persona creation.

1 Introduction

Personas is a technique that supports designing and engineering interactive systems with focus on the end-users. The common understanding of the personas technique is that a persona is a description of a fictitious person [4, 13] based on data collected about the target user group. The common way to represent a persona is as a text describing, and a photo depicting, the fictional user [4, 25]. Personas has been promoted as a strong technique for providing software developers with an understanding of the prospective users of their software [5]. Personas also provides the software developers with empathy for, and engagement in, the end-users [10].

Matthews et al. [15] found that designers who had a very positive attitude towards personas were primarily those who had done extensive work with personas and had some training in the creation of personas, and used them as described by the literature. Those who had worked less with personas had a moderate or neutral opinion, and those who had not worked with personas had a negative or indifferent opinion.

This paper reports from a case study of experiences with creation and use of personas in software development practice. The case study is based on interviews with four developers who are or have been working with personas in practice. Our focus is on comparing the literature with the experiences and the perceived strengths and weaknesses of the persona technique from the perspective of the software development industry. The following section presents work related to this study. Section 3 describes the method used

S. Sauer et al. (Eds.): HCSE 2014, LNCS 8742, pp. 251–258, 2014.
© IFIP International Federation for Information Processing 2014

for data collection. Section 4 presents the results derived from the interviews. Section 5 discusses the results compared to experiences about personas reported in the literature and provides the conclusion.

2   Related Work

Definition of Personas. The literature originally defined personas as a text and a photo describing the character [4, 6]. This then developed into posters, websites and handouts [14]. Personas are considered to be most useful if they are developed as whole characters, described with enough detail for designers and developers to get a feeling of its personality [1, 5, 14]. The benefits of personas are that they enable designers to envision the end-user's needs and wants, remind designers that their own needs are not necessarily the end-users' needs, and provide an effective communication tool, which facilitates better design decisions [7, 8, 9, 16].

Creating Personas. Before creating personas, a comprehensive study of the target user group is suggested. It has been suggested to acquire this information through interviews with the target user group [23] or observational studies of them [24]. Yet Chapman and Milham argue that it is not possible to verify that the created personas actually reflect the target user group [3]. It has been suggested to create 3-5 personas [26, 27], but the amount of users' one persona can represent has been questioned [3].

Personas Critique. Personas have been characterized as unreliable and not well communicated. In addition, developers lack understanding of the technique, personas are non-scientific, they are not able to describe actual people, and they prevent designers from meeting actual users [1, 11, 17].

Personas in Practice. An inquiry of design teams in 13 Danish companies reported that personas help keep the focus on user needs instead of what the developers and designers like, and help in gaining an understanding of how the product can create value for end-users [12]. A different study has described how designers are using personas contrary to the original intended usage; instead of creating personas on research results, designers tend to base the personas on their own experiences and thoughts [2]. This will make it even harder to ensure that the right personas are created to represent the relevant user groups [3]. Problems in application of the personas technique caused by the mindset of the developers have also been reported [1, 13]. It has been suggested to overcome this by regularly sending information about the personas to the development team [14, 18]. It seems difficult in practice to avoid making stereotypes when creating personas, and using personas does not solve the problem that Cooper originally intended to solve [28].

Combining personas and agile development, e.g. XP, has also been explored. In this case, the customer preferred a persona without a picture, merely describing a job title and maybe a name, but they do not support this as it will take away the developers' empathy for the users. Moreover, by using personas integrated in XP, the developers felt confident to make decisions without involving the onsite customer every time [21].

3   Method

We have conducted a case study about the use of personas as a development technique in four software development organizations, including if and how practitioners use personas and how they actually use this technique in practice.

Respondents. We did a survey to identify software developers who had different types of experience with using personas as part of the software development process. This involved several developers who had volunteered to participate in an interview about personas usage. From this group, we identified four different kinds of software developer experience with personas:

- Wants to start using personas as a development technique.
- Has formerly used personas as a development technique.
- Is currently using personas as a development technique.
- Has knowledge about it but never used it as a development technique.

The respondents were working as software developers or project managers. None of them had any education in user experience. All respondents had worked in the industry for at least ten years and been in their current organization for at least two years. Their organizations use an agile software development method.

Data Collection. The interviews were conducted as semi-structured qualitative interviews [19]. The interviews lasted between 22 and 55 minutes. They were recorded and then fully transcribed.

Data Analysis. All interviews were analysed using grounded theory and open coding with the Dedoose tool (https://app.dedoose.com/App/?Version=4.5.98). This resulted in seven categories that are used to structure the presentation of our findings.

4   Findings

This section presents the findings based on the analysis of the interviews. The findings are divided into seven sub-sections in accordance with the coding categories.

4.1   Learning to Create Personas

The respondents learned about the personas technique in different ways. Their first meeting with personas seems to mainly have happened by chance. Two respondents describe it this way:

R2: The first time I heard about personas was at a session with the humanities department four or five years ago. ... Microsoft has created a number of personas describing the users some years ago. They encourage us, as Microsoft consultants, to use these in our development process.

R1: I have a background as a software developer but in my former employment I worked very closely with user experience designers.

One respondent came from a smaller company where he learned about several usability techniques and why it was important to understand and represent the users' in the development process.

4.2   The Basis for Creating Personas

The respondents use different ways of collecting data for the creation of personas. Yet all of them depend either on information they already have or information the customers have. None of the respondents get money or time allocated specifically to gather information about the target user group.

R1: If we don't have enough information ourselves to create the personas we will ask our customers about their usage of the existing systems.

A respondent explained that he was creating personas a bit differently than suggested by the literature. He primarily thought about the existing users and the archetypes that were standing out.

R3: We know our users quite well. Our personas are based on real users, like "can this user understand this?" We use them like personas archetypes. We do not use personas formalized. Unformalized we use personas quite a lot. Personas are based on the users who are critical towards our system; the people that make noise if they have a problem.

R2: To me a persona does not have to be too detailed in the description of the person.

None of the respondents remembered reading specific literature about personas. They had mainly learned the dos and don'ts about personas from others, or from their own experiences.

4.3   Usefulness of Personas

Personas are considered particularly useful when the developers are missing information about users and their work. One respondent mentioned geographical distance between designers and developers as a condition for usefulness:

R3: I find personas useful if the distance between designers and developers is substantial and they are not working side by side all day.

Another respondent explained that he found personas very useful as a substitute for onsite customers:

R1: If there is no onsite customer or employee that knows the field we are developing for very well, personas seems to be very usable. The further the designers and developers are from the users, the more value personas can bring to the development process.

This respondent's company does considerable work for the health sector, and they used to have a former nurse employed to help them understand that domain. However, this was no longer an option, so they needed to find new techniques to bring an understanding of the user groups into the development process. He thought personas could do that.

Another respondent gave an example of where he found personas to be useful;

R2: We are creating ERP solutions. I feel that personas are a relevant tool for us. Because we are developing very specific software solutions for our customers.

This respondent also outlined different opinions about the usefulness of personas:

R2: One of my colleagues approached me one day and said the following "we live by creating solutions, not drawings." I understand his position but personally I feel that drawing up the organization first can help me understand their needs.

4.4   Strengths of Personas

The respondents expressed different expectations about the benefits of using personas in the development process:

R4: I believe using personas would have helped us develop a more user-friendly system.

R1: Personas can help keeping the developer's focus on the users' needs. Personas will provide the software developer with the ability to understand the users' perspective.

R2: I think that personas can provide the security for us not developing the wrong system for our user group.

One respondent added that he found personas especially useful if using a development method like the waterfall method. His argument was that when using the waterfall method the developers have only one possibility to get everything right.

R3: If using the waterfall development method you have to get everything right the first time. When developing agile it is not as critical if we make a mistake, we can change that in the next iteration as a new iteration starts every two weeks.

4.5   Redundancy of Personas

Two respondents stated that personas are unnecessary if user experience designers or expert users are part of the project team, so design decisions are not only left to the developers:

R4: When design is not left to the developer but is in place long before the developers begin to create the software.

R3: If you have an employee who is an expert user and knows what the user group need, personas are unnecessary.

4.6   Weaknesses and Limitations of Personas

The respondents agreed that using personas incorrectly can have substantial negative impact on software or product development. They also agreed that personas should not be used if there is insufficient data or if the creators are unfamiliar with personas.

R2: If the choice you make when creating the personas is wrong they will work against the design.

Another respondent raised the concern that he felt constrained by some formalized personas. Every time he was in doubt he went to look at the persona, but this meant that he got boxed in, and it stopped him from looking outside of the box.

R3: When using personas formalized you might be a bit constrained, always going to look at the posters with the personas [...] To me it works better if I just keep them in my head. Of course our company is not that large anyway so I can just go talk to the developers if I need to change something.

Another respondent had drawn a similar conclusion:

R1: What tends to go wrong in software development is that developers tend to lock on some user requirements pretty early in the process, without documentation, and then describe the entire solution. If the user requirements or the solution change at some point, the developers tend to forget the user and their needs somewhere in the process.

Using personas requires a certain level of maturity. Another respondent's current organization was not using personas:

R1: "We are not using the personas technique at the moment. I have worked with personas in my last employment and found them very useful. I would like to introduce personas in my current employment but the company needs to be at a higher level of maturity before it would make sense. We simply have larger issues at the moment than this".

4.7   Personas with Other Techniques

The respondents stated that scenarios are very usable in combination with personas.

R4: Scenarios are often used in combination with personas.

R3: We have a community around our product and we host meetings with user groups, where we meet three times a year and discuss new releases and improvements.

Three respondents described that they are primarily using user stories to document the users' needs. The user stories are described by two respondents as being used instead of developing a specification of requirements.

R3: We use common sense and we are not afraid of making a mistake because it is okay if we do not get it right the first time.

5   Discussion and Conclusion

This paper has reported from a case study of experiences with creation and use of personas in software development practice. There are still only few studies of the actual use of personas in software development practice [20]. The purpose of this case study was to identify in detail how practitioners in the industry create and use personas in their development processes.

In many development situations, users do not know what they want, thus it is the designer's job to find out. Pruitt and Grudin [14] argue that a good design does not come from users, but from designers. This is because users do not really know what they want until they get it. It is described in the literature that personas is a useful technique to keep the developers focused on the users and their needs and give them empathy towards the personas and the end-users [5, 10].

We found that the respondents perceived personas as a technique that supports designing and engineering interactive systems with a focus on the end-users. Matthews et al. [15] found that mainly developers who have been working with personas are positive in regards to a technique like personas. That was the same impression we got from our respondents. A technique like personas is also still suffering from seeming unnecessary to some developers; e.g one respondent explained that his colleague told him creating background material or drawings was a waste of time.

The practitioners do not use personas as suggested in the literature. Instead, data is collected before creating personas and it is mainly collected within their own or the customers' organization, or personas are created on the basis of real users.

Baird [22] argued that personas could be developed in a workshop while discovering requirements. One of our respondents described how they both used personas and hosted meetings with their user group regularly. These meetings were also used to get to know their users and to help get an understanding of the customers' needs.

Personas are primarily considered useful if designers and developers are not working closely together to ensure that the developers understand the intended users and use, or merely as a representation of a user if there is no onsite costumer available.

Using personas has also been described as being risky. If the personas created are targeting a wrong user group, the software solution could end up being developed for the wrong users.

Scenarios and user-stories are considered useful in combination with personas. In particular, user stories have been used to describe user situations and as a requirements specification.

The results presented in this paper are qualitative. They are based on four developers who have been interviewed in depth. The number of respondents is obviously a limitation of this study; yet only few software companies are using the personas technique in their development process, so it is very challenging to find even a few respondents with experiences from using the personas technique. It would be interesting to conduct a more extensive series of interviews practitioners about their use of personas and study how that influence the quality of the systems they develop.

References

1. Blomquist, Å., Arvola, M.: Personas in action: Ethnography in an Interaction Design Team. In: Proc. of NordiCHI, ACM 1-1-58113-616-1/02/0010 (2002)
2. Chang, Y., Lim, Y., Stolterman, E.: Personas: From Theory to Practices. In: Proc. of NordiCHI, pp. 439–442 (2008)
3. Chapman, C.N., Milham, R.: The Personas' new clothes: Methodological and practical arguments against a popular method. In: Proc. of HFES, pp. 634–636 (2006)
4. Cooper, A.: The Inmates Are Running the Asylum. SAMS, Indianapolis (1999)

5. Cooper, A., Reimann, R.: About face 2.0: The essentials of interaction design. Wiley Publishing (2003)
6. Cooper, A., Reimann, R., Cronin, D.: About Face 3.0: The Essentials of Interaction Design. Wiley (2007)
7. Long, F.: Real or Imaginary - the Effect of Using Personas in Product Design. In: IES Conference, 2009 Dublin: Irish Ergonomics Review (2009)
8. Ma, J., LeRouge, C.: Introducing User Profiles and Personas into Information Systems Development. In: AMCIS 2007, paper 237 (2007)
9. Miaskiewicza, T., Kozarb, K.A.: Personas and User-centered Design: How Can Personas Benefit Product Design Processes? In Design Studies 32(5), 417–430 (2011)
10. Nielsen, L.: Engaging Personas and Narrative Scenarios. PhD Series, vol. 17. Samfundslitteratur, Copenhagen (2004)
11. Nielsen, L.: Personas - User Focused Design. Human-Computer Interaction. Springer (2012)
12. Nielsen, L., Nielsen, K.S., Stage, J., Billestrup, J.: Going global with personas. In: Kotzé, P., Marsden, G., Lindgaard, G., Wesson, J., Winckler, M. (eds.) INTERACT 2013, Part IV. LNCS, vol. 8120, pp. 350–357. Springer, Heidelberg (2013)
13. Pruitt, J., Adlin, T.: The Persona Lifecycle: Keeping People in Mind Throughout Product Design. Morgan Kaufmann, San Francisco (2006)
14. Pruitt, J., Grudin, J.: Personas: Practice and theory. In: Proc. of DUX (2003)
15. Matthews, T., Judge, T., Whittaker, S.: How do designers and user experience professionals actually perceive and use Personas? In: Proc. of CHI 2012. ACM (2012)
16. Grudin, J., Pruitt, J.: Personas, Participatory Design and Product Development: An Infrastructure for Engagement. In: Proc. of PDC, pp. 144–161 (2002)
17. Bak, J., Nguyen, K., Rissgaard, P., Stage, J.: Obstacles to usability evaluation in practice: a survey of software development organizations. In: Proc. of NordiCHI (2008)
18. Faily, S., Flechais, I.: Persona cases: A technique for grounding Personas. In: Proc. of CHI, pp. 2267–2270 (2011)
19. Kvale, S.: Interview. Hans Reitzel, København (1997)
20. Billestrup, J., Stage, J., Nielsen, L., Nielsen, K.S.: Persona usage in software development: Advantages and Obstacles. In: Proc. of ACHI, pp. 359–364 (2014)
21. Powell, S., Keenan, F., McDaid, K.: Enhancing Agile Requirements Elicitation With Personas. IADIS International Journal on Computer Science and Information Systems 2(1), 82–95 (2007)
22. Baird, S.: Using Personas To Discover Requirements (2002), http://philarnold.co.uk/wp-content/uploads/2009/10/User-Personas.pdf (December 21, 2013)
23. Levin, D.: Which Personas are you targeting? 5 Minute Whitepaper (2004)
24. Quesenbery, W.: Using Personas: Bringing Users Alive. STC Usability SIG Newsletter-Usability Interface (2004)
25. Nielsen, L.: A model for Personas and scenarios creation, Roskilde, Denmark, p. 71 (November 27, 2003)
26. Adlin, T., Pruitt, J.: The essential persona lifecycle: Your guide to building and using personas. Morgan Kaufmann, Burlington (2010)
27. Friess, E.: Personas and decision making in the design process: an ethnographic case study. In: Proceedings of CHI 2012, pp. 1209–1218. ACM (2012)
28. Turner, P., Turner, S.: Is stereotyping inevitable when designing with personas? Design Studies 32(1), 30–44 (2011)

Improving UX Work in Scrum Development: A Three-Year Follow-Up Study in a Company

Kati Kuusinen

Tampere University of Technology, Tampere, Finland
kati.kuusinen@tut.fi

Abstract. This paper presents a three-year follow-up study considering the improvement process of user experience work in a software company utilizing Scrum. Problems encountered in the organization included managing the product vision, timing of UX, lack of cooperation among disciplines, and understanding user needs. We also observed changes in the organization over two years. They included ceasing the centralized UX team and dividing the UX specialists over business lines. UX specialists were given influential roles in regard to product decisions – such as nominated as product owners.

Keywords: User experience (UX), Scrum, Agile development.

1 Introduction

Agile methods [5] are commonly utilized in industrial software development. However, guidance on those methods still lacks user experience (UX) [4] activities. Current recommendations for agile UX development suggest dividing the work into activities that are conducted within agile development and activities that are prior to development Sprints as design upfront work [1]. They also typically separate UX related work to its own stream to be conducted by separate UX specialists. However, organizations using such practices struggle with issues such as balancing the amount of design upfront work, and communication between developers and UX specialists [1]. Separating the UX designer to another stream seems to keep the UX designer out of the core team, which hinders within-project communication and endangers the realization of UX design as the product vision gets blurred [3].

In this paper we report a three-year follow-up study where a company advanced in Scrum[1] and with an established UX team aimed at a better integration of those disciplines. We started the study in 2011 by a current state analysis to explore the situation of that time and to enable and focus improvements. We conducted an international web survey with 31 open- and 19 closed-ended questions, followed by 17 theme interviews [6]. Moreover, during 2012 and 2013, the organization adopted new ways of working and we measured their impact with surveys and interviews.

---

[1] Schwaber, K. Agile project management with Scrum, 1st ed., Microsoft Press. 2004.

S. Sauer et al. (Eds.): HCSE 2014, LNCS 8742, pp. 259–266, 2014.

2   Research Process

The studied company was mainly producing specialized software that was supplied via internet service providers (ISP) for consumers. The main product of the company was a software system with massive yearly releases. Large multinational ISPs were dominant when deciding of the feature content for the next release. The company had about 800 employees mainly in Finland, France, and Malaysia. The company was utilizing their own Scrum-based process model in their development. During 2011 the company had a centralized UX team with about 15 members and a few distributed UX specialists. In the beginning of 2013 the UX team as such was ceased and the UX specialists were distributed through the new business lines.

Study Conducted in Year 2011. We started the study in 2011 with a current state analysis to determine where and how to change working practices in order to improve the UX work in the company. Of the company employees working in development related roles from Finland, France, Malaysia and Russia, 76 responded to a web survey. Participant roles included developers, managers, architects, product owners, scrum masters, UX specialists, and quality engineers. The survey consisted of 50 questions (31 open- and 19 closed-ended) on processes and tools, collaboration and communication, and concepts and knowledge in the company [6]. Moreover, we conducted 17 interviews on UX specialists, product line managers, product owners, scrum masters, architects, developers, and quality engineers on the Helsinki site.

Monitoring the Organization Performance in Year 2012. The cooperation between the researcher and the organization was smaller during 2012. The researcher mainly observed a new practice in the organization and discussed and gave some guidance to a few members of the organization as they implemented changes in the organization.

Study Conducted in Year 2013. We started the second current state analysis with a preliminary mapping consisting of five interviews in spring 2013. The interview data was enriched with unofficial "corridor discussions" and some email discussions. The aim of the preliminary mapping was both to gain a high-level understanding of the current state in the agile UX work and to create a preliminary list of possible changes to enable further ideation and discussion. We conducted the actual round of measurements inside one business line in October 2013 by surveying and interviewing six persons working for the business line at the Helsinki site of the company. First, all the participants filled in a short web survey individually (Table 1) and later we interviewed them in pairs. The participants represented the same business line from where the majority of the participants of the 2011 study were. We selected participants using theoretical sampling; with an approach that does not aim at representative sample but a sample that offers to compare to previous findings [2].

Change (Question 6): as the business lines in the company had been rearranged recently, we asked respondents to compare the current situation within the business line to the situation that prevailed a year ago in the organization the respondent were then working for. We use the abbreviations of the studied areas presented in Table 2 throughout this paper.

Table 1. Survey questions, their types and used scales

---

1. The overall satisfaction of UX related work in the business line
    Measured on a scale from 1 (not at all satisfied) to 7 (completely satisfied)
2. Issues in UX related work that the respondent is currently most dissatisfied with
    Open-ended question, listing of 0-3 issues
3. Issues in UX related work that the respondent is currently most satisfied with
    Open-ended question, listing of 0-3 issues
4. Means to improve the current situation
    Open-ended question, text area
5. Level of performance on certain areas of UX related work and their importance to project success. The studied areas (11 items) are listed in Table 2.
    Fourfold table: x-axis: performance from poor to excellent, y-axis: importance from insignificant to significant.
6. The change within last year in the level of performance on the studied areas (areas are listed in Table 2)
    Change was evaluated on the following scale: worsened greatly, worsened somewhat, worsened slightly, no change, improved slightly, improved somewhat, improved greatly

---

Table 2. Studied areas of agile UX work. Level of performance and importance for project success and experienced change were measured for these areas (see items 5 and 6 in Table 1).

Abbreviation	Studied area
A	**Agility** of UX work
T	**Timing** of UX work
W	**Welcoming** late change
C	**Competence** in the project team
B	Maintaining the **big picture** of the project
U	**Understanding** user needs
M	**Meeting** user needs
F	Getting user **feedback**
P	Cooperation between **product owners** (PO) and UX specialists (UXS)
D	Cooperation between **developers** and UX specialists
Q	UX implementation **quality**

3   Results

Next, we present the results from our study in two parts. First, we briefly revisit findings from the study conducted during 2011 already reported in [6]. Then, we concentrate on the results of the study conducted in 2013, and address the changes that can be observed.

3.1   Year 2011 – Analyzing the Problems in Agile UX Work

The company had had some issues in integrating UX work into other agile development practices. They wanted to clarify their understanding of the problems in order to improve the situation. In a web survey answered by 76 R&D related employees and with 17 interviewees we determined the following: 1) Which issues are considered as the biggest challenges in the agile UX work; 2) Which tasks are considered as the most important duties of the UX team; and 3) How the employees would improve the agile UX work and communication between different R&D roles.

The top three challenges in agile UX work included managing the big picture of the project, changing the UX team's way of working from traditional waterfall practices to agile practices, and proper timing of UX work in agile process. Other major challenges were lack of cooperation between different roles, and being able to understand user needs and fulfilling them by the software (Figure 1).

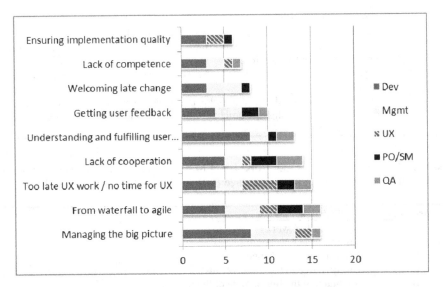

Fig. 1. Biggest challenges in agile UX work by respondent role (results 2011). Horizontal axis presents the amount of respondents. Legend: QA = quality assurance, PO/SM = product owner/ scrum master, UX = UX specialist, Mgmt = manager, Dev = developer. Total number of respondents was 60; each named 1-3 issues.

Study participants emphasized the most that they would like to have closer collaboration between UX specialists and other development roles. The most often mentioned manner of improving the cooperation was to include UX specialists in Scrum teams instead of having them work in a separate UX team.

3.2   Year 2012 – Implementing New Practices in R&D

The company implemented a method called "UX review board" to raise the visibility and understanding of UX related problems of products [6]. The aim was to get UX issues into backlog items to ensure and fasten the process of actually fixing those. The practice improved the visibility and understanding of UX issues. However, it did not work as planned – in many cases the product owner agreed the found issues are severe but still did not welcome them in the backlog as the PO felt the backlog was already overloaded with other issues. Singh [7] reported similar problems; priority of UX tasks remained low and thus they rarely got implemented.

The company adopted a new role of UX engineer to the R&D organization. The role was to work inside Scrum teams as a link between UX designers and developers. UX engineers were people with both coding and UX skills. First, the company had difficulties in recruiting such multi-talents. Later, they noticed they did not manage to maintain the work contents of the role as planned; UX engineers were observed to mainly concentrate on implementing the UI. It became evident that it required changes on the organization level to improve the impact of the agile UX work; the organization structure seemed to hinder from improving the effectiveness of the UX work.

3.3   Year 2013 – Changing the Organization Structure

There were plans to make noticeable changes on the organization level as the previous attempts had not had a desired effect. We started a second round of current state analysis in the beginning of 2013. We used a more lightweight approach than previously to save time and costs. We started by preliminary theme interviews, continued with an expert evaluation and group discussion, and finally conducted a web survey and structured pair interviews. Next, we present the results.

Background Mapping. The idea of preliminary interviews and discussions was to gain understanding on how employees would like to change the current state and which issues they consider the major challenges in agile UX work at the moment. A researcher interviewed five persons from the organization and based on the findings formed a suggestion on how to improve the current state of agile UX work. The main items of the suggestion were the following:

- "Away from silos"; UX needs to be considered in every phase from roadmap to delivery and it must be everybody's concern, and team performance metrics should include a UX-related instrument.
- Mutual project goals, support goal-setting; developers still need more understanding of UX specialists' work contents and goals.
- Spread UX mindset in the organization; continuing the "cultural change"; increasing the understanding of the importance and meaning of UX work.
- Prototype and utilize multi-phase testing on actual users.
- Emphasize early cooperation and iterative way of working.

Expert Evaluation: Comparing the situations of years 2011 and 2013. During summer 2013, an experienced UX specialist walked through the report of the study conducted in 2011 and commented on how they thought the situation had changed since. Next, we list the found issues and the comments of the UX specialist. Found issues are numbered and comments of the UX specialist are started with "UXS:" and printed in italics.

1. UX work is not really integrated with R&D ways of working. (2011)
   - UXS: *"To the best of my knowledge, this is not true anymore. **All the UX team's work I see is done in close collaboration with developers.**"* (2013)

2. It seems that the importance of UX work is generally acknowledged but there is a wish that it should not cost or take time. (2011)
   - UXS: *"This, I think has improved ... projects try find **special sprints to clean up UI** ... or **there really is no work on UI that is not involving the UX team**."* (2013)
3. UX issues are not ordered together with other issues in backlog. Lack of considering UX when creating the minimum viable product.
   - UXS: *"Both issues are (slowly) improving."* (2013)
4. Inadequate communication between architects and the UX team. (2011)
   - UXS: ***"This has improved greatly. Architecture is one of the main issues affecting the UX as experienced by consumers."*** (based on experiences in development of two separate products) (2013)
5. UX work is often conducted in reactive manner. The UX team needs to hurry to get ahead of implementation, but they report often failing in doing so. (2011)
   - UXS: *"In my experience UX team(s) are **quite busy**. ... In the projects I have been involved in the **design has not been reactive**. ... The work is in any case **creative collaboration** - so agile."* (2013)
6. UX work is not properly integrated with the R&D work. (2011)
   - UXS: *"To some extent I do feel UX will always be a little outside of development; it is a different mindset with different educational background and **as a discipline it is UX team's role to challenge**."* (2013)

3.4   Measurement of the Situation after the Organizational Level Change

The organization was rearranged and the centralized UX team as such was ceased in fall 2013. UX specialists were divided to different product lines, and they were given more influential positions in the organization.

Issues in UX Related Work That Respondents Were Most Satisfied with. We asked the participants to list issues that they are most satisfied with in the current ways of working. In general, participants reported that the organization has positive and active attitude; work gets done, tasks are novel and interesting, and new technologies and tools are adopted. Both developers' and UX specialists' skills in UX and attitude towards it were appreciated. UX specialists' cooperation with developers, product management, and marketing were all mentioned. Also, user participation both in planning and feedback gathering was considered good.

Nominating an experienced UX specialist as a product owner had given the person more influence on the product vision. However, it was criticized that it was more of a career decision than actual change on the process level: if the person e.g. chooses to leave the company, it is not a company policy to nominate another UX aware person to replace them.

Issues in UX Related Work That Respondents Were Most Dissatisfied with, and Means to Improve the Current Situation. Diversity and poor quality of used tools caused dissatisfaction. Both own and several third party UI frameworks were in use which was reported to cause extra work. In addition, delivering several clients instead of building one product with several touchpoints was criticized. Also, it was mentioned that the current development tool did not allow creating high-quality UX.

There was still a small number of UX specialists in the company compared to the amount of UX work. UX specialists were overwhelmed with work and that led to implementing new features without UX design, or with *"very basic design"* that was mentioned to be often late. Also, both an architect and a UX specialist reported that the visibility of the contents of concept and design work and timing of those tasks should be improved: *"...the implementation request often comes as a surprise, or I find out after the implementation has begun"* – an architect.

Level of Performance on Studied Areas and Their Importance to Project Success. We asked the participants to evaluate both the importance of the studied areas to project success (from unimportant to important) and the performance of their organization in those areas (from poor to excellent) on a fourfold table (Figure 2). The most important areas for project success were maintaining the big picture of the project (76.7), understanding user needs (75.0), project team competence (74.5), and proper timing of UX work (71.7). The organization performed best on maintaining the big picture (56.2), project team competence (55.2) and getting user feedback (53.3).

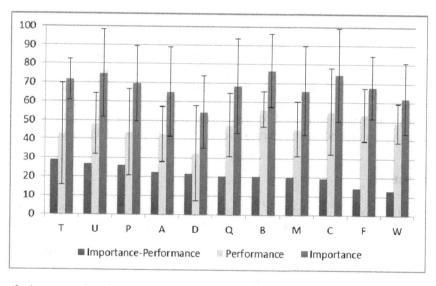

Fig. 2. Averages of performance and importance (middle and rightmost columns) on certain areas (letters T-W) and their standard deviations arranged by the difference between the importance and performance (leftmost bars without standard deviation lines). T = Timing of UX work, U = Understanding user needs, P = PO-UXS cooperation, A = Agility of UX work, D = Developer-UXS cooperation, Q = Quality of UX implementation, B = Big picture maintaining, M = Meeting user needs, C = Competence in project team, F = Getting user feedback, and W = Welcoming late change.

There were largest gaps between importance and performance in the following: timing of UX work (29.0), understanding user needs (26.8) and cooperation between UX specialists and product owners (26.0). Participants agreed the most on their level of performance in big picture management (SD=9.6), and welcoming late change (SD=10.3). Largest values of standard deviation were measured for timing of UX work (27.0) and cooperation between developers and UX specialists (25.3). Both the lowest and highest assessments of performance were given by a developer and an architect. It probably indicates that there are project or individual-specific ways of working inside the business line.

4   Summary and Conclusions

This paper presents a three-year follow-up study considering the improvement process of agile user experience work in a software company. In the initial state the organization was following Scrum methodology in software development and it had an established UX team. However, the organization had problems with integrating the work of these two disciplines. The major problems included managing the big picture of the project (product vision), timing of UX work, lack of cooperation between disciplines, and understanding and fulfilling user needs. We conducted major changes in the organization over two years. Changes included ceasing the centralized UX team as such and dividing the UX specialists over different business lines. UX specialists were given more influential roles in regards to product level decisions. These practices were reported to improve the big picture management and understanding user needs. However, there were significant differences in evaluations between individuals in timing of UX work, cooperation between UX specialists and other disciplines, and the agility of UX work. This indicates that the practices still are strongly person-dependent and there is need for more established approaches.

References

1. da Silva, T., Martin, A., Maurer, F., Silveira, M.: User-centered design and Agile methods: a systematic review. In: Proc. of the International Conference on Agile Methods in Software Development (Agile 2011) (2011)
2. Eisenhardt, K.M.: Building theories from case study research. Academy of Management Review 14(4), 532–550 (1989)
3. Hodgetts, P.: Experiences integrating sophisticated UX design into agile process. In: Proc. AGILE 2005 Conference (2005)
4. ISO 9241-210:2010. Ergonomics of human-system interaction. Part 210: Human-centered design for interactive systems
5. Highsmith, J., Cockburn, A.: Agile software development: The business of innovation. Computer 34(9), 120–127 (2001)
6. Kuusinen, K., Mikkonen, T., Pakarinen, S.: Agile user experience development in a large software organization: Good expertise but limited impact. In: Winckler, M., Forbrig, P., Bernhaupt, R. (eds.) HCSE 2012. LNCS, vol. 7623, pp. 94–111. Springer, Heidelberg (2012)
7. Singh, M.: U-SCRUM: An Agile Methodology for Promoting Usability. In: Proc. of AGILE 2008, Toronto, Canada, August 4-8, pp. 555–560. IEEE Computer Society (2008)

Model-Based Development of Adaptive UIs for Multi-channel Self-service Systems

Enes Yigitbas[1], Holger Fischer[1], Thomas Kern[2], and Volker Paelke[3]

[1] University of Paderborn, s-lab - Software Quality Lab,
Zukunftsmeile 1, 33102 Paderborn, Germany
{eyigitbas,hfischer}@s-lab.upb.de
[2] Wincor Nixdorf International GmbH,
Heinz-Nixdorf-Ring 1, 33106 Paderborn, Germany
thomas.kern@wincor-nixdorf.com
[3] Hochschule Ostwestfalen-Lippe, University of Applied Sciences,
Liebigstrasse 87, 32657 Lemgo, Germany
volker.paelke@hs-owl.de

Abstract. Self-Service Systems are technically complex and provide products and services to end users. Due to the heterogeneity of the users of such systems and their short residence time, the usability of a system's user interface is of great importance. Currently, an intuitive and flexible usage is often limited because of the monolithic system architecture of existing Self-Service Systems. Furthermore, today's Self-Service Systems represent the one-and-only endpoint of communication with a customer when processing a transaction. The integration of the customer's personal computing devices, like desktop PC, notebook, and smartphone is not sufficiently covered yet. In order to tackle these problems, we have established a methodology for developing adaptive UIs for Multi-Channel Self-Services where a customer may, for example, start a transaction on a PC at home, modify it with the smartphone, and finally finish it at a Self-Service terminal. In this paper we describe our integrated model-based approach for the development of adaptive user interfaces for distributed Multi-Channel Self-Service Systems.

Keywords: MBUID, Self-Service Systems, user interface, model-based development, usability, adaptive user interfaces, user experience.

1 Introduction

Due to new interaction techniques possible today (e.g. multi-touch or tangible interaction) and distributed interfaces transcending the boundaries of a single device, software developers and user interface designers are facing new challenges. It is no longer sufficient for a Self-Service System to provide a single "one-size-fits-all" user interface.

By nature, customers of Self-Service Systems like automated teller machines (ATMs), ticketing machines, or postal Self-Service kiosks comprise a very heterogeneous group of users. Nearly everybody, from the young to the very old,

S. Sauer et al. (Eds.): HCSE 2014, LNCS 8742, pp. 267–274, 2014.

from the technically skilled to the completely unskilled, is a potential user of such systems. Some of these users may have cognitive or physical disabilities regarding vision, hearing, or may be sitting in a wheelchair.

Today's personal computing devices provide a level of convenience and user experience, which customers also expect from public Self-Service Systems. Customers do not only want to finish the task at hand within the shortest amount of time, they also would like to have a personalized experience and want to enjoy their interaction with the system. One possible solution is the development of user interfaces, which are personalized in their appearance and which are adaptive to the user's interaction with the system and the context of use.

To make things even more complex, a Self-Service System should no longer represent the one-and-only endpoint of communication with a customer when processing a transaction. Instead, the customer's personal computing devices, like desktop PC, notebook, and smartphone may all be involved in the process.

Imagine a distributed, networked Multi-Channel Self-Service System where the purchase of a ticket is initiated by selecting an appropriate train connection at the PC at home. On the way to the train station, additional seat reservation is booked and arrangements for the luggage are made on a smartphone. Finally, the ticket is printed at the Self-Service ticket machine.

Developers of such systems are faced with the following challenges:

1. Manage high complexity: Sharing an application's user interface and client-side logic across multiple heterogeneous devices in order to support distributed business transactions requires changes to the system's architecture.
2. Increase efficiency of multi-platform software development across heterogeneous computing platforms (Windows, iOS, Android, Windows Phone etc.).
3. Implement software that adapts itself to differences in system functionality and user interface.
4. Integrate user centred design into the development process, extending the existing methods to cover the necessary adaptation options.

According to Petrasch [1], the effort of implementing an application's user interface constitutes at least 50% of the total implementation effort. Developing separate applications for each potential device and operating system is neither a practical, nor a cost effective solution. If we also consider multi-modal environments, such attempts tend to become nearly impossible.

Model-based User Interface Development (MBUID) [2] suggests a solution to these problems. In this paper, we will show a concept how MBUID can be combined with self-adaptive approaches to generate user interfaces for Multi-Channel Self-Service Systems.

2   Background and Related Work

Focusing on the topic of model-based user interface development of adaptive Self-Service Systems, multiple topics have to be taken into account: The possibilities and different levels of adapting a system and frameworks for implementation.

2.1 Adaptation

Developing software with a user interface is getting more and more interactive and complex. Developers require a thorough understanding of the users of a system and their needs and pain points to create an adequate user interface. With Self-Service Systems in mind, the time users spend interacting with the system is rather short. Therefore, the interface should be as simple as possible, while providing the necessary information, working within existing processes and matching the needs of a wide range of users (e.g. young people, older people, people with special needs). One possible solution is to create user interfaces which can be adapted or adapt themselves to the various skills and preferences of the users. Norcio and Stanley consider that the idea of an *adaptive UI* is straightforward since it simply means that: The interface should adapt to the user; rather than the user must adapt to the system [13]. A classification of different adaptation techniques was introduced by Oppermann [11] and refined by Brusilovsky [8]. UIs with adaptation capabilities were proposed in the context of various domains ([12], [9]). Besides works dealing with the quality of adaptive UIs ([14], [10]), there are also proposals for integrating adaptive UI capabilities into enterprise applications (e.g. [15]).

2.2 Model-Based Development

Model-based development methods have been discussed in the past for various individual aspects of a software system and for different application domains. This applies to the development of the data management layer, the technical functionality and to the development of a user interface [4].

The CAMELEON Reference Framework (CRF) [3] provides a unified framework for model-based and model-driven development of user interfaces. Several approaches have proposed a model-based development of user interfaces based on the CRF ([5],[6]). Also the aspect of UI adaptation was analyzed within the CAMELEON-project [17] or in the context of UsiXML [16].

However, the combination of both aspects: multi-channel interaction and adaptive UIs is a promising perspective which is not yet fully covered in the application domain of Self-Service Systems. Therefore in our approach for model-based user interface development we combine ideas from the field of MBUID, adaptive UIs and multi-channel interaction.

3 Adaptive UIs for Multi-channel Self-service Systems

The workflow of processing a transaction on a Multi-Channel Self-Service System is divided into five main steps:

In the first step the end user performs a login using his desktop (PC) or smartphone (S) to start the interaction with the Self-Service System. After successful login, the customer is able to create, edit and delete his orders on the desktop pc, smartphone or at the ATM. If the order is completed, the coupling between

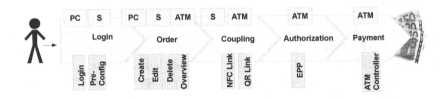

Fig. 1. Transaction workflow on a Multi-Channel Self-Service System

involved devices in the transaction process is established. This is coordinated by a connection manager which makes use of Near Field Communication (NFC) and QR Code technology to couple corresponding devices like the smartphone and the ATM. In the next step authorization of the user is approved using an Encrypting PIN Pad (EPP). Finally, the outcome or service of the Self-Service System is delivered by the ATM.

In our methodology, we are pursuing a model-based development approach based on the CAMELEON Reference Framework (CRF). In order to support the analysis and design phase during the development of distributed, adaptive user-interfaces we have designed a target architecture which pays special attention to aspects of adaptation and integrates them into the model-based development process for user interfaces. Figure 2 shows the target architecture of our solution based on the CAMELEON approach.

At the level of conceptual modeling (Computation Independent Model, CIM) a task model and a user model (representing different user groups or individuals) are created as input for the creation of an abstract model of the user interface at the level of platform-independent modeling (Platform Independent Model, PIM). Another conceptual model describes the context of use in the form of contextual factors, such as the localization of the user (Context Model). This model is used together with a Platform Model to implement the model-to-model transformation (M2M) from the Abstract User Interface Model (AUI) into the Concrete User Interface Model (CUI) at the level of platform-specific modelling (Platform-Specific Model, PSM). This translation step will be supported by the use of appropriate tools. The concrete user interface model consists of a set of coupled partial models for the respective platforms. With the aid of specific generators and interpreters required for a concrete platform, a suitable user interface will be generated from the respective sub-model, which can then be run on this platform.

This model-driven development approach will also support the dynamic adaptation of the user interface at runtime. For this purpose, an Adaptation Model is created in addition to a monitoring concept that describes the adaptation of the user interface (as well as the functionality coupled thereto). From the resulting Adaptation Models the Adaptation Manager is derived. This is a software component that observes the adaptable software and controls the adaptation according to the Adaptation Model. It is contemplated to supplement the

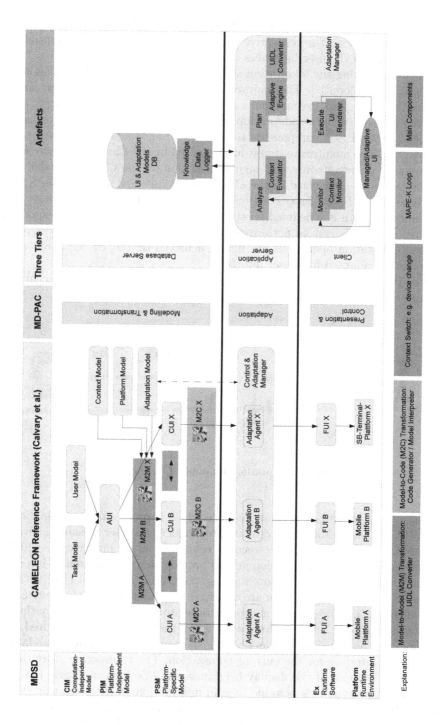

Fig. 2. Architecture: Model-based UI Development View

Adaptation Manager by dedicated sub-components or Adaptation Agents. The latter interoperate on the respective platform instances and are responsible for the adaptation of the user interfaces and their coupled functionality.

For implementing the adaptation steps, our target architecture makes use of IBM's MAPE-K loop [7]. The main components of the MAPE-K loop, namely monitor, analyze, plan, execute and knowledge are embedded in our target architecture to provide runtime adaptation. For managing the adaptation process, we mapped the MAPE-K components to corresponding components in our target architecture. The monitoring step is implemented by the *Context Monitor* which continuously observes context change information on the Context Model. This information is then analyzed by the *Context Evaluator* and stored in the *Knowledge* base by the *Data-Logger* component. With the help of the *Knowledge* base, an adaptation plan is scheduled by the *Adaptive Engine*, so that corresponding adaptation changes can be performed by a *UIDL Converter*. The effect of the planned adaptation operations are finally achieved by the *UI Renderer* which generates the adapted final user interfaces.

In order to exemplify the idea of adaptation in our target architecture, an example walkthrough is depicted in Figure 3.

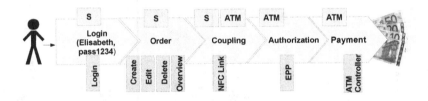

Fig. 3. Adaptation: Example Walkthrough

It shows an exemplary process instance which is processing a transaction on a Multi-Channel Self-Service System. After login of the user Elisabeth with her password, the *Context Monitor* records relevant context information which is needed to perform the transaction and to provide an appropriate user interface. In this case her age, transaction starting time, and her device type with the corresponding operating system are observed. In a next step the *Context Evaluator* analyzes the context information in order to infer possible information for adaptation purposes. In this example the age of the user and often required/used functions are analyzed to decide whether she needs a simple, big, standard or expert user interface for the current transaction. The transaction start time is analyzed to evaluate if the display brightness shall be increased, and based on the used device type it is possible to gain information on the operating system and whether the device supports for example NFC coupling with the ATM. After evaluating these factors an adaptation schedule is planned. In our process example the user profile is set to the standard mode because Elisabeth often makes use of the functions create, edit, delete and overview. Based on other context information, the adaptation schedule also contains a rule to set the brightness to high and to establish automatic device coupling between her smartphone and the ATM.

4   Conclusion and Outlook

In this paper, we presented a concept for the efficient and effective development of adaptive user interfaces. By analyzing use cases and current practice in the application domain of Self-Service Systems we identified the need for tools and techniques, which support the creation of user interface solutions that adapt themselves to the user, the environment and the context of use. Based on this operating concept, we established technological and methodological requirements and started to address them with the development of appropriate tools and techniques. Therefore we developed a model-based approach for the implementation of adaptive user interfaces that extends the CAMELEON reference framework. In this connection we described our target architecture, which pays special attention to aspects of adaptation and integrates them into the model-based development process for user interfaces to enrich UIs of Self-Service Systems with adaptivity capabilities. Our framework is currently not completely supported by tools and further work will be done on the implementation of tools for the creation of the required models and to automate their translation into a concrete UI expression.

Acknowledgement. This paper is based on some of the work within "Ko-MoS", a project of the "it's OWL" Leading-Edge Cluster, partially funded by the German Federal Ministry of Education and Research (BMBF).

References

1. Petrasch, R.: Model Based User Interface Design: Model Driven Architecture und HCI Patterns. In: GI Softwaretechnik-Trends, Mitteilungen
2. Puerta, A.: A Model-Based Interface Development Environment. IEEE Software 14(4), S.40–S.47 (1997)
3. Calvary, G., Coutaz, J., Thevenin, D., Limbourg, Q., Bouillon, L., Vanderdonckt, J.: A Unifying Reference Framework for Multi-target User Interfaces. In: Interacting with Computers, pp. 289-308 (2003)
4. Hussmann, H., Meixner, G., Zuehlke, D. (eds.): Model-Driven Development of Advanced User Interfaces. SCI, vol. 340. Springer, Heidelberg (2011)
5. Link, S., Schuster, T., Hoyer, P., Abeck, S.: Modellgetriebene Entwicklung grafischer Benutzerschnittstellen (Model-Driven Development of Graphical User Interfaces). i-com 6(3), 37–43 (2008)
6. Botterweck, G.: A Model-driven Approach to the Engineering of Multiple User Interfaces. In: Kühne, T. (ed.) MoDELS 2006. LNCS, vol. 4364, pp. 106–115. Springer, Heidelberg (2007)

7. Kephart, J.O., Chess, D.M.: The Vision of Autonomic Computing. Computer 36(1) (2003)
8. Brusilovsky, P.: Adaptive Hypermedia. User Modeling and User-Adapted Interaction 11, 1–2 (2001)
9. Jameson, A.: Adaptive interfaces and agents. In: Jacko, J.A., Sears, A. (eds.) The Human-Computer Interaction Handbook, pp. 305–330. L. Erlbaum Associates Inc., Hillsdale (2002)
10. Lavie, T., Meyer, J.: Benefits and costs of adaptive user interfaces. Int. J. Hum.-Comput. Stud. 68, 8 (2010)
11. Oppermann, R.: Individualisierte Systemnutzung. In: Paul, M. (ed.) GI - 19. Jahrestagung, I, Computergesttzter Arbeitsplatz, pp. 131–145. Springer, London (1989)
12. Stephanidis, C., Paramythis, A., Sfyrakis, M., Stergiou, A., Maou, N., Leventis, A., Paparoulis, G., Karagiannidis, C.: Adaptable and Adaptive User Interfaces for Disabled Users in the AVANTI Project. In: Campolargo, M., Mullery, A. (eds.) IS&N 1998. LNCS, vol. 1430, pp. 153–166. Springer, Heidelberg (1998)
13. Norcio, A.F., Stanley, J.: Adaptive Human-Computer Interfaces: A Literature Survey and Perspective. IEEE Transactions on Systems, Man, and Cybernetics 19, 399–408 (1989)
14. Gajos, Z.K., et al.: Predictability and accuracy in adaptive user interfaces. In: Proc. of the SIGCHI Conference on Human Factors in Computing Systems (CHI 2008) (2008)
15. Akiki, P.A., et al.: Integrating adaptive user interface capabilities in enterprise applications. In: Proc. of the 36th Int. Conf. on Software Engineering (ICSE 2014) (2014)
16. Mezhoudi, N.: User interface adaptation based on user feedback and machine learning. In: Proceedings of the Companion Publication of the 2013 International Conference on Intelligent User Interfaces Companion (IUI 2013 Companion), pp. 25–28. ACM, New York (2013)
17. Balme, L., Demeure, A., Barralon, N., Calvary, G.: CAMELEON-RT: A Software Architecture Reference Model for Distributed, Migratable, and Plastic User Interfaces. In: Markopoulos, P., Eggen, B., Aarts, E., Crowley, J.L. (eds.) EUSAI 2004. LNCS, vol. 3295, pp. 291–302. Springer, Heidelberg (2004)

On the Delivery of Recommendations in Social Software: A User's Perspective

Nan Jiang and Raian Ali

Faculty of Science and Technology,
Bournemouth University, United Kingdom
{njiang,rali}@bournemouth.ac.uk

Abstract. Recommendation is a popular feature of social software. Recommendations could be made by the software autonomously or by social contacts who are often aided by the software on what to recommend. A great deal of emphasis in the literature has been given to the algorithmic solution to infer relevant and interesting recommendations. Yet, the delivery method of recommendation is still a widely unexplored research topic. This paper advocates that the success in deducing recommendations is not the sole factor for "recommendees" to consider. Users have their own requirements on the way a recommendation is made and delivered. Failure in meeting user expectations would often lead to the rejection of the recommendations as well as the violation of user experience. In this paper, we conduct an empirical research to explore such user's perspective. We start with qualitative phase, based on interviews, and confirm and enhance the results in a quantitative phase through surveying a large sample of users. We report on the results and conclude with a set of guidelines on how recommendations delivery should be designed from a user's perspective.

Keywords: social software, recommender systems, user-centric design.

1   Introduction

Recommender systems are designed to help people make better choices when they had limited sufficient personal experience or knowledge of the different alternatives and available options in a large information space [1]. A famous example is item-to-item product suggestions in e-commerce. These systems have become very popular since they were first proposed and developed [2]. Recommender systems utilize information about the users, including their navigation path, actions, and personal characteristics to deduce items and subjects they would be interested in. Techniques like collaborative filtering are examples of how such inference works [3, 4].

The success of recommender systems has been amplified when they were integrated with social software. Such integration allows the recommender system to utilise not only the user's personal profile and history of actions, but also their social space including information related to their group memberships and the characteristic of their contacts [5]. Recommender systems have become an integral part of almost all popular social networks supporting the operation of the network itself, e.g. by recommending the utilization of certain features, or a third party, e.g. adverts.

S. Sauer et al. (Eds.): HCSE 2014, LNCS 8742, pp. 275–282, 2014.

A recommender system could act on behalf of users to search and offer potentially interesting information. It could also support a user to recommend subjects to social contacts who would potentially be interested in them, e.g. recommending a group to join or another contact to link to. In such context of use, recommender systems would be seen human-centred software and should be engineered with this observation in mind. Some recommendation systems are designed to support enterprises and businesses such as predicting the users' trends and recommending certain actions and marketing certain items at a specific time. In such usage, the engineering of recommendation delivery to fit users' expectations, in this case the business analysts and decision maker, is not a main issue. Business users use the system with sufficient subject background and deliberate use of the system for this purpose. These systems will not be discussed in this paper.

Research on recommendation systems has given a great deal of emphasis on enhancing the ability and the efficiency of predicting the right recommendations. The research on personalising recommendation systems has also the same goal with an emphasis on learning and aligning recommendation with user's profile [5]. Little emphasis has been given to the way users would like to receive recommendations and what recommendations are done for them. A relevant, even highly interesting, recommendation would be overlooked and rejected if the delivery method is not appropriate or certain meta-data describing the recommendation are missing, e.g. why and why now a recommendation is triggered.

This paper advocates the need to design the delivery of recommendation in a systematic way so as to improve the user perception of recommendations and avoid violating user experience. As a preliminary step towards achieving this goal, we conduct an empirical study and explore users' view of the current recommender systems in social software and how they would like such systems to operate. Certain results would be still generalizable to other domains like e-commerce. Our results inform the research in this domain towards a human-centric design of recommender systems.

The paper is structured as follows. In Section 2 we describe our research method and report on the results. In Section 3, we discuss a set of recommendations on the design of recommendations delivery. We draw our conclusions in Section 4.

2   A User's Perspective of Recommendations Delivery

The fundamental functionality of social software is to support establishing and maintaining relationships and communication between contacts. Recommender systems were seen useful for boosting such functionality through predicting and offering information, e.g. contacts, groups and services, deduced from a user's social context. Moreover, since word-of-mouth recommendations are already common social activities in everyday real world, it was natural to try and imitate them in social software. Recommendations in social software could also come directly from contacts who are often aided by suggestions from software on what to recommend. Since a recommendation is ultimately meant to target a set of "recommendees", no matter where it was produced from, the perception of those recipients on its delivery should be first understood in a user's perspective. Our study to understand that has the following grounds:

- *User's Knowledge of Recommendations.* Recommender systems rely on prediction algorithms to provide choices for users. This means that better algorithms will lead to better recommendations. This will in turn lead to better user experience in terms related to the relevance of the recommended choices. Studies on user experience often focus on the design and evaluation of recommender systems from this perspective [6-8]. Limited emphasis is given to how users would like to be approached. Their usage of recommendations, their familiarity with recommendations and the suitable frequency to produce/receive recommendations are typically overlooked aspects although they could be critical factors.

- *User's Attitude to Software-Mediated Social Recommendations.* Social recommendations refer to word-of-mouth recommendations provided by a user's contacts. For example, uses could share an interesting article with their colleagues or put it in the bulletin-board. Such recommendations are already a part of everyday life. When these recommendations are mediated through social software, they tend to have a different set of trust, understanding and privacy issues in comparison to real life settings [9]. That is, the medium of interaction has a major effect.

- *User's Preferences on Recommendation Acquisition and Interaction.* There is an increasing awareness in recommender systems research of the need to make the recommendation process more transparent to users. Such transparency would lead to a better user satisfaction [10, 11]. In a user-centric view, the process only includes two stages, acquisition and communication. The former refers to how recommendations can be acquired and the latter to how to present recommendations.

Informed by the three aspects discussed above, we follow a sequential exploratory mixed methods design approach [12] to identify users' concerns on the recommender systems integrated with social software. The first phase is qualitative (interviews) and meant to get insights from an elite group of users which will then inform the design of the next quantitative phase (questionnaire) which involves a large sample of users. The quantitative phase confirms and enhances the results of the qualitative phase.

2.1   Qualitative Phase

A total number of 12 questions were created based on the three aspects discussed above. Table 1 shows how each aspect was reflected by interview questions where the third aspect was separated into acquisition and interaction. The actual questions are omitted due to the space limit but the question topics are summarised in the table.

Table 1. Categorisation of interview questions

Categories	Topics	Question No.
Knowledge level	Recognition, Usage, Frequency	Q1, Q2, Q3, Q4
Attitude	Recommendations group members, Recommendations from others	Q5, Q6, Q7, Q8
Acquisition	Proactively, Passively	Q9, Q10
Interaction	Modes, Configurations	Q11, Q12

Postgraduate student participants, (n=7, 5 males and 2 females), studying different subjects and aging between 23 and 30 were recruited for the interview where all of them are active users on social networking sites (e.g., Facebook, Twitter and the like). The interviews lasted between 30 and 45 minutes each and they were audio recorded and transcribed. These transcripts were then analysed following the general qualitative analysis process.

Since all participants are active users in social networking sites, all of them were fully aware of the two different types of recommendations (from software and from contacts). They all stated explicitly that they receive recommendations very frequently. By analysing the interviews data, we identified five categories representing their perception on the delivery of recommendations and how the different facets of that delivery affected their acceptance of the recommendations and their user experience:

- *Relevance.* All participants agreed that the first and foremost thing they would consider for accepting a recommendation is its relevance to their interests and needs. For example, *"I got annoyed by a recommendation as it is something that I don't need or want to know"* or *"if it is something that I am not interested, I just ignore it"*. This is perhaps the facet which is most researched in the literature.

- *Source.* Recommendations from real people were more likely to be considered than those from the software. One obvious reason is the Bandwagon effect. That is, *"the more people who recommend it, it means more people like it, so for me I might take a look at it"*. Moreover, when comparing recommendations from the general public to contacts and group members, participants stated they would consider more seriously recommendations from the latter as *"we tend to have same interests same topic to talk and chat or discuss"*, *"if it is from my group member and I joined the group then I am open to recommendations from them"*, *"I am very glad to accept recommendations from my group members"*.

- *Credibility.* No matter whether a recommendation comes from a real person or the software, credibility of the source is always important. For recommendations from real people, *"I need to know the level of expertise they have in recommending what they are recommending"* or *"I do sometimes ask my contacts for recommendations as I know some of them have the knowledge and will help me"*. For recommendations from the software, *"if the software is making recommendations, I need to know the grounds it used to make recommendations"* and *"if it is software recommending I will have problem unless it's very well written software and has been proven to me that it works"*.

- *Privacy Issues.* Most participants were concerned about the privacy issues when they were sent recommendations. They need to know what software or a contact knew about them and how in order to recommend an item. For example, *"sometimes I get annoyed by recommendations so it might be part of the risk of you joining software* (as it will monitor your activities)*"* and *"you cannot* [know why you are being sent a recommendation] *especially when it is sent by your friends"*.

- *Interaction.* Participants suggested that it would be very desirable to configure the frequency and interaction style of the delivery. For example, *"I would like to decide when I receive recommendations and when not and how I will receive them"*.

Other participants emphasized that a notification sound or some similar mechanisms can be used to know whether a recommendation is coming from a contact or a software. Moreover, some users *"would like to see a way to subscribe to someone's recommendation list and control the subjects of recommendations and decide what to receive"*.

2.2   Quantitative Phase

The questionnaire consisted of 17 questions where 13 of them related to the five categories identified in Section 2.1 and the rest gathered personal information and options such as whether the participants want to the results. The survey was released on the researchers' social networking sites and via emails to contacts. 137 people, 69 males and 68 females, studying/working in nine industry sectors responded to the survey. Figure 1 shows their age distribution.

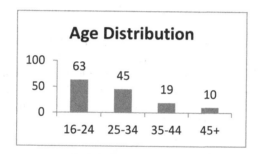

Fig. 1. Age distribution of respondents

- *Would you consider recommendations in social software as part of your social activities?* Yes: 39%, *Partially* 51%, *No*: 9%, *Other*: 1%.   **Themes**: General.
- *How does the type of recommender affect your willingness to look at the recommendations?* When it is from software, I tend to ignore it: 50%, When it is from software, I tend to consider it: 35%, When it is from a person (contact), I tend to ignore it: 18%, When it is from a person (contact), I tend to consider it: 62%, Other: 1%. **Themes**: Source, Credibility.
- *How would you feel about sending your own recommendations to other contacts?* I am open to that: 57%, I do not tend to do that: 44%.   Other: 2%.   **Themes**: Privacy, Source, General.
- *Would you like to be able to ask for recommendation explicitly when you need that? That is, you may announce that recommendations on a certain topic are welcome?*   Yes: 86%, No: 13%, Other: 2%. **Themes**: Privacy, Interaction.
- *Do you tend to follow the advice given in recommendations?* Considerably Yes: 33%, Sometimes: 54%, Often No: 16%, Other: 2%. **Themes**: General.
- *Would the relevance of recommendation to what you are indeed interested in motivate you to look at it?* Yes: 88%, No: 11%, Other: 1%. **Themes**: Relevance.

- *Would you like the recommender (software or human contacts) to respect the time when you are busy and stop sending recommendations?* Yes: 91%, No: 7%, Other: 2%. **Themes**: Interaction, Privacy.
- *When the item being recommended to you is becoming increasingly popular, would that increase your willingness to look at the recommendation?* Yes: 73%, No: 22%, Other: 6%. **Themes**: Source, Credibility.
- *To give you the right recommendation, the recommender (software or human contact) would need to know about you, e.g. who you are, where you are, what you usually use, etc. How do you feel about that from privacy perspective?* Extremely cautious: 42%, Moderately cautious: 23%, I want to be aware of what the recommender can know about me: 34%, I want to be able to control what the recommender can know about me: 40%, I do not care about privacy in the case of recommender systems: 2%, Other: 1%. **Themes**: Privacy, Interaction.
- *How important is it for you that the software gives you the ability to control recommendations (from whom, on what, how they are presented to you, etc.?* Very important: 67%, I would like to see: 33%, Not important: 4%, Other: 0%. **Themes**: Interaction, Privacy.
- *Does the way the recommendation is delivered to you (with sound notification, as pop-up, email, etc.) affect your willingness to consider it?* Yes, this significantly matters: 77%, No, this does not matter: 21%, Other: 5%. **Themes**: Interaction.
- *Which of the following you would like to control?* The time when I get recommendation (morning, afternoon, weekend, etc.): 57%, How many times I get recommendation a day: 69%, The topic on which I get recommendation: 79%, The delivery of recommendation (audio, pop-up, email, etc.): 67%, The device I am using when I get a recommendation: 45%, The size of recommendation, e.g. simple, complex, and the number of items included in it: 45%, Other: 3%. **Themes**: Interaction.

We allowed users who choose "Other" to comment on their choice and add further comments. Interesting additional insights came from those comments. Some users indicated that their acceptance of a recommendation relates to the application domain and subject of recommendation "*I find App Store recommendations very useful. I don't want to have to trawl through a number of poorly constructed ones*" and "*I only tend to use YouTube when I have a video in mind so I never use the recommendations here*". Interestingly, some users worry about the automated inference which led to the recommendation in quite a detailed way. This is particularly true for the new "digital-native" generation of users "*I take time to always view the suggestions that are being recommended to me*" and "*I try to establish whether they used collaborative or content-based filtering*" and "*I feel very worry about the spam recommendations*". Some users indicated that recommendation could harm the recommended item if not presented well.

3   Recommendations

Based on the results from both phases, an initial list of recommendations are worth to be noted when engineering the recommendation delivery. Figure 2 presents succinctly the three macro recommendations which could also be seen as research challenges for the design of human-centred recommendation delivery.

Fig. 2. Three recommendations for human-centred recommendation delivery

- **Control.** It is important to allow users to control the way in which a recommendation is made and delivered. To achieve this, the recommendation system should enjoy certain degree of variability and alternatives which will enable users to choose and customize their choices. Moreover, developers should explore what users would like to control and customize which could be differ between application domains, environments, and other dimensions of the context of use.
- **Awareness.** Users would be positive to and even trust a recommender that provides explanation or hints on how a recommendation was made and for what reason(s) it was delivered at a certain time. It is essential that the explanation should be simple and informative in order to increase trust and maintain user experience at the same time. It also needs to explore what metadata about recommendation to communicate to the user, e.g. the inference steps, the history of actions made by users or their social contacts which led to deduce a recommendation, etc. Similar to our previous discussion about Control, this set of metadata is not expected to be "one size fits all" and ach context of use may require a different set.
- **Adaptivity.** Users' preferences of being able to control recommendations in certain ways (e.g., forms, delivery) does not typically mean they are willing to spend much time and effort on that. It may turn to be a burden if a user has to specify that on a case-by-case basis. Users should only provide policies and preferences at a high level of abstraction using their terminology and expect the recommender to interpret that and make its own judgement for each individual case. The challenge is that users typically specify their preferences using terms fuzzy by nature, e.g., "busy" and "interesting". This makes it hard to have an interpretation which reflects users' real intention and, consequently, leads to poor adaptation decisions.

4   Conclusions

In this paper we argued that recommendation delivery should be engineered in a way that enhances users' perception of recommendations and maximises user experience. Current research on recommender systems has largely focused on the inference of recommendations, i.e. its relevance. Topics around the user's perspective have only received limited attention to date. Our results show that users are keen to see recommenders systems which are configurable and more sensible to their preferences and social settings. Our study highlights the need for a human-cantered engineering for recommender systems and provides initial insights towards such an approach.

Acknowledgement. The research was supported by an FP7 Marie Curie CIG grant (the SOCIAD Project) and by Bournemouth University through the Fusion Investment Fund (the BBB and VolaComp and BUUU projects).

References

1. Resnick, P., Varian, H.R.: Recommender systems. Communications of the ACM 40(3), 56–58 (1997)
2. Goldberg, D., Nichols, D., Oki, B.M., Terry, D.: Using collaborative filtering to weave an information tapestry. Communications of the ACM 35(12), 61–70 (1992)
3. Linden, G., Smith, B., York, J.: Amazon. com recommendations: Item-to-item collaborative filtering. IEEE Internet Computing 7(1), 76–80 (2003)
4. Good, N., Schafer, J.B., Konstan, J.A., Borchers, A., Sarwar, B., Herlocker, J., Riedl, J.: Combining collaborative filtering with personal agents for better recommendations. In: Proceedings of AAAI/IAAI, pp. 439–446 (2003)
5. Cho, Y.H., Kim, J.K., Kim, S.H.: A personalized recommender system based on web usage mining and decision tree induction. Expert Systems with Applications 23(3), 329–342 (2002)
6. Pu, P., Chen, L., Hu, R.: Evaluating recommender systems from the user's perspective: survey of the state of the art. User Modeling and User-Adapted Interaction 22, 441–504 (2012)
7. McNee, S., Riedl, J., Konstan, J.: Making recommendations better: an analytic model for human-recommerder interaction. In: Proceedings of 24th International Conference Human Factors in Computing Systems (CHI), pp. 1103–1108 (2006)
8. Ozok, A.A., Fan, Q., Norcio, A.F.: Design guidelines for effective recommender system interfaces based on a usability criteria conceptual model: results from a college student population. International Journal of Behaviour Information Technology 29, 57–83 (2010)
9. Knijnenburg, B.P., Willemsen, M.C., Gantner, Z., Soncu, Newell, C.: Explaining the user experience of recommender systems. User Modeling and User-Adapted Interaction 22, 441–504 (2012)
10. McSherry, D.: Explanation in Recommender Systems. Artificial Intelligence Review 24, 179–197 (2005)
11. Tintarev, N., Judith, M.: A survey of explanations in recommender systems. In: IEEE 23rd International Conference on Data Engineering Workshop (2007)
12. Creswell, J.W., Clark, V.L.P.: Designing and conducting mixed methods research. SAGE Publications, Inc. (2011)

Persona as a Tool to Involving Human in Agile Methods: Contributions from HCI and Marketing

Leydi Caballero[1], Ana M. Moreno[2], and Ahmed Seffah[3]

[1] Instituto Tecnológico de Conkal, Km 16 Old Road Motul, Yucatán México
leydi.caballero@itconkal.edu.mx
[2] Universidad Politécnica de Madrid, Campus Montegancedo 28660 Boadilla del Monte, Spain
ammoreno@fi.upm.es
[3] University of Valenciennes, Le Mont Houy F59313 Valenciennes Cedex 9, France
ahmed.seffah@univ-valenciennes.fr

Abstract. Human centricity refers to the active involvement in the overall product lifecycle of different human actors including end-users, stakeholders and providers. Persona is one of the different tools that exist for human centricity. While marketing is the original domain in which persona was introduced, this technique has also been widely used in user-centered design (UCD) design. In these two perceptions, persona has demonstrated its potential as an efficient tool for grouping the users or customers and focusing on user or customer needs, goals and behavior. A segmentation technique is generally used with persona in order to group individual users according to their common features, identifying within these groups those that represent a pattern of human behavior. This paper investigates how persona has been used to improve the usability in the agile development domain, while studying which contributions from marketing and HCI have enriched persona in this agile context.

Keywords: Persona, Agile Usability, HCI methods in software engineering.

1 Introduction

The active involvement of customers, citizens and employees in the co-creation process of innovative solutions and products helps to understand human behaviors and factors that affect the quality of work, services and products. This active involvement can help to answer the designers and developers questions such as:

- What factors drive the use of the products or services? How do people actually use the services and in which context?
- What factors drive the adoption and acceptability of the product by a target community?
- What new services can we use or do we need to improve the communication line between the developers, brokers and users of a service?
- How does your target audience feel about themselves in the context of using your products or services? Do they look more satisfied, smart, or informed?

S. Sauer et al. (Eds.): HCSE 2014, LNCS 8742, pp. 283–290, 2014.

The persona technique has been used successfully in marketing. In this context, this technique can give us a general scope of its advantages and disadvantages when the understanding of behavior of the final client is a crucial factor. Additionally, in recent years the concept of "persona" has been investigated as a powerful design tool focused on improving the design and usability of software development through the definition of user representations after learning and analyzing users' goals and behavior. The concept of "persona" in the HCI community was introduced by Alan Cooper in "The inmates are running the asylum" as part of his method Goal-Directed design (GDD) [1]. HCI focuses on improving software design from a usability perspective taking into account the user experience and skills. Looking for a new and better process to design Cooper [1] asserts that persona represents an efficient tool for communication and interaction.

On the other hand, agile methods constitute a software development approximation widely used nowadays [2, 3]. A core principle of the agile manifesto (www.agilemanifesto.org) emphasizes the continuous delivery of valuable software. This requires the correct identification of user needs and an adequate understanding of user priorities and goals [4]. Even when some voices in the agile community have claimed the adding values of HCI methods in explicitly developing for customer needs, in general, usability and user interaction factors, do not have yet the necessary relevance in the agile approximations. Among the supporters of the integration between HCI and agile, we find Ambler [5] who claims that good end product usability can be ensured only by systematic user centered design activities during the agile development iterations. Jokela and Abrahamsson [6] state that without explicit user experience practices added to agile methods, good software usability would be more or less a coincidence resulting from customer and/or developer intuition. Patton [7] pointed that before the first line of code can be written someone needs to decide how a specific user will interact with the software to achieve her goals. In sum, the use of HCI tools would help agile teams to identify properly and from the beginning of the development process the final users in order to develop for them. This would avoid waste of effort and time achieving the objectives defined by the principles of the Agile Manifesto. Persona is one of the HCI tools that have been used for this aim.

In what follows, we explore the characteristics and perceptions of persona in marketing, HCI and agile while identifying the contributions from the first two fields to the persona technique used in agile development.

2   Persona in Consumer Research

The essence of the marketing concept is to achieve the company's objectives by directing a coordinated marketing effort at identifying and satisfying consumer's wants and needs [8].

Segmentation was adopted to help marketers to better meet the needs of specific groups of consumers, dividing the total potential markets into smaller, homogeneous segments for which they could design specific products [9]. Solomon [10] describes the market segmentation as a process that identifies groups of customers who are similar to one another in one or more ways, and then devises marketing strategies.

Engel et. al. [11] argue that each of us is a distinct market and the objective of segmentation is to identify groups within the broader market that are sufficiently similar in characteristics and responses to warrant separate treatment. Therefore, to better meet the customer's needs, the marketers must divide consumers in different groups (segmentation) according to common needs, attitudes or characteristics (consumer behavior).

In marketing research, the basic usage of persona arises from the concept of community of individuals introduced by Jenkinson [12]. He pointed that a group connotes a community of individuals, that is, individuals who have something in common. He specifies the difference between "segment" and "grouping". Segment implies dividing a population into groups using factors such as age, gender, interests, etc. Grouping means merging people to form a class of consumers who share common characteristics with tailored solutions.

In [13] Jenkinson proposed to implement an enriched segmentation model that the companies must communicate to staff and senior management converting the community segments into real living people using day-in-the-life archetype descriptions as Customer Prints or personas.

3   Persona in HCI

Persona in HCI was presented as part of the effective mental tools considered in Cooper's method Goal-directed design. Cooper [1] describes persona as a powerful communication and interaction design tool. Although persona does not deal with real people they are represented along with their goals with significant rigor and precision synthesized directly from observations of real people [14]. Nielsen [15] pointed that personas are considered a method to communicate data about users and to aid in the perception of users. Instead of project participants having individual understandings they share a perception of the users that is built on field data and not on preconceived ideas.

Sharp et al. [16] describe the persona process related with Cooper's definition as the collection of attributes for a "typical user" called a user profile. The segments defined in marketing to learn and identify behaviors of the customers are applied, in a similar way, when the personas are defined in software design. Any product may have a number of different user profiles representing specific, individual human beings that the designers can focus on and design the product for [16]. These representations are analyzed and grouped by their similarities and this allows us to segmenting them and prioritizing, avoiding user's representations that eventually will not be representative users.

Like an actor represents a character in a movie or novel and through the history we understand their feelings, goals and behaviors, personas represent people who have their own stories that help the development team to understand the user. Quesenbery in [17] asserts that storytelling makes persona work; when we create a short anecdote to imagine how our persona might interact with our product we are creating a story that shows the persona in action and that helps to understand how to better design for him or her.

Despite the potential advantages of using persona, this technique has also been criticized mainly due to the fictitious or figurative descriptions generated to describe real people; using figurative models it can be difficult to know what is an accurate reflection of real user characteristics and what is mere concoction [17]. Another issue is the time consuming for persona during the development process [18].

4   Persona in Agile Methods

In order to explore how persona has been used in agile approximations we made a literature review. We searched in the following databases: IEEExplore Digital Library, Elsevier ScienceDirect, ACM digital library, Springer, Scopus. We queried these databases covering publications from mid-2001 until mid-2013 according to the following search criteria: (Usability OR Human-computer interaction OR User experience OR HCI) AND (Persona) AND (Agile OR Agile method OR Agile Development OR Agile Practice OR Agile Project OR SCRUM OR Extreme programming OR XP).

Table 1 shows a summary of the papers where we found relevant information about the use of persona in agile projects. In this table we show the source of the persona technique used by each author (mainly the HCI or the marketing version); the adaptation, if any, of persona to the agile domain; and the phase in the agile process where persona or its variants have been applied.

Regarding the phase in the agile development process where persona was applied, we identified two moments that we referred to as the Exploratory phase and the Refinement phase. During the Exploratory phase, personas are identified at the beginning of the project before working on any agile cycle and before any code is released. By this way a whole or partial perspective of the goals and speculations of the user is gathered to improve the results from the cycles or sprints derived and from the observations and feedbacks received. In the Refinement phase, that is, through the agile cycles, the personas defined in the Exploratory phase are evaluated using each cycle's feedback. This can help to determine if the personas must remain as were previously defined, be modified, eliminated or merged with others. In this phase, new personas can be also created.

Table 1. Persona in Agile projects

Author/s	Ref.	Source of Persona	Concept	Agile Moment
S. Chamberlain et. al.	[19]	HCI-Cooper	Persona	Exploratory phase
J.Haikara 2007	[20]	HCI-Cooper	Persona	Exploratory phase Refinement phase
D.Sy 2007	[21]	HCI-Cooper	Persona	Exploratory phase
Z. Hussain et. al.	[22]	HCI-Cooper	Extreme Persona	Exploratory phase Refinement phase
P.Wolkerstorfer et. al.	[23]	HCI-Cooper	Extreme Persona	Exploratory phase Refinement phase
M.Najafi et. al.	[24]	HCI-Cooper	Persona	Exploratory phase
M. Singh 2008	[25]	HCI-Cooper + Marketing	User persona	Exploratory phase
D.Broschinsky et.al.	[26]	HCI-Cooper + contextual design	Persona	Exploratory phase
L. Cho 2009	[27]	HCI-Cooper	Persona	Exploratory phase Refinement phase
J.Gonzalves et. al.	[28]	HCI-Cooper	Persona	Exploratory phase

In [19], Chamberlain and Sharp introduced "up-front design methods" where personas are defined based on significant user research carried out before any coding is done. Sy [21] also used persona at the start of the project, in particular in the cycle zero. The author claimed that this helps developing brief and vivid descriptions of target users and workflows. Similarly, Najafi et. al. [24] considered HCI methods in the sprint zero of a Scrum process. In this case, the user experience team specifically uses this sprint zero to understand the users, explore their context and identify their goals. They did these exploratory tasks using personas.

Singh [25] used Coopers' persona and describes a user persona as an archetypal user resulting from a combination of market research, ethnographic studies and anecdotal observations. The author proposes the U-Scrum model which incorporates a usability product owner from the beginning of the project. His role is to work with the Scrum product owner to achieve an agreement on the user experience. He works with the marketing team defining personas at the beginning of the process. In [26] personas were also brought before the development started to help developers know their users and become familiar with them. Personas descriptions are validated with customers and developers on-site. During the subsequent agile iterations, the personas are refined based on the revision meetings but preserving the essential of the original descriptions.

The software tool presented by Gonzalez et.al. [28]combines Scrum and Cooper's GDD methodology [14]. The purpose of the tool is to develop a system of low-fidelity prototyping and aims to help identifying and defining the personas as part of the cycle zero before the agile sprints.

Haikara [20] extended an interaction design process that exploits personas during the exploratory phase. In the first planning day, the primary persona is identified and subsequently in this phase persona expectations are refined. Subsequently persona definitions are used to keep in mind the persona definition in order to have a clear target audience that the development team should focus on.

Wolkerstorfer et. al. [22] and Hussain et. al. [23] extended the XP paradigm of small iterative steps and refactoring to persona resulting an "extreme persona". At the beginning of the process, the users are investigated through user studies to develop personas. At the end of each iteration the vision about the users is broadened. This helps in extending the personas for next cycle refactoring or if the knowledge reveals that current personas do not cover the new insights new personas will be developed.

In [27], the agile process uses Feature teams [29] self-organized to complete design, planning, and construction within the same sprint. Each sprint has explore and refinement phases. As the software evolved through the sprints, new functionalities are built into existing components. The initial set of persona is then updated or new personas are created.

5   Concluding Remark

We have seen how persona has been used in agile to help agile teams to get a good interaction design without breaking agile values and principles. Most agile authors that apply persona, use it according to the HCI philosophy for providing a more holistic model of the target users and their contexts. HCI advocates knowing and learning about the goals and behavior of the users at the beginning of the software development to identify the real end users and develop for them assuring by this way delivering useful software.

On the other hand, we have also seen how the marketing idea of persona as a vehicle for knowing the customer's behavior and for identifying the end customer that will use the product fits with the need to know the user's needs and goals in agile software development, to identify final users and develop for them. Particularly in agile the idea of segmentation has been applied with persona to identify the end users that will use the product delivered.

However, the original idea (from both HCI and marketing) regarding the creation of a complete up-front design that allows getting all the details from the final users of the system can be in contradiction with the agile philosophy. That's why the literature we surveyed showed that the traditional way of using persona has, in some cases, been adapted or "agilized"; allowing the partial application of the technique at the beginning of the agile project and its refinement and completion during the agile iterations. This agilized persona contributes to address the time restrictions that drive the agile development process.

The agile literature we have analyzed provides evidence that persona helps not only HCI designers to develop usable user interfaces but also agile developers and other stakeholders to elicit the client requirements and to engage client in the development lifecycle. We confirm the Cooper's [14] assertions that persona is powerful tool to:

- determine what a product should do and how it should behave,
- mediate the communicate line between stakeholders, developers and other designers,
- build consensus and commitment to the design from both the HCI and system/functionality perspectives,
- measure the design's effectiveness,
- contribute to other product-related efforts such as marketing and sales plans.

Persona is a flexible technique to be tailored for different development methods, projects and users.

References

1. Cooper, A.: Inmates Are Running the Asylum, The: Why High-Tech Products Drive Us Crazy and How to Restore the Sanity. Sams (1999)
2. Hussain, Z., Slany, W., Holzinger, A.: Investigating Agile User-Centered Design in Practice: A Grounded Theory Perspective. In: Holzinger, A., Miesenberger, K. (eds.) USAB 2009. LNCS, vol. 5889, pp. 279–289. Springer, Heidelberg (2009)
3. Dyba, T., Dingsoyr, T.: Empirical studies of agile software development: A systematic review. Inf. Softw. Technol. 50, 833–859 (2008)
4. Beck, K., Beedle, M., van Bennekum, A., Cockburn, A., Cunningham, W., Fowler, M.: Agile Manifesto, http://www.agilemanifesto.org

5. Ambler, S.: Tailoring Usability into Agile Software Development Projects. In: Law, E.-C., Hvannberg, E., Cockton, G. (eds.) Maturing Usability SE - 4, pp. 75–95. Springer, London (2008)

6. Jokela, T., Abrahamsson, P.: Usability Assessment of an Extreme Programming Project: Close Co-operation with the Customer Does Not Equal to Good Usability. In: Bomarius, F., Iida, H. (eds.) PROFES 2004. LNCS, vol. 3009, pp. 393–407. Springer, Heidelberg (2004)

7. Patton, J.: Designing Requirements: Incorporating Usage-Centered Design into an Agile SW Development Process. In: Wells, D., Williams, L. (eds.) XP 2002. LNCS, vol. 2418, pp. 1–12. Springer, Heidelberg (2002)

8. Loudon, D.L., Della Bitta, A.J.: Consumer behavior: concepts and applications. McGraw-Hill, New York (1979)

9. Schiffman, L.G., Kanuk, L.L.: Consumer behavior. Prentice Hall, Upper Saddle River (1997)

10. Solomon, M.R.: Consumer behavior: buying, having, and being. Pearson Prentice Hall, Upper Saddle River (2006)

11. Engel, J.F., Blackwell, R.D., Miniard, P.W.: Consumer behavior. Dryden, Chicago (1990)

12. Jenkinson, A.: Beyond Segmentation. J. Targeting, Meas. Anal. Mark. 3, 60–72 (1994)

13. Jenkinson, A.: What happened to strategic segmentation? J. Direct, Data Digit. Mark. Pract. 11, 124 (2009)

14. Cooper, A., Reimann, R., Cronin, D.: About Face 3. The essentials of Interaction Design. Wiley Publishing (2007)

15. Nielsen, L.: Personas in Cross-Cultural Projects. In: Katre, D., Orngreen, R., Yammiyavar, P., Clemmensen, T. (eds.) Human Work Interaction Design: Usability in Social, Cultural and Organizational Contexts SE - 7, pp. 76–82. Springer, Heidelberg (2010)

16. Sharp, H., Rogers, Y., Preece, J.: Interaction Design beyond human-computer interaction. John Wiley & Sons (2007)

17. Pruitt, J., Adlin, T.: The persona lifecycle: keeping people in mind throughout the product design. Morgan Kaufmann Publishers (2006)

18. McGinn, J. (J.), Kotamraju, N.: Data-driven persona development. In: Proceedings of the SIGCHI Conference on Human Factors in Computing Systems, p. 1521. ACM Press (2008)

19. Chamberlain, S., Sharp, H., Maiden, N.: Towards a framework for integrating agile development and user-centred design. In: Abrahamsson, P., Marchesi, M., Succi, G. (eds.) XP 2006. LNCS, vol. 4044, pp. 143–153. Springer, Heidelberg (2006)

20. Haikara, J.: Usability in Agile Software Development: Extending the Interaction Design Process with Personas Approach. In: Concas, G., Damiani, E., Scotto, M., Succi, G. (eds.) XP 2007. LNCS, vol. 4536, pp. 153–156. Springer, Heidelberg (2007)

21. Sy, D.: Adapting Usability Investigations for Agile User-centered Design. J. Usability Stud. 2, 112–132 (2007)

22. Hussain, Z., Lechner, M., Milchrahm, H., Shahzad, S., Slany, W., Umgeher, M., Wolkerstorfer, P.: Agile User-Centered Design Applied to a Mobile Multimedia Streaming Application. In: Holzinger, A. (ed.) USAB 2008. LNCS, vol. 5298, pp. 313–330. Springer, Heidelberg (2008)

23. Wolkerstorfer, P., Tscheligi, M., Sefelin, R., Milchrahm, H., Hussain, Z., Lechner, M., Shahzad, S.: Probing an agile usability process. In: Proceeding twenty-sixth Annu. CHI Conf. Ext. Abstr. Hum. factors Comput. Syst., CHI 2008, p. 2151 (2008)

24. Najafi, M., Toyoshiba, L.: Two Case Studies of User Experience Design and Agile Development. In: Agile 2008 Conference, pp. 531–536. IEEE Press (2008)

25. Singh, M.: U-SCRUM: An Agile Methodology for Promoting Usability. In: Agile 2008 Conference, pp. 555–560. IEEE (2008)

26. Broschinsky, D., Baker, L.: Using Persona with XP at LANDesk Software, an Avocent Company. In: Agile 2008 Conference, pp. 543–548. IEEE (2008)
27. Cho, L.: Adopting an Agile Culture A User Experience Team's Journey. In: 2009 Agile Conference, pp. 416–421. IEEE (2009)
28. Gonçalves, J., Santos, C.: POLVO - Software for prototyping of low-fidelity interfaces in agile development. In: Jacko, J.A. (ed.) Human-Computer Interaction, Part I, HCII 2011. LNCS, vol. 6761, pp. 63–71. Springer, Heidelberg (2011)
29. Frank, A., Hartel, C.: Feature Teams Collaboratively Building Products from READY to DONE. In: Agile Conference, AGILE 2009, pp. 320–325 (2009)

Seeding the Design Process for Future Problems

Peter Newman[1], Stephen Forshaw[2], Will Simm[1], Maria Angela Ferrario[3],
Jon Whittle[1], and Adrian Friday[1]

[1] School of Computing and Communications, Lancaster University
[2] Lancaster Institute for the Contemporary Arts, Lancaster University
[3] Lancaster University Management School, Lancaster University
Lancaster LA1 4WA, UK
{p.newman,s.forshaw,w.a.simm,m.a.ferrario,
j.n.whittle,a.friday}@lancaster.ac.uk

Abstract. Designing with the community brings about a number of
benefits, including tacit and contextual knowledge about the problem
domain; this is especially apparent in rural settings. However, designing
for problems that have yet to embed themselves in the fabric of society *(i.e. future problems)* poses a number of challenges, as they typically
present intangible scenarios and concepts that have yet to be experienced
by the wider-community. Using the *OnSupply* project as a case study,
we share our experience in working with the Tiree community to address
a future problem through a technology-mediated enquiry. Furthermore,
we present a novel process that uses creative workshops augmented with
physical artefacts to inform and learn from the community about a problem space, and to seed the design of a system that addresses it.

Keywords: User-driven, Creative workshop, Design, Future problem.

1 Introduction

Designing systems with the user community can often lead to the development
of *appropriate* solutions, which is a consequence of the user being the *expert of
their own experience* [1]. Working with the community is even more crucial in
rural settings, as systems are *almost invariably tailored for urban users* [2]. As
such, it is important not to overlook rural communities when developing systems
that may affect all segments of society, as there will often be different cultural,
societal, and technological constraints as compared to an urban environment.

However, there are circumstances where the intention is to design a system
to address a problem that has yet to establish itself in the fabric of society
(i.e. *future problems*). As these problems often describe intangible scenarios and
concepts that have yet to be experienced by the wider-community, designing in
a bottom-up, user-centric manner can pose a number of challenges:

- *Lack of domain expertise.* The involvement of users is often intended to draw
  upon their expert knowledge of the current system (i.e. *domain experts*);
  however, designing in a community-driven manner for an unfamiliar domain
  potentially means that the traditional level of expertise is not present.

S. Sauer et al. (Eds.): HCSE 2014, LNCS 8742, pp. 291–298, 2014.

– *Lack of visibility/tangibility.* As future problems often describe emergent, abstract problems, they are typically less visible to the greater society, meaning that the users must first be convinced of its existence and importance before any fruitful dialogue may occur.

In this paper, we describe our experience of using creative workshops augmented with physical artefacts to help support the discussion and design of a system that addresses a future problem. This is done by gradually immersing the intended end-users into the problem context through the use of game-based scenarios and physical artefacts. We present *OnSupply* as a case study, which describes a possible future scenario where the supply of power cannot meet the current pattern of demand placed upon the grid.

2   Designing the Future

The development of systems and strategies to address future problems (i.e. scenarios) can be seen in a number of domains, including air traffic control and power generation [3,4]. However, there are few research initiatives that investigate the design and planning of such systems in a community-driven context. Instead, the majority of work focuses on design with expert users.

The use of media as a means to help vision future technology is sometimes used to help design for the future. Macini *et al.* present *ContraVision* [5], which demonstrates a fictional *future technology* to users through a video that uses both positive and negative scenarios to elicit reactions from the user. Another example of using scenarios and users to vision future technologies is seen in the works of Go *et al.* and Carroll *et al.* [6,7], who both present novel participatory design approaches for the design of future systems (i.e. mobile phone and virtual learning environment). However, whilst these approaches attempt to elicit the design constraints and requirements of systems for the future, they typically involve the use of domain experts to elicit design considerations.

3   Supporting the Creative Process

There are a number of methods that have been explored to support discussion in a workshop setting. One well known method is that of Six Thinking Hats, which was presented by De Bono [8] in 1985, and describes a way of assigning a role to play for each participant. Creativity is another dimension to consider in a workshop setting, and can often be encouraged by the presence of physical artefacts. Indeed, physical artefacts often play a crucial role in design, a sentiment shared by Hansen and Dalsgaard [9]. Maiden *et al.* [10] present one such method, which aids the creative process through the use of physical artefacts and lucid workshops. In a similar vein, Vyas *et al.* attempt to support the sharing of artefacts and related notes through a mobile application called CAM [11]. Although this demonstrates that physical artefacts have been applied to design in the computing domain, there is a lack of examples showing the use of physical artefacts to design in a non-expert setting.

4   Design Using Physical Artefacts

To address the challenges described in Section 1, we present a process that uses physical artefacts, scenario-based games, and creative workshop sessions to teach, inform, and learn from the participants about the problem space. Through this process and by involving them in the design of the end system, we aim to encourage and maintain interest from the community, and foster the creation of *proxy* domain experts within the pool of participants.

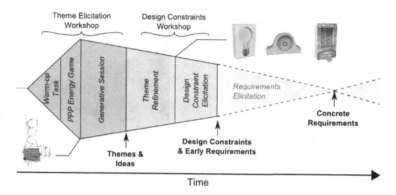

Fig. 1. Overview of the process used to elicit themes and design constraints

This process is embodied by two phases, which are illustrated in Figure 1. The purpose of two workshops is to give the facilitators time to realise the elicited themes from the first workshop as low fidelity physical artefacts, which we would subsequently present back to the community. The use of physical artefacts and game-based scenarios helps to mitigate the *lack of visibility/tangibility* of a future problem by allowing the participants to physically engage with the problem context. This provides an element of learning through *experience* and *concrete example*, which are important parts of the learning cycle [12].

5   Case Study : OnSupply

Recently, there has been a gradual shift in the UK from conventional coal-fired power stations to less carbon-intensive methods of power generation, such as renewable (e.g. wind turbine, photovoltaic etc.) energy [13]. However, as renewable energy is often time and weather dependent, the output of these low carbon alternatives can shift quickly, leading to a highly variable supply of electricity. Further compounding this problem is the *gap* between the decommissioning of current, older-generation power stations, and the commissioning and construction of new ones [14]. The Catalyst project [15] *OnSupply* is working with the island community of Tiree in a bottom-up approach to realise the future systems needed to help communities adapt to a highly variable energy supply.

5.1   Overview

We held two 90 minute workshop sessions on Tiree in an attempt to elicit design constraints for a digital intervention from the island community. Through an open invitation in the local newsletter, we attracted participants from a wide variety of different backgrounds, including the local school headteacher, an electrical engineer, a local artist, and older teenagers.

(a) 3D printed *Inter-dimensional Energy* prop

(b) *Ping pong ball dispenser* from scenario-based game

Fig. 2. Physical artefacts used during the first workshop

5.2   Theme Elicitation Workshop

The first workshop was intended to engage with the adults and teenagers on the island, encourage ideation around the utilisation of a variable energy supply, and help position the participants within the described future problem space. The following describes the tasks within the first workshop.

— *Warm-up task.* The main purpose of the warm-up task was to break down any barriers between the participants and the facilitators. Borrowing from the *Neutral-Zone Metaphor* technique [16], *Inter-dimensional Energy* was presented to the participants as a fictional, alien power source that suffered from intermittent black-outs — akin to the island's power infrastructure. It was represented as a small glass vial enclosed in a 3D printed plastic manifold (see Figure 2a), and the participants were asked to imagine ways that they may harness it as an energy source.
— *Scenario-based game.* As supply-driven energy use is not the currently established model of energy consumption, a way was needed to present it in a manner that was both understandable and interesting to different backgrounds. In order to achieve this, the Ping Pong Power (PPP) game was developed to help the participants better visualise variable energy supply. The aim of the game involved the participants needing to power a number of household appliances using dispensed ping pong balls (*energy*) (see Figure 2b). To gradually ease participants into the problem context, rules were slowly introduced to the game to mimic the properties of variable supply.

– *Theme generation task.* The aim of the generative task was to give the participants of the workshop a chance to reflect on the previously played PPP game. Because the game and *OnSupply* are so closely linked, we expected that any ideas generated would encompass both real-world and in-game mechanisms to help better utilise energy/balls. During this task, the participants were encouraged to write down any ideas they had.

Theme Elicitation Results. In total, 16 participants attended the workshop, with an age range of 16–60. During the warm-up session, approximately 40 *ideas* for utilising the fictional inter-dimensional energy were suggested, with ideas ranging from *charge a battery* to *cook[ing] popcorn*. Although these ideas had no bearing on those generated in the *generative* task, they played an important role in encouraging the participants to engage with each other — in part spurred on by witnessing lighthearted and *out-worldly* ideas being presented by the rest of the group. Furthermore, the PPP game and its physical artefacts (ping pong ball dispensers) appeared to generate excitement, as evidenced by exclamations of *"Catch it!"* and *"Come on, come on!"* in reference to the dispensed balls, and laughter and excitement being witnessed throughout the task. Finally, the *generative* task resulted in a number of themes that suggest the participants were interested in ways to store, forecast, and predict generated electricity; these themes are brought forward in the next workshop.

5.3   Design Constraints Workshop

The second workshop was intended to build upon the themes elicited in the first workshop, and to refine them into a set of design constraints. As this workshop relied on the participants to understand the problem context, they were selected from the pool of people who attended the first workshop, and from other previous engagements with the community. The workshop consisted of the two elements: *Theme refinement* and *Design constraint elicitation.*

– *Theme refinement.* This part involved a brief overview of the themes (and thus artefacts) generated by the previous workshop, which had since been embodied in a number of low fidelity physical artefacts (or *sketches*). The design of these sketches was informed by our notes of the island, and *designer instinct*; in total, 5 sketches were made (see Figure 3), and they were distributed around a table central to the participants.
During their development, it was important to consider the perception the participants had towards the sketches, and if they would feel free to draw on, alter, and potentially discard them. As such, they were made from low fidelity materials (e.g. craft foam) as a way to decrease their perceived value.
– *Design constraint elicitation.* The final part of the second workshop included a short period to reflect upon any new themes and comments placed on the table by the participants. During this latter half of the session, the participants were prompted to list the desirable (and undesirable) features of any

future system that may be used to address the proposed problem. Once the session had ended, the participants were invited to present to the rest of the group and provide an explanation of the constraints they wrote, and why they were important to them. This would give the rest of the group an opportunity to raise any issues or conflicting viewpoints.

Fig. 3. Number of physical sketches presented to participants. (Left to Right) : Lightbulb Sketch, Clock Sketch, Haptic Sketch, Zoltar Sketch, and Target Sketch

Design Constraints Results. In total, 8 participants were involved in the *Design constraints workshop*, the majority of which were invited back from the previous workshop; these participants were invited back based on their continued correspondence with us. From the initial themes brought forward from the first workshop, over 60 individual design artefacts were generated by the participants, including sketches and comments drawn on the main worksheet.

The low fidelity sketches played an important roll in the seeding of this discussion, which is demonstrated by the participants often picking up, playing with, and annotating the sketches — akin to *show and tell*. Further evidence of the sketches being used to inspire ideation can be seen in comments written on the table worksheet, such as *"clock = great, [needs] forecasting in real-time"* and *"It should have tactile feedback for the sight/hearing impaired"*; the latter comment was made in context of the *Haptic* sketch. These comments were predominantly placed in close proximity to the physical sketches.

6 Reflections

The workshops seemed to be well received by the island community, a sentiment echoed by one of the participants — *"[...] I think for me, this whole thing shows the importance of how productive collaboration can be, and how it can facilitate this kind of brainstorming session [...]"*. As a vehicle to engage with the community, the workshops were equally successful as a means to convey the properties and concepts of a future problem (i.e. intermittent and variable energy supply). This was evident in the understanding of the problem context shown by the participants after the warm-up tasks and during the second workshop.

As noted during the session, there was also evidence to suggest that the sketches were used to help inspire ideation and acted as *talking points* between the participants; indeed, participants would often gesticulate with the sketches to convey an idea. We would go further to suggest that the presentation of themes and physical sketches also helped to focus the design artefacts being generated by providing a focal point for the participants to discuss.

6.1 Lessons Learnt

From these workshops, we have learnt a number of valuable lessons that may help other creative workshops; these lessons are:

- *Physical over abstract.* During our first workshop, we found that the verbal description of a concept (such as *OnSupply*) wasn't sufficient for a participant to fully understand and visualise it. Our experience shows that using physical props is very useful in conveying ideas to and between the participants.
- *Allow time for reflection.* There was the temptation to hold both workshop sessions as one larger session; however, due to the time constraints of the participants, we decided to split the workshop into two. Consequently, we were able to spend more time analysing the results from the first part of the process, and develop higher fidelity sketches. Furthermore, we believe this gave the participants more time to reflect on the first workshop.
- *Know the context.* An important factor to the success of these workshops has been the other engagement opportunities that surround it. Through interviews and other ethnographic efforts, we feel we have gained a level of understanding of the island context, which has better equipped us to analyse the data we have gathered. As such, we urge the reader to get to know the culture of the workshop participants to better design around and with them.

7   Conclusion

Designing with a community plays an important role in the development of ICT systems, as it allows for the development of *appropriate* solutions to the problems identified by the community. However, designing for *future problems* in a user-centred manner can be challenging, especially as these problems provide a context that may be unfamiliar to those involved.

This paper has presented our experience of eliciting design constraints for a *future problem* through the use of playful, creative workshops in a user-centred manner using physical props and scenario-based games. Through these creative workshops, we have been able to facilitate an ongoing dialogue with the Tiree community, whilst distilling and disseminating the properties of the energy scenario. Although the results of this work are promising, we feel that further evaluation to fully gauge the efficacy of this approach is needed.

The future direction of this work includes revisiting Tiree with early prototypes inspired and guided by the design constraints elicited during the workshops described herein. We also hope to continue with the workshop participants as lead users by involving them in iterations of these prototypes.

References

1. Sanders, E.B.N., Stappers, P.J.: Co-creation and the new landscapes of design. Co-design 4(1), 5–18 (2008)
2. Siew, S.-T., Yeo, A.W.: Employing participatory action research to augment software development for rural communities. In: Proc. of the 25th BCS Conference on Human-Computer Interaction, BCS-HCI 2011, pp. 171–176. British Computer Society, Swinton (2011)
3. Hunter, G., Ramamoorthy, K.: National airspace strategies for future demand scenarios in inclement weather. In: The 24th Digital Avionics Systems Conference, DASC 2005, vol. 1 (October 2005) 3.E.2–31–12
4. Widen, J.: Correlations between large-scale solar and wind power in a future scenario for sweden. IEEE Transactions on Sustainable Energy 2(2), 177–184 (2011)
5. Mancini, C., Rogers, Y., Bandara, A.K., Coe, T., Jedrzejczyk, L., Joinson, A.N., Price, B.A., Thomas, K., Nuseibeh, B.: Contravision: Exploring users' reactions to futuristic technology. In: Proc. of the SIGCHI Conference on Human Factors in Computing Systems, CHI 2010, pp. 153–162. ACM, New York (2010)
6. Carroll, J., Rosson, M., Chin, G., Koenemann, J.: Requirements development in scenario-based design. IEEE Transactions on Software Engineering 24(12), 1156–1170 (1998)
7. Go, K., Takamoto, Y., Carroll, J.: Designing a mobile phone of the future: requirements elicitation using photo essays and scenarios. In: 18th International Conference on Advanced Information Networking and Applications, AINA 2004, vol. 2, pp. 475–480 (March 2004)
8. De Bono, E.: Six Thinking Hats. Little, Brown Book Group Limited (1985)
9. Hansen, N.B., Dalsgaard, P.: The productive role of material design artefacts in participatory design events. In: Proceedings of the 7th Nordic Conference on Human-Computer Interaction: Making Sense Through Design, NordiCHI 2012, pp. 665–674. ACM, New York (2012)
10. Maiden, N., Jones, S.: The rescue requirements engineering process: An integrated user-centred requirements engineering process, version 4.1. Technical report (February 2004)
11. Vyas, D., Nijholt, A., van der Veer, G.: Supporting cooperative design through "living" artefacts. In: Proceedings of the 6th Nordic Conference on Human-Computer Interaction: Extending Boundaries, NordiCHI 2010, pp. 541–550. ACM, New York (2010)
12. Kolb, D.: Experiential learning: experience as the source of learning and development. Prentice-Hall (1984)
13. UK Government: UK Renewable Energy Roadmap Update 2013 (2014)
14. EDF Energy: The Energy Gap (2014), http://www.edfenergy.com/energyfuture/key-info/the-energy-gap
15. Whittle, J., Ochu, E., Ferrario, M.A., Southern, J., McNally, R.: Beyond Research in the Wild: Citizen-Led Research as a Model for Innovation in the Digital Economy. In: Proc. Digital Futures (2012)
16. Forshaw, S., Cruickshank, L., Dix, A.: Collaborative Communication Tools for Designing: Physical-Cyber Environments. In: Proc. of HCI 2012 - The 26th BCS Conference on Human Computer Interaction (2012)

Usability of Single- and Multi-factor Authentication Methods on Tabletops: A Comparative Study

Anders Bruun[1], Kenneth Jensen[1,2], and Dianna Kristensen[1,3]

[1] Aalborg University, Selma Lagerlöfs Vej 300
DK-9220 Aalborg Oest
bruun@cs.aau.dk
[2] Analytech, Bøgildsmindevej 21
DK-9400 Nørresundby
keje89@gmail.com
[3] DanDomain, Normansvej 1
DK-8920 Randers NV
dhk@dandomain.dk

Abstract. With the introduction and adoption of tabletop technologies a need for different user authentication mechanisms has arisen. Tabletops support close collaboration between users, typically in close physical proximity and such settings are more vulnerable to shoulder surfing attacks compared to desktops settings where users are more distantly located. Previous studies on desktop interfaces have shown that multi factor authentication provides a higher level of security than single factor authentication. This study extends previous work by comparing the usability of several authentication methods applied in tabletop settings. The aim of the study is to contribute with proposals on which authentication methods to apply when engineering user interfaces for tabletop devices. We compare single factor and multi-factor authentication mechanisms from a usability perspective.

Keywords: Usability, tabletop, multi-factor, authentication, TUI.

1 Introduction

Tabletop technologies are applicable in public and private spaces where large interfaces foster collaboration between users interacting with digital information [8]. Although promising, we also find new security shortcomings within tabletop settings as the nature of these devices is for co-located collaboration. One such shortcoming is that of shoulder surfing attacks, which is when a person makes malicious observations to obtain e.g. write access in personal documents belonging to one of the collaborators. In the case of collaborative settings with tabletops the authentication information is relatively easy compromised as everyone around the tabletop can see what everyone else does [8]. Another security threat is smudge attacks, which is when fingerprint oil is left on a display when using direct touch to interact. Such oil traces can be used to deduce authentication credentials [1]. Thus, close physical proximity in collaborative settings decrease the level of security.

S. Sauer et al. (Eds.): HCSE 2014, LNCS 8742, pp. 299–306, 2014.

In conventional desktop settings several authentication methods have been proposed for validating users and to grant permission to access personal data. A common knowledge-based authentication approach is the username/password combination. Literature reports of three authentication factors: K*nowledge factor* (information you know), *possession factor* (physical object you possess) and the *inheritance factor* (biometric properties you possess) [7, 10].

The growing risk of compromising passwords and usernames (not only in tabletop settings) has led to alternative methods accommodating a higher level of security. One such method is multi-factor authentication which is considered stronger than single factor authentication [2, 10]. Multi-factor authentication combines two or more of the above authentication factors e.g. a password (knowledge factor) and a keycard (possession factor) for authentication.

Currently, only a few studies concern security aspects of tabletop technologies [8]. Also, the focus in authentication research has primarily been on security aspects and lesser on usability aspects. Examples of studies emphasizing security over usability are [8, 10, 11]. Design of security systems often conflicts with usability concerns, although the two aspects are important to address [2, 4]. Gutmann and Grigg [4] for instance state that users ignore secure systems and choose those that are more usable, i.e. usability is prioritized over security. Thus, the aim of the study presented in this paper is to compare different single- and multi-factor authentication methods with respect to usability concerns.

2   Related Work

In this section, we present related work within single and multi-factor authentication methods in relation to desktop and tabletop technologies. Recent research has been on multi-factor authentication methods [5, 8, 10] on various systems.

Braz et al. [2] presents a comparative study of authentication methods applied on traditional desktop applications in which they compare existing methods such as password, proximity card, multifunction card, public key, fingerprint etc. They compare authentication methods on the parameters of advantages and disadvantages in relation to security, usability and input time. Findings of that study indicate that the highest level of security can be found in the three methods of voice (inheritance), password and PIN (knowledge). The three systems with the highest level of usability are: Password, PIN and retina/iris scanning. They conclude that there is a need for more focus on usability to make reliable, effective and usable authentication systems [2].

Kim et al. [8] specify methods for one-factor authentication on tabletops. The aim was to reduce the risk of shoulder surfing. That study was based on one user logging into the system and two observers that afterwards tried to login as that user, hereby simulating a shoulder surfing attack. Findings in that study are based on measures of task completion times and number of successful shoulder surfing attacks.

Marquardt et al. [9] specify a system using a fiduciary-tagged glove. Fiduciary-tags are like barcodes and QR codes. By placing 15 tags strategically on the glove to identify which part of the hand is actually touching the surface their system enhanced gesture recognition and thereby expanded the interaction possibilities. The glove also makes it possible to identify a specific user, as the glove is meant to be a unique possession [9]. In terms of related work we did not find any studies comparing single and multi-factor authentication methods on tabletop technologies.

3   Method

In this study the two independent variables are: One-factor and two-factor authentication methods. These two variables have been chosen based on the popularity in modern systems and because they will likely require different completion times. We set up four authentication conditions: Three based on single-factor and one on multi-factor. The four conditions were evaluated by measuring task completion times and the System Usability Scale (SUS) [3].

Throughout the study we applied Microsoft Surface 2.0 as the tabletop device. We chose to create a similar layout of all developed prototype designs in order to avoid experimental bias related to differences in designs.

3.1   One-Factor Authentication

We designed and developed three prototypes for one-factor authentication. Two of these focus on the knowledge factor through the use of a username/password combination and a username/PIN combination. The third condition focuses on the possession factor by using a Tangible User Interface (TUI).

We evaluated knowledge factor authentication through the use of PIN and Password as Braz et al. [2] found these to have the highest level of security and usability in desktop settings. In collaborative settings around a tabletop it is not enough to settle for just a PIN or a password as is the case on e.g. a laptop or a mobile phone where the devices are personal. As the tabletop is shared among multiple users, the individual person needs to be identified as anyone around the tabletop could enter a PIN/password. To accommodate this situation we added the established knowledge factor of username hereby keeping the conditions in a single-factor mode.

Authentication based on possession is evaluated through the use of a TUI based on fiduciary tags, which Marquardt et al. [9] found to be a feasible authentication method.

Username and PIN Condition (UsPi). In the UsPi condition participants applied a combination of a username and PIN for authentication. User input was made through an onscreen QWERTY keyboard and a numpad was provided for entering the PIN. See Fig. 1 for an example.

Username and Password Condition (UsPa). In the UsPa condition the user uses a combination of a username and password. The purpose is to use this condition as a benchmark for the four other conditions, as this is a common authentication method applied in traditional desktop settings.

Tag. In the tag condition the participants applied a TUI. The TUI is implemented using a fiduciary tag, which is a paper-based 8 bit picture code that Microsoft Pixelsense recognizes. With the Tag condition the user just places the TUI on the tabletop in order to authenticate.

Fig. 1. UsPi prototype, knowledge factor authentication

3.2   Two-Factor Authentication

The second variable is two-factor authentication, where we designed and developed one prototype focusing on a combination of using a TUI and PIN.

Tag and PIN Condition (TaPi). The TaPi condition uses a TUI with a PIN input. The process to authenticate is first to place the TUI. When the TUI is registered by the tabletop, a numpad appears relative to the TUI. The user then enters a four digit PIN and presses OK.

3.3   Participants

Each system was evaluated by university students. The experiment had 16 participants of which two were female. Participant's mean age was 24 (SD=3.66). They had one to eight years of experience using touch devices, such as tablets and smartphones. Only two had previous experience using tabletops. Participants were familiar with single- and multi-factor authentication methods on conventional desktop and laptop PCs.

3.4   Procedure

The study was conducted within a lab facility at the university and the room was darkened to limit interference of sunlight on the tabletop. The experiment was conducted as a within-subject study, i.e. each condition had 16 participants. To reduce ordering bias the usage of prototypes was randomized.

The procedure of the experiment was as follows: 1) Participants filled the demographic questionnaire, 2) Participants were informed of the purpose and procedure, 3) Credentials for authorization (in written form) was given to the participants, 4) Participants tried to authorize themselves using the credentials, 5) After successful (or unsuccessful) attempts for each prototype, participants filled in the SUS questionnaire, 6) Repeat steps 4 and 5 until participants completed all four conditions and 7) Participants were interviewed to elaborate on their opinion on the different prototypes.

3.5 Data Analysis

The data analysis was conducted by the two last authors of this paper who analyzed all data. For each participant we collected four videos, four SUS questionnaires and one interview of five to 15 minutes. In total we collected 64 videos, 64 SUS questionnaires and 16 interviews. Each video was analyzed and usability problems were noted. Afterwards the two last authors made a comparison of the identified problems. To validate the qualitative video analysis the agreement between the evaluators was calculated based on the measure of any-two agreement. In this study the two authors agreed on 22 of the 44 identified problems, i.e. an any-two agreement of 50%. The any-two agreement for this study is at the higher end compared to the agreement of 6% to 45% mentioned in [6].

4   Results

In this section we present our findings. First, the SUS scores are presented. Secondly task completion time results are presented followed by qualitative results from the interviews and video analysis of usability problems.

4.1   System Usability Scale

Table 1 provides a summary of the average SUS scores given for each of the four prototypes. This shows that the UsPi prototype scores lowest with an average of 68.75 (SD=19.3) while the TaPi and Tag prototypes scores highest with 92.5 (SD=9.9) and 90.2 (SD=7.5) respectively.

Table 1. SUS scores for each of the prototypes and user

	UsPi	UsPa	TaPi	Tag
Avg (SD)	68.75 (19.3)	84.1 (13)	92.5 (9.9)	90.2 (7.5)

A one-way ANOVA test shows significant differences between one or more of the conditions (df-resid=60, F=10.56, p<0.001). A Tukey's pair-wise comparison test reveals significant differences between the UsPi prototype and all other prototypes (0.001<p<0.01). There are no significant differences between the UsPa, TaPi and Tag prototypes (p>0.1). Thus, the UsPi protype receive significantly lower SUS scores than all other prototypes.

4.2   Task Completion Times

Table 2 shows an overview of the task completion times for all participants. The slowest condition on average is the UsPi prototype with a mean of 34.4 (SD=28.8) seconds while the fastest is the Tag prototype with 3.6 (SD=0.8) seconds.

Table 2. The Completion time in seconds for each prototype and user

	UsPi	UsPa	TaPi	Tag
Avg (SD)	34.4 (28.8)	29.2 (16.9)	10.4 (3)	3.6 (0.8)

A one-way ANOVA test on the task completion times show significant differences between one or more of the prototypes (df-resid=60, F=12.32, p<0.001). A Tukey's Pair-wise comparison test reveals significant differences between the UsPi/UsPa prototypes compared to the TaPi/Tag prototypes (p<0.001). Completion times between the UsPi and UsPa prototypes are not significant (p>0.1). Also, we found no significant differences between the TaPi and Tag prototypes (p>0.1). Thus, the UsPi and UsPa prototypes have significantly longer completion times than the TaPi and Tag prototypes.

4.3   Qualitative Data

We gathered two types of qualitative data in our study. The first were the results of the preference questions asked in the post test interview, the second were the usability issues extracted from videos. The most severe usability problems are presented here and all relate to platform and implementation issues.

We identified a tag-flickering problem in the prototypes based on a TUI (TaPi and Tag). The TUI began to sporadically flick causing the tabletop device to lose track of the TUI. Participants also mentioned confusion in the interpretation of how to use the progress bar in case of the UsPi prototype. A participant mentioned: *"I was confused on how to continue and tried to press the keyboard and the progress bar [while pointing at the four spaces in the UsPi prototype]"*. One participant also experienced problems with the keyboard in the UsPi prototype: *"I searched for the Tab button but could not find it at all, and then I was in trouble of how I should continue from here"*.

5   Discussion

In relation to task completion time, the possession-based TUI prototypes were significantly faster than the knowledge based. As expected, the single-factor Tag prototype was faster than the multi-factor TaPi prototype. Although faster, the Tag prototype received lower SUS ratings compared to the TaPi prototype. This indicates that task completion time is not corresponding entirely to the satisfaction ratings provided in the SUS scores. This is also supported by the finding of the UsPa prototype having significantly longer task completion time, yet similar SUS ratings compared to the TaPi and Tag prototypes. When asked which of the prototypes participants preferred, most mentioned TaPi followed by Tag. Thus, although the Tag prototype resulted in faster completion times it was not the preferred authentication method. An explanation for this observation is related to security concerns. We asked participants if the type of personal information accessed would affect their choice of authentication method. Several mentioned that they wanted to use TaPi for authenticating access to personal information while some also mentioned that they would apply a TUI for less critical information access. This indicates that participants were willing to use an authentication method that takes more time to complete in order to increase security in collaborative settings, i.e. they felt less secure using single-factor authentication based on possession only. Furthermore, some of the participants stated a concern towards the ease of replicating the particular fiduciary tag applied in our case. A consequence of the ease to replicate it is that malicious people can easily create another tag and hereby a false identity. So, in general the tag alone is not perceived to be secure enough for participants. The preference of the Tag and PIN combination could also be attributed to the novelty of this type of user interface, which could make it more interesting for first time users compared to the well-known Username/Password combination. UsPi performed worst in terms of SUS ratings and task completion times. This is likely because the username and PIN combination is rarely used elsewhere, which is also reflected in some of the severe usability problems identified. In terms of related work, both TUI prototypes had average completion times in same range as those identified by Braz et al. [2] in desktop settings. However, findings in [2] and our study cannot be compared directly as desktops and tabletops are two very different technologies with varying interaction patterns. Nevertheless it shows that similar task completion times can be obtained in tabletop settings.

In sum, the fastest of our authentication methods was the Tag and second fastest was TaPi, both having average completion times in same range as in related work dealing with desktop settings. The condition which had the highest level of usability was TaPi while the second highest score was attributed to the Tag prototype. In contrast, the widely used single-factor method of username and password received a slightly lower SUS score and it had significantly longer completion times.

6 Conclusion

The aim of the study was to contribute with proposals on which authentication methods to apply when engineering tabletop devices and user interfaces. We have emphasized a usability perspective in a comparison of single-factor and multi-factor authentication methods. We found that the combination of a TUI and PIN (TaPi) provided the highest level of usability. However, TaPi was not the fastest authentication method, but participants perceived TaPi authentication to be the most secure. Surprisingly, the well-established single factor authentication method based on username and password was not preferred. These are key points to consider when engineering user interfaces for tabletop technologies.

Authentication is typically conducted several times during a day. For this reason it would also be relevant to extend our work with longitudinal studies of usability, i.e. the usability of first time usage is only a subcomponent in the evaluation of authentication methods for tabletops.

References

1. Aviv, A.J., Gibson, K., Mossop, E., Blaze, M., Smith, J.M.: Smudge attacks on smartphone touch screens. In: Proc. WOOT. USENIX Association (2010)
2. Braz, C., Jean-Marc, R.: Security and usability: the case of the user authentication methods. In Proc. IHM. ACM (2006)
3. Brooke, J.: SUS-A quick and dirty usability scale. In: Jordan, P.W., Thomas, B., Weerdmeester, B.A., McClellan, A.L. (eds.) Usability Evaluation in Industry. Taylor and Francis (1996)
4. Gutmann, P., Grigg, I.: Security Usability. Security & Privacy 3(4), 56–58 (2005)
5. Harini, N., Padmanabhan, T.R.: 2CAuth: A New Two Factor Authentication Scheme Using QR-Code. International Journal of Engineering and Technology (2013)
6. Hertzum, M., Jacobsen, N.E.: The evaluator effect: A chilling fact about usability evaluation methods. International Journal of Human-Computer Interaction 13(4), 421–443
7. Jin, A.T.B., Ling, D.N.C., Goh, A.: Biohashing: two factor authentication featuring fingerprint data and tokenised random number. Pattern Recognition 37(11), 2245–2255 (2004)
8. Kim, D., Dunphy, P., Briggs, P., Hook, J., Nicholson, J.W., Nicholson, J., Olivier, P.: Multi-touch authentication on tabletops. In Proc. CHI. ACM (2010)
9. Marquardt, N., Kiemer, J., Greenberg, S.: What caused that touch?: expressive interaction with a surface through fiduciary-tagged gloves. In: Proc. ITS. ACM (2010)
10. Sabzevar, A.P., Stavrou, A.: Universal Multi-Factor Authentication Using Graphical Passwords. In Proc. SITIS. IEEE (2008)
11. Qin, Y., Yu, C., Jiang, H., Wu, C., Shi, Y.: pPen: enabling authenticated pen and touch interaction on tabletop surfaces. In: Proc. ITS. ACM (2010)

User Centered Inclusive Design
for People with Dyslexia:
Experiences from a Project on Accessibility

Dominik Rupprecht, Rainer Blum, and Birgit Bomsdorf

University of Applied Sciences, Department of Applied Computer Science, Fulda, Germany
{dominik.rupprecht,rainer.blum,
birgit.bomsdorf}@informatik.hs-fulda.de

Abstract. User participation is a key element in user centered design of interactive systems. However, applying established methods is not straightforward while realizing a system for people with cognitive impairment due to their specific, heterogeneous needs and abilities. This paper presents experiences from conducting a user centered inclusive design process within an ongoing project. It aims at the development of a web application for people with dyslexia caused by cognitive impairment. A distinctive feature is the intended use of the application: It must support the counseling interviews for planning the real life inclusion of the target group. In addition, it must enable cognitively impaired as well as non-impaired people using it cooperatively. One of the most challenging issues was how and when to involve cognitively impaired users.

Keywords: User Centered Design, Inclusive Design, Accessibility, User Participation, Methods and Techniques, Dyslexia.

1 Introduction

In user centered design (UCD) the focus throughout the development process is on the users' needs and (dis-)abilities. Applying traditional methods, however, is not straightforward while realizing a system for people with cognitive impairment. For example, most of the well-known methods of user participation, a key element in UCD, rely on face-to-face meetings that are not easily applicable, because of a lack of knowledge of the diverse, heterogeneous characteristics of the user group. Furthermore cognitively impaired may be unable to concentrate on a topic or to utter a want.

All in all, designing interactive systems for and with people with disabilities and their involved personal supporters (caregivers, relatives) is highly complex because of the resulting multi-faceted interplay of needs, abilities, and objectives. Involving people with disabilities in the design process, even though challenging, is important to increase the understanding about these complexities and enables to create more meaningful and useful systems for them. We adapted in a current project, similar to Newell et al. [1], traditional UCD methods aiming at a user centered inclusive design process. This contribution presents lessons learned, particularly in facing the challenge of involving people with cognitive impairment – and additional stakeholders.

S. Sauer et al. (Eds.): HCSE 2014, LNCS 8742, pp. 307–314, 2014.
© IFIP International Federation for Information Processing 2014

As the focus is on UCD methods, usability problems are only mentioned but not reported in detail.

In the remaining part of this section the project background is introduced and related work is reported. Section 2 shows the involvement of the clients throughout the project. The third section outlines the usage of guidelines for the target application. The final section gives a summarization and a short outlook on ongoing work.

1.1   Background of the Project

The main objective of the project referenced in this paper is the investigation of how interactive web forms can be accessible for people with dyslexia caused by cognitive impairment. The proof-of-concept example is a specific form intended to discuss and plan central aspects of the daily life of individuals with impairments. This form is used once a year in collaboration with the concerned persons to perform counseling interviews. The aim is to determine required help and integration services. In these interviews information on the current situation, impairments and wishes of the impaired people are collected. This builds the basis for granting vital support activities in the areas of self-care, living and working for the next months. The currently used form is a PDF document of eight pages crowded with arrays of questions. During the interviews it is used by assistants not only to collect the needed data, but to keep track of the whole process.

Three different stakeholders are involved in the project: The first user group in focus are people with dyslexia attributable to cognitive impairments, in the following referred to as "clients". The second group comprises caregivers and relatives of the clients guiding the counseling interviews, referred to as "assistants". The last group consists of the marketer of the form (the current PDF form and the upcoming web application), a small-sized enterprise with years of experience in providing trainings for using the form.

1.2   Related Work

McCarthy and Swierenga [2] give an overview of the literature considering dyslexia and accessibility produced until 2010. The authors highlight that much work has been done in the topics of dyslexia and web accessibility separately. But there is only a small amount of work addressing both aspects at once. They also report that most efforts are focused on how to support users that are blind or have low vision.

De Santana et al. [3] give a good and comprehensive overview over existing guidelines regarding people with dyslexia. They present 41 guidelines to support three website stakeholders: Developers, designers and content producers. These guidelines were gathered on websites discussing dyslexia and accessibility and are based on available sets of guidelines like the Web Content Accessibility Guidelines (WCAG) [4]. The authors divided the guidelines in the following groups: navigation, colors, text presentation, writing, layout, images and charts, end user customization, markup, and videos and audios. One conclusion the authors draw is that end user customization is an important step to achieve accessibility considering dyslexia. But they identified only two guidelines and recommended a deeper study on end user customization.

The Web Accessibility Initiative (WAI) [5] of the W3C proposes an analysis procedure when working with guidelines containing three phases: evaluation by experts, automatically or manual conformity assessment and user evaluation. For the conformity assessment the WebAIM [6] project created a checklist (Cognitive Web Accessibility Checklist) and the self-acting evaluation tool WAVE [7] based on the WCAG guidelines.

Newell at al. [1], [8] point out the need for a shift of paradigm towards a "User Sensitive Inclusive Design" extending the methodologies of the UCD. The authors show challenges when working with people with disabilities and point out differences to the UCD. Challenges we identified also in our project are:

- Users may not be able to communicate their thoughts,
- Users may not be the purchaser of the final product,
- Users with disabilities may have specialized and little known requirements and
- Different user groups may provide very conflicting requirements for a product.

Differences we also identified in our project are:

- Much greater variety of user characteristics
- Difficulty of finding and recruiting "representative users"
- Conflicts between accessibility and ease of use for less disabled people
- Possible conflicts of interest between accessibility for people with different types of disabilities

Existing methods and approaches are a good starting point to support the work with disabled users. Newell et al. [1] points out that the designer should develop an "empathetic relationship" with disabled users, rather than rely on standards and guidelines. Thus, following the idea of participatory design, the authors underline the importance of the involvement of the impaired users from the beginning. Furthermore, they suggest to begin the design process with only a narrow list of features to get products that are usable by the target user group and to avoid function-overloaded products the users cannot work with.

They also argue for the use of personas in the early project phases. Personas are descriptions of hypothetical archetypes of actual user groups and are developed based on identified user profiles. Zhang et al. [9] make use of personas in the early design and also in the evaluation phases. In their methods, called "persona self-guided evaluation method" and "persona think-aloud method", experts act from the perspective of the persona. These methods cannot fully replace user testing, but enable designers to create a better product when the target user population is not accessible. Working with personas can be helpful to avoid ethical and legislative barriers in working with impaired people. Another approach to this is proposed by Newell et al. [1]: Instead of asking experts to adopt the roles of personas they had well-briefed professional actors working to a well-crafted script in the phase of design. The actors provided a personification of the target user and throughout improvisation interacted with the designers or the users. The authors showed that this method can be a powerful tool of communication between designers and users of technology and in raising the designers' awareness of the challenges when working with disabled people.

There are some projects working with people with dyslexia or cognitive impairments, too. For example Sutcliff et al. [10] investigated an e-mail system for users with cognitive impairments (e.g. attention span problems, working memory limitations, mild problem-solving and language disorders). They showed that with cognitively impaired people, often, training is no solution when there are problems with the user interface. Or Hagelkruys et al. [11] who are working on the ongoing LITERACY web portal to improve social inclusion of youth and adults with dyslexia. They use additional tools like screen reader to support people with dyslexia. The usage of those tools is not part of this paper, but is considered in our development.

2   Involvement of Clients

At the beginning of the project all members of the project consortium assumed that substantial contributions of the clients for the analysis could not be expected due to their cognitive and verbal impairments (compare to [8]). Within the early phase of gathering requirements only assistants and the marketer were involved but no clients. However, members of the development team visited six clients in their daily environment like the foster homes they are living in to get a better understanding of the target group (compare to [1]). Out of their observations and statements of the caregivers different client profiles were built containing information about their computer skills like Internet usage, their form of dyslexia and additional physical impairments. This was the basis for building personas to be used at least in the first development and evaluation steps.

During the process the importance to get information from both the clients and the caregivers was underlined and increased. On the one hand, more skills of the clients were observed than the caregivers knew of. On the other hand, the evaluation recordings were analyzed together with caregivers, because the clients have learned to pretend and fake social interaction skills – thus some of their impairments were not visible at first glance.

Early on in the first four months of the project it became clear that the clients could be involved more often. So the project consortium decided to shorten the planned development cycles and to include the clients directly in the process instead of the personas ahead of the original schedule.

To get a greater user base in order to prevent the need of redesign in later phases of the project the initial group of six clients was extended over the course of the project up to eleven clients. With each extension the range of client profiles grew based on the additional information and the existing personas had to be altered and additional ones had to be created. For example, all clients from the beginning were familiar to the web and to browsers. Subsequently, clients without these abilities joined in, resulting in a very heterogeneous group of clients. With each addition more assistants joined in, too. All of the clients were familiar to the counseling interviews and the original PDF form. Not only in the meetings with only the assistants and the marketer but in general each of them favored a different group of clients. Hence it was harder to come up with coherent solutions, and from time to time the focus was on a subgroup but mostly the design considered the whole group. It is still challenging to specify priorities of user profiles or of impairments to lead the design processes.

Prototypes of different fidelity and type were utilized throughout the development process. As also suggested by Zhang et al. [9] we started with sketches and paper prototypes to come up with a number of different ideas. Based on selected solutions simple HTML pages were created including only parts of the intended system. Later on we used interactive prototypes using the wireframe and rapid prototyping tool Pidoco [12]. It enabled us to realize interactive low-fidelity prototypes very fast to get feedback on them and to evaluate those involving assistants and the marketer.

Even the first evaluations were conducted with the clients and not by using personas as projected before. This decision resulted from the positive experiences. The evaluations with the clients were conducted as field tests taking place in their familiar surroundings. They were performed in form of a user test combined with further standard usability methods like questionnaires and scenario-based tasks the user were asked to perform as well as audio and video recording. The recordings were analyzed together with the caregivers and assistants so that they could individually interpret the reactions and statements of the clients.

For the different client groups nearly identical scenario-based tasks and test settings were implemented. We started with the first HTML prototype with only limited functionality to check the hierarchy, navigation structure and simple input fields. The clients understood that the prototype did not represent the whole PDF form they are familiar with and no problems with this artificiality of the system were observable. Whether or not the clients realized the artificial situation became not clear, but this was not a problem, too. But quickly we realized that the process of filling out the PDF form is really essential to the life of the clients. The clients were enthusiastic being part of the test and started to work on their participation in life. For example, they were not in favor to fill in "only" test data but wanted to have their actual data filled in. Therefore, a person of the evaluation team had to assist them by instructing them how to type single words. In subsequent evaluations we considered bigger parts of the counseling interviews and followed the known counseling procedure.

With each of the conducted four iterations the range of functions and the level of detail of the implementation grew resulting in an evolutionary prototyping with a fully functional demonstrator version of our application at the end.

Other variations from the original procedure based on the PDF form were that the clients wandered from one topic to another and didn't focus on the given task. Sometimes the clients only wanted to show what they could do with the computer, regardless if it was on subject or not.

As mentioned above clients are used to hide their impairments and have strategies to avoid attracting attention. This made it difficult to get information from the clients about their opinions of the tested prototypes. Most of the time it seemed that the clients had two strategies: providing answers that they assumed the observers wanted to get or providing answers by which they hoped to avoid follow-up questions. When they were asked to mention positive and negative points about the application, almost all answers were that everything is all right – although problems were observed. Particularly in the first two prototypes clients were not aware of most of the interactive elements and navigation possibilities. However they were not pointed to the problems (afterwards) not to unsettle them and to keep up their motivation to participate.

3   Guidelines

Another part of our approach was consulting existing accessibility guidelines. The summary of de Santana et al. [3] was a good starting point. Typical guidelines like avoiding scrolling, recommended text size or the use of short, simple and direct sentences were considered throughout the design phases. We also used the mentioned WAVE tool [7] to automatically check against the common accessibility guidelines.

Additionally the project consortium committed to advance guidelines. It was discussed which (minimal) mental model of the application the users should be required to build and what the clients are capable of. We wanted to use as few different concepts as possible (compare to [1]) that have to be understood by the clients (easy-of-use), because training of using the interface was not possible (see [10]).

It was not possible to show the entire hierarchy and structure of the eight-page PDF form at once. The form was therefore split up resulting in a hierarchical structure. According to the assistants' and marketer's previous knowledge about the clients the number of layers of the hierarchy was reduced to four (more width, less depth), each layer containing a set of elements that could be shown only partially. The main question at this point was how to support the clients to move through the hierarchy even if they are unable to build a mental model of it. This could be split up into:

- How to show that there is more to find in lower levels?
- How to show that there is more on the same level?

We re-formulated such questions from the client perspective using simple language (e.g. if at a current subordinate node of the hierarchy a set of elements exists that could not be presented at a time: "How to show, that there is more?" "How to show, that there is a sub-layer?"). This helped us in different ways: Fist it supported the developers to empathize with the clients and to get the perspective of the clients. Second it helped in communicating with the assistants, because this communication can be difficult as they come from different backgrounds and have different jargons (compare to [8]). Further guidelines refer to the visual design of the interface, e.g.:

- No use of 3D elements: A use of three-dimensional elements in the interface was not possible, because this representation would demand too much cognitive resources of the clients to understand and work with it.

Other examples of guidelines and conflicts between them are:

- Prevent distractions: Each webpage should contain only one input field. The attention of the clients should be targeted only at one information unit at a time to prevent distraction. At the same time, however, every option should be visible. Following "out of sight, out of mind" an invisible option will most likely be forgotten. In the current prototype some pages contain more than one input field to preserve information. Additionally, each webpage contains as many visual clues as possible to navigate to the remaining input fields.

- Control: No use of a wizard to guide the users. Some of the assistants and the marketer wanted that the clients are enabled to have free control over the dialog and navigation. The clients should be able to visit the pages in an arbitrary order not to force a specific sequence in filling out the form. Later on assistants and marketer agreed with the developers that software assistants such as a wizard are needed.

- Always save automatically: The clients do not have to save their inputs explicitly, e.g., by a "Save"-UI-Element. The behavior of the application should be like filling out a paper based form, where you do not need to save the inputs separately. This was in conflict to the assistants' expectation, who were missing the explicit and familiar saving function when working with the application.

General applicability of these guidelines is still under investigation. Nevertheless, these guidelines often served us within the project to find a common sense. Every time an additional feature was under discussion, it was counter-checked to the guidelines. For example, based on their own "prevent distraction" guideline the assistants and the marketer were convinced not to demand too much additional functionality per page.

4   Conclusion and Future Work

In this paper we presented experiences from adapting UCD for a user centered *inclusive* design process within a project aiming at the inclusion of people with dyslexia caused by cognitive impairments (clients). The proof-of concept application was taken from the domain of digital forms the clients have to understand and interact with.

One finding is that real clients could be involved much earlier than assumed before. Their contribution to the analysis and evaluation is essential even if this contribution is more difficult to achieve due to the cognitive and verbal impairments. In our project the clients were highly encouraged to work with us. They were proud to take part and working with us was a welcome distraction of their daily life. All in all, they asked to be more involved. For the developers this was a very positive experience, too, and they are willing to expand client participation even though it is more challenging and time consuming. Statements and behavior of the clients have to be analyzed very carefully since the clients are used to "fake", i.e. they develop strategies to hide their impairments. Not only because of this but in general, working with the assistants and caregivers is very important due to their specific knowledge and expertise about their clients.

Throughout the project the use of rapid prototyping and of the developed guidelines proved to be valuable to find solutions. The prototypes essentially supported communicating design ideas within the project team (assistants, marketer, and developers). New features were easily counter-checked against the guidelines. The impact on the whole system of features to be implemented was rapidly checked by new prototype versions.

One challenge for the developers was to implement "simple" solutions, e.g. "no use of 3D elements" (see above). However, reactions of the stakeholders to the current system were positive. One of our next step is to evaluate, if the developed application can improve the counseling interviews and thus the inclusion of impaired people.

Acknowledgement. This project (HA project no. 310/11-55) is funded in the framework of Hessen ModellProjekte, financed with funds of LOEWE – Landes-Offensive zur Entwicklung Wissenschaftlich-ökonomischer Exzellenz, Förderlinie 3: KMU-Verbundvorhaben (State Offensive for the Development of Scientific and Economic Excellence).

References

1. Newell, A.F., Gregor, P., Morgan, M., Pullin, G., Macaulay, C.: User-Sensitive Inclusive Design. Univ Access Inf. Soc. 10(3), 235–243 (2011)
2. McCarthy, J.E., Swierenga, S.J.: What we know about dyslexia and Web accessibility: a research review. Univ. Access Inf. Soc. 9(2), 147–152 (2010)
3. de Santana, V.F., de Oliveira, R., AAlmeida, L.D.A., Baranauskas, M.C.C.: Web Accessibility and People with Dyslexia: A Survey on Techniques and Guidelines. In: Proceedings of the International Cross-Disciplinary Conference on Web Accessibility, W4A 2012, pp. 35:1–35:9. ACM, New York (2012).
4. Web Content Accessibility Guildlines (WCAG) 2.0, W3C Recommendation, (December 11, 2008), http://www.w3.org/TR/WCAG20/
5. Web Accessibility Initiative (WAI), http://www.w3.org/WAI/
6. WebAIM – web accessibility in mind, http://webaim.org/articles/evaluatingcognitive
7. WebAIM: WAVE – web accessibility evaluation tool, http://wave.webaim.org/
8. Newell, A.F., Gregor, P.: User sensitive inclusive design. – in search of a new paradigm. In: Scholtz, J., Thomas, J (eds) Proceedings on the 2000 Conference, Arlington, Virginia, United States, pp. 39–44 (2000)
9. Zhang, H., Hung, Y.-H., Dhillon, G.S., Yang, Y., Mccrickard, D.S.: Social Reader: a Cognitive Stimulation Approach towards Helping Dyslexics. In: International Conference on Kansei Engineering and Emotion Research (2012)
10. Sutcliffe, A., Fickas, S., Sohlberg, M.M., Ehlhardt, L.A.: Investigating the usability of assistive user interfaces. Interacting with Computers 15(4), 577–602 (2003)
11. Hagelkruys, D., Struhár, J., Motschnig, R., Balharová, K.: Including Dyslexic Users in the Early Design of the LITERACY Portal. In: Proceedings of the Iadis International Conference: Interfaces and Human Computer Interaction, pp. 273–277. IADIS, Praha (2013)
12. Pidoco – The Rapid Prototyping Tool, http://pidoco.com

End-User Software Engineering: Toward a Future Beyond the Silos

Margaret Burnett

School of EECS, Oregon State University
Corvallis, OR 97331 USA
burnett@eecs.oregonstate.edu

Abstract. This paper summarizes the keynote address on the future of end-user software engineering. We believe the future that we envision has implications for not only end-user software engineering, but also for "classic" software engineering.

Keywords: End-user software engineering (EUSE), end-user programming, end-user development.

From End-User Programming to End-User Software Engineering

End-user programming has become pervasive in our society [3], with end users programming simulations, courseware, spreadsheets, macros, mashups, and more [1, 2]. In this talk, we will consider what happens when we add to end-user programming environments consideration of the software lifecycle beyond the "coding" phase. Considering other phases is necessary, because there is ample evidence that the programs end users create are filled with errors [1]. To help address this problem, we have been working on a software "engineering" methodology designed specifically for end users.

Because the user may have no expertise or even interest in software engineering, we do not propose to transform end users into engineers. Rather, most end-user software engineering research strives to tightly integrate elements of design, implementation, component integration, debugging, testing, and maintenance, supported behind the scenes by analysis and inferential reasoning, to help the user reason about the dependability of their software as they work with it, in a manner that respects the user's problem-solving directions to an extent unprecedented in existing software development environments [2].

In this talk, we briefly describe the present state of end-user software engineering, and then focus on challenges in moving forward—specifically, the challenges of avoiding becoming over-siloed. We then show that focusing on the in-the-moment intents of end-user developers can be used to derive a number of promising directions forward for end-user software engineering researchers, and how theories can help us further de-silo future end-user software engineering research. Finally, we discuss how overcoming challenges for the future of end-user

S. Sauer et al. (Eds.): HCSE 2014, LNCS 8742, pp. 315–316, 2014.

software engineering may also bring direct benefits to the future of "classic" software engineering.

Biography: Margaret Burnett's research is in human issues of software development, which lies in the intersection of HCI and software engineering. Her current research focuses on end-user programming, end-user software engineering, information foraging theory as applied to programming, and gender issues in those contexts. End-user software engineering is the first research area to rigorously consider the problem of dependability in end-user programming, and Burnett led in founding this research area. Her team's "WYSIWYT" systematic testing approach for end-user programmers initiated the groundwork, and in 2003, she co-founded and became Project Director of the EUSES Consortium. Under her leadership, this collaboration grew to 10 institutions whose contributions have helped ordinary end users achieve up to 10 times greater effectiveness at guarding against software defects, receiving wide recognition for technical quality (11 Best Paper recognitions for the project). Burnett's awards for her own work include several Best Paper recognitions, IBM's International Faculty Award, and the NSF Young Investigator Award. She was recently honored with her university's Excellence in Graduate Mentoring Award, College of Engineering's Research Award, College of Engineering's Research Collaboration Award, and the Elizabeth P. Ritchie Distinguished Professor Award. She also serves on a variety of HCI and Software Engineering conference program committees, and currently co-chairs the Academic Alliance of the National Center for Women & Information Technology (NCWIT).

Acknowledgments. This talk is an expanded version of a talk given at the ICSE'14 "Future of Software Engineering" track; both are based on an invited paper co-authored by Burnett and Myers [1]. We'd like to acknowledge the many researchers whose pioneering works have helped establish the area of end-user software engineering. We also thank the students and collaborators who contributed to our own work in end-user software engineering. This paper was supported in part by the National Science Foundation under grants 1240957, 1314384, 1302113. Any opinions, findings and conclusions or recommendations expressed in this material are those of the author(s) and do not necessarily reflect those of the National Science Foundation.

References

1. Burnett, M., Myers, B.: Future of End-User Software Engineering: Beyond the Silos. In: ACM/IEEE International Conference on Software Engineering: Future of Software Engineering Track (ICSE Companion Proceedings), pp. 201–211. ACM Press (2014)
2. Ko, A., Abraham, R., Beckwith, L., Blackwell, A., Burnett, M., Erwig, M., Scaffidi, C., Lawrance, J., Lieberman, H., Myers, B., Rosson, M., Rothermel, G., Shaw, M., Wiedenbeck, S.: The State of the Art in End-User Software Engineering. ACM Computing Surveys 43(3), Article 21, 44 pages (2011)
3. Scaffidi, C., Shaw, M., Myers, B.: Estimating the Numbers of End Users and End User Programmers. In: IEEE Symposium on Visual Languages and Human-Centric Computing, pp. 207–214. IEEE (2005)

How People Really (Like To) Work
Comparative Process Mining to Unravel Human Behavior

Wil M.P. van der Aalst

Eindhoven University of Technology, P.O. Box 513, 5600 MB, Eindhoven,
The Netherlands
w.m.p.v.d.aalst@tue.nl

Abstract. Software forms an integral part of the most complex artifacts
built by humans. Communication, production, distribution, healthcare,
transportation, banking, education, entertainment, government, and
trade all increasingly rely on systems driven by software. Such systems
may be used in ways not anticipated at design time as the context in
which they operate is constantly changing and humans may interact
with them an unpredictable manner. However, at the same time, we
are able to collect unprecedented collections of event data describing
what people and organizations are *actually* doing. Recent developments
in process mining make it possible to analyze such event data, thereby
focusing on *behavior* rather than correlations and simplistic performance
indicators. For example, event logs can be used to automatically learn
end-to-end process models. Next to the automated discovery of the real
underlying process, there are process mining techniques to analyze bottlenecks, to uncover hidden inefficiencies, to check compliance, to explain
deviations, to predict performance, and to guide users towards "better"
processes. Process mining reveals how people really work and often reveals what they would really like to do. Event-based analysis may reveal
workarounds and remarkable differences between people and organizations. This keynote paper highlights current research on *comparative process mining*. One can compare event data with normative process models
and see where people deviate. Some of these deviations may be positive
and one can learn from them. Other deviations may reveal inefficiencies,
design flaws, or even fraudulent behavior. One can also use *process cubes*
to compare different systems or groups of people. Through slicing, dicing, rolling-up, and drilling-down we can view event data from different
angles and produce process mining results that can be compared.

1 Events Are Everywhere!

The term "Big Data" is often used to refer to the incredible growth of data in
recent years. However, the ultimate goal is not to collect more data, but to turn
data into real value. This means that data should be used to improve existing
products, processes and services, or enable new ones. This explains the need for
more *data scientists* [3]. A data scientist should be able to answer questions of
the kind: *What happened?*, *Why did it happen?*, *What will happen?*, and *What is*

S. Sauer et al. (Eds.): HCSE 2014, LNCS 8742, pp. 317–321, 2014.
© IFIP International Federation for Information Processing 2014

the best that can happen? [3]. These questions all refer to the *behavior* of people, organizations, and systems. Hence, we consider *event data* to be most important source of information.

1.1   Internet of Events

Events may take place inside a machine (e.g., an X-ray machine or baggage handling system), inside an enterprise information system (e.g., a order placed by a customer), inside a hospital (e.g., the analysis of a blood sample), inside a social network (e.g., exchanging e-mails or twitter messages), inside a transportation system (e.g., checking in, buying a ticket, or passing through a toll booth), etc. In all of the above examples, software is instrumented to record events. These events tell us how people and organizations behave and use the systems at their disposal.

In [3], we coined the term the *Internet of Events* (IoE) to refer to all event data available. The IoE is composed of:

- The *Internet of Content* (IoC): all information created by humans to increase knowledge on particular subjects. The IoC includes traditional web pages, articles, encyclopedia like Wikipedia, YouTube, e-books, newsfeeds, etc.
- The *Internet of People* (IoP): all data related to social interaction. The IoP includes e-mail, facebook, twitter, forums, LinkedIn, etc.
- The *Internet of Things* (IoT): all physical objects connected to the network. The IoT includes all things that have a unique id and a presence in an internet-like structure. Things may have an internet connection or tagged using Radio-Frequency Identification (RFID), Near Field Communication (NFC), etc.
- The *Internet of Locations* (IoL): refers to all data that have a spatial dimension. With the uptake of mobile devices (e.g., smartphones) more and more events have geospatial attributes.

The above sources of event data not only reflect the abundance of event data, they also illustrate our reliance on complex software artifacts. Software forms an integral part of the most complex artifacts built by humans. Software systems may comprise hundreds of millions of program statements, written by thousands of different programmers, spanning several decades. Their complexity surpasses the comprehensive abilities of any single, individual human being. Moreover, *software must run in an ever changing context composed of different software components, different hardware configurations, may be applied in ways not anticipated at design time.* Classical modeling approaches have failed to cope with this complexity. This makes it essential to learn from systems "in vivo". We can only learn how people use systems by observing them both in their natural habitat. The event data that are omnipresent make this possible.

1.2   Event Logs

Process mining provides a powerful way to analyze operational processes based on event data. Unlike classical purely model-based approaches, process mining

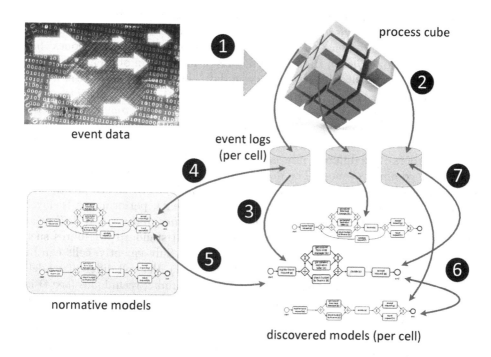

Fig. 1. Overview of comparative process mining using process cubes: ❶ store events in the process cube, ❷ materialize the events in a cell as an event log that can be analyzed, ❸ automatically discover models per cell (e.g., a BPMN or UML model), ❹ check conformance by replaying event data on normative (process) models, ❺ compare discovered models and normative models, ❻ compare discovered models corresponding to different cells, and ❼ compare different behaviors by replaying event data of one cell on another cell's model

is driven by "raw" observed behavior instead of assumptions or aggregate data. Unlike classical data-driven approaches, it is truly process-oriented and relates events to high-level end-to-end process models [1].

Event logs serve as the starting point for process mining. An event log can be viewed as a multiset of *traces* [1]. Each trace describes the life-cycle of a particular *case* (i.e., a *process instance*) in terms of the *activities* executed. Often event logs store additional information about events, e.g., the *resource* (i.e., person or device) executing or initiating the activity, the *timestamp* of the event, or *data elements* recorded with the event.

2 Comparative Process Mining

Process mining can be used to analyze event data. The spectrum of available techniques is broad and includes techniques to automatically learn end-to-end process models, to check conformance, to analyze bottlenecks, to predict performance, etc. For an overview of available techniques see [1] or processmining.org. Here we would like to focus on *comparative process mining*, i.e., techniques that compare behavior either in the form of models or in the form of event logs [2, 5].

As Figure 1 shows, it all starts with event data. These event data are stored in a so-called *process cube* [2] with dimensions based on the event's attributes (see ❶ in Fig. 1). Note that in a process cube, there is no fixed assignment from events to cases (process instances). The same event may belong to different cells (e.g., people can work in two departments), different cases (e.g., a delivery may refer to multiple orders), and different processes (e.g., the sales and distribution processes may share common events). The dimensions may refer to groups of customers (gold versus silver customers), periods (2013 versus 2014), locations (Eindhoven versus Berlin), departments (sales versus procurement), performance (delayed or not), etc. These dimensions can be used to *slice, dice, roll-up,* and *drill-down* event data [2]. Events can be assigned to cases and standard attributes such as *activity, resource,* and *timestamp* can be chosen. Subsequently, cells can be materialized into concrete event logs (see ❷ in Fig. 1). Per cell different models can be *discovered* using dozens of different process mining techniques (see ❸ in Fig. 1). For example, one can automatically discover Petri nets or BPMN models from such event logs. Using *conformance checking* techniques one can also compare the event logs to normative process models (see ❹ in Fig. 1). These techniques quantify the conformance level and diagnose differences, e.g., highlighting activities that are skipped frequently [4]. It is also possible to compare discovered models with normative models (see ❺ in Fig. 1). Using the dimensions in the process cube one can also quickly compare different groups of cases, periods, locations, etc. For example, one can compare the models constructed for an array of cells (see ❻ in Fig. 1). What are the differences between the cases that got delayed and the cases that were able to meet the deadline? Why did the bottleneck shift from the back-office to the front-office in Spring 2014? Such questions can be answered using comparative process mining. Often we also compare a discovered process model for one cell with the event log of another cell (see ❼ in Fig. 1). Through conformance checking we can then analyze the differences at a very detailed level. For example, by replaying the event log of 2014 on the model constructed for 2013, we may see remarkable differences and immediately inspect the underlying event data.

3   Learning from Positive Deviants

As Figure 1 indicates, conformance checking can be done with respect to a normative model or the model constructed for another cell. The term "normative model" suggests that deviations are bad. However, there are many examples of *positive deviants*, i.e., cases that are non-conforming but also better performing (successful exceptions). The term "positive deviance" refers to approaches used to identify people (but also organizational entities and process variants) whose uncommon but successful behaviors or strategies enable them to find better solutions to a problem than their peers [6]. Positive deviance has been been applied in healthcare, education, agriculture, public administration, production, and services. The concept is simple: *look for outliers who succeed against all odds rather than sicking to a normative process model.* Comparative process mining –as explained using Fig. 1– is a powerful tool to distinguish between positive deviants, mainstream behavior, and negative deviants.

Process discovery and conformance checking techniques have matured over the last decade and are well-supported by the process mining framework *ProM* (`processmining.org`). However, better support for process cubes and an improved symbiosis between data and process mining are needed to provide a comprehensive toolbox for positive deviance. This way we can truly exploit the torrents of event data surrounding us.

References

[1] van der Aalst, W.M.P.: Process Mining: Discovery, Conformance and Enhancement of Business Processes. Springer, Berlin (2011)

[2] van der Aalst, W.M.P.: Process Cubes: Slicing, Dicing, Rolling Up and Drilling Down Event Data for Process Mining. In: Song, M., Wynn, M.T., Liu, J. (eds.) AP-BPM 2013. LNBIP, vol. 159, pp. 1–22. Springer, Heidelberg (2013)

[3] Aalst, W.M.P.: v.d.: Data Scientist: The Engineer of the Future. In: Mertins, K., Benaben, F., Poler, R., Bourrieres, J. (eds.) Proceedings of the I-ESA Conference. Enterprise Interoperability, vol. 7, pp. 13–28. Springer, Berlin (2014)

[4] van der Aalst, W.M.P., Adriansyah, A., van Dongen, B.: Replaying History on Process Models for Conformance Checking and Performance Analysis. WIREs Data Mining and Knowledge Discovery 2(2), 182–192 (2012)

[5] van der Aalst, W.M.P., Guo, S., Gorissen, P.: Comparative Process Mining in Education: An Approach Based on Process Cubes. In: Lesage, J.J., Faure, J.M., Cury, J., Lennartson, B. (eds.) 12th IFAC International Workshop on Discrete Event Systems (WODES 2014). IFAC Series, pp. PL1.1–PL1.9. IEEE Computer Society (2014)

[6] Pascale, R., Sternin, J., Sternin, M.: The Power of Positive Deviance: How Unlikely Innovators Solve the World's Toughest Problems. Harvard Business Review Press (2010)

Author Index